What the Faith Is All about

A Study of the
Basic Doctrines of
Christianity

ELMER L. TOWNS

D0104036

 L I V I N G   S T U D I E S
Tyndale House Publishers, Inc.   Wheaton, Illinois

All Scripture quotations are from the
King James Version of the Bible.

Third printing, November 1985
Library of Congress Catalog Card Number 83-70235
ISBN 0-8423-7870-7, paper

C O N T E N T S

INTRODUCTION

According to my research on church growth, I found that the greatest curriculum need of Christian education in the 80s is Bible doctrine written in the language of the people. Since a researcher ought to place confidence in the findings of his exploration, I determined to write a book on Bible doctrine for the average Christian. Also, my major in seminary was theology and I have taught that subject for over twenty years. A book on doctrine gave me an opportunity to put the results of my studies into print.

First, I determined to write for contemporary Bible students, not for theologians. This meant I had to deal with the sophisticated and complicated issues facing modern Christians, without getting bogged down in ecclesiastical tangents or concerning myself with all the issues discussed in seminaries. I trust this is a simple book to understand as I have tried to explore the incomprehensible nature of God. It is still true that "profound truth is discovered in a simple expression."

In the second place, I used selected theological words but tried to interpret them for the average layman by giving a biblical background, resulting in a definition. When the readers know correct theological terms, they have a basis for understanding the doctrine involved.

In the third place, I have tried to make this book practical. Many times I have heard that theology dries up soul-winning. Also it is said that theology may be true in the classroom but does not work in the church. I disagree with both of those statements. If doctrine is truly biblical, it will motivate the students to win souls for Jesus Christ. Also, if doctrine is presented correctly in the classroom, it is practical for the church. As a result, I tried to end each chapter with a practical section, applying the lesson to life.

This book is adaptable for use in classes, in the Sunday school, or home Bible cells. There are fifty-two chapters, one for each week of the year. A daily Bible reading suggestion is tied to each chapter so that the serious student of Bible doctrine can cover every major doctrine in his daily devotional reading in one year.

Finally, due credit must be given to two of my students at Liberty Baptist Seminary for their contribution to this manuscript. It is only coincidental that both are from Canada, but this fact only adds to my appreciation for their educational system. Mr. Douglas Porter worked on research and composition, while Miss Margaret Barr typed and retyped the manuscript. Mrs. Marie Chapman read the text critically to strengthen its contribution.

May God use this book for its intended purpose.

Elmer L. Towns

PART ONE
INTRODUCTION

ONE
UNDERSTANDING
CHRISTIANITY

And the disciples were called Christians first in Antioch. Acts
11:26

INTRODUCTION

Someone has said, "Christianity is Jesus Christ." That embryonic answer is an adequate description, but the problem
is that many people do not understand who Jesus Christ is.
The popular conception of Christ is not always correct. Even
in the Scriptures, individuals did not always properly understand Christ. To illustrate, observe the two disciples on the
road to Emmaus on the first Easter Sunday afternoon. They
thought they knew Christ and were even discussing the
events of Jesus' death, burial, and resurrection. But they
were wrong in their understanding of him. When Jesus
joined them and spoke to them, they did not recognize him
because their eyes were blinded with unbelief (Luke 24:16,
31).

These were his disciples who now were perplexed at the
events of the morning. They had heard reports that someone
had stolen his body or that he had disappeared. Obviously,
these two disciples had apparent spiritual needs, just as
many in today's world have needs. How Jesus met their
needs, then, is an indication of how he meets needs today.

Jesus began teaching these two disciples at the first books

of the Bible (the Law) and surveyed Old Testament history to the last books (the Prophets). Some might think Jesus would have comforted them with a psalm or a devotional challenge. Instead, he met their needs by laying the foundation of biblical teaching. "He expounded unto them in all the scriptures the things concerning himself" (Luke 24:27). The basis of his ministry to them was doctrine. The verb for "teaching" is the same root from which we get the word "doctrine."

The church has the same mandate today; our lives and ministry must be based on sound doctrine. But most people are afraid of the word "doctrine." The world thinks that doctrine is dusty and irrelevant, or hidden in old theology books. But biblical doctrine is as spiritually alive as a new born-again Christian. It is as practical as a growing Sunday school and as enjoyable as reading a favorite text.

Christian doctrine is similar to the wrench in a plumber's toolbox—it is there to fix something. Those who just keep the wrench shiny are similar to the theologian who is always perfecting his doctrine but does not apply it to his life or ministry. Others deny the "doctrine wrench" illustration by saying, "That sermon is good in theory [doctrine] but it will never work in life." They are wrong. When true doctrine touches life, it is always practical.

The Bible and doctrine walk hand in hand with practical Christianity. "All scripture is given by inspiration of God, and is profitable for doctrine, for reproof, for correction, for instruction in righteousness: That the man of God may be perfect, throughly furnished unto all good works" (2 Tim. 3:16, 17). Therefore, the purpose of Bible doctrine is *the communication of the gospel to people at a point of need.* The first section of this chapter will deal with the topic: *What is man's point of need?* The second topic in this section is, *What is communication?* The third section is, *What is the Gospel?* The answer to these questions formulate the necessity and function of doctrine.

CHRISTIAN DOCTRINE SPEAKS TO THE POINT OF NEED

All doctrine begins with God and has its eternal existence in God, but there was no need of doctrine until God created man. As soon as man was created, a need existed. Man was made in the image of God, which means among other things that he had the ability to reason. His intellectual ability reflects the thought processes of God. Man also had emotions, as expressed in the feelings of love and hate, to mention just two. Finally, man was a volitional being who could decide his own fate. So, when Satan came and tempted, "Ye shall be as gods," man, who had the ability to make a moral choice, fell into sin. Sin produced the greatest need in man and doctrine is the channel through which God told how he would meet that need.

Man is cut off from God. Not only Adam and Eve, but everyone from that time forth was excluded from God's presence. The Scriptures teach, "For all have sinned and come short of the glory of God" (Rom. 3:23). This included every child who was born in the line of Adam and Eve, since "as by one man sin entered into the world, and death by sin;...so death passed upon all men, for all have sinned" (Rom. 5:12).

Man's sin is classified into three aspects. First, anything less than God's perfect holiness is sin. Sin is similar to an arrow falling short of the target. It did not attain to the perfect standard. So every person born into the world does not measure up to God's perfect standard.

Rebellion is the second aspect of sin, usually translated "transgression." Sin is the breaking of God's law, either volitionally or ignorantly. God prohibits the worship of idols, but man sins when he falls upon his face and worships a wooden statue. He has transgressed God's commandment.

The third aspect of sin is inherent wickedness or moral impurity. This is described as filth or uncleanness and is abhorred by God, who is pure and holy.

The result of sin is that it blinds the sinner (2 Cor. 4:3, 4; Eph. 4:17). Usually man does not recognize that he is a sinner and that he is cut off from God. Therefore a sinner needs the gospel communicated to him at his point of need, to reveal to him that he is a sinner.

Man becomes his own point of reference. When Satan promised Eve, "Ye shall be as gods" (Gen. 3:5), he fulfilled that promise. As a result, each man today is his own standard of measurement. Each has become the focus of the circle in which he lives. A wise man once observed, "There is some divinity in us all." By that he meant that each man justifies his own actions and thinks that everything he does is perfect, or at least almost perfect.

The Fall of man has created an upside-down condition. Instead of man's placing God on the throne, man sits there in supreme ignorance that he has usurped the place of God. Doctrine teaches man that God must be placed on the throne and only when man understands God's nature and program can man begin to get his problem solved.

Man suffers alienation and isolation. Too often it has been said that sin is punished after death. That is only part of the picture. People also suffer the consequences of sin in this life. Sin results in isolation or alienation from God. Spiritual death is the ultimate form of isolation from God. As a result of man's sin, he needs eternal salvation to bring him into fellowship with God. But there is a second problem. Modern education speaks of "felt needs," those problems we are aware of, and "ultimate needs," usually the problems that are real but unexperienced. The "ultimate need" is salvation for man to be rejoined to God from whom he was cut off. But let us not forget the "felt need," the deliverance from the affliction in this life that also springs from our sin.

Isolation from God may not be a felt need, but severe depression is an experience that needs immediate help. To this person, the doctrinal message of fellowship with God may not be enough, but it is the foundation of all ministry to that person. Since man is a social creature, his problem of isolation may be the root of many of his other mental or psychological problems.

The answer to isolation is that God took the initiative with man. "When the fulness of time was come, God sent forth his Son" (Gal.4:4). And again we read "God . . . hath in these last days spoken unto us by his Son" (Heb. 1:1, 2).

Man is filled with anxiety. Any life that is separated from ultimate authority is like a boat without an anchor; it is drifting. A person may be anxious because he does not have all the answers to the questions raised by others, or even the questions asked in his heart.

Every person has within his heart a need, something missing that only God can fill. He knows that something is missing but he usually refuses to identify it as God. He looks for answers elsewhere and does not find any. He becomes his own point of reference, but he makes mistakes and is aware of his own stupidity.

People are anxious because they have a problem keeping their emotional lives together. God should function in man's immaterial nature, but the vacuum created by his absence produces anxiety. "Anxiety" is another word for fear, depression, jealousy, or any other condition that keeps man in an emotional disequilibrium.

Man searches for meaning. Because man is isolated and affected by sin in every part of his life, the lack of meaning in life becomes a felt need. Those who are slaves to drugs know that narcotics do not lead to happiness or meaning. The same can be said for wealth, fame, or even success.

Some people do not know where to go or how to get where they want to go. But they want to go somewhere. They are like a fine-tuned car that has a full tank of fuel but is without direction or purpose. Others are bewitched or have dropped out of the human race. They have no drive or no desire. They are like a car without fuel, without a battery, and with a rusting engine. Both have problems with meaning—they have not found the secret in life. They need the revelation of God that gives his purpose for which men should live.

Man marches inevitably toward death. We are frightened when we see a young friend struck down with cancer, and yet thousands die annually of some form of cancer. We experience the same fear when a child is killed or we hear of a young son who is missing in war.

The threat of death is all about us. Then we look within our decaying bodies and realize death is our enemy. We are spirits that want to rise above the limitations of the body. Yet we see dimly because our eyes are wearing out. Our arms ache because of arthritis. Even the thirty-year-old feels the inevitable rising tide of age when a younger man takes his place on the team.

The Bible teaches that "the wages of sin is death" (Rom. 6:23), and the ultimate need of man is an explanation for death. A little boy was standing next to his father on the front seat of their Mercedes Benz. The father had given his son everything. Then the little boy asked, "Does everyone have to die?" The father thought a moment then answered, "Yes." The young son pondered that answer, then blurted out, "Even if they are lucky?"

THE PURPOSE OF CHRISTIAN DOCTRINE IS COMMUNICATION

The word "communicate" actually means "to have in common." When we communicate with a friend, the two of us have something in common. Language is the usual means of communication. Though much of human communication is nonverbal, language difficulty is the most significant cause of communication failures.

God communicated to man in many ways but the greatest was Jesus Christ. Christianity is a relationship between God and man, based on the life, death, and resurrection of his Son, Jesus Christ. Now, every person who is saved has a living relationship to God. Those Christians who allow their relationship to God to affect their whole personality prosper.

Christians are expected to reach out in relationships to other people—to the unsaved in soul-winning and to other Christians in fellowship. Every man is potentially a loner, but he can reach out of his shell for meaningful relationships when he has a full understanding of the relationship between God and himself. It takes strength to reach to another person. The ultimate strength is in Jesus Christ who forgives our sins, gives us meaning in life, and gives us strength to rise above our circumstances.

The record of God's communication to man is the Word of God. But it is more than a history of how God has reached out to man. It is the basis of man's communication with God today. Since the Bible is the communication of the gospel to people at their point of need, then it must be rational and logical. God reveals himself as rational and logical. Since the Bible teaches that man is made in the image and likeness of God, we may conclude that human beings are rational and logical, and that the channel of communication between God and man proceeds in a logical and rational manner.

When God speaks to man (revelation) it will follow rational and logical means. We can conclude that God is not illogical nor does he do foolish things. When man seeks God he cannot forsake his God-given intellect, nor can he find God by seeking the Lord in foolish ways. The channel of communication between God and man runs in both directions, and Christianity must always be rational. That does not mean we will understand all the Bible nor does it mean God will reveal everything to us. But it does mean that God will never ask us to violate our minds to be Christians.

When the gospel is presented to us, it must be communicated to us so that we understand it. (That does not mean the content is changed but that the method of expressing it is revised.) Since we are rational and logical beings, the gospel must be communicated to us in a rational manner. This means that the gospel must be systematic in content and presentation. From this we get the term "systematic theology." However, this book uses the biblical term "doctrine" instead of the word "theology."

Several steps are taken in making doctrine systematic and logical. First, we must look at all of the facts on every topic of doctrine. We begin by looking at biblical content, but we also include truth from any and every source: biology, history, sociology, and philosophy. As an illustration, when we are studying the nature of God we must consider all the facts of God that are taught in the Bible concerning the nature of God. But we also include all information concerning him that we learn from nature.

Second, we must classify the facts into a consistent whole. This means that the verses which deal with the holiness of God must be correlated with those that teach the justice of God. Then we write the results of our study into statements that give a total picture of the person of God.

Finally, we must analyze all of our statements, making sure they are consistent, so that we do not contradict ourselves.

But also, we analyze them to make sure our statements correspond to the reality of the world and the people who live here. The final result is doctrine. Now we must express it as simply and clearly as possible, so that others will be able to understand the total revelation of God on each subject.

The final step in communication between God and man is worship. Since man is spiritual he has an innate desire to worship someone. The problem is that man, the worshiper, has invented his own ways to worship God or has created his own gods to worship. God recognized this weakness and commanded that we should have no other gods before him (Exod. 20:3).

But the obvious question remains: "Which worship is correct?" Actually, this book is not an apologetic answer to the philosophical questions of man. The answer to true worship is found in what Jesus told the woman at the well. "God is a Spirit: and they that worship him must worship him in spirit and in truth" (John 4:24). God must be worshiped according to truth, which is biblical doctrine. But to worship God by correct doctrine is only part of worship. The worship of God must also be an expression of the deepest feelings in the heart of man, which is what is meant by worshiping him in spirit.

THE CONTENT OF CHRISTIAN DOCTRINE IS GOD'S GOOD NEWS

We have talked of man's need and God's method of communication to him. Now we come to the content of the gospel, or what must be believed to solve man's problem. This is the basis on which God meets the need of man. The word "gospel" means "good news" and is usually applied to mean the good news of salvation. The gospel is the first message of good news that God gave to sinful man. After Adam and Eve sinned, the Lord came walking in the cool of the Garden looking for man. Even though man had hidden, God, who knows all things, knew where Adam was hiding. God took the initiative. God wanted to save Adam—that is the good news. And the good news (gospel), which is doctrine, grows out of the first encounter of God and man after man had sinned.

The gospel has two aspects, a proposition and a Person. The average church member thinks of only one concept, that the gospel is a propositional statement of faith. Many people miss Christianity because they think it is belief in a historical statement.

The gospel—a proposition. The basis of good news is the death and resurrection of Jesus Christ. This message is best expressed in these words of Paul: "I declare unto you that gospel which I preached unto you, . . . that Christ died for our sins according to the Scriptures; and that he was buried, and that he rose again the third day according to the scriptures" (1 Cor. 15:1-4). The gospel message is simply the death, burial, and resurrection of Jesus Christ for our sins. Those who deny the reality of these truths deny the foundation of Christianity. This gospel must be affirmed in our doctrinal statements. For a person to be saved, mere mental agreement to a propositional statement is not enough.

The gospel—a Person. The gospel is more than a proposition; it is a Person—Jesus Christ. A person's becoming a Christian involves more than giving mental assent to the fact of the death, burial, and resurrection of Jesus. The gospel enters our lives when Jesus Christ enters our hearts. "But as many as received him [Christ] to them gave he power to become the sons of God" (John 1:12).

By definition we have said that the purpose of doctrine is the communication of the gospel to people at their point of need. We communicate doctrine not only by writing and speaking it in words. The gospel is a Person—Jesus Christ. Therefore to be doctrinally correct, we must know the content of Christianity and be in right relationship to Jesus Christ.

A few years ago when the street people were converted, they were called "Jesus people." They claimed to have a deep relationship to Jesus Christ, but many of them ignored doctrine. On the other extreme are some orthodox churches that correctly teach the Word of God, but their legalistic approach to Christianity has squeezed an emotional or spiritual relationship to Jesus Christ out of the church. Both extremes are unbiblical. A person must be correct in his relationship to the

Person of Jesus Christ. And correct words are the vehicle that expresses a man's doctrine. One cannot have Christianity without Christ; and the revelation of Christ is the substance and content of doctrine.

CONCLUSION

This doctrine book is written to communicate doctrine for the modern-day Christian. It is written to the head and to the heart. Sound doctrine proves itself sound if it can be related to the needs of man.

DAILY READINGS

☐Monday: *Romans 3:10-26*   ☐Tuesday: *John 3:1-18*
☐Wednesday: *Romans 5:1-21*   ☐Thursday:
Hebrews 11:1-6, 32-40   ☐Friday: *Matthew 28:1-20*
☐Saturday: *1 Thessalonians 4:1-18*   ☐Sunday:
Revelation 19:1-21

TWO
UNDERSTANDING FAITH

And Jesus, answering, saith unto them, Have faith in God.
Mark 11:22

INTRODUCTION

Several years ago a group of high school students from America spent three weeks in Osaka, Japan, at the world's fair. The students decided to take the subway into the downtown area to purchase some souvenirs. After spending several hours taking pictures and buying souvenirs, the students decided to return to their local residence. Arriving at the station, they saw the subway train pull up. They quickly paid the fare and jumped on board. As the train doors closed, the students learned they had gotten on the wrong train. Instantly their confidence was shattered. Though they had sincerely believed they were right just moments earlier, they now knew they were sincerely wrong.

The object of our faith is more important than the sincerity of our belief. The man who thinks he is right but is not sure may be far better off than the one who is "sure" but is absolutely wrong. The credibility of our faith begins with objective truth and ends with internal trust. This chapter analyzes the six types of faith that describe the believer's relationship to God.

DOCTRINAL FAITH

Someone may ask, "How can I get more faith?" Paul wrote, "Faith cometh by hearing, and hearing by the word of God" (Rom. 10:17). The source and foundation of all faith is the Bible.

If we want faith, we must begin with a correct understanding of the Word of God. The more we know of the Bible, the more faith we can have, and the more correctly we know the Bible, the more effective our faith.

This book, *What the Faith Is All About,* covers all the major aspects of the Bible so that our faith may have a broad foundation. Throughout the New Testament the phrase "the faith" and "doctrine" are used interchangeably. When faith has an article preceding it as in "the faith," it means "the statement of faith." Therefore, to have correct faith, we must have an accurate statement of doctrinal faith.

The apostle Paul certainly recognized the importance of correct doctrine. He constantly opposed those who sought to change the faith. Perhaps he was concerned about accurate doctrine because of his own experience. When Saul of Tarsus was persecuting the church, he thought his doctrine was accurate and that he was serving God. But when he met Christ on the Damascus road, he gained a living faith which changed what he believed and how he lived. Paul talked about those who had "departed from the faith" (1 Tim. 4:1) and "denied the faith" (1 Tim. 5:8). At the end of his life, the apostle was able to say, "I have kept the faith" (2 Tim. 4:8). Jude challenged his readers to "earnestly contend for the faith" (Jude 3).

If we want to have a growing biblical faith, we need to ground it upon a correct knowledge of God. A certain woman once heard someone compliment her great faith. "I have not a great faith," she responded, "I have a little faith in a great God."

Doctrinal faith is both the beginning and the test of our Christianity. If our statement of faith is wrong, then our personal faith is misplaced. We must begin with a correct statement of faith, and build saving faith thereupon. Then we are meeting some of the important conditions to correctly experience a life of faith and continue to learn about doctrinal faith.

SAVING FAITH

A person becomes a Christian by faith. "For by grace are ye saved through faith" (Eph. 2:8). When the Philippian jailor was troubled about his salvation, he was exhorted to exercise belief, the verb expression of faith. "Believe on the Lord Jesus Christ, and thou shalt be saved, and thy house" (Acts. 16:31). When Nicodemus failed to understand how he could enter into a relationship with God, Jesus said, "For God so loved the world, that he gave his only begotten Son, that whosoever believeth in him should not perish but have everlasting life" (John 3:16). Apart from faith, personal salvation is impossible.

Personal salvation is experienced by the inner person. Since humans are composed of intellect, emotion, and will, faith comes through a proper exercise of these three aspects of personality.

Our faith must be grounded on correct knowledge. A person cannot put his trust in something he does not know about, nor can he honestly trust something that is proven false to him. A person must first know the gospel, which means he has an intellectual knowledge of salvation. But knowledge alone will not save him.

The Bible seems to make a distinction between "believe that" and "believe in." In the first place, one can believe that his team will win or believe that a job is superior. This belief is opinion, but is not deep conviction, i.e., based on the object of his faith—Jesus Christ. When a person "believes in," the belief is based on a careful weighing of the evidence. When we say "believe in" we are speaking of a moral expression or a moral experience.

The Gospel of John uses the word "believe" ninety-eight times and ties faith to the object of belief. We are exhorted to "believe in Jesus Christ." As a result, the important aspect of belief is what you believe, not just the measure of your belief. Therefore, to have saving faith, a person must believe that

God exists. He must believe that he himself is a sinner (Rom. 3:23). He must believe that God will punish sin (Rom. 6:23), and that Christ has made a provision for his salvation (Rom. 5:8). A person must believe these truths, which means he accepts them intellectually, but mere intellectual assent to biblical truth is not enough to save.

Our faith will have an emotional expression. Knowledge about God is the foundation of saving faith, but such faith will extend to the individual's emotional responses as well. Solomon wrote, "Trust in the Lord with all thine heart, and lean not unto thine own understanding" (Prov. 3:5). Jesus repeated this truth, "Thou shalt love the Lord thy God with all thy heart, and with all thy soul, and with all thy mind" (Matt. 22:37). This means that intellectual belief is not enough. A person cannot trust his own understanding about God. Although emotions are involved in faith, faith is more than emotional feeling. Our emotional response to the gospel must be founded upon an intellectual understanding of the Scripture.

Your faith must be a volitional response. A third aspect of saving faith is an expression of volitional faith. A person is saved as a result of an act of his will whereby he relies on Christ as proclaimed in the gospel. Paul told the Roman Christians, "Ye have obeyed from the heart that form of doctrine which was delivered you" (Rom. 6:17). When a person accepts Jesus Christ as his Savior (John 1:12), it is a conscious act whereby he invites him into his heart (Eph. 3:16).

JUSTIFYING FAITH

Whereas saving faith is an experimental encounter with Jesus Christ, the next expression, justifying faith, is nonexperiential. Justifying faith is belief that we have been justified or declared righteous. Justification is not something that we feel with our senses. It is something that happens to our record in heaven. God is the One who performs the act of justification (Rom. 8:34). Man is the one who receives the action and is justified (Rom. 5:1). Justification is the judicial act of

God whereby he justly declares righteous all those who believe in Jesus Christ.

Abraham is the first person in the Bible described as having been justified by faith. This is not to say that he was the first person to be a child of God. "He [Abraham] believed in the Lord; and he [God] counted it to him [Abraham] for righteousness" (Gen. 15:6). God made a promise to Abraham which he accepted as possible, and God rewarded him for his faith.

Justification is an act whereby our legal position in heaven is changed. Being justified is similar to the act whereby the U. S. government declares that an alien has become an American citizen. The moment the person is pronounced a citizen, nothing happens to him internally. His thought processes remain the same as does his personality and his pattern of speech. The only actual change is his legal standing. But as he becomes aware of the benefits of being an American, he may shout, cry, or break out into a grin. It is simply an emotional reaction to a legal action.

In the same way, justification changes our legal standing in heaven. We become children of God. In response to this new relationship the new Christian may respond emotionally.

The basis of justifying faith is a double transference that happens at salvation. Our sin was transferred to Jesus Christ; he became our sin. The preposition "for" is the key word, indicating Christ died for us (Gal. 2:20), he gave his life for the church (Eph. 5:25), and he gave himself for the sins of the world (John 1:29). The second transference is that the perfection of Jesus Christ was credited to our account. When God looks at us in judgment, he sees the righteousness of his Son. "For [God] hath made him to be sin for us [the first step of transference]... that we might be made the righteousness of God in him [second step of transference]" (2 Cor. 5:21).

INDWELLING FAITH

The Bible teaches that a person cannot overcome sin and sinful habits by himself. Faith is the secret of the victorious Christian life. "This is the victory that overcometh the world, even our faith" (1 John 5:4).

Even beyond living a triumphant life, a person can walk in moment-by-moment communion with God. A medieval monk described this victory as "practicing the presence of God." This life of victory and fellowship is made available by the indwelling of Jesus Christ. When a person becomes a Christian, Christ comes into his life. The believer has union and communion with Christ (John 15:5). Not only does Christ dwell within the believer, the power of Christ is available to him. Paul testified, "Christ liveth in me: and the life which I now live in the flesh I live by the faith of the Son of God" (Gal. 2:20). The secret of victorious living is allowing the life of Jesus Christ to flow through us. The believer must surrender his fears and rebellion to Christ. In so doing, he finds new faith to overcome his problems. Paul described this "new faith" that comes from Christ, "the promise by faith of Jesus Christ [that] might be given to them that believe" (Gal. 3:22).

Every Christian has access to the "faith of Jesus Christ." Yet many Christians are defeated and discouraged because they have not allowed Christ's power to flow out of their lives.

To get this victory a Christian must first recognize that faith comes from Christ and is described as "Christ's faith" (Gal. 2:16; Eph. 3:12; Phil. 3:9). Second, a person must yield (the nature of faith is trusting) and allow Christ to work through him. And third, the Christian must constantly obey the direction of the Word of God so that he can continually have power for victory.

The agent of faith. An agent is one who acts on behalf of another. The Holy Spirit, the agent of faith, acts on behalf of Jesus Christ to plant faith in a person's heart. The Holy Spirit is one who initiates the faith process by convicting or causing a sinner to see his sin (John 16:8, 9). By the work of conviction, the Holy Spirit is working in a sinner's heart to make him aware that he is a sinner, that Jesus is God's standard of righteousness, and that Christ's death on the cross paid the debt for sin. The ability to believe comes from the Holy Spirit. Paul declared that "your faith should not stand in the wisdom of men, but in the power of God" (1 Cor. 2:5).

The instrument of faith. Indwelling faith is placed in our hearts as we read the Scriptures. When Paul says, "Faith cometh by hearing, and hearing by the word of God" (Rom. 10:17), he is saying that the Bible is the tool in the hand of the Holy Spirit to place faith in the human heart. Just as a carpenter uses a hammer to build things, so God uses the Bible as an instrument of faith. When a minister is quoting the Bible, God may be using the Scriptures in a negative way to break up unbelief (Jer. 23:29) or to cut out prejudice or ignorance (Acts 5:33). But the Scriptures received in the heart also have the positive force of implanting a new nature in the convert (2 Pet. 1:4), to give him faith to believe (Rom. 10:8).

DAILY FAITH

When we live by faith we are being set apart to God, which is the meaning of "sanctification." The Bible teaches that "positional sanctification" is a past action on Calvary. Progressive sanctification is being carried out daily, and future sanctification will take place when we arrive in the presence of God. Daily sanctification requires an exercise of faith, "for we walk by faith, not by sight" (2 Cor. 5:7).

As we live by faith, God is able to use us and cause us to grow in grace. Sometimes daily growth seems minute or even nonexistent to a casual observer. We may sometimes become frustrated with the apparent lack of progress, not able to see the forest for the trees. It is good from time to time to look back and see how God has been working in our lives.

As a bricklayer places one brick upon the other, building a large tower, he may feel his progress is insignificant. Yet, the tower will be built one brick at a time. It is the same in our Christian lives. God makes the big changes through a series of little ones. We must learn to trust God for the little things so we can enjoy great growth. We must trust God daily so we can enjoy yearly gain. Like any other growing experience, living by faith is taking one step at a time.

We grow in faith through the Word of God. As we make the Word of God a part of our lives by reading, studying, and memorizing, we begin to grow in faith (1 Pet. 2:2). Every

Christian needs to hear the Word of God taught and preached regularly (Ps. 1:1-3).

We grow in faith by following biblical principles. A growing faith is an obedient faith. Usually, the exercise of faith will be rational, in keeping with what God wants done. We must put complete trust in the principles of the Bible and not trust our feelings. Faith is not a blind leap into the dark. Faith is following the light of God's Word.

We grow in faith through seeking the Lord. The doctrine of "seeking" the Lord is not usually emphasized, but it is biblical to search for God. "When thou saidst, Seek ye my face; my heart said unto thee, Thy face, Lord, will I seek" (Ps. 27:8). Our faith will grow as we seek God. First, we will begin to recognize the issues that keep us from God. Then, as we search for a better relation with the Savior, we will come to know God experientially.

We grow in faith through confessing our sins. No Christian will live a sinless life, but God is constantly cleansing us through the blood of his Son. "If we walk in the light, as he is in the light, we have fellowship one with another, and the blood of Jesus Christ his Son cleanseth us from all sin" (1 John 1:17). When we as Christians do sin, God will forgive and cleanse us if we confess our sins to him (1 John 1:9). Every time we recognize sin in our lives and rid ourselves of its hindrance, we grow in faith.

We grow in faith by surrender. The Christian must constantly surrender to the lordship of Christ. We do this once when we are saved, but there are also subsequent times to surrender to Christ. As we yield our lives to the Lord, we are growing in grace (Gal. 3:3; Col. 2:6). Paul challenged the Romans to "present your bodies a living sacrifice, holy, acceptable unto God, which is your reasonable service" (Rom. 12:1).

We grow in faith through constant communion. If we want a growing faith we must have a constant communion with Jesus Christ. As we spend time in prayer, Bible study, and fellowship with Christ, we will develop our faith more fully. Jesus recognized that we would become like those we spend time with (Matt. 10:25). As we spend time with the Lord, we will become more Christlike in our faith.

We grow in faith through the testing of difficult experiences. Once we are saved, our faith is nurtured as we grow from victory to victory. Paul describes this "from faith to faith, as it is written, the just shall live by faith" (Rom. 1:17). God wants us to have faith in himself because that pleases and glorifies him. But living faith is not something we receive as one takes a vitamin pill. With the opportunity of taking a step of faith there is the risk of success or failure. When we successfully trust God we should learn through the experience and grow thereby. Faith must come from man's heart, which is governed by his free will. Therefore, to develop a person's faith, God will sometimes maneuver a man into a corner so that the creature is forced to look to his Creator in faith. Through such experiences, man has an opportunity to grow in his faith.

THE GIFT OF FAITH

The gift of faith is one of the gifts that the Holy Spirit supernaturally gives men to serve God (Rom. 12:7; 1 Cor. 12:9). This is more than saving faith which is also called a gift. The gift of faith is considered to be a serving gift, or an ability whereby a person serves God by exercising faith. Not everyone has all of the gifts, so not everyone has the gift of faith. Paul explained that the gifts differ: "Having then gifts differing according to the grace that is given to us" (Rom. 12:6). God has given some this special gift of faith to enable them to carry out their ministry in a more effective way.

If God has given us the gift of faith, we need to exercise it faithfully in keeping with well-balanced Christianity. Paul said, "Though I have the gift of . . . faith, so that I could remove mountains, and have not charity, I am nothing" (1 Cor. 13:2).

The Bible teaches that the proper use of our gifts increases the effectiveness and usefulness of those gifts (Matt. 25:14-

34). It also teaches that we can desire and pray for more gifts (1 Cor. 12:31). Therefore, it is possible for us to have more faith to trust God for bigger things than we have now. If we are faithful in small things, God will give us more faith. Note that Abraham was weak in faith but grew spiritually so that Paul described him as "strong in faith" (Rom. 4:19, 20).

CONCLUSION

The ultimate human expression of Christianity is an act of faith. To the casual observer, "faith" is simply defined as "reliance, trust, or dependence." Yet to the careful student of the Scripture, faith has at least six expressions. First, we must know correct doctrinal faith, which is called a statement of faith. Second, we become a Christian by experiencing saving faith in Jesus Christ. Third, we must have justifying faith. Fourth, we must let the faith of Christ flow through us; this is called indwelling faith. Fifth, we live the Christian life by daily faith. Finally, if we grow in our spiritual gifts, we can exercise the "serving gift" of the Holy Spirit, called faith, whereby some serve God and magnify him by the expression of great faith for accomplishments in their Christian service.

DAILY READINGS

☐Monday: *Romans 10:1-17*   ☐Tuesday: *John 20:19-31*
☐Wednesday: *Genesis 15:1-21*   ☐Thursday: *1 John 5:1-21*
☐Friday: *Psalm 27:1-14*   ☐Saturday: *Romans 12:1-16*
☐Sunday: *Mark 11:12-33*

PART TWO
UNDERSTANDING THE DOCTRINE OF THE BIBLE

THREE
REVELATION

The secret things belong unto the Lord our God: but those things which are revealed belong unto us and to our children for ever, that we may do all the words of this law. Deuteronomy 29:29

INTRODUCTION

Just before his death, Sir Walter Scott was taken into his library and seated by a large window where he could view the scenery. As he sat there, he called to his son-in-law to "get the Book" and read to him. During his lifetime, Scott had collected one of the world's largest private libraries, so his son-in-law asked the logical question, "From what book shall I read?" Scott's reply was simple: "There is but one."

Later, the son-in-law wrote, "I chose John 14. He listened with mild devotion and said, when I had done, 'Well, this is a great comfort. I have followed you distinctly, and I feel as if I was to be myself again.' "

For many years, all kinds of people have held the Bible in high esteem, yet more recently, it has become popular to criticize and even ridicule the Bible. A closer look at the Bible will assure us that it is the very Word of God and help us realize that its greatest critics are those who have never read its pages. The Bible is the greatest Book in the world because it is the special revelation of God. By the expression "greatest Book" we mean it is the greatest in subject matter, greatest in influence on lives and nations, and it answers the greatest need in man, salvation.

THE DEFINITION OF REVELATION

Revelation was the act of God which gave men knowledge about himself and his creation, including knowledge which man could not have otherwise known. The act of revelation by God is described in several places in the Bible. "The secret things belong unto the Lord our God: but those things which are revealed belong unto us and to our children forever that we may do all the words of this law" (Deut. 29:29). In the New Testament we read, "God, who at sundry times and in divers manners spoke in time past unto the fathers by the prophets, hath in these last days spoken unto us by his Son" (Heb. 1:1, 2).

Revelation is an act of God. Peter tells us "No prophecy of scripture is of any private interpretation. For the prophecy came not in old time by the will of man: but holy men of God spake as they were moved by the Holy Ghost" (2 Pet. 1:20, 21). Even though God used over forty men to record the Bible, they did not write the Bible as other men wrote their books. The message of the Bible originated with God and concerns God. But God is unknowable and man cannot understand his Maker apart from a decision by God to let man know.

Because God is love, which means God wants to share himself with man, God chose to tell man about himself. Therefore, God acted to reveal himself and his will. Man did not stumble onto facts about God nor did man think up truth about God. All that anyone knows about God came from God. This is called the act of revelation which was "forever settled in heaven" (Ps. 119:89) before it was ever written on earth. Therefore, the real Author of Scripture is God the Holy Spirit. Actually, the Holy Spirit and approximately forty men of God were the coauthors of the Bible. These human authors simply recorded the things that God revealed to and through them.

When a photographer shoots a picture of a landscape, we respect him for his skill, yet no one seriously considers him the creator of the subject of the picture. Yet as we compare his picture with those taken of the same scene by a beginner, we can see the evidence of the photographer's skill. An extremely good photographer is able to communicate his personality through his work. So it is with the Bible. It is God's revelation recorded by men. Sometimes we can see characteristics of a particular writer in a book, but there can be no question that the Bible is the very Word of God.

God gives this revelation to man. The Bible is a personal book; it is written to and for men. When a person is saved, he feels the Bible has a personal message from God to him, even though the Word of God is addressed to all. Moses told Israel the "things that are revealed belong unto us and to our children forever" (Deut. 29:29). The psalmist interacted personally with Scripture, noting, "I have more understanding than all my teachers; for thy testimonies are my meditation" (Ps. 119:99). A thousand years later the apostle Paul agreed, writing, "These things were our examples" (1 Cor. 10:6), and he wrote to the Romans, "That which may be known of God is manifest in them; for God hath shewed it unto them" (Rom. 1:19). The act of revelation began in the heart of a personal God who wanted to reveal himself to people.

Revelation was the communication of truth man could not otherwise know apart from God. Because God is infinite, man could never understand him. The nature and plan of God are contrary to sinful man, so finite humans could not understand God if they would try (1 Cor. 2:9-11). But man will not understand because sin is rebellion against God. And man could not understand God if he wanted to, for only God can understand God. Therefore, God chose to reveal everything we know about himself to us.

Christians have recognized this truth because they have been aided by God to understand his revelation. Even the infidel Rousseau said, "I must confess to you that the majesty of the Scriptures astonishes me; the holiness of the evangelists speaks to my heart, and has such strong and striking characters of truth, and is, moreover, so perfectly inimitable, that, if it had been the invention of men, the invention would be greater than the greatest heroes."

But the Bible also is a revelation concerning sin. The world says sin is fun. God says sin is rebellion, filthy, and abnormal. If natural man were writing the Bible, he would not paint sin black, allow sinners to go to hell, or describe the destructiveness of iniquity. But God hates sin, so his Book condemns all men because all are sinners (Rom. 3:23). So the Bible is not a Book that man would choose to write. Because the Bible reveals God, it is a Book that man could not write if he would, and because the Bible reveals the condemnation of men, it is a Book he would not write if he could.

Revelation is both partial and complete. This apparent contradiction of terms needs some clarification. By "complete" we mean that the revelation of God is finished, completely written, containing all that God wants us to know about him. The Christian does not expect to find some new truth that needs to be added to the Bible. In fact, the final words of the closing chapter of the Book of Revelation make it clear that this is a completed Book. "For I testify unto every man that heareth the words of the prophecy of this book, If any man shall add unto these things, God shall add unto him the plagues that are written in this book" (Rev. 22:18). Even though these words were written about the Book of Revelation, they are relevant to all the Bible.

The Bible is complete, yet in its completed form it is only a partial revelation of God. We do not know everything there is to know about God. "The secret things belong unto the Lord" (Deut. 29:29). When John wrote the Revelation, he was prevented from recording some things God had revealed to him (Rev. 10:4). Paul had a similar experience where "he was caught up into paradise, and heard unspeakable words, which it is not lawful for a man to utter (2 Cor. 12:4).

God has wisely seen fit not to reveal some things to us. Many things about God are still hidden and unrevealed. We can be certain that the revelation God has given us is enough to accomplish his purpose in our lives. God's revelation to man is not a complete revelation of all truth, but it is as complete as it needs to be.

THE IMPORTANCE OF REVELATION
Revelation is important for many reasons.

Salvation is found only in God's revelation. After Jesus rose from the dead, "then opened he their understanding, that they might understand the scriptures, And said unto them, Thus it is written, and thus it behoved Christ to suffer, and to rise from the dead the third day: And that repentance and remission of sins should be preached in his name among all nations, beginning at Jerusalem" (Luke 24:45-47). The records of history tell us of the death of Christ, but only the Bible tells us it was for our salvation. "Christ died [history] for our sins [revelation]" (1 Cor. 15:3).

The Bible reveals the Person of God. God has revealed his existence in general ways to all men through nature, conscience, and history. But God has used the special revelation of Scripture and Christ to reveal his Person. Men cannot arrive at the right ideas about God by themselves. The only ideas that are correct about God are those that he has revealed about himself. His names (titles), his attributes, and his plan can only be found in this Book.

Revelation is foundational to all doctrine. The Bible says, "All scripture is given by inspiration of God, and is profitable for doctrine" (2 Tim. 3:16). Doctrine is simply the teaching of God concerning a particular subject. If God did not reveal (teach) anything on a particular subject, there would be no doctrine.

Revelation is foundational to the Christian life. "All scripture . . . is profitable for doctrine, for reproof, for correction, for instruction in righteousness: That the man of God may be perfect [mature], throughly furnished unto all good works" (2 Tim. 3:16, 17). The Bible is the Christian's "how-to" manual on how to please God. "This book of the law shall not depart out of thy mouth; but thou shalt meditate therein day and night, that thou mayest observe to do according to all that is written therein: for then thou shalt make thy way prosperous, and then thou shalt have good success" (Josh. 1:8).

THE MEANS OF REVELATION

Revelation is usually discussed in two categories, called "general revelation" and "special revelation." General revelation is given to all persons and man needs no help to understand it. General revelation comes to us from nature to reveal the existence and power of God (Rom. 1:18-20). General revelation also comes from the conscience (Rom. 2:14, 15) and, finally, from the existence of law in or through history (Rom. 2:1). Special revelation comes to us from Scripture in particular and through the revelation of God in Jesus Christ specifically (John 1:10).

HOW GOD REVEALS HIMSELF	
General Revelation	*Special Revelation*
History (1 Cor. 10:1-6)	Bible (Deut. 29:29;
Conscience (Rom. 2:14-16)	2 Pet. 1:20, 21)
Nature (Ps. 19:1-6;	Christ (John 1:14, 18)
Rom. 1:18-21)	

When the Wise Men came from the east seeking the newborn king (Matt. 2:1-11), God must have allowed them to understand something of what he was doing. That was, in part, general revelation which came to them in nature. Their consciences might have influenced them to seek to worship the newborn King of the Jews. Their examination of natural revelation led them to Jerusalem, where they encountered special revelation. There they heard a verse of Scripture (Mic. 5:2) that directed them to Bethlehem. In Bethlehem, they had their fullest revelation of God as they worshiped the baby King, the Word that became flesh (John. 1:14).

People should respond to what God teaches them through natural revelation. That information will never save them, but it points them to the special revelation, the Bible, where they learn of the Person of God and his salvation. Special revelation far surpasses the revelation from history, conscience, and nature. As we study the Bible, we will be constantly pointed to Christ. Someday Christ shall return and "then shall [we] know even as [we are] known" (1 Cor. 13:12).

THE PURPOSE OF REVELATION

God has revealed his Word for a purpose. Too often the Bible is used in Christian homes for little more than a display. Christians, by not reading the Scriptures, rob themselves of much blessing that could be theirs to enjoy.

A revelation of our sin. The Bible reveals the secrets of our heart. Many times moral codes and guides for living do not help us because of cultural overtones. But since the source of the Bible is God, and he is the Savior of men, it is only natural that he would reveal the sins that keep us from him (Rom. 3:9-20). Therefore, we would expect God to speak through his Word to all people in every situation.

After a missionary had been in China for some time, he finally finished translating the New Testament. It was generally well received by the Chinese until they read Romans. Then the missionary was challenged. "You told us your Book was very ancient; but you wrote about our sin since you have come and learned about Chinamen." God who knows the heart of all men, has revealed the sinful nature of men in the Bible. Now this message should be taught to the entire world without fear that it may not apply to some cultures.

A revelation of Christ. God's revelation is primarily a revelation of Christ. Jesus said he was the central theme of Scripture (John 5:39). The central theme of the final book of the Bible, "the Revelation of Jesus Christ" (Rev. 1:1), is the central theme of the Bible.

A revelation of eternal life. The Bible shows us how to have both eternal life and the assurance of it, which was John's chief reason for writing the fourth Gospel (John 20:31). One of John's themes was that we could know the certainty of our salvation (1 John 5:13). Christianity is not like other religions, where the followers can never be assured of their eternal salvation. Assurance is possible because of the revelation of God.

A revelation of God's expectations for us. The Bible gives us a standard by which to live. God revealed the law to Moses so that Israel would obey it (Deut. 29:29). The Scriptures were given so the Christian might grow spiritually (2 Tim. 3:17). It is our Christian duty to do all that is commanded of us (Luke 17:10). Our only biblical guarantee to success in the Christian life is tied to obedience to the biblical standards of our life (Josh. 1:8).

When we purchase a major appliance, we receive a manual that tells how the appliance should work and what is to be done if a problem arises. God has also given us a manufacturer's manual—the Bible—to reveal how to live and what steps to take to achieve success.

The revelation of wisdom. The Bible gives wisdom and understanding to its students. This is something for which every Christian can pray (James 1:5). God, who is the source of wisdom gives it to us as we study the Bible. This is especially true of the Proverbs (Prov. 1:2, 5), but also true of the Bible as a whole (Ps. 19:7). The Christian with a good comprehension of Scripture should be wiser concerning the decisions of life than those who do not know and apply it to life (Luke 16:8).

A revelation of victory. The Word of God has the power to keep a Christian from sin. God, knowing that men would face the problem of sin, revealed a way of escape to help the Christian live a clean life (Ps. 119:9-11) and overcome temptation (1 Cor. 10:13). Even Jesus used the Scriptures when he was tempted by Satan (Matt. 4:1-11). Throughout history, Christians have found the Bible an indispensable aid in overcoming temptation. In the flyleaf of his Bible, Dwight L. Moody wrote, "This Book will keep you from sin, or sin will keep you from this Book."

The Bible prepares the Christian for spiritual battles as he struggles against evil forces in the world. Paul experienced these same battles in his life and ministry. As a result, he concluded that "above all" the Christian needed "the sword of the Spirit which is the word of God" to gain victory in these spiritual battles (Eph. 6:16, 17).

The Bible is an understandable Book. This does not mean

that everyone will understand it, or that anyone will understand all of it. It does not mean we will understand everything the first time we read it, but the Bible can be understood by those who properly attempt to understand it. This of course assumes that the Holy Spirit is teaching us as we read.

Through the Bible, God teaches us his will. If we accept the truths and apply them to our lives, we will continue to discover more. If we rebel against God by rejecting his teaching, the presence of sin in our lives will soon hinder our understanding of the Bible. One of the greatest causes of disagreement among Christians about some passages in Scripture is their spiritual blindness due to their lack of yieldedness to God. To understand the Bible, it is important that we be both hearers and doers of the Word (James 1:22).

When we read the Bible and come across something we do not understand, we should set it aside and learn what we can in other places. It may be that upon reading the same passage days or even years later, the truth of that verse may suddenly become clear to us. In the meantime, we are able to understand and apply other parts of the Bible.

CONCLUSION

When we receive a personal letter from a friend we have not seen for some time, such a letter is not just glanced at and thrown in the trash can. We probably read it again and again to learn what new things have taken place in our friend's life.

The Bible is God's revelation of himself to us. Any person who wants to know God and live for him will continually read the Word of God. No one will ever find God by accident. A person must determine to seek him.

DAILY READINGS

☐Monday: *Psalm 119:1-24*   ☐Tuesday: *Psalm 119:25-48*
☐Wednesday: *Psalm 119:49-72*   ☐Thursday:
Psalm 119:73-96   ☐Friday: *Psalm 119:97-120*   ☐Saturday:
Psalm 119:121-144   ☐Sunday: *Psalm 119:145-176*

FOUR
INSPIRATION

All scripture is given by inspiration of God, and is profitable for doctrine, for reproof, for correction, for instruction in righteousness: That the man of God may be perfect, throughly furnished unto all good works. 2 Timothy 3:16, 17

INTRODUCTION

The Bible is unique among the books of the world. For years it has been studied for its quality of style and beauty. More copies of this Book have been published than any other book in history. While in every respect the Bible is a superb example of good literature, it is more than a good book. It is the actual words of God.

The French philosopher Voltaire sat one day to rewrite Psalm 51 in poetic form. All went well until he came to verse 10, "Create in me a clean heart, O God!" Voltaire, though the chief opponent of Christianity in his day, attempted to translate the verse into his poem. As he wrote, a sudden realization of the terror of hell came upon him. He tried to shake the feeling, but found himself unable to write. Later he confided to his friends that he could not think of that experience without an inner fear that haunted him.

Why does the Bible have such a profound impact on people? Because it is a message from God, called "the revelation of God," and because of the way God guarantees the accuracy of recording the Bible through what is called "inspiration."

The authorship of the Bible makes this Book even more unique. Written by over forty authors over a period of 1600 years, amazingly this collection of epistles, sermons, poems and narratives demonstrates a single theme, that of God's love for mankind and all that such love implies. These writers were not all scholars. Moses and Paul probably received the finest education available in their day. Others were raising cattle and sheep for a living when they recorded their contributions. At least four writers were accustomed to living in the royal household of the land, while the background of another was that of fishing in the Sea of Galilee. Some were raised in morally upstanding homes, but at least one was a tax collector, which was considered by the Jews of that day a disgraceful occupation. With all these contrasts, it is miraculous that such a Book as the Bible, with such a harmonious theme and single purpose, was produced.

The Bible is God's revelation of himself to man. When we understand this principle we begin to understand the character of the Bible. Since God is who he is, then what is true of him must be characterized in the Book that describes him. God is the Source of this revelation (Deut. 29:29). Christ, the Son of God, is the central theme of the Bible (John 5:38). The Holy Spirit is the divine Author of Scripture (2 Pet. 1:20, 21). Therefore, the Bible is the revelation of God, from God and written by God. The Greek word Paul used actually described the Bible as being "breathed-out from God" (theopneustos) (2 Tim. 3:16) and Jesus spoke of "every word that proceedeth out of the mouth of God" (Matt. 4:4). The words of the Bible are the words of God written by men. This process is called the "inspiration of the Scriptures."

THE MEANING OF INSPIRATION

Inspiration recognizes the role of the Holy Spirit in producing the Scriptures. Paul's use of the term theopneustos communicated the idea of God "breathing out" the Scriptures. Since "spirit" in the original language can also mean "breath," the process of "out-breathing" may rightly be the work of the Holy Spirit as he inspired the Scriptures. Based on the nature of God, the result makes them accurate and inerrant (authoritative), since God is incapable of error. Inspiration applies to every word of the Bible. When we use this term, we are referring to the supernatural guidance of the writers by the Holy Spirit which resulted in every word being accurate and reliable in the original manuscripts. When we talk about the authorship of Scripture, we recognize dual authorship. God wrote the Bible using human authors.

Inspired guidance. Inspiration recognizes the supernatural work of the Holy Spirit upon the writers. Not everyone uses the word "inspiration" with this meaning. Sometimes people use the word to describe the "enthusiasm" of a brilliant artist or athlete. We must define the word as it is used in its context in Scripture. The Bible says "holy men of God spake as they were moved by the Holy Ghost" (2 Pet. 1:21). This process was something beyond the natural. These men were "moved" (picked up and borne along) as they wrote God's message. Therefore, inspiration means an author was guided to go where God wanted him to go, not where he chose.

Inspired writers. Inspiration also incorporates the personality of the writer into the final product. Some have argued in the past that God dictated to the writer who simply recorded it, much as a secretary would type a letter that the boss had dictated. This is called the dictation theory. There are many places where the Scriptures were dictated directly by God (cf. Rev. 2:1—3:22); at other times, the style of the writing and the selection of words reflect the personality and background of the writer. This is especially evident when we read the four Gospels.

Matthew was a Jewish tax collector, impressed with the fact that he had found the King of the Jews. His Gospel begins with a royal genealogy and the arrival of kings from the east to worship Christ. Mark, a young disciple of Peter, seems to reflect Peter's activism in his Gospel. The key word "straightway" or "immediately" makes it appear Jesus is always on the move, doing something as a servant. Luke's Gospel is more methodical, reflecting his historical investigation into the facts. Luke the medical doctor reflects the humanity of Christ and his key word is "the Son of man." The fourth Gospel, written by one "whom Jesus loved," seems to be obsessed with love for Jesus and his love for others. His key word is "believe."

Though each of the four Gospels reflects a different style of the writer and a different perspective of Jesus Christ, they do not contradict each other. They harmonize completely to give us the fully inspired, accurate record of the life of Christ.

Inspired words. Inspiration applies to more than thoughts or impressions of the authors. Inspiration means the words are placed there by God. Every word in the Bible is inspired equally, though some may have a greater influence on our lives than others. Though much of the content of what the writers included was known to them, the Holy Spirit was sovereignly directing them in what to include and to exclude. So the Holy Spirit's ministry extends to the very words. "We have received, not the Spirit of the world, but the Spirit which is of God, that we might know the things that are freely given to us of God. Which things also we speak, not as the *words* which man's wisdom teacheth, but which the Holy Ghost teacheth" (1 Cor. 2:12, 13, italics added.)

A man in a sailboat is dependent upon both the wind and his own skills in sailing a designated course. In the same way, God communicated his revelation to the world in an accurate and reliable Book, every word chosen by the moving of the Holy Spirit of God, yet expressed through the personality of the human author.

There is a similarity between the inspired Word (the Bible) and the incarnate Word (Jesus Christ). Both are fully God without question and both are fully man without sin or error. When they speak it is the authoritative Word of God in all purity, judgment, and truth.

Inerrant and authoritative results. Because the Bible is inspired by God, it is completely accurate and reliable. The Bible differs from other good books in its content, method of writing, and the final result. It is not like *Aesop's Fables* or

The Arabian Nights, a collection of stories that may or may not be true but have good morals. The doctrine of biblical accuracy and reliability is called "inerrancy." This is dealt with further in Chapter 5. If we believe the Bible is inspired by God, we must also accept that it is inerrant. An error in the Bible, as God originally communicated it would reflect a flaw in the character of its Source and Author, God.

THE MANNER OF INSPIRATION

The Hebrew Christians were told, "God, who at sundry times and in divers manners spake in time past unto the fathers by the prophets, Hath in these last days spoken unto us by his Son" (Heb. 1:1, 2). God used a variety of ways to reveal his inspired Word to the men, who then wrote it down for us. Sometimes these men were aware of the significance of what they were recording and why they were writing (John 20:30, 31; Rev. 1:1-3), but on other occasions, they did not realize the full truth they were communicating. Concerning those who wrote the messianic prophecy, Peter said, "Unto whom it was revealed that, not unto themselves, but unto us they did minister the things, which are now reported unto you by them that have preached the gospel unto you with the Holy Ghost sent down from heaven; which things the angels desire to look into" (1 Pet. 1:12). Peter was saying that some authors did not fully understand the message they wrote, but today we can examine its content to understand its meaning. The following chart compares some of the different ways God has used to reveal his inspired Word.

THE MANNERS OF INSPIRATION/REVELATION (Heb. 1:1)
1. Dreams—Dan. 7:1
2. Visions—Ezek. 1:1
3. The actual voice of God—Lev. 1:1
4. Symbols/object lessons—Jer. 19:1-15
5. Dictation—Rev. 2:1–3:22
6. Eyewitness reports—1 John 1:1-3; Rev. 1:2
7. Guidance of the Holy Spirit—2 Pet. 1:21
8. Experience of men/testimony—Ps. 23; 51
9. Historical research—Luke 1:1-4
10. Jesus Christ—John 1:14; Heb. 1:2

Even though God used a variety of different methods to produce the Bible, every verse is as inspired as the next. Every verse of Scripture is authoritative. Jesus acknowledged that not one letter or even one part of a letter would be changed until all Scripture was fulfilled (Matt. 5:18). There is no such thing as a degree of inspiration on a particular part of Scripture that is greater or lesser than in another part of Scripture. Although there were varying degrees of knowledge about the subjects on which they wrote, the authors wrote exactly what God wanted written. God used a variety of ways to give us his word (poetry, history, testimony, law, epistles, or biography), yet every word is his Word, complete and inerrant as a result of the inspiration of the Holy Spirit (2 Tim. 3:16; 2 Pet. 1:21).

THE PROOF OF INSPIRATION

The proofs that the Bible is the inspired Word of God are seen in the Bible itself and in the influence it has had. Since every book communicates in part the nature of its author, the Bible and God share a common character in many respects. That the Bible is understandable in spite of the depth of its simplicity is another mark of the hand of God in this Book. Finally, the influence of the Bible in the lives of its readers demonstrates the work of God himself in human lives.

The character of the Bible. Since an author's personality is reflected in his journalism, the character of God is reflected in the Book he wrote. A closer look at the Scriptures will demonstrate that many of those attributes ascribed to God are also true of the Bible. The holiness of God is prevalent in the Scriptures themselves. It has always seemed appropriate to call it the "Holy Bible." God is a comforting God, and his Word is a source of comfort and encouragement to the reader. Both God and the Bible are eternal and life-giving. The following chart illustrates the revelation of these and other attributes of God and the Bible.

The understandable nature of the Bible. Only God could write a Book like this one. Though the Bible is the result of men who worked within cultural limitations, it is not limited to a

The Character of:	God	Bible
1. Holiness	Isa. 6:3	Ps. 119:3, 9-11
2. Truth	John 17:3	Ps. 119:43, 143
3. Justice	1 John 1:9	Ps. 119:149
4. Power	Nah. 1:2	Ps. 119:114, 116-120
5. Love	1 John 4:8	Ps. 119:32
6. Goodness	Ps. 119:68	Ps. 119:66
7. Righteousness	Ps. 119:137	Ps. 119:138
8. Purity	1 John 3:3	Ps. 119:140
9. Wisdom	Jude 25	Ps. 119:98-100
10. Life-giving	Isa. 40:31	Ps. 119:50
11. Comforting	2 Cor. 1:3	Ps. 119:50, 76
12. Mercy	Ps. 119:64	Ps. 119:58
13. Faithfulness	Ps. 119:90	Ps. 119:86
14. Immutability	Heb. 1:12	Ps. 119:89
15. Joy-producing	Jude 24	Ps. 119:111
16. Wonder	Isa. 9:6	Ps. 119:18, 129
17. Eternity	Ps. 90:2	Ps. 119:144

particular culture. Men in China find the truths of this Book just as applicable to their lives as men in Africa and America. With the exception of the names of various individuals, which would be strange to anyone of a different background than that of the context, most of the Bible can be understood by a school child.

Some studies place the Bible at a sixth-grade readability level. Despite its simplicity, it has a depth of teaching that men have spent a lifetime trying to learn. God inspired this Book realizing it would be a tool for his servants. Few of those servants would be well educated by the world's standards (1 Cor. 1:26-31), so God had to remove as many barriers as possible for them to use his Word. Yet at the same time, the well-educated man is challenged by its profound truth and expression.

No matter what a person's background, he has a responsibility to learn more of the Bible and perfect his skills in studying and using it. Paul advised Timothy, "Study to show thyself approved unto God, a workman that needeth not to be ashamed, rightly dividing the word of truth" (2 Tim. 2:15).

The influence of the Bible. The Bible can have a definite positive influence on the life-style of its readers, even though some have misapplied its truths and entered into grave error. Actually the Bible's influence begins at our conversion. Paul rejoiced that the Romans had "obeyed from the heart that form of doctrine which was delivered unto [them]" (Rom. 6:17). The things a person must know to be saved are found in the Bible. Peter observed that we are "born again, not of corruptible seed, but of incorruptible, by the word of God, which liveth and abideth forever" (1 Pet. 1:23).

The life-style of a Christian ought to be different from that of the unsaved. This is accomplished in four phases, according to 2 Timothy 3:16. Phase one involves building a doctrinal base. Our lives are a result of what we believe. Phase two involves being reproved by the Bible. Reproof means we are shown what we are doing is wrong. If God convicts us of something we are doing, it is important that we obey his instructions. Phase three is correction. It should be easier to do the right thing than to stop the wrong. Whenever the Bible tells us something is wrong, it will also tell us what is right. The final phase is instruction in righteousness, which means building a life-style that naturally avoids the failures of our former life-style. While the Christian does not always have a transformed life-style overnight, every Christian has the power to make progress in his life.

THE EVIDENCE OF INSPIRATION

The total message of the Bible is a supernatural one which only God could reveal to his spokesmen. They recorded the activities and conversations of God at times and places where no man was present to observe. That which was otherwise hidden from man and known only by God was revealed or shown by God to them. Yet, some read the Bible and miss this principle. The Bible teaches that its message came from God and the source of its words are from God. Those who deny the revelation and inspiration of the Bible claim that God gave only an impression or an experience. They deny verbal inspiration, but a close study of the following authors reveals their attitude toward being a divine instrument for communicating the message to men.

Moses. Moses did not attempt to hide his source in recording Scripture but readily acknowledged the fact of revelation. "The secret things belong unto the Lord our God; but those things which are revealed belong unto us and to our children forever, that we may do all the words of this law" (Deut. 29:29).

At his trial, Stephen recognized that the writings of Moses were the revelation of God by the Holy Spirit. After highlighting some of what Moses taught in relation to Christ, Stephen said, "Ye stiffnecked and uncircumcised in heart and ears, ye do always resist the Holy Ghost; as your fathers did, so do ye" (Acts 7:51). Resisting the words of Moses is here equated with resisting the Holy Spirit. That which Moses recorded was revealed to him by the Holy Spirit.

David. Another major contributor to the Old Testament, David, had a special relationship with the Holy Spirit. Jesus said, "For David himself said by the Holy Ghost" (Mark 12:36). This introduction to an Old Testament quote demonstrated the method of inspiration in Scripture. It recognizes that David was used of God to record Scripture. In doing so, God permitted David the full use of his faculties and personality so that it is accurate to say, "David himself said" at the same time he spoke "by the Holy Ghost." An understanding of inspiration must recognize that both are true without affecting a compromise upon the other. "For the prophecy came not in old time by the will of man: but holy men of God spake as they were moved by the Holy Ghost" (2 Pet. 1:21).

In his desire to be right with God, David once prayed, "Cast me not away from thy presence; and take not thy holy spirit from me" (Ps. 51:11). As he recorded the Psalms, he was recording what the Holy Spirit had revealed to him in his walk with God. The New Testament church recognized, "Thou art God, which hast made heaven, and earth, and the sea, and all that in them is: who by the mouth of thy servant David..." (Acts 4:24, 25). This powerful verse shows that the people of the New Testament recognized that the Creator also spoke through human authors by inspiration.

The prophets. As we read the writings of the major and minor prophets we cannot help but be impressed with their reliance upon God for their message. Again and again we read, "Thus saith the Lord." Isaiah said, "The Spirit of the Lord God is upon me, because the Lord hath anointed me to preach good tidings unto the meek; he hath sent me to bind up the brokenhearted, to proclaim liberty to the captives, and the opening of the prison to them that are bound" (Isa. 61:1).

God told Jeremiah, "Behold, I have put my words in thy mouth" (Jer. 1:9). Ezekiel began his prophecy acknowledging, "I saw visions of God" (Ezek. 1:1). Even the minor prophets acknowledged the work of God. "This is the word of the Lord...not by might, nor by power, but by my spirit, saith the Lord of hosts" (Zech. 4:6). The prophets gave abundant witness to speaking God's Word.

Disciples. Jesus promised his disciples that the Holy Spirit would reveal himself to them so they could record the Word of God. "Howbeit when he, the Spirit of truth, is come, he will guide you into all truth: for he shall not speak of himself; but whatever he shall hear, that shall he speak: and he will shew you things to come" (John 16:13).

It is interesting in the light of this promise to see how one of these disciples began the final book of the Bible. "The Revelation of Jesus Christ, which God gave unto him, to show unto his servants things which must shortly come to pass; and he sent and signified it by his angel unto his servant, John" (Rev. 1:1). It should also be noted that John "was in the Spirit on the Lord's day" (Rev. 1:10) when he received this revelation and at least seven times in the Revelation Jesus says, "He that hath an ear, let him hear what the Spirit saith unto the churches" (Rev. 2:7, 11, 17, 29; 3:6, 13, 22). This promise, fulfilled in the ministry of John, was also fulfilled in the ministries of Peter and Matthew as they recorded what the Holy Spirit revealed to them for eternity.

Paul. The apostle Paul acknowledged that God had given him a special revelation. He spoke of "my gospel, and the preaching of Jesus Christ, according to the revelation of the mystery, which was kept secret since the world began, But now is made manifest" (Rom. 16:25, 26). Concerning his revelation, the apostle stated in another place, "But God hath revealed them unto us by his Spirit" (1 Cor. 2:10). The Holy Spirit had a ministry in the life of Paul where the message of God was revealed to him to teach it to others (1 Cor. 2:12, 13). Very quickly in the early church, the epistles of Paul were collected and studied as equal to the Old Testament Scriptures (2 Pet. 3:15, 16). Those that read the Scriptures recognized that Paul's writings were accepted on the same level as Moses and the writers of the Old Testament.

CONCLUSION

God has inspired a single Book for our edification. He used a number of different men and methods to reveal his Word, yet the Holy Spirit governed the writers in such a way that the end result is the very Word of God. The Christian can turn to the Bible with confidence that he is going to hear personally and authoritatively from God. Every Christian needs to allow God to use the Bible in his life to accomplish the will of God.

The children's story *Peter Pan* is based upon the idea of a boy who decided he would never grow up. This story is an amazing commentary on many Christians. Many persons have been born again and have apparently decided to never grow up. For us to ignore all that God has given us is like going to a huge banquet and not so much as drinking a glass of water. A poor diet can stunt the growth of a child. The same holds true of the Christian who ignores his Bible.

DAILY READINGS

☐Monday: *Psalm 19*   ☐Tuesday: *1 Peter 1:13-15*
☐Wednesday: *2 Peter 1:12-21*   ☐Thursday: *Hebrews 4:9-16*
☐Friday: *2 Timothy 3:15—4:8*   ☐Saturday: *Isaiah 40:1-8*
☐Sunday: *James 1:19-27*

FIVE
INERRANCY AND CANONICITY

*For verily I say unto you, Till heaven and earth pass, one jot or
one tittle shall in no wise pass from the law, till all be fulfilled.*
Matthew 5:18

INTRODUCTION

There was a time when it was not known that oil existed in
the Middle East in general and Egypt in particular. The story
of the initial discovery is a remarkable demonstration of one
man's faith in the integrity of the Bible.

One of the directors of the company was a Christian who
practiced reading the Scriptures. One day, while he was
reading through Exodus, one verse stood out in particular.
He read concerning the mother of Moses, "And when she
could not longer hide him, she took for him an ark of bul-
rushes, and daubed it with slime and with pitch, and put the
child therein; and she laid it in the flags by the river's brink"
(Exod. 2:3). Being an oil man, his mind went into overdrive
when he read the word "pitch." He knew pitch was a by-
product of oil, and if a slave could find pitch in Egypt, there
must be oil somewhere nearby. On the basis of one word in
one verse, Charles Whitsholt was sent to Egypt by Standard
Oil to find oil.

The amazing accuracy of the details of the Bible also had a
tremendous impact over a hundred years ago on a young En-

glish scholar named Ramsey. Like many intellectuals of his day, Ramsey believed the Bible was unreliable. Unlike his contemporaries, he set out to prove it. He traveled to the Near East to gather evidence to prove his point. As he searched and dug in ruins, he soon discovered the New Testament was extremely accurate even to the smallest detail. The lesson learned so impressed the young student that he entered the ministry. Even today, the works of Sir William Ramsey are considered by many as important contributions to biblical studies.

Today it has become popular among some evangelicals to question the integrity of the Bible yet still to claim to believe it is inspired. The amazing accuracy and reliability of the Bible is the natural by-product of supernatural inspiration.

THE INERRANCY OF THE BIBLE

As we look back into history, the great theologians and Bible teachers of the past didn't address themselves to the problem of inerrancy because inerrancy was assumed. But that has all changed. Today, the issue of inerrancy is one of the most important questions currently faced by Christians.

According to a contemporary scholar, James Montgomery Boice, "Inerrancy states that what is inspired is also authoritative." Historically, Christians have believed in verbal inspiration, that every word of the Bible as it was originally given, in Hebrew, Aramaic, and Greek, is inspired by God. By this they have assumed that every word was therefore accurate and authoritative, as the author meant it to be. The Bible is not deceitful or fraudulent.

Today, some people are wavering, teaching that the Bible is inspired but that the part of Scripture which speaks of geography, history, and creation may not be accurate. Some critics suggest the Bible is inspired and accurate in matters relating to God and doctrine, but when the Bible speaks on science, it contains scientific inaccuracies. There are many good reasons to reject this suggestion.

The Bible teaches inerrancy. Paul wrote, "All scripture is given by inspiration of God" (2 Tim. 3:16). Peter claimed,

"Holy men of God spake as they were moved by the Holy Ghost" (2 Pet. 1:21). When New Testament writers quoted from the Old Testament, they considered they were quoting God. This is seen in one of the prayers of the early church. "Lord, thou art God, who hast made heaven, and earth, and the sea, and all that in them is; who by the mouth of thy servant, David, has said . . ." (Acts 4:24, 25). The writer to the Hebrews wrote, "As the Holy Spirit said . . ." (Heb. 3:7) and then went on to quote David.

Even while some New Testament books were being written, other New Testament books were already recognized as Scripture. Peter wrote, "Even as our beloved Paul . . . hath written unto you; As also in all his epistles, speaking in them of these things; in which are some things hard to be understood, which they that are unlearned and unstable wrest, as they do also the other Scriptures" (2 Pet. 3:15, 16). Peter classified Paul's writings with the other Scriptures and in fact was saying Paul's writings are Scripture.

Jesus testified to biblical inerrancy. Jesus used the Bible authoritatively during his ministry. When he was tempted by Satan to sin, three times he said, "It is written" (Matt. 4:1-11). He appealed to the Scriptures to defend his actions (Matt. 26:54-56; Mark 11:15-17). He claimed the "Scriptures cannot be broken" (John 10:34, 35). What he was saying was that "the Scriptures cannot be treated as if events never happened."

Jesus believed every letter of Scripture was accurate. He taught "till heaven and earth pass, one jot or one tittle shall in no wise pass from the law, till all be fulfilled" (Matt. 5:18).

Most of the Old Testament was originally written in Hebrew. The *yod* was the smallest letter of the Hebrew alphabet. *Caph* and *beth* are very similar letters, distinguished only by an extended line at the base of the letter *beth*. Many Bible commentators believe that Jesus was referring to these letters when he said not one "jot or tittle" would change a letter in the Hebrew alphabet much less a word. As far as Jesus was concerned, even the smallest letter of the alphabet or an otherwise insignificant mark distinguishing two letters "shall in no wise pass from the law till all be fulfilled." Had the Bible been originally written in English, Jesus might have said "not one dot over an *i* or one crossing of the *t* would pass from the law." Jesus obviously believed in inerrancy.

In Exodus 3:6, God is recorded as saying, "I am the God of thy father, the God of Abraham, the God of Isaac, and the God of Jacob." Yet, these three men were dead when Moses heard this message from God. Jesus argued on the basis of the tense of the verb when he confronted the Sadducees who did not believe in the resurrection or life beyond the grave. Here Jesus said, "God is," not "God was." Even though Abraham, Isaac, and Jacob were dead when God spoke to Moses, they had not ceased to exist. "God is their God because they are alive with him." For Jesus, not only the spelling of the words but the tenses of the verbs were important and inerrant in the Scripture.

The apostles believed in inerrancy. Paul had no question but that he was proclaiming the Word of God as he wrote. He told the Corinthians, "If any man think himself to be a prophet, or spiritual, let him acknowledge that the things that I write unto you are the commandments of the Lord" (1 Cor. 14:37). John referred to his writings as "the record that God gave of his Son" (1 John 5:10).

Concerning the Old Testament authors, Peter wrote, "Unto whom it was revealed, that not unto themselves, but unto us they did minister the things, which are now reported unto you by them that have preached the gospel unto you with the Holy Ghost sent down from heaven; which things the angels desire to look into" (1 Pet. 1:12).

The writers of the New Testament claimed to be speaking by the Holy Spirit. This was in fulfillment of Jesus' promise to his disciples that "the Holy Ghost...shall teach you all things" (John 14:26). When these men wrote, they were aware that they were speaking God's message, not that which they had themselves developed (Acts 2:4; 4:3, 31; 13:9; Gal. 1:1, 12; 1 Thess. 2:13; 4:28; Rev. 21:5; 22:6, 18, 19).

The character of God demands inerrancy. The real issue of inerrancy is centered in the character of God. Some who deny inerrancy will eagerly point out that the Bible is God's revelation, but they do not necessarily believe the Bible is completely accurate. But we recognize the Bible comes from God, and the perfect nature of God would make it impossible for him to write a book that was not perfect. God, because he is God, could not have produced other than an inerrant revelation of himself. If a choice is to be made, the Bible says, "Let God be true, but every man a liar" (Rom. 3:4). Twice the Bible says it is impossible for God to lie (Titus 1:2; Heb. 6:18). The divine attribute of truth is also ascribed to the Bible (Ps. 119:160; John 17:17).

The argument against inerrancy today states, "God inspired the Scriptures but he included some things he knew were wrong because the people of that time thought they were right." There were times when God responded on the basis of man's understanding of nature. When Joshua prayed for the sun and moon to stand still (Josh. 10:12), he evidently didn't understand what caused the sun and moon to move across the sky. Obviously, it was the earth's turning that God stopped, which gave the appearance of the sun and moon standing still, to give Joshua a longer day to finish the battle. But this accommodation of God to man's understanding in no way lessens the inerrancy of God's Word.

THE RELIABILITY OF THE SCRIPTURES

It would be foolish to try to argue that the Bible is a textbook of mathematics. Any reader would realize that it contains some arithmetic, but not a presentation of the science of mathematics. However, anything the Bible says about mathematics is reliable. Apparent numerical inconsistencies, such as the ages of certain Old Testament kings, are cleared up by treating them as different methods of counting rather than as errors. The same could be said about botany, geology, history, or any other subject. God's nature would prohibit him from writing a book to accurately reveal himself, yet use innovative data from history or physical science.

Science and the Bible. There is no proven fact of science that creates an inexplicable problem for any verse of Scripture; however, some theories of science disagree with Scripture.

But, as has happened on many occasions, after examination and testing, many of the theories of men have been proven false. More and more scientists are now accepting the biblical accounts of creation and flood as an accurate scientific explanation of the events that happened. Simple medical advances, such as isolating those with contagious diseases, washing hands thoroughly, and giving careful thought to diet, were all part of the Mosaic writings. Some argue the Bible is unscientific when idioms like the "sun rising" (Eccles. 1:5) or the "dew falling" (Num. 11:9) are used, but somehow the same critics fail to apply the same standards when the same phrases are used by meteorologists on television today.

History and the Bible. Whenever there has been a conflict between the Bible and another document of antiquity, further study has shown the Bible to be reliable. The Bible was written largely by eyewitnesses to the events recorded in its pages (2 Pet. 1:16; 1 John 1:1-3). Most historians, like Luke (Luke 1:1-4), tried to uncover primary sources when they were preparing to write about historical events. Many of the passages in Scripture were written by witnesses of the facts. This should be proof enough of the credibility of God's Word, yet the eyewitnesses also had the enabling of the Holy Spirit by inspiration to record an accurate Book.

Archaeology and the Bible. One of the strongest arguments for the reliability of the Bible is archaeology. Professor H. H. Rowley says, "It is not because scholars of today begin with more conservative presuppositions than their predecessors that they have a much greater respect for the patriarchal stories than was formerly common, but because the evidence warrants it."

Another archaeologist, Sir Fredrick Kenyon, observes, "Archaeology has not yet said its last word; but the results already achieved confirm what faith would suggest, that the Bible can do nothing but gain from an increase of knowledge." As you read the writings of the archaeologists today, it is evident that a profound respect for the accuracy and historicity of Scripture exists in their minds.

Prophecy and the Bible. Over 40 percent of the Bible was prophetic when it was written. Some Scriptures told of nations which would be judged by God, and they were judged. Others dealt with the future of individuals, and they too were fulfilled. Hundreds of prophecies concerning the coming of Jesus to save men were literally fulfilled during his lifetime. The odds of this happening by chance are 1 in 10^{23} or about the same as a blindfolded man finding on the first try a particular silver dollar thrown into a pile of silver dollars large enough to cover the state of Texas two feet deep. The following chart illustrates some of those prophecies fulfilled in Jesus' life.

EVENT	FORETOLD	FULFILLED
1. Virgin birth	Isa. 7:14	Matt. 1:23
2. Descendant of Abraham	Gen. 12:2, 3	Matt. 1:1
3. Birthplace	Mic. 5:2	Matt. 2:1
4. Miracles performed	Isa. 35:5, 6	Matt. 9:35
5. Use of parables	Ps. 78:2	Matt. 13:34
6. Resurrection	Ps. 16:10	Acts 2:31
7. Betrayed by friend	Ps. 41:9	Matt. 10:4
8. Crucified with thieves	Isa. 53:12	Matt. 27:38
9. Prayed for persecutors	Isa. 53:12	Luke 23:24
10. Gambling at the cross	Ps. 22:18	John 19:23, 24

THE CANONICITY OF THE BIBLE

Some religious groups today accept the Bible as one of their religious books but they also accept other so-called "revelations from God." We deny that any of these claims are accurate. The sixty-six books of the Bible form the completed canon of Scripture. "Canon" comes from "reed or measurement." A canonical book is one that measured up to the standard of Scripture. Today, books in the canon are those that are universally recognized by Christians on the official list of books of Scripture. Christianity accepts sixty-six books of the Bible, thirty-nine Old Testament books and twenty-seven New Testament books.

Josephus, a Jewish historian during the life of Christ, testified that the books of the Old Testament were brought together during the reign of Artaxerxes Longimanus (464 to
424 B.C.) during the life of Ezra the Scribe (Neh. 8:1, 4, 9, 14;
7:6, 11; 12:26, 36). H. C. Theissen notes:

*By the end of the second century all but seven books, Hebrews,
II and III John, II Peter, Jude, James and Revelation, the so-
called antilegomena, were recognized as apostolic, and by the
end of the fourth century all the twenty-seven books in our
present Canon were recognized by all the churches of the West.
After the Damasine Council of Rome A.D. 332 and the third
Council of Carthage A.D. 397 the question of the Canon was
closed in the West. By the year 500 the whole Greek-speaking
church seemed also to have accepted all the books in our
present New Testament.*

The early Christian church used four criteria to determine
what books appeared in the canon. First, they included books
that were written by apostles or an author in special relationship to an apostle, such as Mark, Luke, and James. Second,
the contents were revelatory in nature; hence, apocryphal,
(of doubtful origin) and pseudepigraphical (written under
pseudonyms or anonymously) books were eliminated. Many
such books appeared around 200 B.C. Third, the church accepted books that were universally recognized as Scripture.
These were the books that were used in preaching and teaching. Finally, the books that were considered inspired or gave
evidence of inspiration where placed in the canon.
    There are several reasons why these sixty-six books were
included in the canon.

The end of doctrinal revelation. God implied in Scripture that
the giving of revelation would terminate and come to an end.
By implication, those who added to revelation would be
judged and those who took away from the revelation would
also receive God's condemnation (Rev. 22:18, 19). This verse
is integrated specifically to the last book of the Bible, and by
application can be extended to all sixty-six books.
    God's wisdom anticipated the tendency towards corrup-

tion of his message, and he issued warnings against those who would "corrupt the Word of God" (2 Cor. 2:12). The same warning was given to those who "pervert the gospel" (Gal. 1:7). Any tendency toward heresy was also condemned by God, apostasy being that which took away from God's message. God warned in the Old Testament not to add to his Word (Prov. 30:6). The New Testament concludes with a similar warning (Rev. 22:18, 19). James spoke of the Bible as the "perfect [complete] law of liberty" (James 1:25), again implying a full system of doctrine. Since God warned that no one could add or subtract from his doctrine, we conclude that the revelation of God in the Bible is complete.

Completion of the task of writing revelation. All the truth that God is going to reveal has been revealed. This means God will not add to the truth about himself that he revealed in the Bible. The task of revealing truth is completed. God began by revealing himself (theology proper) and ends with the doctrine of eschatology (the last things). Everything that man needs on every subject has been revealed, but this does not include everything that man wants to know. Since this revelation is complete in content, there came a time when Jude could say, "the faith which was once delivered unto the saints" (Jude 3). We do not need additional revelations from God, therefore the canon is closed.

Prophetic office. Revelation was recorded by "holy men of God . . . as they were moved by the Holy Ghost" (2 Pet. 1:21). When Paul says that the church was built upon the apostles and prophets (Eph. 2:20), he was indicating that these two offices were recipients of revelatory truth.

Acceptance by spiritual people. A message from God is recognized by people who have his Spirit. One of the criteria to determine the canon is its recognition and acceptance by the church. We believe that the message of God is spiritually discerned, and that only those who possess the Holy Spirit can recognize God's Spirit (1 Cor. 3:6-9). Jesus said, "My sheep hear my voice and follow me" (John 10:24). In essence, God's people will recognize his voice in the written page and obey his commandments. But at the same time, they will recognize that certain claims to inspiration are false claims. While this is a subjective argument and will not stand alone, it will support the other arguments for a closed canon. There has been no large movement by evangelical Christians to recognize a new, inspired book.

The acceptance of the Old and New Testament and the apparent indestructibility of the canon are additional arguments for a closed canon. When the Bible is read alongside its contemporary literature, the mark of God becomes even more obvious in its pages.

CONCLUSION

There is no good reason for anyone to doubt the authority and accuracy of the Bible. The foundation of Scripture is the basis for Christian living (Matt. 7:24-27). And when the Bible is applied to the lives of Christians, it becomes a further source to demonstrate its credibility. Paul used this argument when writing to the Corinthians, "Ye are our epistle written in our heart, known and read of all men" (2 Cor. 3:2). People today will not recognize the Bible for what it is until they see it lived out in our lives.

Mahatma Gandhi has been identified as one of the most influential men of this century. This Hindu leader brought democracy to the nation of India. He was a man who had at one time seriously considered converting to Christianity. After studying Christianity and Christians, Gandhi is reported to have said, "I would be a Christian, if it were not for Christians." He failed to see the principles of the Bible lived out in the lives of Christians.

DAILY READINGS

☐Monday: *Matthew 5:17-20*   ☐Tuesday: *John 17:9-19*
☐Wednesday: *John 10:22-42*   ☐Thursday: *Matthew 12:38-41*
☐Friday: *2 Corinthians 2:14—3:3*   ☐Saturday:
Mark 7:1-13   ☐Sunday: *Luke 24:13-29*

SIX
HOW TO
INTERPRET THE BIBLE

Open thou mine eyes, that I may behold wondrous things out of thy law. Psalm 119:18

INTRODUCTION

After the events of the resurrection morning, two disciples made their way home to Emmaus from Jerusalem. They were joined by Jesus as they walked, but at first they did not recognize him. As they talked, Cleopas, one of the two, was surprised that the stranger did not seem to have heard the reports of the crucifixion and resurrection of Jesus.

Jesus responded by explaining the Scriptures, showing how the Messiah was to suffer and be raised from the dead. Though the two disciples were familiar with the Scriptures, they had not previously understood them. Later that evening, as they sat with Jesus and he broke bread in their sight, the Bible says, "Their eyes were opened, and they knew him; and he vanished out of their sight. And they said one to another, Did not our heart burn within us, while he talked with us along the way, and while he opened to us the scriptures?" (Luke 24:31, 32).

DEFINITION OF ILLUMINATION

What Jesus did with those two disciples on the Emmaus road is what the Holy Spirit does with Christians in their Bible study today. Because the Bible is a spiritual book, the Christian needs spiritual help when he comes to interpret it. As we come to read the Bible, the Holy Spirit aids us in understanding the Scriptures. Theologians call this aspect of the Holy Spirit's work "illumination."

Illumination is the ministry of the Holy Spirit which enables us to understand and apply the spiritual message of the Scriptures. When a Christian sits before an open Bible and begins to discover the truths of Scripture, this ministry of the Holy Spirit enables him to understand the message of Scripture.

Illumination is a ministry of the Holy Spirit. Some things cannot be learned apart from supernatural aid. The Holy Spirit directly illuminates men's understanding. Later John wrote, "By this know ye the Spirit of God: every spirit that confesseth that Jesus Christ is come in the flesh is of God" (1 John 4:2). One of the reasons every Christian has the Holy Spirit is "that we might know the things that are freely given to us of God" (1 Cor. 2:12). Spiritual illumination is one of the distinguishing marks of the saved, as spiritual blindness is a mark of the unsaved. "But the natural man receiveth not the things of the Spirit of God: for they are foolishness unto him: neither can he know them, because they are spiritually discerned" (1 Cor. 2:14).

Illumination results in an understanding of the Scripture. The Holy Spirit, who inspired men to write the Scriptures in the past, instructs Christians who read the Scriptures today. The author of a book is always the one who best understands his writing. In the same way, the divine Author of Scripture is best suited to teach us the things of God. Jesus told his disciples, "when he, the Spirit of truth, is come, he will guide you into all truth;. . .he shall take of mine and shew it unto you" (John 16:13-15).

In the experience of some of these early disciples, the Holy Spirit ministered through revelation to write the Scripture. Today the same Holy Spirit takes the inspired Word and ministers in our lives through illumination (1 Cor. 2:12-16).

Illumination is dependent upon a man's relation with God.
God never forces his truth upon any individual. Sometimes
we miss out on what God wants to give us because of our unwillingness to cooperate with him. When we come to interpret the Bible, we must be careful not to allow sin to hinder
the Spirit of God. We must be willing to respond positively to
the Scriptures if we expect God to teach us. David prayed,
"Teach me, O Lord, the way of thy statutes; and I shall keep it
unto the end. Give me understanding, and I shall keep thy
law; yea, I shall observe it with my whole heart" (Ps.119:33,
34).

THE NEED FOR ILLUMINATION

The Holy Spirit helps us focus on the important truths we
need to know. Actually, our spiritual illumination is more
than an aid to natural understanding; the Bible describes our
problem as hardness of heart.

Hardness is the inability or the unwillingness to understand the spiritual message of the Scriptures. Some men have
known more of the Bible than some Christians in terms of
actual content, but they did not understand the spiritual
truth of redemption, repentance, and regeneration. The Bible speaks of three occasions when spiritual discernment
was not possible.

Israel's hardness of heart. The Bible speaks of a partial and
temporary insensibility of the nation of Israel. The Jews, who
had the Scriptures and should have welcomed their Messiah,
rejected him and called for his crucifixion. "He [Jesus] came
unto his own [the Jews], and his own received him not" (John
1:11). Paul spoke of "blindness [hardness]" as happening to
Israel (Rom. 11:25). Israel's rejection is temporary. The time
is coming when many Jews will turn to Christ (Rom. 11:26;
2 Cor. 3:14, 15). God's temporarily setting aside the nation he
loves so much ought to be a warning to Christians not to reject the teaching of the Scriptures.

The blindness of unbelief. The Bible also identifies a type of
blindness of unsaved people. John wrote, "He that hateth his

brother is in darkness, and walketh in darkness, and knoweth not where he goeth, because that darkness hath blinded his eyes" (1 John 2:11). This blindness is overcome with the light of the gospel. Writing of the birth of Christ hundreds of years before the event, Isaiah wrote, "The people that walked in darkness have seen a great light; they that dwell in the land of the shadow of death, upon them hath the light shined" (Isa. 9:2). From the Fall of man to the spread of Christianity to the Gentiles, Gentiles knew nothing but spiritual darkness. Unsaved heathen today are still in this blindness.

Jesus told Nicodemus that, apart from a spiritual rebirth, he could not "see the kingdom of God" (John 3:3). Writing to the Corinthians (primarily Gentiles) Paul wrote, "But if our gospel be hid, it is hid to them that are lost: In whom the god of this world hath blinded the minds of them which believe not, lest the light of the glorious gospel of Christ, who is the image of God, should shine unto them" (2 Cor. 4:3, 4). Satan has imposed a blindness upon both unsaved Jew and Gentile to prevent them from seeing (understanding) the gospel and believing in Christ.

Even after salvation, it is possible for a Christian to hinder the work of the Holy Spirit by allowing sin to continue in his life. Paul exhorted the Colossian Christians to "walk worthy of the Lord" in order to be "increasing in the knowledge of God" (Col. 1:10). If we try to interpret the Bible knowing there is unconfessed sin in our lives, the Holy Spirit will not be able to show us all we need to learn.

THE WORK OF THE HOLY SPIRIT IN ILLUMINATION

Illumination is one of the many present-day ministries of the Holy Spirit to Christians. He can reveal to us important spiritual truths we could not otherwise know. While we normally think of illumination in terms of helping the Christian understand the Bible, it occurs as conviction to the unsaved.

Conviction to the unsaved. Conviction is clearly the work of the Holy Spirit. Jesus said, "When he is come, he will reprove [convict] the world of sin, and of righteousness, and of judgment" (John 16:8). The word "convict" means "to rebuke or to cause to see." Before a person receives Christ as Savior, the main work of the Holy Spirit is to help that individual to see his need for the Savior. The Holy Spirit convicts by causing the sinner to see his sin, to see the righteousness of Jesus Christ, and to see the sin judgment of the cross (John 16:9-11). When the sinner is convicted of (sees) his sin, he is rebuked or convicted. Then he is motivated to seek salvation.

Understanding to the saved. The other aspect of this ministry of the Holy Spirit is in helping the Christian to understand the Bible. As a Christian reads his Bible, the Holy Spirit causes that man to understand God's plan for his salvation. The same man without the Holy Spirit would be unable to uncover spiritual truth from the passage, "but he that is spiritual judgeth all things" (1 Cor. 2:15). As we seek to interpret and apply the Bible to our lives, we realize that the Holy Spirit is our Teacher (John 14:26; 16:13, 14). Spiritual illumination is also called the anointing of the Holy Spirit (1 John 2:20, 27).

The next two sections examine the principles which must be obeyed when we come to study the Bible. Both are important. The man who is spiritually right with God, yet fails to give attention to the normal rules of language interpretation will miss out on the message of Scripture. The man who follows these principles of interpretation exactly but is not walking in fellowship with God will also miss important lessons when he attempts to interpret the Bible.

SPIRITUAL PRINCIPLES OF INTERPRETING THE BIBLE

If God used holy men of God to write his Book, he wants holy men of God to interpret his Book. If we are not in proper relation with God, it is not realistic to think we will be able to interpret the Bible rightly.

Prayer. Every Christian needs to pray as he comes to study the Bible. The Bible is God's revelation to man. As we come to hear what God has to say, we need to talk to God. David prayed, "Open thou mine eyes, that I may behold wondrous things out of thy law" (Ps. 119:18). This ought to be our prayer as we come to interpret the Bible.

Cleansing. Sin in the life of a Christian will hinder the Holy Spirit from illuminating the Scriptures. It is important that we are not harboring unconfessed sin in our lives if we expect God to teach us through the Bible. Because no one is perfect, we need constantly to apply the principle of 1 John 1:9 to maintain our fellowship with God. "If we confess our sins, he is faithful and just to forgive us our sins, and to cleanse us from all unrighteousness." Naturally, the Christian must strive to live a pure life, but when we fail, God is willing to forgive if we will confess.

No one can have a cleansed life until he first receives Christ as personal Savior. Jesus told his disciples "that except your righteousness shall exceed the righteousness of the scribes and Pharisees, ye shall in no case enter into the kingdom of heaven" (Matt. 5:20). The righteousness Jesus requires of his disciples is not a superior list of standards or perfect life-styles. Rather, everyone should receive the righteousness of God by faith (Rom. 3:24, 25).

At salvation, we are first cleansed, but as we live in this world, we are contaminated by the affairs of life. When we sin, we need to be cleansed so we can restore our broken fellowship with God. Jesus said, "He that is washed needeth not save to wash his feet, but is clean every whit: and ye are clean, but not all" (John 13:10).

Comparing Scripture. The Bible is the best interpreter of itself. As we study the Bible, we should learn to compare the Scriptures we are studying with other relevant passages of Scripture to interpret the Bible.

LITERARY PRINCIPLES OF INTERPRETING THE BIBLE

Conservatives believe in a "historical grammatical" interpretation of the Bible. This basically means that we study the Bible within its historical context. In other words, we interpret the Bible as we would normally interpret any literary work, using the normal rules of grammar.

Historical context. As we come to interpret a passage, we must consider the historical context of the passage. Since the author spoke to a historical setting, we must understand something about that background to interpret the text.

Also, the more we know about the author, the easier it will be to determine what he wanted to say in the passage. The Bible was written by men to other individuals or groups. The good interpreter of the Bible will also interpret a passage in light of the recipients of the message. We should also consider the place of the passage in the context of the total message of the book in which it is found.

Grammatical context. Words are important. God inspired the words of Scripture. When both the Old and New Testaments were being written, God chose to use Hebrew and Greek, explicit languages to write his Word. God chose to give his Word first to people in a culture that was very careful about the words used. When we interpret the Bible, we should use our knowledge of grammar to interpret the passage.

Literal meaning. The Bible should be interpreted literally, which means we should seek the obvious meaning of words, context, and language. When we interpret literally, we seek the literal meaning of the author when he wrote or spoke the message of God. We should not seek for a hidden or mystical meaning. If God had written his message in esoteric pictures, there would be no objectivity to Christianity. Anyone could make a passage mean anything he desired. Hence, there could be no Christianity.

Do not stumble over the word "mystery" in Scripture (Eph. 3:8). A mystery was part of the message of grace that was hidden in the Old Testament, but revealed in the New.

Figurative language. The Bible contains much figurative language, such as metaphors, simile, parables (extended metaphors), and many other figures of speech. It is generally clear when figurative language appears that a clear understandable message is being taught. To interpret the Bible the reader must search for the literal meaning the author had in mind when he used the figurative language.

The principle of interpreting Scripture according to the meaning of the author should remind us that the Bible has two authors—human and divine. Therefore, we must follow human laws of interpretation to understand Scripture. But we must also follow the spiritual principles of illumination to understand the mind of the Holy Spirit.

CONCLUSION

God has given us a revelation of himself in the Bible. He did not give it to us to frustrate us with something we could not understand. He also gave each Christian the Holy Spirit to illuminate the Scriptures, so that the message of God could be understood. As we study the Bible, we need to apply sound principles of interpretation. While we recognize that man will sometimes disagree, we believe the problem stems from wrong application of literary principles or spiritual problems in the believer's life. But when diligently applied, you can begin to understand God's message in the Bible.

DAILY READINGS

☐Monday: *Luke 24:30-43*   ☐Tuesday: *Luke 24:44-53*
☐Wednesday: *1 Corinthians 2:9-16*   ☐Thursday: *Psalm 51*
☐Friday: *Psalm 139*   ☐Saturday: *Ephesians 3:1-12*
☐Sunday: *2 Corinthians 4:1-7*

PART THREE

UNDERSTANDING THE DOCTRINE OF GOD

SEVEN
WHO GOD IS

Hear, O Israel: The Lord our God is one Lord: And thou shalt love the Lord thy God with all thine heart, and with all thy soul, and with all thy might. Deuteronomy 6:4, 5

INTRODUCTION

"Who is God?" is one of the most frequently asked questions by both children and philosophers alike. When we study about God, we are studying about the One who affects us most. He is the Creator and Sustainer of all life and will reward those who commit their lives to him. But most people appear to live without recognizing God. He is called the all-knowing One, yet so few know much about him. He is a God of order, yet the discussion about God ends in confusion. When a crisis of life comes suddenly upon us, we find ourselves searching for God, yet not quite sure who God is.

THE DIFFICULTY OF KNOWING GOD

We must be aware of the source of the staggering problem that confronts us as we seek to know God. To understand fully the nature and existence of God is an impossible task for us in this life (1 Cor. 13:12). God cannot and never will be fully comprehended by human minds. The very nature of unlimited reality can never be understood by a limited mind. The very words we use to describe God are finite words and cannot adequately describe an infinite God. Beyond these problems, God has withheld himself. "No man hath seen God at any time" (John 1:18). Therefore, the following observations on the nature of God are, at best, like man attempting to describe the nature of the sun—calculated opinions based on partial facts.

WHO IS GOD?

Men have tried for centuries to adequately define God. Many theologies and catechisms have been produced in this effort. They have found how difficult it is to produce a simple statement defining God in his totality. A definition of God will include seven aspects. The Scriptures define God as: (1) Spirit, (2) a Person, (3) life, (4) self-existent, (5) unchanging, (6) unlimited by time or space, and (7) a unity, which means God is one God.

Every definition must have a definitive term, such as "the man is a husband." The definitive term "husband" gives meaning to the word being defined. The following chart gives seven definitive terms that give meaning to the nature of God. Notice each definitive term contains a specific truth about God. When all are placed together, a picture of God's nature as he has revealed himself, is seen.

WHO IS GOD?	
God is	Spirit
	A Person
	Life
	A self-existent Being
	Unity (one God)
	Unchangeable
	Eternal and limitless

God is Spirit. Jesus told the Samaritan woman, "God is a Spirit: and they that worship him must worship him in spirit and in truth" (John 4:24). Even though the *King James Version* uses the article "a" with Spirit, God should not be referred to as a Spirit, which means "one of many." The original languages should be interpreted to read "God is spirit," which describes his nature.

As Spirit, God is not limited by a physical body. "Spirit" means incorporeal being. God is a real Being who does not exist in or through a physical body (Luke 24:39). Although God is said to have hands (Isa. 65:2), feet (Ps. 8:6), eyes (1 Kings 8:29) and fingers (Exod. 8:19), he is not to be understood as having a physical body. God attributes human form and personality to himself in order to relate to humanity in terms meaningful to us. In some passages God is also said to have wings (Ps. 17:8; 36:7) and feathers (Ps. 91:4), but this figurative language, depicting God as a protecting mother bird, does not imply that God has a physical body.

A spirit is also invisible. Though God was in the pillar of fire that led Israel through the wilderness, he was never visible to the nation (Deut. 4:15). There are some passages in Scripture where it seems that men actually saw God (Gen. 32:30; Exod. 3:6; 34:9, 10; Num. 12:6-8; Deut. 34:10; Isa. 6:1). Actually, it would be more correct to say these men saw a reflection of God, but did not see him directly. The only ones who have seen God are those who saw Christ, "the image of the invisible God" (Col. 1:15). Because God is invisible Spirit, no one has ever seen him (John 1:18; 1 Tim. 1:17).

The second commandment is a ban on the making of idols. It prevents the use of idols in religious service. God prohibits idols for many reasons but one of them was because God is Spirit.

God is a Person. Most of the religions of the world portray God as an impersonal Being or a force. The Bible paints a totally different picture of God. He has all of the characteristics of personality.

A basic characteristic of personality is self-awareness, the ability to know oneself. When God told Moses, "I am that I am" (Exod. 3:14), God was describing himself according to his own perception. He was aware of who he was.

God also has self-determination, the second characteristic of personality. Self-determination implies freedom and God is free to do whatever he chooses. Hence, being a person is equated with freedom. The opposite of freedom is determinism and there is nothing that makes God do or be anything. God is free to follow the direction of his nature. Hence, when man is made in the image of God, man is a free being, responsible to his Maker.

Self-determination involves accepting the responsibility for one's life. The self-determination of God is seen in that he exists by himself and perpetuates himself by his nature (Job 23:13; Rom. 9:11; Heb. 6:17).

Personality also implies intelligence. God is said to know (Gen. 18:19; Exod. 3:7) and have known (Acts 15:18). The infinite wisdom and omniscience of God is clearly taught in the Bible (Jer. 39:19).

Another characteristic of personality is emotion. Some may not use the word "emotion" relating to God, but rather the word "sensibility." However, emotions are attributed to God. Note the following feelings that are present in God: Genesis 6:6 (grief); John 3:16 (love); Psalm 103:8-13 (kindness); Exodus 3:7, 8 (empathy); John 11:35 (sorrow); Psalm 7:11 (anger).

Because God is a Person, he also has a will, the volitional aspect of personality. He has the ability to make his own decisions and choose his own actions (John 4:34; Rom. 12:2). The acts of God are not responsive to outside stimulus as ours sometimes are. When God acts, his volition is motivated according to his predetermined will.

If we possessed the infinite understanding as does the will of God, we would find God's activities very predictable. Paul urged the Romans, "Present your bodies a living sacrifice, holy, acceptable unto God,...that ye may prove what is that good, and acceptable, and perfect will of God" (Rom. 12:1, 2).

God is life. Joshua told his people, "Ye shall know that the living God is among you" (Josh. 3:10). Young David recognized that Goliath was defying "the living God" (1 Sam. 17:26) and not just Israel. Later he wrote, "For with thee is the fountain of life" (Ps. 36:9). Peter called Jesus "the Son of the living God" (Matt. 16:16). The Bible makes frequent reference to the "living God." He is both the source and sustainer of life (John 5:26). In essence, life comes from the nature of God, because God is life. When God gives life to something, he gives a part of his nature to it. All life comes from "the life" (John 14:6).

God is self-existent. One of the common names for God in the Old Testament is "Jehovah." The name comes from the verb "I am." In Exodus 3:13-15, Moses confronted Jehovah in a burning bush. When Moses asked for an identification of God, the answer given was, "I am that I am." The name implied not only that God always was, is, and will be, but that God is independent of any other thing. "Jehovah," therefore, means "the self-existent God." Others interpret the name to mean also "the one who is utterly trustworthy and reliable." Man exists in dependence upon food, water, and air, but God exists independently. From before birth man is dependent upon others, but God is dependent only upon himself.

God is immutable. By definition, God is perfect and cannot become better (Ps. 102:25-27). If he became less than perfect, he would not be God. God is therefore immutable; he cannot change.

The Bible states, "God is not a man, that he should lie; neither the son of man, that he should repent" (Num. 23:19). To deny the immutability of God, some have pointed to the biblical accounts of God repenting. A close look at these accounts (Gen. 6:6; 1 Sam. 15:11) reveals that it was men, not God, that changed. When men sinned, God was consistent in his nature to judge sin. The word "repent" used in these references refers to an expression of sorrow rather than a change of character or nature.

When men sought to live for God, God was still consistent in his nature to reward believers. The changing life-styles of men caused the consistent behavior of God to appear to change, but the change was not in God. God is unchangeable.

God is unlimited in time and space. God is unlimited by time. The Bible describes him as the one who "inhabiteth eternity" (Isa. 57:15). Paul called him "immortal" (1 Tim. 1:17). Abraham recognized "the everlasting God" (Gen. 21:33). Moses observed "even from everlasting to everlasting, thou art

God" (Ps. 90:2). The psalmist wrote, "But thou art the same, and thy years shall have no end" (Ps. 102:27).

Time is the measurement of events that appear in sequence. Since God created the world, he existed before the first event. God never had a beginning point. He always existed. And God will continue without a terminal point. This is why Christ was called the Alpha and Omega, the Beginning and the End.

Neither is God limited by space. Space is all the area where there is physical reality and being. Space is the distance between objects. God is independent of space. His existence goes beyond the farthest located object. The presence of God never ends. Paul told the Athenian philosophers that "God that made the world and all things therein, seeing that he is Lord of heaven and earth, dwelleth not in temples made with hands" (Acts 17:24). Solomon observed that "the heaven and heaven of heavens cannot contain him [God]" (2 Chron. 2:6).

Both time and space are results of God's creative act. He himself exists beyond time and space. God is infinite, while time and space are limited. God alone exists in the universe without limitations. If another God did exist, then God would not be the self-existent, all-powerful, unlimited God. It is axiomatic that two unlimited beings cannot occupy the same space. If another God did exist, then God could not be an unlimited God. The infinity and immensity of God are strong arguments for the sovereignty of God in the universe.

God is one. "Hear, O Israel: The Lord our God is one Lord" (Deut. 6:4). There can only be one God. To speak of more than only one supreme, absolute, perfect, and almighty being called God makes about as much sense as talking about a square circle. The meaning of words would become useless and truth would collapse. "Thus saith the Lord the King of Israel, and his redeemer the Lord of hosts; I am the first, and I am the last; and beside me there is no God" (Isa. 44:6). When we talk about the Trinity, we are still talking about one God in three personalities. The idea of God as a Trinity was suggested in Hebrew thought by the name of God, *Elohim,* which is a plural. Elsewhere in Scripture, God is also spoken of as plural, such as: "Let us make man in our image" (Gen. 1:26, italics added).

THE NECESSITY OF KNOWING GOD

Those who choose to deny the existence of God spend time justifying their reasons for so doing. Some who cannot deny God find themselves hating God and rebelling against him. Then there are those who seek God honestly. But behind all the reasons why men seek or rebel against God is one obvious fact: a person's understanding of God sometimes determines the reason to search him out or to flee from his presence.

Seeking knowledge of God is a clear command in the Bible. "Be still, and know that I am God" (Ps. 46:10). When troubles come upon us, it is often then that we find "God is our refuge and our strength, a very present help in trouble" (Ps. 46:1). As David gave his son Solomon the plans for the temple, he said, "Know thou the God of thy father, and serve him with a perfect heart and a willing mind: for the Lord searcheth all hearts, and understandeth all the imaginations of the thoughts: if thou seek him, he will be found by thee; but if thou forsake him, he will cut thee off forever" (1 Chron. 28:9). The unexpected twist is that, when we are seeking God, he is searching for us.

Knowing God is a prerequisite to knowing ourselves. In order to better know ourselves, we must have a better understanding of God, for the Bible says, "God created man in his own image, in the image of God created he him; male and female created he them" (Gen. 1:27). The more we can learn about God, who he is and what he is like, the more we will learn about ourselves. The most revealing thing about a man is his idea of God. Subconsciously, he strives to become like his God. Societies built upon a low view of God are called "primitive." Those which have recognized the master design of the universe created by an omnipotent God are called "advanced."

Knowing God is foundational for knowledge. Jesus said, "I am...the truth" (John 14:6). Whatever is true in the universe is founded upon the nature of God. This is because one of the descriptions or definitions of God is "truth." The Book of Proverbs has a great deal to say about wisdom and practical principles of living. Most Bible commentators agree that the wisdom that Solomon wrote was a typical picture of Christ.

Knowing God is one of the benefits of eternal life. When Jesus prayed in the garden before his betrayal, he identified this truth: "And this is eternal life, that they might know thee, the only true God, and Jesus Christ whom thou hast sent" (John 17:3). It is impossible to know God without being saved. Jesus said some will claim a right to enter the kingdom based upon their charitable works. "Then will I [Jesus] profess unto them, I never knew you: depart from me, ye that work iniquity" (Matt. 7:23). The only way to know God is by faith (Heb. 11:6). By faith we must accept what God says about himself as true.

Knowing God promotes spiritual growth. The apostle Paul constantly desired to mature in his spiritual life. One of the motivating factors in his life of continual spiritual growth was a deeper knowledge of God. He wrote the Philippians that he forsook all "that I may know him, and the power of his resurrection, and the fellowship of his sufferings" (Phil. 3:10). Peter gave the same exhortation to Christians in 2 Peter 3:18.

Knowing God precedes loving God. People do not fall in love with strangers, whether the stranger is a man or God (note Jer. 9:23, 24). The greatest commandment of Scripture is to love God (Matt. 22:35-38). Before we can love God and obey Scripture, we must first know the God we are commanded to love.

HOW TO KNOW GOD

The Bible commands that we know and love God for himself. This creates a dilemma for mankind. Job experienced this dilemma when he cried out, "Oh that I knew where I might find him! that I might come even to his seat!" (Job 23:3). The question is sometimes asked, "How can a man know God?"

By faith. It is impossible to know God apart from faith. Faith is accepting what God says about himself. The Bible says, "But without faith it is impossible to please him: for he that cometh to God must believe that he is and that he is a rewarder of them that diligently seek him" (Heb. 11:6).

By the Word of God. The Bible is the object of our faith, what God has said about himself.

By desire. Some people are perfectly content to deny the existence of God without any serious consideration of the subject. These people are prevented from knowing God because they do not want to know God. Unless men have a desire to know God, they will never know him. Why? The Bible says, "And ye shall seek me, and find me, when ye shall search for me with all your heart" (Jer. 29:13).

By involvement. Our knowledge of God can grow just as our knowledge of a friend grows. This requires involvement with God on our part. This is more than learning the content of Scripture. We must apply scriptural content to our lives. Jesus said, "Not everyone that saith unto me, Lord, Lord, shall enter into the kingdom of heaven; but he that doeth the will of my Father, which is in heaven. Many will say to me in that day, Lord, Lord, have we not prophesied in thy name? and in thy name cast out devils? and in thy name done many wonderful works? And then will I profess unto them, I never knew you: depart from me, ye that work iniquity" (Matt. 7:21-23).

CONCLUSION

Knowing God is the highest privilege afforded to men. Unfortunately, most people fail to recognize the priority that ought to exist in this area. If the greatest commandment is to love God with our total being, this must precede our effective service for him. Only as we study the Word of God and apply its principles to our lives will we come to know God as we should.

DAILY READINGS

☐Monday: *Deuteronomy 6:1-15*   ☐Tuesday: *Psalm 46:1-11*
☐Wednesday: *Matthew 22:34-46*   ☐Thursday: *Isaiah 40:18-31*   ☐Friday: *Psalm 103:1-22*   ☐Saturday: *Psalm 33:1-22*   ☐Sunday: *Psalm 90:1-17*

EIGHT
THE ATTRIBUTES OF GOD

The fear of the Lord is the beginning of wisdom: and the knowledge of the holy is understanding. Proverbs 9:10

INTRODUCTION

Our understanding of God is extremely important. A culture usually does not advance beyond its view of God. Our highest thoughts are our thoughts of God. That toward which we strive determines the limits of our success. We tend to become like our expectations of God.

For the Christian, understanding the nature of God is even more important. The first commandment states, "Thou shalt have no other gods before me" (Exod. 20:3). If we are mistakenly reverencing an idea of God contrary to the biblical description of God, then we are living in violation to the law of God. While God does judge us according to the light each of us has received, those of us with access to the Bible will be held accountable for reading it and learning about God.

If we were to study the great awakenings of the past, such as under the preaching of Jonathan Edwards, we would soon recognize that a fresh glimpse of God was one of the chief factors in bringing about revival. If we were to hear the testimonies of the great men of the past, we would discover that many of them had a turning point in their lives when they recognized God in all his glory. When we have a biblical idea of God, we have a basis upon which we will grow spiritually.

The key to understanding God is seen in understanding his attributes. A. W. Tozer defined an attribute as "something that is true about God." The attributes of God are those virtues or qualities which manifest his nature. The *Westminster Shorter Catechism* lists four attributes (holiness, justice, goodness, and truth) in its definition of God. "God is a Spirit, infinite, eternal and unchangeable, in His being, wisdom, power, holiness, justice, goodness and truth."

We have classified his attributes into six categories, even though we do not know exactly how many he has. One theologian said, "God has a thousand attributes." Charles Wesley, the hymn writer, described God's attributes as "glorious all and numberless." Because God has only partially revealed himself to us, we do not know everything about his existence; therefore, we cannot say exactly how many attributes he possesses.

THE ABSOLUTE ATTRIBUTES OF GOD

In considering the attributes of God, it is possible to discuss them in terms of his *absolute* and *comparative* attributes.

THE ATTRIBUTES OF GOD	
Absolute	Comparative
1. Holiness	1. Omniscience
2. Love	2. Omnipresence
3. Goodness	3. Omnipotence

Holiness. Holiness is the first description that comes to our mind when we think of God. Holiness is the standard, the "what" as love is the "how." God is holy and apart from everything that is sinful. The root meaning of "holiness" is a verb meaning "to separate or to cut off." The primary meaning of holiness implies separation. As holiness applies to our lives, it includes both separation *from* sin and separation *unto* God. The holiness of God makes it impossible for God to commit or even look upon sin.

The holiness of God is both passive and active. The Bible talks about "God, who cannot lie" (Titus 1:2). Another way of saying the same thing about the active holiness of God is to recognize that he speaks the truth always (John 17:17; Rom. 3:4). The holiness of God is the primary motive in all God's action. It is that which God desires us to remember most, and is the means by which he glorifies himself. Holiness denotes the perfection of God in all his moral attributes.

The word "holiness" is synonymous with God. David said, "He sent redemption unto his people: he hath commanded his covenant for ever: holy and reverend is his name" (Ps. 111:9). Isaiah wrote about "the high and lofty One that inhabiteth eternity, whose name is Holy" (Isa. 57:15). Jesus called the Father "Holy Father" (John 17:11), and instructed his disciples to pray, "Hallowed be thy name" (Matt. 6:9). The angels around the throne of God will eternally shout the chorus, "Holy, holy, holy, Lord God Almighty, which was, and is, and is to come" (Rev. 4:8; cf. Isa. 6:3).

It is important that we recognize the holiness of God because so much of our relationship with God is dependent upon it. When we realize God is so holy that he must judge all sin, we begin to understand the necessity of coming to God through Jesus Christ. When Jesus hung on the cross and cried out, "My God, my God, why hast thou forsaken me?" (Matt. 27:46), God was actually unable to look upon his own Son as he died, bearing our sins. An understanding of the holiness of God reminds us of the degree to which God loves us. "For God so loved the world, that he gave his only begotten Son" (John 3:16).

God's attitude toward sin that demanded our salvation, also demands of us a holy life. The central theme of Leviticus is, "Ye shall be holy: for I the Lord your God am holy" (Lev. 19:2). Isaiah observed that, although God can hear and answer prayer, "Your iniquities have separated between you and your God, and your sins have hidden his face from you, that he will not hear" (Isa. 59:2). David said, "If I regard iniquity in my heart, the Lord will not hear me" (Ps. 66:18). The holiness of God demands that he judge the continual practice of sin in the lives of Christians.

Love. Another attribute of God that readily comes to mind is love. When children are asked to describe God, they most often respond by saying, "God is love" (1 John 4:8, 16). Love is basically an outgoing attribute, as expressed in an act whereby God gives to those outside himself.

Lewis S. Chafer described love as "a rational and volitional affection having its ground in truth and holiness, and is exercised in free choice." Henry Thiessen called love "that perfection of divine nature by which he is eternally moved to communicate himself." Love is the attitude that seeks the highest good in the person who is loved.

It may be possible to give without loving, but it is impossible to love without giving. Therefore, love involves giving oneself to another. Jesus said, "Greater love hath no man than this, that a man lay down his life for his friends" (John 15:13). John later wrote that the greatest love expressed by God was to give his life as a propitiation (atoning sacrifice) for our sins (1 John 4:10).

The love chapter of the Bible, 1 Corinthians 13, describes love in terms of giving. The word "love" in this chapter, translated "charity," is an old, out-of-date word. "Charity" today means giving time and money to a worthy cause. Charity originally meant giving of oneself to those people whom we think are worthy. Today that idea is conveyed by the word "love."

Perfect love is the opposite of selfishness. It gives itself in devoted sharing to the object of its love. Only those who are strong can love because they must reach out of themselves to others. God, who is the source of all strength, is also the source of all love. He can give himself and never empty himself or divide himself. He can love perfectly and continually. The Bible speaks of both "the God of love" (2 Cor. 13:11) and "the love of God" (2 Cor. 13:14).

Goodness. When parents teach their children to pray, they often teach them to say before eating, "God is great, God is good...." The goodness of God is another of the absolute attributes of God. In a broad sense, the goodness of God includes all the positive moral attributes of God.

When Jesus told the rich young ruler "There is none good

but one, that is, God" (Mark 10:18), he was relating a truth the young man already knew. When God told Moses his name, he said, "The Lord, the Lord God, merciful and gracious, longsuffering, and abundant in goodness and truth, keeping mercy for thousands, forgiving iniquity and transgression and sin" (Exod. 34:6, 7). Moses later told the nation, "He [God] will do thee good" (Deut. 30:5).

The goodness of God is an attribute reflected in his various actions. The mercy of God is an expression of his goodness. Henry Thiessen described mercy as "the goodness of God manifest towards those who are in distress." His mercy is eternal in quality, but expressed only at his choice.

God's mercy is available to a wide range of individuals. The Bible speaks of mercy to the church (2 Cor. 1:3), mercy to believers (Heb. 4:16), mercy to Israel (Isa. 54:7) and mercy to those who are called (Rom. 9:15, 18). The mercy of God is demonstrated according to the will of God. "I will make all my goodness pass before thee...and will show mercy on whom I will show mercy" (Exod. 33:19).

The grace of God is another expression of God's goodness. The grace of God, according to Thiessen, "is the goodness of God manifested towards the ill-deserving." The grace of God is the opposite of the justice of God. Grace is God giving to man the exact opposite of what he deserves. Man deserves condemnation, but he receives eternal life. Man deserves hell, but he may receive heaven.

God's grace is the motive behind our salvation. The Bible teaches, "The grace of God that bringeth salvation hath appeared to all men" (Titus 2:11). Paul wrote, "For by grace are ye saved through faith" (Eph. 2:8). Early, in the same epistle, he wrote, "In whom we have redemption through his blood, the forgiveness of sins, according to the riches of his grace" (Eph. 1:7).

A third aspect of the goodness of God is his benevolence. Thiessen says, "The benevolence of God is the goodness of God manifested in his care of the welfare and needs of his creatures and creation." Jeus taught the benevolence of God. "He maketh his sun to rise on the evil and on the good, and sendeth rain on the just and on the unjust" (Matt. 5:45). Paul and Barnabas pointed to God's benevolence as a witness of the gospel. "He left not himself without witness, in that he did good, and gave us rain from heaven, and fruitful seasons, filling our hearts with good and gladness" (Acts 14:17).

Finally, the long-suffering of God reflects God's goodness. The word "long-suffering" means slow to become angry. God is described as long-suffering (Rom. 2:4) because he waits for men to repent and believe on him. Long-suffering is the patience of God whereby his love overshadows his holiness. God exercises long-suffering, hoping that men will trust him and turn to him in salvation.

THE COMPARATIVE ATTRIBUTES OF GOD

The absolute attributes of God are those things man cannot know apart from the revelation of God to him. If any man has holiness, love, or goodness, he first recognized it in God and then received it from God. The comparative attributes of God show that human abilities reflect God's divine nature. Every man has a degree of power, but only God possesses omnipotence. Every man has presence, but only God is omnipresent. Every man has some knowledge, but there is only One who is omniscient.

These three attributes of God may be defined by a comparison of degrees which God and man share the same. Psalm 139 lays a foundation for understanding the comparative attributes of God. The omniscience of God is seen in Psalm 139:1-6, the omnipresence of God is seen in Psalm 139:7-11, and the omnipotence of God is seen in Psalm 139:12-16.

Omniscience. When we say God is omniscient, we mean he possesses perfect knowledge of all things. The prefix "omni" means "all" and the word "science" comes from a Latin root meaning "knowledge." The omniscient God has all knowledge in the world. God has never had to learn anything. He has never forgotten anything he ever knew. God knows everything possible. That means he knows and understands the sum total of all the world's knowledge and even those things mankind has yet to discover.

David wrote, "Great is our Lord, and of great power: his

understanding is infinite" (Ps. 147:5). Jude identified God as "the only wise God" (Jude 25). Most Bible commentators agree that wisdom in Proverbs is personified in Christ. As a Christian seeks guidance in the daily affairs of his life, it is good to realize that God guides him because God knows the answers to questions the Christian has not yet fully comprehended.

Omnipresence. One of the most difficult of the attributes of God to comprehend is his omnipresence. God is everywhere present at the same time. The perfections of God demand that he exist everywhere at the same time. This does not mean that God is "spread out" so that part of him exists here and another part of him is in a room down the hall. Everything of God is here, in the room down the hall, and in every other place at the same time.

Throughout time people have assumed the existence of God. The psalmist said, "Thou art there" (Ps. 39:7-9). Hagar cried out in the desert, "Thou God seest me" (Gen. 16:13). The fact of God's omnipresence is a constant source of guidance, comfort, and protection for the believer. We can never find ourself beyond the presence of God.

Omnipotence. The power of God is beyond human comprehension. The Bible teaches that "[God is] upholding all things by the word of his power" (Heb. 1:3). When we say God is omnipotent, we mean God can do everything he wants to do. He can do anything that is in harmony with his nature. He can do the impossible (raise the dead) and the improbable (walk on water; John 6:19). "With God all things are possible" (Matt. 19:26).

There are some things God cannot do, but this does not limit his omnipotence. God cannot look on sin (Hab. 1:13), deny himself (2 Tim. 2:13), lie (Heb. 6:18), or be tempted into sin (James 1:13). If God could do any of these things, he would not be God. This limitation represents things contrary to his nature. It is still proper to say God can do anything he wants to accomplish.

CONCLUSION

When great men of God have been exposed to the nature and attributes of God in the past, it has been a time of personal renewal. This was David's experience in Psalm 139.

DAILY READINGS

☐Monday: *Revelation 4:1-11*   ☐Tuesday: *Isaiah 6:1-13*
☐Wednesday: *Psalm 139:1-24*   ☐Thursday: *Psalm 91:1-16*
☐Friday: *Psalm 66:1-20*   ☐Saturday: *Psalm 68:19-35*
☐Sunday: *1 Corinthians 13:1-13*

NINE
THE LAW OF GOD

The law of God is in his heart; none of his steps shall slide.
Psalm 37:31

INTRODUCTION

How many times have you been driving down the highway, cruising at a comfortable speed, when suddenly a flashing red light appeared in your rearview mirror? At that moment you were reminded of the role that the law plays in your life. Probably you did not fully appreciate the place of the law in your world. When you get caught, it is often hard to see any good in the law, but it is there.

One of the realities of life is that we live under many forms of law. The natural laws of the universe sustain our very existence. The civic laws of our society protect us and give us a limited sense of security. The social customs taught us in our developing years provide for us a standard by which we relate to others. Besides these, we encounter laws at work and play. The biblical view of the law reveals truth about God and what he expects from us, aiding us in our spiritual growth and development.

THE DEFINITION OF THE LAW OF GOD

The moral law of God is more than the Ten Commandments or Moses' 632 rules and regulations to the Jews. The law of

God is more than the idea of right and wrong that exists as an attitude or idea in the mind of God. The law of God is an expression of the will and nature of God. The law of God is a revelation of God himself. To a great extent, God controls his creation through his laws. The law carries out his desire in heaven and earth.

The law is absolutely necessary to all human existence. The laws of nature control physical life, social laws control society, and spiritual laws control the spiritual realm. Therefore, just as law is necessary for administration, so God's rule over the earth is carried out through his laws.

The nature of law implies a penalty for its violation, which is the foundation of all government. The certainty of the penalty for violating any law depends upon the credibility of the one who enacts the law. Since God exists, and he rules by his laws, he will penalize those who break his law. This is another way of saying that no one has power to rule unless he has power to enforce penalties.

The justice of God requires that he judge those who violate his law. God's justice also requires that he equally assign the appropriate criminality of the nature of the violation of the law. Since God's rule is universal (he knows all things and is everywhere at the same time), then those who violate his law cannot escape his judgment. Every person who has broken God's law and those who have not lived up to standards of God's law will be weighed in God's scale of justice and punishment will be meted out, to the sinner or to the one who takes his place, according to the degree of criminality. This means that a degree of criminality will be attached to every sin or violation of God's law.

Judgment cannot be fully carried out during a person's lifetime on earth because sin cannot be correctly estimated until all of the person's intentions, violations, and influences are evaluated. Man is part of God's universe which itself is a unity. Therefore, every thought, word, and act of man will have an influence upon God's universe. Just as every man is tied to those who have gone before him and lives in a world that is the result of the influence of his fathers, so every man will pass his influence on to his children. Therefore, every man will be accountable for all of his failures and violations of the law.

Since God is impartial, he must judge every violation of his law, both the intent and the action. Therefore, no one can be finally judged while he is living because the influence of where he has violated the law has not yet ceased. The existence of the law of God implies there is a future judgment.

The nature of law implies that man is being judged on earth. God expects him to live by the law, hence, God is testing his creatures to see if they will live according to his standard. The consequence of breaking the law may be suffered while man is here on earth (Acts 5:1-23), but the moral punishment cannot be inflicted until the trial is over.

Because of his nature, God cannot overlook the violation of his law. To do so, he would deny his nature. Also, God cannot treat the violation of his law lightly. The truthfulness of God indicates that he knows everything that has happened. Since he cannot ignore anything within his responsibility, he must punish every violation of his law.

God cannot forgive those who have violated his law by his mere prerogative. If he could do that, he would have to ignore his law, which means that he would ignore his standard and deny himself.

Because of the law of God, each person had to be punished for violating that law. But Christ lived under the law and perfectly kept the law (Matt. 5:17). He never sinned (1 Pet. 2:22) and thereby became eligible to become a substitute for those who violated the law. He paid the price demanded by God's justice for those who broke his law, "Having abolished in his flesh the enmity, even the law of commandments contained in ordinances" (Eph. 2:15), making it possible for everyone to be saved. Faith in Jesus Christ is the sole condition for the sinner to be forgiven of his violation of the law. Therefore, a person can be saved because Christ has blotted "out the handwriting of ordinances that was against us, which was contrary to us, and took it out of the way, nailing it to his cross" (Col. 2:14).

The natural law of God. This world is the product of the creative will of God. Its complexities are kept functioning in order by God. The Bible says, "By him all things consist [hold together]" (Col. 1:17). God has established the natural laws of the universe. "While the earth remaineth, seedtime and harvest, and cold and heat, and summer and winter, and day and night shall not cease" (Gen. 8:22). The laws of this universe were established by God and are maintained by God to carry out his plan in the world. When a scientist determines the course of a rocket that will arrive at another planet several years from now, he is able to do so after careful study of those laws upon which our universe functions. The laws of the universe reflect a rational, orderly, and consistent God. And, by implication, the law implies a God of judgment when we disobey him, because there are always consequences when a law is violated.

The moral law of God. Because God is a moral being, he expresses himself through moral law. It has not always been popular to proclaim, "Thus saith the Lord," but it is a message that needs to be enunciated again and again. The law of God by definition is a moral law. The Bible is also called "the perfect law of liberty" (James 1:25), the standard for one's spiritual life. It is given that "the man of God may be perfect, throughly furnished unto all good works" (2 Tim. 3:17). The apostle Paul strongly opposed those who wanted to live apart from the law. Some in that day taught that the Christian was free from the moral standards of the law of God because they were under grace. Paul asked these people, "What shall we say then? Shall we continue in sin that grace may abound? God forbid. How shall we, that are dead to sin, live any longer in it?" (Rom. 6:1, 2). Notice the things that are prohibited in this dispensation: Ephesians 4:25 (lying), Ephesians 4:28 (theft), James 4:11 (gossip), Matthew 5:28 (lust), and Matthew 5:22 (anger).

The social law of God. The Jewish rabbis often talked about the two tables of the law. The first table related to a man's relationship with God and included the first four commandments. The final six dealt with a man's relation with other men. James emphasized the keeping of this second table of the law in his brief epistle. "If ye fulfil the royal law according to the scripture, Thou shalt love thy neighbour as thyself, ye do well" (James 2:8). Every Christian needs to recognize the place of the law of God in establishing good relations with others. Since we are all made in the image of God, the principles of how we relate to one another also come from God and are his sacred laws. Beyond these are many other laws that guide a person in the total relationship with himself and mankind.

The spiritual law of God. The final aspect of the law of God is that part which deals with a man's relationship with God. When Jesus was challenged to identify the most important commandment of the law, he immediately responded, "Thou shalt love the Lord thy God with all thy heart, with all thy soul, and with all thy mind. This is the first and great commandment" (Matt. 22:37, 38).

THE NATURE OF THE LAW OF GOD

The law of God is an expression of the will and nature of God. That being true, everything that is true about law is a reflection of the nature of God. Likewise, everything that is true about God, will be reflected in his laws.

Characteristics of the law. A law is the expression of the will of the lawgiver. If the legislators of our government desire to pass a fifty-five-mile-per-hour speed limit, it becomes law. If they are opposed to such a law, it would never be proclaimed. The law of God is an expression of the will of "the Lord thy God, which have brought thee out of the land of Egypt, out of the house of bondage" (Exod. 20:2). When God gave Israel his law, he revealed his nature as the basis of that law. He is saying, "Because I am who I say I am, this is the way I want you to live."

A law is also a standard to be obeyed. The speed limit does not exist as a revenue-making device. It exists to let motorists know what is expected of them. While God is willing to forgive us when we sin, he is also concerned that we obey him. Even God's anointed King Saul had to be reminded that "to obey is better than sacrifice" (1 Sam. 15:22). Jesus said, "So likewise ye, when ye shall have done all those things which are commanded you, say, We are unprofitable servants: we have done that which was our duty to do" (Luke 17:10).

A law also comes with a penalty for disobedience. When we are caught driving too fast, we pay a fine. For various crimes, there are various penalties reflecting the seriousness of the crime. Breaking the law of God is an affront to the Person of God. When we understand this, we understand the penalty for sin, "For the wages of sin is death" (Rom. 6:23). The word "death" refers not only to the end of our physical life on earth, but includes our eternal separation from God. It is described vividly in John's vision of the end times. "And death and hell were cast into the lake of fire. This is the second death" (Rev. 20:14).

Similarities between the law and God. If we were to list the attributes of God, we would have a list of the characteristics of the law of God. Many Christians think of the law in strictly negative terms. They often quote the apostle Paul, not understanding the context in which Paul wrote. Although Paul opposed those who preached salvation by law as another means of salvation, Paul had some positive words to say about the law itself.

THE ABSOLUTE ATTRIBUTES OF GOD AND LAW	
The Nature of Law	*The Nature of God*
Law is holy—Rom. 7:12	God is holy—1 Pet. 1:16
Law is good—Rom. 7:16	God is good—Mark 10:18
Law is spiritual—Rom 7:14	God is Spirit—John 4:26

The law is holy. God is a holy God. This is the central theme of the third book of the Bible. Many theologians consider holiness to be the chief attribute of God. It seems strange that Paul, who preached Christian liberty and opposed legalistic Judaizers, is the one to recognize the holiness of the law. It was not the law Paul opposed but rather the abuses of the law by heretics. But the law is holy because it is an expression of God who is holy. And the law demands that everyone who is a sinner (unholy) be punished. But the law of holiness is later solved by the law of love.

The law is good. Jesus was emphatic that "None is good, save one, that is, God" (Luke 18:19). If goodness exists in anything else, it is only as God has provided it. Therefore, the law does not contain goodness, it *is* good. The reader of this passage cannot be mistaken about Paul's attitude toward the law. Every Christian needs to realize the law is something desirable and attractive, even in the mind of God's inspired writers of Scripture. If men could have perfectly obeyed the law (which they could never do) they would have been good. Christians who live in opposition to the law of God are really in opposition to the expression of the will and nature of God.

The law is spiritual in essence. God is in essence Spirit, which is reflected in his law (Rom. 7:14). In his own strength it is not possible for man to keep God's laws because of man's carnality and the natural evil desires of his heart. But as Christians we do not live by law. We live by the power of the indwelling Holy Spirit. If the Christian were to perfectly follow the Holy Spirit, he would fulfill the "spiritual law of God."

THE PURPOSE OF THE LAW OF GOD

To reveal the nature of God. Since man could not know God, God gave his law to Moses and Israel to teach us about himself. The psalmist often referred to the Bible, God's revelation of himself to mankind, as "the law of the Lord." As we study the Word of God and attempt to keep the law of God, we will learn more about the God we serve.

To provide a standard of life. As Moses instructed the people in the law, he consistently challenged them to "observe to do all that is written." When Moses died and Joshua was left to lead Israel, he was commanded to "observe to do according to all that is written therein" (Josh. 1:8). While the keeping of the law was never taught as a means of earning salvation, it is the standard by which God directs his creation and will judge all things. One should not confuse, however, dietary and sanitation laws given by God to Israel during their wilderness journey with moral laws, as binding on all generations. For example, we do not refrain from eating pork or shellfish today, since Paul has declared all food clean that is eaten with thanksgiving (Rom. 14:6; 1 Cor. 10:30). Such temporary regulations were obviously not intended to be a part of the universal moral standards by which we are to live.

To instruct Israel concerning their Messiah. Paul recognized the typical significance of the law (1 Cor. 10:11). John the Baptist drew upon the teaching of the law when he announced, "Behold the Lamb of God" (John 1:29). The writer of Hebrews went to great lengths to quote the law and apply it to Jewish Christians. With the record of the first advent of Jesus Christ available to us today, we are not ignorant of how the atonement of Christ fulfilled the sacrificial law. But, prior to Calvary, the Jews were reminded with each sacrifice that the day was coming when God would "provide himself a lamb for a burnt offering" (Gen. 22:8).

To reveal sin in our life. "For until the law sin was in the world; but sin is not imputed when there is no law" (Rom. 5:13). The law revealed that sin is transgression against God. Knowledge of the law does not make us sinners; we are sinners because we break God's law, whether or not we know about the law we break. But the preaching of the law makes us realize we are sinners, and that includes everyone, "For all have sinned, and come short of the glory of God" (Rom. 3:23).

The law reflects the glory of God and shows how far we miss his standard. Many times a revival team visiting a church will produce a spiritual checklist of what God says is wrong and what we ought to be doing instead. As people see their lives in the light of the law of God, they often experience personal conviction that leads to genuine repentance.

To lead us to Christ. The chief desire in the heart of God is "all men to be saved, and come unto the knowledge of the truth" (1 Tim. 2:4). The law is one of the tools God uses to accomplish this goal. "The law was our schoolmaster to bring us unto Christ, that we might be justified by faith" (Gal. 3:24). The law has never been able to save an individual but it is used by the Holy Spirit to bring a person to conviction, to the place where he trusts Christ personally as his Savior.

THE CHRISTIAN AND THE LAW OF GOD

The Christian is not expected to keep the entire Mosaic law, as the Jew in the Old Testament. Jesus came to fulfil the law (Matt. 5:18), the moral aspects of the moral law, and to be the sacrifice that fulfilled completely the sacrificial law. All of the law's requirements were satisfied in him. What we could never do, Christ did in his life (he never sinned); in his death on the cross he fulfilled the demands of the law for a perfect sacrifice (Col. 2:14, 15; Eph. 2:15). This does not mean that Christians are exempt from the law. This practice, called "antinomianism," was one which Paul specifically dealt with in Romans 6. Actually, the moral demands of the law of God are still operative for the Christian, but in a new and spiritual way.

The great commandment. Jesus identified our love for God as the single greatest commandment (Matt. 22:37, 38). Love for God was the standard of conduct and the practice of the New Testament church. The keeping of this commandment carries a special promise. "Delight thyself also in the Lord; and he shall give thee the desires of thine heart" (Ps. 37:4).

The royal law. James instructed the readers of his letter to love their neighbors and "fulfil the royal law according to the scripture" (James 2:8). John also had the same emphasis (1 John 4:7-11). Our love for others reflects God's love for us. This is one of the distinguishing marks of a Christian (John 13:33, 34).

The law of Christ. "Bear ye one another's burdens, and so fulfil the law of Christ" (Gal. 6:2). Living for others, rather than self, is another aspect of the law of God that a Christian must obey. The child of God ought to seek always to help others up, not tear them down. When another Christian is burdened, it is our responsibility as members of the family of God to comfort, pray for, counsel, and in other ways help that burdened brother.

The law of liberty. It was so called because it sets us free from the bondage of sin. "So speak ye, and so do, as they that shall be judged by the law of liberty" (James 2:12). This law of liberty is identified earlier by James as the Word of God (James 1:22-25). The Christian must come to realize that obedience to the Bible is obedience to God. Jesus requires total obedience of the law of liberty as part of the duty of every Christian (Luke 17:10).

DAILY READINGS

☐Monday: *Matthew 5:17-32*   ☐Tuesday: *Matthew 5:33-48* ☐Wednesday: *Matthew 22:34-40*   ☐Thursday: *Exodus 20:1-17*   ☐Friday: *Deuteronomy 6:1-19*   ☐Saturday: *Galatians 3:1-14*   ☐Sunday: *Romans 7:1-14*

TEN
THE WORK OF GOD

The king's heart is in the hand of the Lord, as the rivers of water: he turneth it whithersoever he will. Proverbs 21:1

INTRODUCTION

In previous chapters we looked at the nature and attributes of God. In this chapter we examine the overall plan that God has for the people and world that he has created. Some have said God has completed his work in this world, as a man winds up a clock which will run down independently. These people treat God as an absentee landlord, not attempting to control what man does day by day, but who will return in the end of this age to ask for an accounting.

Others conceive of God as the architect of this universe and that he has preconceived every small detail. Man will fit into God's minute blueprint, exercising very little of his own free will. This view teaches that God has determined and is daily controlling every aspect of life, down to the smallest detail. God is the Author of life, and man is simply the key on the typewriter he has chosen to use. They see God as a divine chess player, guiding the chess pieces through life. The people God guides are like actors chosen to perform in a play.

In truth, God is a God of love, and that love moves his entire being to take interest in the affairs of his people. God is not ignoring all that takes place on the earth. He is vitally interested and involved in the smallest and apparently least significant events in our lives. As we understand the work of God, we will better understand God's specific will in our lives.

DEFINITION OF THE WORK OF GOD

When we talk about the work of God, we are referring to the outworking of his external plan for this life, based upon his wise and holy purpose, whereby God controls and oversees all that comes to pass. Everything was created and exists for his glory. The work of God is founded upon his self-existence; and, because God always has existed, he knew all things from all eternity. Therefore, his work fits into one eternal and unchangeable plan, that all come to the saving knowledge of his Son, and through this salvation God is glorified—the ultimate will of God.

The work of God is based upon God's sovereignty. From "before the foundation of the world" (1 Pet. 1:20), God had foreordained his plan to save men. While God's purpose was determined in eternity, his work is performed in time. However, a few facts must be kept clearly in mind.

Some theologians emphasize that God works in salvation by choosing certain individuals, that Christ died for them, and that the Holy Spirit sovereignly brought them to salvation. Others emphasize that God offers salvation to all men because Christ died for the sins of the world. Although these views seem contradictory, the Bible seems to teach that both are true (2 Thess. 2:13, 14).

The ultimate source of our salvation is the Lord (Jonah 2:10). The apostle Paul used several words to describe God's sovereignty; "predestinate," "foreknowledge," "chosen," "called," "the counsel of God," "God's will," and "God's good pleasure." A proper understanding of these words will help us understand God's work in salvation. These words are used in Scripture in relationship to God's programs, principles, and plans that relate to salvation, sanctification, and God's ultimate glorification. We know that God has an eternal plan for the salvation of those who call upon him.

One of these words is "predestinate"—*proorizo* (Acts 4:28; Rom. 8:29; Eph. 1:5, 11, translated "determine"). This word means "to decide upon beforehand." God originated a plan for man's salvation and offered it to everyone who would respond in faith. The apostle wrote of God's predestined plan for the world because he loves the world he created (John 3:16), then he died for the sin of the world (John 1:29), and calls everyone to partake in that plan. Therefore, "predestinate" deals primarily with those who respond to his plan (Rom. 8:28, 29).

Another of these words is "foreknowledge"—*proginosko*. Foreknowledge speaks of God's knowledge of the future (Acts 2:23; 26:5; Rom. 8:29; 11:2; 1 Pet. 1:2, 20; 2 Pet. 3:17). Foreknowledge means foreordination (Acts 2:23; 1 Peter 2:20). Those whom God foreknew, those upon whom he set his love beforehand, he ordained to be conformed to the image of his Son.

On the day of Pentecost, the apostle Peter vividly illustrated the harmony that exists between the sovereignty of God and man's personal responsibility. Even though the cross was in the eternal plan of God and a part of his sovereign will, those who crucified Christ did so as a rebellious act of their will. God had predetermined the plan, which Peter said, "Him, being delivered by the determinate counsel and foreknowledge of God, ye have taken, and by wicked hands have crucified and slain" (Acts 2:23).

Paul used the word *eklegomai*, translated sometimes "chosen," to describe the people God will save (1 Cor. 1:27, 28; Eph. 1:4). The word is also translated "elect" (Rom. 11:7; Col. 3:12; 1 Thess. 1:4). Those who responded to God's call were those that God had chosen for salvation. God's election is an exercise of his choice (John 15:16; 1 Peter 2:9), as he gives salvation as a free gift to those whom he has chosen (Eph. 2:4-10; 2 Tim. 1:9; Titus 3:4-7).

The word "call"—*kletos*—originates out of his sovereignty (Rom. 1:1, 6, 7; 1 Cor. 1:26; 7:20; Eph. 1:18; 4:1; 2 Thess. 2:11). Those whom God has elected hear his call to salvation. Jesus said, "He that is of God heareth God's words; ye therefore hear them not, because ye are not of God" (John 8:47). Those who have been given to Christ hear him (John 10:25-28). The command to preach the gospel is not a contradiction of the truths concerning election. The invitation to receive Christ is the means used by God to call out those whom he has chosen.

Paul used the verb *protitheemi*, translated "purpose," in terms of his overall plans (Rom. 1:13; 3:25; Eph. 1:9). The other word, *boulee*—"counsel"—also carries the same meaning (Acts 13:26; 20:27; Eph. 1:11). These words relate to the volitional nature of God, that he can translate his desires into an organized program relating to his creation. God's will is related to his knowledge, here the word *eudokia*—"good pleasure" [of his will]—relates to sovereignty (Eph. 1:5). These words describe the initiative God has taken in salvation, but they never deny man's moral responsibility before God. The basis of God's acts of sovereignty is his nature, "For it is God which worketh in you both to will and to do of his good pleasure" (Phil. 2:13).

At times God calls, expecting man to answer and at other times God punishes so man will respond. On other occasions, God sovereignly directs through inner direction such as giving a burden to men (Isa. 21:1, 11, 13). The Christian can be led of the Spirit both consciously (Rom. 8:14) and when he is captive to circumstances (Acts 21:14). Whether God leads directly or indirectly, by leading or pushing, by enticement or by compulsion, God works all things to his glory (Rom. 8:28). But in freedom, man will sin and miss God's best road, or man will reject and go to hell. And in the final analysis, God's sovereignty cannot be man's defense at the judgment. Because man was created in the image of God, so each man is responsible for his free choice.

The work of God is based upon God's wisdom. God does everything in infinite wisdom and holiness. Sometimes this may not be readily seen by us, but with Paul we must recognize "the depth of the riches both of the wisdom and knowledge of God! how unsearchable are his judgments, and his ways past finding out!" (Rom. 11:33). We need to be reminded constantly that "the foolishness of God is wiser than men" (1 Cor. 1:25).

Habakkuk failed to understand that God had a wise plan on earth, so he encountered problems trying to understand the work of God. He knew that God's people had sinned and deserved the judgment of God. Habakkuk could not understand why God did not judge them. Then he began to see how God was working to raise up a wicked nation to judge Judah. The Old Testament prophecy of Habakkuk records the intellectual struggles of a prophet trying to understand the work of God.

The work of God is consistent with his nature. There is nothing and no one capable of motivating God's work apart from his nature. There was no one to advise and counsel God or influence any of his decisions (Isa. 40:13, 14). The nature of God demands the sovereignty of God in all areas of his work.

Some have misunderstood the sovereignty of God by denying it or misapplying it. Those who deny it fail to recognize that "salvation is of the Lord" (Jonah 2:9). If God is sovereign in the matter of salvation, it is easier to understand the security of the believer. We are neither saved nor kept by our own works. "Wherefore he is able also to save them to the uttermost that come unto God by him, seeing he ever liveth to make intercession for them" (Heb. 7:25).

The work of God is committed to glorify God. God has "created all things, and for [his] pleasure they are and were created" (Rev. 4:11). The psalmist wrote, "The heavens declare the glory of God" (Ps. 19:1). Paul told the Ephesians that their conversion was performed "to the praise of the glory of his grace" (Eph. 1:6). The purpose of God's work is to bring glory to himself. The responsibility of all creation is to glorify God. If in our lives and conversation we bring dishonor to God, we have failed to do the will of God. When we do what God desires, we will naturally glorify God and direct honor to him.

The work of God is both passive and active. Sometimes the work of God is active. This occurs when God causes things to happen to us according to his plan for our life. Understanding what we need and what is best for us, God will sometimes direct the circumstances around us to provide experiences, opportunities, and provisions to aid us in our lives.

At other times, the work of God is passive. The classic example of this is found in the life of Job. God allowed the devil to hinder the life of Job but not the purpose of God. When the devil was permitted on two occasions to test Job, on both occasions divine limits were set on the testings. God used the devil to accomplish something in the life of Job while God remained passive. Today, when God allows the same to be accomplished in our lives, we have the promise of divine limits set by a God who knows us better than we know ourselves. "God is faithful, who will not suffer you to be tempted above that ye are able; but will with the temptation also make a way to escape, that ye may be able to bear it" (1 Cor. 10:13).

THE CONTENT OF THE WORK OF GOD

God is at work in three specific areas of our lives: the physical, social, and spiritual.

The physical work of God. All about us, we can see the work of God in the physical universe. The world was created by God and is sustained by God (Ps. 33:6-11). The atmosphere, seasonal changes, heat, and rain are all "acts of God." Sometimes we call a terrible storm an "act of God." While this is true, it is also an act of God when the sun rises on a clear summer day and when it hides behind a cloud during a refreshing spring shower. Our physical bodies are one of many amazing creations that exist in this world to remind us of the work of God. When we consider the intricacies of the body we begin to recognize the immense wisdom and creativity of God. The human body is limited and directed through human nature. God put a human nature in man and God works his purposes in the world through that avenue.

God does his work in other areas of our physical world. He has established the boundaries of the nations and the general course of human history. God is at work today in the internal and international affairs of many nations as he prepares all nations for the end times.

The work of God in society. God has established three institutions upon which our society rests: the family, government, and church. These three institutions are the foundation of society. God accomplishes his work through these institutions.

If these crumble, as some observers believe they may be doing today, the lives of many will crumble with them. It is important that we see God at work in the family, government, and church, and that we seek to work with, rather than against God in these areas.

Marriage was ordained of God from the beginning. The plan of God has always been one man for one woman for one lifetime. God never intended that the family should be destroyed by divorce. Marriage is the legal and socially accepted practice which meets the cultural need for children to be born and trained by their parents. The traditional family is more than a tradition. It is the design of God.

Government too is a divine institution (Rom. 13:1-3). It was established because the nature of God demands order. Even the worst form of government is better than anarchy. According to the Bible, government leaders are ministers of God. Although the establishment of government was by God, he is not responsible for bad leaders. The laws of governments ought to reflect the law of God. Christians are responsible to support, honor, and pray for all in authority. It is hard to understand how Christian leaders can support anti-God revolutionary movements committed to overthrowing their governments. This is directly opposed to the social work of God. Christians in every age have had to make difficult decisions concerning their support of governments that oppose the laws of God.

The third institution established by God was the church. It too is foundational to our society, acting as the social conscience of the community. Jesus pictured the church as aggressively opposing and defeating the strongholds of the devil in the world (Matt. 16:13, 18).

Each of these three institutions has a role to play in carrying out the work of God in our society. We need to recognize the divine authority which established these three institutions.

God's eternal work—salvation. This third aspect of the work of God deals with the salvation and spiritual growth of men. God permitted sin to enter the world but also determined to provide for man's salvation. Lewis S. Chafer observed, "God determined not to hinder the course of actions which His creatures pursue, but He does determine to regulate and control the bounds and results of man's actions."

God's provision for man's salvation is twofold. First, he provided the means of salvation in the blood of Christ. Man is unable to save himself. Jesus alone was a suitable sacrifice to effect the forgiveness of sins. Second, God provides the messengers of salvation. God calls individuals into the ministry of proclaiming the gospel. Beyond that, he has directed that every Christian should be a witness, actively involved in bringing the message of salvation to every creature.

THE STRATEGY OF THE WORK OF GOD

God works through the law of nature. God, the Creator of this universe, has established the natural order of the universe. "While the earth remaineth, seedtime and harvest, and cold and heat, and summer and winter, and day and night shall not cease" (Gen. 8:22). When God works, he will normally work within the laws of nature. This work of God is often referred to as Providence.

God works through the laws of human personality. God made us the way we are. Our nature is a product of his work and we should allow him to work through the strengths and limitations of our personalities. When God works, he often uses people to accomplish his goals. In doing so, he considers the laws of human personality. God will use us to accomplish that for which we are best suited. "The king's heart is in the hand of the Lord, as the rivers of water: he turneth it whithersoever he will" (Prov. 21:1). The word "heart" often represents the seat of intellect, emotions, and will in an individual, the real person. Today we define the term "personality" as the sum total of all we are. Each personality rests in the hand of God to be directed and used by him in his work according to his will.

God works through circumstances. God is sovereign in all the affairs of life. Because he is in control, he can direct our circumstances to accomplish his work. Paul told the Corinthians that "a great door and effectual is opened unto me" (1 Cor. 16:9). At other times God led in the life of Paul by closing doors of opportunity (Acts 16:6, 7). Back of circumstances we know that "All things work together for good to them that love God" (Rom. 8:28).

God works through the Bible. God always reserves the right to work beyond his natural laws within the boundaries of his supernatural laws. All of his laws have unity and God will never work contrary to his laws. The Bible is God's revelation of himself. As such, God would never contradict his nature by working inconsistently with biblical revelation. Jeremiah experienced the way God used the Word of God in his life to accomplish the work of God in his life (Jer. 20:9).

DISCOVERING HOW GOD WORKS IN OUR LIVES

God has probably directed our lives as we have sought his will on specific matters. The following twelve principles reveal how God can guide his children today.

DISCOVERING GOD'S PLAN FOR YOUR LIFE
1.   Commit yourself to do God's will (John 7:17; Rom. 12:1, 2).
2.   Look for God's will in the Bible (Ps. 119:105).
3.   Pray for guidance in applying God's will (Luke 18:1).
4.   Make sure your motives are pure in seeking God's will (Matt. 6:22).
5.   Begin by doing what you know is right (Rom. 12:2).
6.   Face your own thoughts, strengths, and weaknesses realistically (1 Cor. 12:11, 29-31).
7.   You will have inner peace if your decisions are correct (Phil. 4:7; Col. 3:15).
8.   Seek spiritual counsel from godly people (Ps. 11:14).
9.   Study circumstances to see whether doors are open or closed (Acts 16:6, 7; 1 Cor. 16:9).
10.   Do not move forward until you know you are obeying the Bible (Isa. 40:31).
11.   Judge decisions by the long look (Rom. 12:2; 8:39).
12.   Be flexible about past decisions you have made regarding the will of God (Phil. 3:13).

CONCLUSION

God is at work in our world today bringing men to a saving knowledge of himself and building them up in their faith. In accomplishing this work, God uses people. It is important that we make ourselves available to God and seek his direction in the affairs of life. As we do the will of God in our lives, we will be cooperating with the work of God in our world.

DAILY READINGS

☐Monday: *Habakkuk 1:1-17*   ☐Tuesday: *Habakkuk 2:1-20* ☐Wednesday: *Habakkuk 3:1-19*   ☐Thursday: *Psalm 19:1-14*   ☐Friday: *Isaiah 40:18-31*   ☐Saturday: *Psalm 33:1-22*   ☐Sunday: *Matthew 19:1-15*

ELEVEN
THE TRINITY

Come near unto me, hear ye this: I have not spoken in secret from the beginning; from the time that it was, there am I; and now the Lord God, and his Spirit, hath sent me. Isaiah 48:16

INTRODUCTION

One of the most difficult and yet most important things to understand about God is that he is triune. God is referred to as three distinct Persons in Scripture, yet at the same time we are taught there is one God. The teaching of one God in three Persons has baffled Christians for centuries as they have sought to understand the complete teaching of the Persons of God in Scripture.

The Father, Son, and Holy Spirit are each distinguishable from the other, yet everything that is true about God is true about the Father, the Son, and the Holy Spirit. Ignoring this simple doctrine can lead to error. When understood, the doctrine of the Trinity forms a foundation to all doctrine we believe.

THE DEFINITION OF THE TRINITY

The doctrine of the Trinity states that God exists in unity and yet exists in three eternal Persons. The members of the Trinity are equal in nature and distinct in Person. The Son was eternally begotten by the Father. "The Lord hath said unto me, Thou art my Son; this day have I begotten thee" (Ps. 2:7). The Son is submissive to do the work of the Father, yet equal in nature to the Father. Jesus prayed to the Father, saying, "I have finished the work which thou gavest me to do" (John 17:4). Then the Father and Son send the Holy Spirit: "The Comforter...whom I will send unto you from the Father" (John 15:26). Therefore, the Father is the head or fount of deity, the Son is the revealer of deity, and the Holy Spirit, who proceeds from the Father and the Son, is the agent that usually carries out the work of deity. In some Scripture references, one Person of the Trinity seems to perform the entire process (Isa. 6:3-9; John 12:37-41; Acts 28:25, 26).

The oldest existing identification of the Trinity is the Athanasian Creed written about A.D. 250. "We worship one God, in trinity, and trinity is unity, neither confounding the persons, nor dividing the substance." About 100 years ago, Robert Dick put the same truth this way: "While there is only one divine nature of God, there are three persons called the Father, Son, and Holy Spirit who possess, not a similar, but the same numerical essence, and the distinction between them is not merely nominal, but real."

THOSE WHO DENY THE TRINITY

The word "trinity" is not found in Scripture, but the idea and doctrine of the Trinity are derived from scriptural foundation. Many groups have gone off into doctrinal error by denying the existence of the Trinity or explaining the Trinity wrongly. Part of understanding what the Trinity is, depends on knowing what it is not.

The Trinity is not equivalent to three Gods. The doctrine of the Trinity does not support the existence of three distinct Gods, an idea which is called "tritheism." Often fundamental Christians are charged by Jehovah's Witnesses and Jews with believing in three Gods, a charge founded upon their misunderstanding of what is meant by the term "trinity."

Christians are monotheists, meaning they believe in one God. "Hear, O Israel: The Lord our God is one Lord" (Deut. 6:4). When we acknowledge that the Father, Son, and Holy Spirit are each part of the Triune God, we still hold to the unity of God.

The Trinity is not three manifestations of God. One of the early heretical groups in the early church taught what was known as Sabellianism or Modalism. They held that the Trinity was three different manifestations of the same God, as water can be seen as ice, liquid, and vapor. They explain "Person" to mean a representation of God, just as man could be father, husband, and brother at one time. According to Modalism, there was only one God who revealed himself as the Father and the Creator in the Old Testament, and that the same Person revealed himself as Redeemer. In this manifestation he is called Jesus. The Holy Spirit is the third manifestation of the same God who relates to people today. Sabellius was wrong in saying: "The only unchanging God is differently reflected upon the world on account of the world's different receptivities."

The basic error of Modalism is that it denies the eternity and distinctiveness of the three Persons of the Trinity. As we will see later, the Father, Son, and Holy Spirit were all involved in the work of creation. All three have existed and worked together since before time began. All three exist in unity in the Godhead.

The doctrine of the Trinity does not teach that the Father created the Son or Holy Spirit. One of the hottest doctrinal controversies of the early church was Arianism. Arius taught that only the Father was eternally God from the beginning. He taught that both the Son and the Holy Spirit were created out of nothing by God before anything else. Because they were created Beings, they could not be considered divine or possessing the attributes of divinity.

The Bible, of course, does not teach the creation of the Son or Holy Spirit, but recognizes the work of both in the creation of all things (cf. John 1:3; Gen. 1:2). Historically, Christians have recognized the error of Arianism and taught the biblical doctrines of the deity of Christ and of the Holy Spirit. Even today, however, there are those, such as the Jehovah's witnesses, who twist the Scriptures to deny the Trinity.

The doctrine of the Trinity does not teach that Christ or the Holy Spirit was a power or attribute of God. A fourth wrong view of the Trinity called Monarchianism, teaches that Jesus was a mere man who was energized by God at the baptism but sacrificed his essential deity at his death. This error misunderstands the truth that Jesus is God. The Bible teaches "the Word [Jesus] was God" (John 1:1). Then, in the same context, we are told "the Word was made flesh, and dwelt among us (and we beheld his glory, the glory as of the only begotten of the Father)" (John 1:14). John described the return of Christ when he "saw heaven opened and, behold, a white horse; and he that sat upon him was called...the Word of God" (Rev. 18:11, 13).

THE OLD TESTAMENT POINTS TO THE TRINITY

There is an element of mystery in doctrines that first appear in the Old Testament before they are more completely revealed in the New Testament. Throughout the Old Testament there are continuous signposts that point to the existence of the Trinity. These are seen in the names of God, the worship of God, and the distinctions made within the Godhead.

The names of God imply the Trinity. God reveals his nature in part through his names. The first name for God used in Scripture is *Elohim*. Even in the first verse of the Bible, a hint of the Trinity is given; the word *Elohim* is plural. If this use of plural were the only teaching we had about God it would not be a strong argument since the Hebrew language elsewhere uses the plural in reference to majesty. "And God said, let us make man in our image, after our likeness" (Gen. 1:26). When man gained a knowledge of good and evil God said, "The man is become as one of us" (Gen. 3:22). Before God judged at Babel, he said, "Let us go down" (Gen. 11:7). Isaiah "heard the voice of the Lord saying, Whom shall I send, and who will go for us?" (Isa. 6:8).

Isaiah records a second name of God which is plural. The name "Maker" (Isa. 54:5) is plural in the Hebrew language. This verse then names three who are God. "For thy Maker is thine husband; the Lord of hosts is his name; and thy Redeemer the Holy One of Israel; the God of the whole earth shall he be called" (Isa. 54:5). These plural names of God suggest what is known as a "plural unity."

The worship of God by use of a trinitarian formula. A second intimation of the Trinity in the Old Testament is seen in the worship of God. Isaiah's vision of God included the threefold designation, "Holy, holy, holy" (Isa. 6:3). When Jacob blessed his son Joseph in the name of God, three times he identified God differently (Gen. 48:15, 16). The Aaronic benediction given by God for recitation by Israel's first priest was also threefold in nature: "The Lord bless thee, and keep thee; The Lord make his face shine upon thee, and be gracious unto thee; The Lord lift up his countenance upon thee, and give thee peace" (Num. 6:24-26). While these are not conclusive in themselves, most biblical theologians agree these threefold emphases in the worship of God allow for the threefold Person of God.

All three Persons are distinguished as God. A third inference of the Trinity in the Old Testament is the practice of distinguishing between God and God. The judgment by the Lord on Sodom and Gomorrah distinguishes between the Lord on earth and the Lord in heaven (Gen. 19:24). More specifically, the Old Testament teaches Jehovah has a Son (Ps. 2:7) who is called God (Isa. 9:6). The Spirit of God is also distinguished in the Old Testament from God (Gen. 1:2; 6:3).

A clear statement points to the Trinity. Probably the clearest statement on the Trinity in the Old Testament is Isaiah 48:16, because it demonstrates an Old Testament belief in the three Persons of the Trinity. God the Son is speaking in this verse. He identifies the Father (Lord God) and "his Spirit" as having sent him. In the next verse the Son is more clearly identified as God. Therefore, this verse identifies three who are God yet it does not deny monotheism. Missionaries to the Jews often use this verse when challenged by Jews that Christians believe in "three Gods." Christians believe in one God in three Persons, just as the Old Testament teaches.

DIRECT TEACHING OF THE NEW TESTAMENT

What was hidden in the Old Testament is clearly revealed in the New. The doctrine of the Trinity that was implied in the Old Testament is clearly taught in the New Testament.

Trinity revealed at the baptism of Jesus. The most vivid illustration of the Trinity is found at the beginning of the earthly ministry of Jesus. He was baptized by John the Baptist in the Jordan River (Matt. 3:16, 17). As *God the Son* was raised from the water, he saw *God the Holy Spirit* "descending like a dove." The Bible also records the voice of *God the Father* breaking the silence of heaven to acknowledge his delight in his Son.

Jesus taught the Trinity (John 14:16, 17). Jesus believed in and taught his disciples the doctrine of the Trinity. When attempting to prepare them for their life of service after his resurrection, he told them he had asked the Father to send the Comforter, which is God the Holy Spirit. By this point in his ministry, the disciples were well aware that Jesus was God the Son. In his instruction concerning the coming of the Holy Spirit, he taught in such a way that assumes the disciples understood the doctrine of the Trinity.

Later the same evening, Jesus made the same reference to the Trinity to the same group. "But when the Comforter [God the Holy Spirit] is come, whom I [God the Son] will send unto you from [God] the Father . . ." (John 15:26). Jesus would have had only to say something once to make it true, but the repetition of this teaching in this context suggests not only was the teaching true, but the learners (disciples) were able to relate to that truth. They were familiar enough with the doctrine of the Trinity to be able to learn new truth built upon old truth.

The New Testament church recognized the Trinity (2 Cor. 13:14). The doctrine of the Trinity was taught in the early church. Two practices of the church revealed that the first Christians were trinitarians. The first is seen in the practice of greetings and benedictions. Christians often greeted one another in the name of the Lord. Even today some Christians will comment, "God bless you" as they part company. When the apostle Paul pronounced his final benediction upon the Corinthian church, he did so in the name of the three Persons of the Trinity. "The grace of the Lord Jesus Christ, and the love of God, and the communion of the Holy Ghost, be with you all" (2 Cor. 13:14).

A second practice in the New Testament church which recognized the Trinity was baptism. Jesus instructed his disciples to baptize converts "in the name of the Father, and of the Son, and of the Holy Ghost" (Matt. 28:19). When a person was baptized, the Father, Son, and Holy Spirit were each identified in the act. Though three were identified, converts were baptized in the "name" singular, reflecting the unity of the Godhead.

Some have misunderstood this point and have argued that the formula of baptism "in the name of Jesus" (Acts 2:38) is different than the formula of Matthew 28:19. Actually this phrase is often used in the Book of Acts to distinguish Christian baptism from the baptism of John the Baptist. Specifically, it called for the recognition of the deity of Christ whom they crucified. Christian baptism was always "in the name of the Father, and of the Son, and of the Holy Ghost" (Matt. 28:19) in obedience to Christ's commandment, hence in "the name of Christ."

The distinct work of each Person of the Trinity points to the Trinity. Much of the work of God is attributed to each member of the Godhead. Hebrews 9:14 illustrates the cooperative efforts of each member of the Trinity in the atonement: God the Son offered his blood through God the Holy Spirit to God the Father for our salvation. In this way, an understanding of the Trinity is foundational to an understanding of the atonement. The author of Hebrews felt this was important when reminding Hebrew Christians in Jerusalem of what God had done for them.

THE ATTRIBUTES OF THE TRINITY

One of the strongest proofs of the Trinity of God is that the Bible reveals that each member of the Trinity possesses the same attributes of God. The following chart reinforces the doctrine of the Trinity by showing that each Person of the Godhead is equal in attributes.

THE WORK OF THE TRINITY

The above chart shows each Person of the Trinity equal in attributes, and, since the attributes are eternal, the Persons of the Godhead are equal. Two absolute forces would conflict with each other if in fact they were not a unified whole. The below chart shows that all three Persons of the Godhead are involved in works that only God can do.

CONCLUSION

Christians believe in one God in three Persons: Father, Son, and Holy Spirit. Each member of this Trinity is God and works in our lives as Christians. As God, each is worthy of our worship and deserving of our obedience. They have revealed themselves and what they expect of us in the Bible. The desire of every Christian ought to be to love, worship, and obey the Triune God.

DAILY READINGS

☐Monday: *Isaiah 48:12-22*   ☐Tuesday: *Matthew 3:1-17*
☐Wednesday: *John 14:15-26*   ☐Thursday:
Matthew 28:1-10, 16-20   ☐Friday: *Corinthians 13:1-14*
☐Saturday: *Hebrews 9:1-15*   ☐Sunday: *Genesis 1:24-31*

THE ATTRIBUTES OF THE TRINITY

Attributes	Father	Son	Holy Spirit
Omnipresence	Jer. 23:24	Matt. 28:20	Ps. 139:7-12
Omnipotence	Rom. 1:16	Matt. 28:18	Rom. 15:19
Omniscience	Rom. 11:33	John 21:17	John 14:26
Immutability	Mal. 3:6	Heb. 13:8	Hag. 2:5
Eternality	Ps. 90:2	John 1:1	Heb. 9:14
Holiness	Lev. 19:2	Heb. 4:15	name "Holy"
Love	1 John 3:1	Matt. 9:36	name "Comforter"

THE WORK OF THE TRINITY

Work	Father	Son	Holy Spirit
Creation of world	Ps. 102:25	John 1:3	Gen. 1:2
Creation of man	Gen. 2:7	Col. 1:16	Job 33:4
Death of Christ	Isa. 53:10	John 10:18	Heb. 9:14
Resurrection of Christ	Acts 2:32	John 2:19	1 Pet. 3:18
Inspiration	Heb. 1:1, 2	1 Pet. 1:10, 11	2 Pet. 1:21
Indwelling of believers	Eph. 4:6	Col. 1:7	1 Cor. 6:19
Authority of ministry	2 Cor. 3:4-6	1 Tim. 1:12	Acts 20:28
Security of believer	John 10:29	Phil. 1:6	Eph. 1:13, 14

TWELVE
THE FATHER

(For after these things do the Gentiles seek:) for your heavenly Father knoweth that ye have need of all these things. Matthew 6:32

INTRODUCTION

A father should be the key individual to make a great impact on the life of his child. But the greatest influence on man will be by the Father in heaven. The concept of the fatherhood of God comes from the first Person of the Trinity, who is addressed as "Our Father which art in heaven" (Matt. 6:9).

In God's original design for the family, he placed a father at the head of the home. God established three institutions—family, government, and church—to assist us in our lives and to demonstrate an aspect of his relationship with us. Often the Bible uses the term "family of God" to speak of the spiritual kinship of all believers with each other and to God. The biblical pattern of the family, when practiced, is a tremendous aid for parents concerned about teaching children the fatherhood of God.

THE CHARACTERISTICS OF A FATHER

When a father properly fulfills his role in the family, he is fulfilling a picture of the heavenly Father's relationship to his children. We should not reverse this picture and say our relationship to God is a reflection of earthly fathers. If we do that, we are making God follow our earthly example. Since God was an eternal Father when man was created in the image of God (Gen. 1:26, 27), he was given the potential role of father to earthly children.

A father gives life to his children. A child is the result of a physical union between a man and a woman. Our heavenly Father is responsible for our spiritual life in a similar way. Every member of the family of God becomes a child of his heavenly Father when he is born again. They are those "which were born, not of blood, nor of the will of the flesh, nor of the will of man, but of God" (John 1:13). Until we have been born again, we are not members of the family of God. Though God is the Father of all by creation, God is not our spiritual Father until we are his children. We can be children of the heavenly Father by placing our trust in Jesus Christ and receiving him as our Savior by faith. "But as many as received him, to them gave he power to become the sons of God, even to them that believe on his name" (John 1:12).

A father loves his child. When a father gives to his children, he is demonstrating the strongest expression of love possessed by human beings. In his teaching, Jesus used the example of a father's willingness to give good gifts unto his children: "If ye then, being evil, know how to give good gifts unto your children, how much more shall your heavenly Father give the Holy Spirit to them that ask him?" (Luke 11:13).

Jesus told the parable of the prodigal son, demonstrating both God's love for sinners and a father's love for his children. The apostle Paul wrote: "For ye have not received the spirit of bondage again to fear; but ye have received the Spirit of adoption, whereby we cry, Abba, Father" (Rom. 8:15). The term *abba* is similar to a child's crying "Daddy." The picture here is one of warmth and compassion between a father and his young child.

A father protects his children. A good father desires to protect his children, which is carried over into his duties and responsibilities. How much more does the supernatural love of God cause him to step in and protect us.

God protects his children today in working all things for good (Rom. 8:28). This does not mean that some will not be martyred or be victims of war or crime. God's protection extends to our spiritual welfare and, in many occasions, our physical protection. "What shall we then say to these things? If God be for us, who can be against us?" (Rom. 8:31).

A father will provide for his family. The father is the provider for the home. The father who loves his family is a willing provider. Our heavenly Father is much more a provider. "Every good gift and every perfect gift is from above, and cometh down from the Father of lights, with whom is no variableness, neither shadow of turning" (James 1:17).

A father will teach and train his children. Part of the biblical responsibilities of being a father is to train up children. "And, ye fathers, provoke not your children to wrath: but bring them up in the nurture and admonition of the Lord" (Eph. 6:4). A good father will be an example and teacher for his children. Our heavenly Father has given us the Holy Spirit. Jesus noted, "I will pray the Father, and he will give you another Comforter" (John 14:16). "The Comforter which is the Holy Spirit, whom the Father will send in my name, he shall teach you all things" (John 14:26).

THE FATHERHOOD OF GOD

Although God is Father of all created, some teach that the fatherhood of God means everyone is a spiritual child of God and because of that everyone is going to heaven. This doctrine, called Universalism denies that all men are sinners and implies that there is no eternal punishment for sin. It denies the necessity of Christ dying for our sins. Hence there is no need of salvation. It claims that all men are born the children of God. Because of the abuse of these humanistic teachings, many conservative Christians will not use the phrase, "the fatherhood of God." However, the Bible teaches that God is the Father of the universe and all people in that universe, but that does not mean everyone is a Christian and that everyone will go to heaven (Gal. 3:26).

The Father of creation. When people describe God the Father, they often use the phrase, "the universal fatherhood of God." This phrase makes God the Father of all living things, including people, by virtue of the fact that he is their Creator. We prefer to use the phrase "the Father of creation," because it identifies God with the reason *why* he is Father. The best verse to identify "the Father of creation" is James 1:17: "Every good gift and every perfect gift is from above, and cometh down from the Father of lights."

When we study the history of an organization or a nation, we find the term "founding fathers." The man who invents or develops some new product is often called the "father" of that product. We use the term "father" to identify its source. Since God is the Creator of all things, he is the Father of the universe.

The national Father of Israel. God has a unique relationship with the nation Israel; he is called its father. Although the doctrine of the Father is fully developed in the New Testament, we have noted that it exists in embryonic form in the Old Testament. Jeremiah put it this way, "I am a father to Israel, and Ephraim is my firstborn" (Jer. 31:9). Israel was a special son to God because he was its source; Israel was loved by Jehovah and he was their teacher, giving them the law to instruct them in the way they should live. God cared and protected Israel as a Father.

The unique Father of Jesus Christ. In an extremely unique way, God is the Father of Jesus Christ, his Son. Jesus was miraculously born of a virgin with no human father. Actually, he existed from before the beginning and simply became a man, while retaining his divinity at his birth. God claims to be the Father of Christ when he calls him "Son," and in "Thou art my Son; this day have I begotten thee" (Ps. 2:7). This does not mean that Jesus Christ was begotten at a point in time. The phrase "this day" means God's eternal day, or a day without time. The Son was always in the process of being begotten by the Father—both Father and Son are eternal. At the baptism of Jesus, the Father himself spoke. "This is my beloved Son, in whom I am well pleased" (Matt. 3:17). Jesus recognized his sonship by telling the Jewish leaders, "My Father worketh hitherto, and I work" (John 5:17). This statement looks innocent to us because we do not see the implication of the original language. The Greek word for "my" is *idios,* by which Jesus meant, "My Father, of whom I am identical." When Jesus called God his Father, he also recognized himself as equal in deity.

Paul related Jesus to God by saying "his dear Son" (Col. 1:13). John called Christ "his only begotten Son" (John 3:16). Jesus recognized this unique relation he had with his God. He used the title "Father" more than any other when referring to God. He distinguished between "my Father" and "your Father." Though he instructed his disciples to pray "our Father," he himself never used the term. He recognized the uniqueness of his relationship with the Father.

A protective father. "A father of the fatherless, and a judge of the widows, is God in his holy habitation" (Ps. 68:5). God is a father to those oppressed who need a father. This verse does not teach that all poor orphans and widows are saved, but rather that God is concerned about those for whom no one else cares. Even among Christians there is a tendency to ignore those who are less fortunate. But God is the defender of those unable to defend themselves. When a Christian is opposing the poor, he is opposing those supported by God. As fathers will sometimes involve themselves in the disputes of their sons, so will the "father of the fatherless" step in for his children.

Redemptive father. The major emphasis in New Testament doctrine is the Father's relationship to redemption. All who are saved are born "of God" (John 1:13). God becomes our Father when we trust Christ as our Savior and gain admittance into the family of God (John 1:12). We immediately, upon salvation, have an intimate relationship with God "whereby we cry, Abba, Father" (Rom. 8:15). We cannot know God as our redemptive Father until we are known by him as his redeemed children.

THE CHRISTIAN AND HIS HEAVENLY FATHER

Many benefits are provided for the Christian by the heavenly Father. "He that spared not his own Son, but delivered him up for us all, how shall he not with him also freely give us all things?" (Rom. 8:32). Because of the Father's love, he gives us all that is good for us (James 1:17). God has provided the following benefits.

Fellowship with the Father. John wrote: "That which we have seen and heard declare we unto you, that ye also may have fellowship with us; and truly our fellowship is with the Father, and with his Son, Jesus Christ" (1 John 1:3). As members of the family of God, we have fellowship with other members of that family, including the Father himself. Often Christians will call each other brother and sister. This recognizes our spiritual kinship. Jesus said, "Call no man your father upon the earth: for one is your Father, which is in heaven" (Matt. 23:9). When we pray to the Father and call him Father, we recognize our spiritual kinship with him.

Access to the Father. Christians can pray and know their heavenly Father hears and will answer their prayers. Jesus taught his disciples to pray, "Our Father" (Matt. 6:9). He said, "Your heavenly Father knoweth that ye have need of all these things" (Matt. 6:32).

Guidance by the Father. Our heavenly Father has provided guidance for his creation. One of the purposes of Scripture is "that the man of God may be perfect, throughly furnished unto all good works" (2 Tim. 3:17). David said, "Wherewithal shall a young man cleanse his way? by taking heed thereto according to thy word" (Ps. 119:9).

Security from the Father. When a person receives Christ personally as Savior, immediately he receives eternal life (John

5:24). By definition, eternal life lasts forever. Our security as Christians is due in part to our relationship with the Father. Jesus said, "My Father, which gave them me, is greater than all; and no man is able to pluck them out of my Father's hand" (John 10:29).

A young child feels secure in his father's arms. The child believes his father would not permit anything to happen to him. The most secure place for the Christian is in his heavenly Father's hand. Our heavenly Father will not allow any harm to come to us that could in any way affect our eternal security.

Inheritance of the Father. Children are entitled to their father's inheritance. As children of God, we too are entitled to an inheritance. "And if children, then heirs; heirs of God, and joint-heirs with Christ" (Rom. 8:17). Jesus said, "In my Father's house are many mansions; if it were not so, I would have told you. I go to prepare a place for you" (John 14:2). Every believer has the promise of God of an eternal home in heaven as part of his inheritance.

CONCLUSION

When we think of God in all his majesty, we are impressed with the sovereignty of God. We need always to recognize that God is a great God and worthy of worship. But Jesus also taught us that God is our heavenly Father. As such he is intimate and personal. When we have a correct understanding of God, we realize he wants both to be our Father and to be worshiped in majesty. Out of duty and desire, the Christian ought constantly to live his life in a way pleasing to his heavenly Father.

DAILY READINGS

☐Monday: *Psalm 103:1-22*   ☐Tuesday: *Ephesians 5:21—6:4*   ☐Wednesday: *Colossians 3:3-21*   ☐Thursday: *1 John 3:1-17*   ☐Friday: *Matthew 6:1-18*   ☐Saturday: *Matthew 6:19-33*   ☐Sunday: *John 5:17-38*

THIRTEEN
THE NAMES OF GOD

His name shall endure for ever: his name shall be continued as long as the sun: and men shall be blessed in him: all nations shall call him blessed. Psalm 72:17

INTRODUCTION

Names are important. Someone has said, "the sweetest sound in any language is the sound of a person's own name." The names of God are also important. The Scriptures record hundreds of names and titles given to God. These names not only identify God but reveal something about his character and nature. Much of the truth of God is capsulized in his names. Therefore, an understanding of God's names will deepen our reverence and love for him.

THE PRIMARY NAMES OF GOD

The following chart will help interpret the interrelationship among the various names of God.

The names of God are one method God has chosen to reveal truth about himself. Some of God's names emphasize his nature. Other names emphasize his special relationship to man. At other times, God gave his name to identify other aspects of truth.

THE NAMES OF GOD IN SCRIPTURE	
Elohim (God)	El-Shaddai, El-Elyon, El-Olam
Jehovah (LORD)	Jehovah-Sabaoth, Jehovah-Jireh, Jehovah-Rapha, Jehovah-Nissi, Jehovah-Shalom, Jehovah-Tsidkenu, Jehovah-Shammah
Adonai (Lord or Master)	

Elohim—God. The most common designation for deity in Scripture is "God." The Hebrew word for "God" is *Elohim.* This term comes from two other Hebrew words, *El* meaning "Strong One," and *ohim* meaning "to swear or bind with an oath." Therefore, God is the Strong One who manifests himself by his Word. This name is used over 2,500 times in the Old Testament, often to remind the reader of the strength or faithfulness of God. Moses wrote, "From everlasting to everlasting, thou art God [*Elohim*]" (Ps. 90:2).

Elohim is the name first used to mention God in the Scriptures. "In the beginning God [*Elohim*] created the heaven and earth" (Gen. 1:1). The final reference to the word "God" in the New Testament is the Greek equivalent *theos* (Rev. 22:19). Usually, the name God (*Elohim*) is used in connection with the unsaved or inanimate objects.

Jehovah—Lord. An unusual problem confronts the study of this second name of God. We really are not sure how to pronounce it. Some scholars say "Yahweh" but others say "Jehovah." To distinguish it from another Hebrew word also translated "Lord," *Jehovah* in most Bible translations is LORD, using small capital letters.

The reason we are not sure of its pronunciation stems from the reverence Jewish scribes gave to it. No one would pronounce it, out of fear of offending God. Whenever a scribe came to the word in copying the Scriptures, some would stop and bathe and put on clean clothes. Others would begin with new pen and ink before writing God's name.

This concern not to dishonor the name of God was also expressed in the reading of the Scriptures. When the reader came to this name for God, he would either pause and omit it or often substitute another name for God in its place. Also, Hebrew language has no vowels in its alphabet so pronouncciation of words is learned orally. Because men did not speak the name, it was not long before others did not know how to pronounce it.

This word *Jehovah* means "to be or become." It comes from the verb "to be" repeated twice. *Jehovah* means, "I am, I am." This is the name whereby God identified himself at the burning bush (Exod. 3:14). This name speaks of both the self-existence of God and his eternity. God is the only one who can say I am, I exist by myself independent of any other. He can always say "I am" because he always was in the past and always will be in the future.

Jehovah is used about 4,000 times in the Bible, usually in association with his people. It has been called "the covenant name of God," as it is often used to identify God in his covenants (Gen. 2:15-17; 3:14-19; 4:15; 12:1-3).

Adonai—Lord. The third name used of God in Scripture is *Adonai*, usually translated "Lord" in our English Bible. Only the first letter is capitalized with *Adonai* Lord, whereas small capital letters are used in *Jehovah* LORD. *Adonai* was first used by Abraham as he sought the will of God in adopting an heir (Gen. 15:2). The term indicates the sovereignty of God. If he is the master, then we are the servants. The master is the one who assumes control of a situation. It is reasonable to assume that the servants will do the master's will. Of all the names used of God, *Adonai* identifies him with the qualities of an earthly master. Hence, it gives human characteristics to God.

The word *Adonai* also implies the possibility of knowing the will of the master. Abraham used the name as he sought to determine a course of action. If the responsibility of a servant is to do the will of his master, it is reasonable to assume the master will make that will known to his servant.

Today Christians often talk about the Lord but show little of allowing him to control their lives. If we recognize him as

Lord, then there is no longer any question of obeying his commandments. When God told Peter to kill and eat unclean animals, three times Peter replied, "Not so, Lord" (Acts 10:9-16). As soon as Peter said "not so," he was at that moment not recognizing God as his Lord.

THE COMPOUND NAMES OF ELOHIM

El-Shaddai—The Almighty God. The primary names of God are sometimes used with other names to identify a specific characteristic of God. The name *El-Shaddai* means "the Almighty God." This name speaks of God's all-sufficiency. When Abraham was ninety-nine years old and still without an heir, "the Almighty God" renewed his covenant with him (Gen. 17:1, 2). This was the God who was able to overcome any obstacle to keep his promise.

The term *Shaddai* means "rest or nourisher." It comes from a root word that means "breast or strength given or sustainer." Though translated "the Almighty God," it also means "the all-sufficient God." Today we can claim the psalmist's promise, "He that dwelleth in the secret place of the Most High shall abide under the shadow of the Almighty [*El-Shaddai*]" (Ps. 91:1).

El Elyon—the most high God. This name is used to identify God, particularly to polytheistic Gentiles. The idea in this name is that the true God of Israel was above all other false gods of the Gentiles. This title is first used in the Scriptures to identify Melchizedek, "the priest of the most high God" (Gen. 14:18). At that time, Melchizedek attributed Abraham's recent military victory to *El-Elyon* (the most high God). He is also understood to be "the possessor of heaven and earth" (Gen. 14:22).

El-Olam—the everlasting God. In his experience with God, Abraham also came to know him as "the everlasting God" (Gen. 21:33). This name indicates God is not limited by time, for he is eternal. Moses wrote, "From everlasting to everlasting, thou art God" (Ps. 90:2). The name *El-Olam* personifies all that is true about the eternity of God.

THE COMPOUND NAMES OF JEHOVAH

Jehovah—Sabaoth—the Lord of hosts. This name emphasizes the power and glory of God. The word "hosts" is used in the Bible to refer to heavenly bodies (Gen. 2:1), angels (Luke 2:13), saints (Josh 5:15), and sinners (Judg. 4:2). It implies the power of the heavenly beings who serve the Lord. As the Lord of hosts, God is working through all these "hosts" to fulfill his purposes. The Christian can be encouraged today as he claims the promise, "The Lord of hosts is with us" (Ps. 46:7).

In discussing the second coming of Christ, David asked and answered a very important question. "Who is this King of glory? The Lord of hosts, he is the King of glory" (Ps. 24:10). The expression "Lord of hosts" is used over 170 times in Scripture to identify the Lord.

Jehovah-Jireh—the Lord shall provide. Probably the single greatest test of faith in the life of Abraham occurred when God called him to sacrifice his son. When Isaac asked his father about the sacrifice animal, Abraham responded, "God will provide himself a lamb for a burnt offering" (Gen. 22:8). Later that same day, God honored the faith of Abraham and prevented the death of Isaac, providing a ram in his place. "Abraham called the name of that place Jehovah-Jireh [the Lord shall provide]" (Gen. 22:14). In the New Testament, Paul may have been thinking of this name of God when he asked, "He that spared not his own Son, but delivered him up for us all, how shall he not with him also freely give us all things?" (Rom. 8:32).

Jehovah-Rapha—the Lord that healeth. God always wants the best for his people. When he brought Israel out of Egypt, he wanted his people to live full and healthy lives. "If thou wilt diligently hearken to the voice of the Lord thy God, and wilt do that which is right in his sight, and wilt give ear to his commandments, and keep all his statutes, I will put none of these diseases upon thee, which I have brought upon the Egyptians; for I am the Lord that healeth thee" (Exod. 15:26). This name of God emphasizes God's concern for our good health.

God is certainly able and does on occasion heal people miraculously, but that is only part of what this name teaches. The context of the revelation of this name is preventive medicine more than curing. No doctor has found a cure for the common cold, but the mother who bundles up her children with scarves, mittens, boots, and snowsuits on a cold winter day has "cured" her children's cold by preventing it. Here God has promised to heal us from the diseases that plagued the Egyptians by providing the resources that are available to those who obey the Lord. Obedience will produce good health.

Jehovah-Nissi—the Lord our banner. When God gave Israel the victory over Amalek, "Moses built an altar, and called the name of it Jehovah-nissi" (Exod. 17:15). The name *Jehovah-Nissi* means "the Lord is my banner" or "the Lord that prevaileth." The emphasis of this name for the Christian is that we are not in the battle alone. As soldiers, we march under the banner and colors of God. The battle itself belongs to God, and victory is already guaranteed. The Christian can therefore serve the Lord with complete confidence in the outcome.

Jehovah-Shalom—the Lord our peace. When God called Gideon to deliver Israel from the oppressive Midianites, "Gideon built an altar there unto the Lord, and called it Jehovah-shalom" (Judg. 6:24). The name *Jehovah-Shalom* means "the Lord is our peace." The building of that altar before the gathering of an army or forming of a battle plan was an act of faith on Gideon's part. The only way one can know *Jehovah-Shalom* is by faith. "Therefore being justified by faith, we have peace with God through our Lord Jesus Christ" (Rom. 5:1). As we seek to live for God consistently, the Bible says, "The God of peace shall be with you" (Phil. 4:9).

Jehovah-Tsidkenu—the Lord our righteousness. When the Lord returns to this world at the end of the age, many Jews will recognize their Messiah and turn to him as Savior. At that time they will know a name of God that every Christian knows experientially, "the Lord our righteousness" (Jer. 23:6). Our admission into heaven is not dependent upon our personal righteousness but rather the righteousness of God applied to our account. Someday this will also be the experience of national Israel and "the Lord our righteousness" will be the prominent name of God in that day.

Jehovah-Shammah—the Lord is there. As Ezekiel concludes his discussion of the eternal city, he records, "and the name of the city from that day shall be, The Lord is there" (Ezek. 48:35). This name of God emphasizes his presence. When God called Moses to lead Israel out of Egypt, he promised, "Certainly I will be with thee" (Exod. 3:12). As we are faithful today in presenting a greater deliverance to the lost by preaching and teaching the gospel, Jesus has promised, "Lo, I am with you alway, even unto the end of the world [age]" (Matt. 28:20). The Lord is present.

THE USE OF THE NAME OF GOD

Taking God's name in vain disobeys a biblical command. Taking God's name in vain is commonly identified as cursing and is definitely prohibited in the Scriptures. "Thou shalt not take the name of the Lord thy God in vain" (Exod. 20:7). On at least six occasions in the Book of Leviticus, Moses writes, "Neither shalt thou profane the name of thy God" (Lev. 18:21, 19:12; 20:3; 21:6; 22:2, 32). That book of the Bible which teaches most about the holiness of God is also that book which reminds us most definitely not to curse.

Christians have a tendency to classify certain commands as more important than others. Actually, it is our duty as Christians to obey all that is commanded (Luke 17:10). We also sometimes wrongly classify sins in terms of what we would never do and those that God understands we will sometimes do. For many Christians, cursing is one of those "understandable sins." They would be surprised to realize that God banned this practice in the context of prohibiting child sacrifices and just before forbidding homosexuality and bestiality (Lev. 18:21-24). In the mind of God, these things were serious enough to cause him to cast out the pagan nations which at that time inhabited the Promised Land.

Cursing is not becoming priests. Moses was instructed to advise Aaron, Israel's first priest, "that they profane not my holy name" (Lev. 22:2). The priest was that individual who represented the people before God. The chief ministry of the priest was prayer. He naturally had a higher view of God than the typical Jew. God specifically told the priest not to desecrate God's name.

The New Testament teaches the priesthood of all believers. Every Christian has access by prayer to God directly through the blood of Jesus (Heb. 4:14-16). We are a part of the "royal priesthood" (1 Pet. 2:8). Just as the Old Testament priest had the highest view of God, so the New Testament priest should have a high view of God. If the Christian "priest" has a correct understanding of who God is, he will not take his name in vain.

Cursing may produce detrimental associations. Many make a practice of cursing or using minced oaths (using a slang word as a swear word such as, darn for damn) in association with God. Some even find swearing or minced oaths somewhat entertaining. The Bible identifies those that curse in a different way. David said, "Thine enemies take thy name in vain" (Ps. 139:20). When a Christian curses, he identifies himself with the enemy of God.

Cursing is also a characteristic of "desperate men." During the Great Tribulation, men who have rejected Christ as Savior will panic in the midst of the judgment of God and blaspheme the name of God (Rev. 16:9). When God allowed Satan to try Job, Job's wife considered the situation desperate and advised Job to "curse God and die" (Job 2:9). The Christian should not panic in the midst of an apparently desperate situation. "Fret not thyself" (Ps. 37:1) is a command every Christian needs to obey daily.

Cursing is incompatible with personal holiness. God told redeemed Israel, "Ye shall be holy; for I the Lord your God, am holy" (Lev. 18:2). In the New Testament, Peter taught his converts, "As he which hath called you is holy, so be ye holy in all manner of conversation [life]" (1 Pet. 1:15). A Christian cannot practice consistent personal holiness and curse. "They shall be holy unto their God, and not profane the name of their God" (Lev. 21:6). It is incompatible to try to live for God in our life-style and dishonor his name in our speech.

Paul charged the Jews in Rome that "The name of God is blasphemed among the Gentiles through you" (Rom. 2:24). He was not here accusing these Jews of cursing but rather of inconsistent lives. While they were concerned about keeping certain laws, they were also slack about observing others; their inconsistency in the name of God being dishonored. Because of the One that name represents and what it stands for, it is imperative that a Christian never dishonor the name of God, verbally or otherwise.

CONCLUSION

God has revealed a great deal about himself in his names. When we actively use his name in vain through cursing or passively by not showing proper respect, we rob ourselves of the blessing of God. As we apply these names of God to our Christian experience, our communion with God will grow deeper and our Christian life will be more fulfilling.

DAILY READINGS

☐Monday: *Genesis 14:17—15:6*   ☐Tuesday: *Genesis 17:1-22*
☐Wednesday: *Genesis 22:1-14*   ☐Thursday: *Judges 6:11-24*
☐Friday: *Exodus 15:22-27*   ☐Saturday: *Exodus 17:8-16*
☐Sunday: Exodus 34:1-17

PART FOUR

UNDERSTANDING THE DOCTRINE OF CHRIST

FOURTEEN
THE PREEXISTENCE
OF CHRIST

*I will declare the decree: The LORD hath said unto me, Thou
art my Son; this day have I begotten thee.* Psalm 2:7

INTRODUCTION

An honest person cannot study the life and ministry of Jesus
Christ as taught in the Bible and not be impressed with his influence. The years Jesus traveled throughout Galilee and
Judea have had a greater impact upon civilization than any
other thirty-year period in the history of the world. Jesus
taught a limited group for a limited time, yet his teachings
have outlived those who taught a lifetime. Though Jesus
Christ was not personally engaged in the arts, he has furnished the theme for more poems and songs, paintings and
sculptures than any artist in history. None of the original
projects that were built by this Carpenter remain in our mu-
seums, yet in almost every city around the world exist build-
ings and structures erected in his honor. The earthly life of
Jesus Christ cannot be denied by an honest student of history.

The Bible teaches that Jesus Christ is the second Person of
the Trinity; as such he is equal with God in nature, yet submissive in office. What the Bible says about God, it also main-
tains about Jesus Christ. And, since God is eternal, Jesus
Christ existed before his birth in Bethlehem. The Son of God

was born into this world as you or I because he had a human birth (see Chapter 16, The Virgin Birth). But the Bible also describes his birth, "the Word became flesh" (John 1:14). Jesus Christ existed from eternity past. Since the evidence in the documents overwhelmingly attests to the life and ministry of Jesus on earth, they also attest to his eternal past. Jesus was the Son of God in the Old Testament; this is the doctrine of preexistence. Jesus Christ has always existed and has no point of beginning. This is the doctrine of eternality.

The eternality of Christ means he is not limited by time, has no beginning, and will have no end. The preexistence of Jesus Christ means he existed before his birth in Bethlehem. Because Christ existed before his earthly birth, his eternality gives him Godlike qualities. This concept of preexistence and the proofs of eternality support the proofs of the deity of Christ.

DEITY IMPLIES PREEXISTENCE AND ETERNALITY

A key to understanding Christ in eternity past is in understanding his deity. Jesus of Nazareth was not just another religious leader who had a following in his day. He was not just a teacher who gave some moral principles for our day. Jesus is God. Since eternal existence is one of the attributes of God, it follows that if Jesus is God, then he must have an eternal past. Though some theologians question the deity of Christ, conservative Bible scholars recognize the Bible contains an abundance of evidence to confirm this doctrine.

The claims of Jesus. Because a man claims to be God does not make his claim true. On the other hand, it is assumed that if God would reveal himself, he would also identify himself by a claim that he is God. This becomes one foundation upon which we consider the deity of Christ. The one who claims to be God would have to demonstrate Godlike moral power of holiness, love, and goodness. He would also have to back up his claim with demonstration of power, knowledge, and omnipresence. Finally, his teachings must be consistent within themselves and correspond to the wisdom of God. The biblical account of Christ gives ample evidence that Jesus claimed he was God.

Jesus often used the term "my Father" when referring to God. This is a common expression today and many Christians say "my Father" when speaking of God. When Jesus said, "my Father," the Jewish leaders recognized that he claimed deity for himself as well as God. "Therefore the Jews sought the more to kill him [Jesus], because he not only had broken the sabbath, but said also that God was his Father, making himself equal with God" (John 5:18). On another visit to Jerusalem, Jesus was asked for a clear statement concerning his claim. He responded, "I and my Father are one" (John 10:30). Jesus understood he was saying, "I am the Son of God" (John 10:36). Certainly his audience understood what he was saying. On several occasions they attempted to kill him for claiming to be God. When the religious leaders finally brought Jesus to Pilate for crucifixion, they accused him of blasphemy. "The Jews answered him, We have a law, and by our law he ought to die, because he made himself the Son of God" (John 19:7).

The teaching of the Bible. Jesus recognized his claim was not enough to make him God. "If I bear witness of myself, my witness is not true" (John 5:31). Jesus was pointing out that any claim, true or false, could be assumed false if unsubstantiated. Jesus pointed his critics to another authority. "Search the scriptures; for in them ye think ye have eternal life: and they are they which testify of me" (John 5:39).

The Bible records many statements concerning the deity of Christ (Heb. 1:8). John says "the Word was God" (John 1:1). Writing hundreds of years before his birth, Isaiah called him "the Mighty God" (Isa. 9:6). Paul was "looking for that blessed hope, and glorious appearing of the great God and our Saviour, Jesus Christ" (Titus 2:13). Paul quotes an early church doctrinal statement, "God was manifest in the flesh, justified in the Spirit, seen of angels, preached unto the Gentiles, believed on in the world, received up into glory" (1 Tim. 3:16). The teaching of both Old and New Testament is clearly that Jesus is God.

The triune nature of God. God is one God in three Persons: Father, Son, and Holy Spirit. Each member of the Trinity is completely God. The deity of the Trinity has been recognized from the beginning. Isaiah recorded the predictive words of Jesus, "Come near unto me, hear ye this: I have not spoken in secret from the beginning; from the time that it was, there am I; and now the Lord God, and his Spirit, hath sent me" (Isa. 48:16). When Christians are baptized, they are baptized "in the name of the Father, and of the Son, and of the Holy Ghost" (Matt. 28:19). The very act which God has prescribed for every believer as he begins the Christian life recognizes the place of Jesus Christ as the Son of God. What is true about God is true of every member of the Trinity of God. If God has existed from eternity past (Ps. 90:2), then every member of the Trinity has existed equally as long.

The heavenly origin of Christ. Christ is eternal. The writer of Hebrews compared Melchizedek to Christ. "Without father, without mother, without descent, having neither beginning of days, nor end of life; but made like unto the Son of God" (Heb. 7:3). When we think of the earthly life of Christ, however, we recognize that he had come from heaven. John the Baptist said, "He that cometh from above is above all: he that is of the earth is earthly, and speaketh of the earth: he that cometh from heaven is above all" (John 3:31). Because of this, John could accept the growing popularity of Jesus at his expense. Jesus told the people of his home region, "I came down from heaven, not to do mine own will, but the will of him that sent me" (John 6:38).

The preincarnate work of Christ. Before Jesus was born as the babe in Bethlehem, he was engaged in the work of creation. "All things were made by him; and without him was not anything made that was made" (John 1:3). In addition to his work in creation, he was also involved in the work of inspiration. Paul described the Scriptures as "the word of Christ" (Col. 3:16). Jesus Christ traveled with Israel throughout the wilderness providing for them. Israel "did all drink the same spiritual drink: for they drank of that spiritual Rock that followed them: and that Rock was Christ" (1 Cor. 10:4). The presence of Jesus Christ protected and sustained Israel as they wandered in the wilderness. Jesus demonstrated his deity by his activity in the Old Testament.

OLD TESTAMENT APPEARANCES TEACH HIS PREEXISTENCE AND ETERNALITY

The preexistence of Christ is further substantiated by the many recorded preincarnational appearances in the Bible. Often the Bible identifies these appearances as those of "the angel of the Lord." A closer look at the references of these events will demonstrate that this angel was more than just another angel; he was God. At other times these were an appearance of Jesus in human form but not identified as an Angel of the Lord.

A Man (Gen. 18:1-33; 32:24-32; Dan. 3:23-29). On at least three occasions, Jesus appeared as a human before the incarnation. On these occasions, he appeared among men as a man. Three men appeared to Abraham and Sarah to confirm God's provision of a son and to inform Abraham of the coming destruction of Sodom and Gomorrah. One of these men is identified as "the Lord" (Gen. 18: 1, 13, 17, 20, 22, 26, 27, 30-33) and also called "the Judge of all the earth" (Gen. 18:15). This man must have been Jesus Christ because "no man hath seen God at any time; the only begotten Son, which is in the bosom of the Father, he hath declared him" (John 1:18). Since Christ is the only one of the three Persons of the Trinity to be seen, we are left to believe this man on this occasion and the angel of the Lord who is called God was in fact the second Person of the Trinity, Jesus Christ. Jesus is the only member of the Trinity to have taken on a physical body at any time.

At a later time, Christ appeared to Jacob and wrestled with him during the night. Jacob recognized the next morning he had met with God. "And Jacob named the place Peniel; for I have seen God face to face, and my life is preserved" (Gen. 32:30).

On a third occasion, Jesus joined the three young Hebrews in Nebuchadnezzar's furnace. Though assured that Nebuchadnezzar had thrown only three men into the furnace, "He answered and said, Lo, I see four men loose, walking in the midst of the fire, and they have no hurt; and the form of the fourth is like the Son of God" (Dan. 3:25).

The Angel of the Lord. By far the most common appearance of Jesus Christ in the Old Testament is as the Angel of the Lord. There can be no question but that he is God. When he appeared, it was usually to an individual who was commissioned to do a special work for God. Jesus took the time personally to enlist that individual in his service.

THE ANGEL OF THE LORD		
Reference	*Occasion*	*Called God*
Gen. 16:9-14	To Hagar	Gen. 16:13
Gen. 22:11-14	Sacrifice of Isaac	Gen. 22:14
Exod. 3:2—4:17	Burning bush	Gen. 3:14
Judg. 6:11-24	To Gideon	Judg. 6:22
Judg. 13:2-23	To Samson's mother	Judg. 13:18, 22

When we consider that Christ would meet with men as he did throughout the Old Testament and then spend a life among men on earth, we cannot help but be impressed with the intense personal concern of Christ. He is intensely interested in our personal lives and takes a personal interest in the problems and decisions which face us day by day. As he existed in the past and demonstrated his interest in the affairs of men, so today he is interested in our problems. He desires to become involved in our lives.

THE NAMES OF CHRIST TEACH HIS PREEXISTENCE AND ETERNALITY

Son of God. One of the many names of Jesus Christ in the New Testament is Son of God. The term "Son of God" is used by Christ when he is referring to his deity. The first reference to the Sonship of Christ is, "I will declare the decree: the Lord hath said unto me, Thou art my Son; this day have I begotten thee" (Ps. 2:7). This verse reveals a conversation between God the Father and God the Son. The Father called the second Person of the Trinity by the name "Son" to whom he said, "I have begotten thee."

Some Bible interpreters raise a question as to when Jesus became the Son of God. Some teach Jesus became the Son of God at the incarnation. To prove this, they use the prediction to Mary by the angel, "He shall be called the Son of God" (Luke 1:35).

Still others say Jesus became a Son of God at his baptism. It was there God broke the silence of heaven to announce, "This is my beloved Son, in whom I am well pleased" (Matt. 3:17).

A third view is that Jesus became the Son of God at his resurrection, because Paul said, "Declared to be the Son of God with power, according to the Spirit of holiness, by the resurrection from the dead" (Rom. 1:4).

Yet another group cites Hebrews 1:1-4, arguing that Jesus became the Son of God by "appointment" at his ascension. All of these fail to recognize the teaching of one of the Bible's best-known verses: "For God so loved the world, that he gave his only begotten Son, that whosoever believeth in him should not perish but have everlasting life" (John 3:16). Jesus was recognized as the Son of God before he came to earth to provide eternal salvation. Jesus was the Son of God even before the first presentation of the gospel in Genesis 3:15, "And I will put enmity between thee and the woman, and between thy seed and her seed; it shall bruise thy head, and thou shalt bruise his heel." This verse recognized the coming of the seed of the woman to bruise the head of the serpent.

The key to understanding when Jesus became the Son of God is to understand the meaning of the word "day" in Psalm 2:7. The word "day" does not refer to a twenty-four-hour period in time. God lives beyond time. This word means an eternal day. Technically this is called *eternal generation*. Jesus did not become the Son of God at a point in time. He has always been in the process of becoming the Son of God in God's eternal day. The conclusion is that there never was a time that Christ was not the Son of God.

Only begotten Son. The Bible identifies angels, Jews, and Christians at various times as sons of God, but the relationship that exists between God the Father and Jesus Christ is different. Jesus is the "only begotten Son of God." The term "only begotten" is used to describe the unique relationship between the Father and Jesus (John 1:14, 18; 3:16; 1 John 4:9). Though any individual who trusts Christ personally for salvation will become a child of God (John 1:12), there is only one "only begotten Son of God." In this phrase Christ expresses the nature of God, just as a son possesses the nature of his father. The only begotten Son of God is just like his heavenly Father, for he is God.

CONCLUSION

The history of Jesus Christ began before Bethlehem. He is God and has always lived and performed the work of God. Even before the incarnation, Jesus was personally involved in the lives of men. Today he lives in heaven with the same interest he has had in eternity. Since he is God, we can trust him not only for our eternal salvation but also for the guidance we need each day.

DAILY READINGS

☐Monday: *John 1:1-18*   ☐Tuesday: *John 14:1-14*
☐Wednesday: *John 5:17-35*   ☐Thursday: *John 5:36-47*
☐Friday: *Judges 13:2-23*   ☐Saturday: *Judges 6:11-24*
☐Sunday: *Genesis 18:1-33*

FIFTEEN
THE OFFICES OF CHRIST

And Simon Peter answered and said, Thou art the Christ, the Son of the living God. Matthew 16:16

INTRODUCTION

In a small business establishment, it is often necessary for an individual to assume multiple roles. He may be in charge of accounting but also be responsible for office staff, or he may also be the sales manager. The same thing is often true in churches. A Sunday school teacher may also serve as an usher, choir member, bus worker, deacon, songleader, or one of hundreds of other responsibilities. This practice of wearing two hats will help us to understand the three offices of Christ. The term "Christ" is a Greek word; its Hebrew equivalent in the Old Testament is "Messiah." These terms could be translated "the anointed One." This title of our Lord recognizes three anointed offices that belong to Christ: (1) Prophet (Deut. 18:15-19); (2) Priest (Heb. 9:14-16); and (3) King (Acts 17:7).

THE PROPHETIC OFFICE OF CHRIST

When Israel was preparing to enter the Promised Land, God instructed them not to learn or practice the false religions of Canaan. Rather than be satisfied with these illegitimate means of gaining spiritual insight, God promised to give the nation prophets who would speak for him. Though each prophet had a message from God for the people, their presence would also serve as a reminder of another promise God made. "The Lord thy God will raise up unto thee a Prophet from the midst of thee, of thy brethren, like unto me; unto him ye shall hearken" (Deut. 18:15). This "Prophet" was none other than Jesus Christ himself.

The prophets of God were often unpopular among their own people because of their message of judgment. Many times the people would rebel against God's message that judged their sin. The prophet was simply doing his job. He represented God before the people and gave them God's message.

If God had a message to give to the world today he could do it any number of ways, for God could do anything. But God has chosen to limit himself to a strategy of using people who know the message to tell others who do not know. In the Old Testament, he would reveal a message to his prophets, who in turn would give the message to the nation. Some of these men described this revelation in terms of vision (Isa. 1:1; Ezek. 1:1). Others simply acknowledged the coming of the Word of the Lord (Jer. 1:4; Jonah 1:1). Commonly, these men simply announced with authority, "Thus saith the Lord" (Obad. 1). Nahum and Habakkuk described their message in terms of a "burden" (Nah. 1:1; Hab. 1:1). These men knew they were speaking on behalf of God.

Jesus, the Word of God, became flesh. This will be one of the titles Jesus holds when he returns: "His name is called The Word of God" (Rev. 19:13). Jesus consciously said and did the will of the Father while here on earth. He told the religious leaders of his day, "The Son can do nothing of himself, but what he seeth the Father do: for what things soever he doeth, these also doeth the Son likewise" (John 5:19). Later in the same conversation Jesus said, "I can of mine own self do nothing; as I hear, I judge, and my judgment is just; because I seek not mine own will, but the will of the Father which hath sent me" (John 5:30).

Prediction—Foreteller. When we think of prophecy, we usually think of predicting future events. In the role of foreteller,

Jesus made several "prophecies" during his ministry: John 14:26 (coming of the Holy Spirit); John 16:16, 17 (ministry of the Holy Spirit); John 14:2, 3 (his return); and, Matthew 16:21 (his death, burial, and resurrection).

A Preacher to people—"Forth-teller." In his wisdom, God has always "sought for a man among them" (Ezek. 22:30) whenever he chose to communicate his message. When people can identify with the messenger, they will respond to the message. To minister to man, Jesus came as a man. "And the Word was made flesh, and dwelt among us (and we beheld his glory, the glory as of the only begotten of the Father,) full of grace and truth" (John 1:14). Jesus became a man, so men could identify with him and his message.

A Hindu heard the message of the gospel but could not understand why Jesus became a man. As he left the meeting, he encountered an anthill in danger of being burned. Concerned about the ants, he tried to rescue them but they ran from him in fear. Suddenly the Hindu realized why Jesus came as a man. Just as an ant was the only one who could warn ants, so Jesus became a man to relate the message of God to other men.

Jesus taught the people the things concerning God. Nicodemus, a Pharisee and ruler of the Jews, acknowledged, "Rabbi, we know that thou art a teacher come from God: for no man can do these miracles that thou doest, except God be with him" (John 3:2). When Jesus taught, "the people were astonished at his doctrine: For he taught them as one having authority" (Matt. 7:28, 29). Several extended discourses of Jesus are recorded in Scripture, including the Sermon on the Mount (Matt. 5—7), the Olivet discourse (Matt. 24—25), and the Upper Room discourse (John 13—16). In these messages of Jesus, the major theme dealt with teaching men how to live for God.

THE PRIESTHOOD OF CHRIST

A second office appointed by God in the Old Testament was that of the priest, whose main function was to represent man before God. The job of Israel's high priest was to appear before God to make intercession for the people. The priest was the one who offered the sacrifice upon the altar. The priest did teach the people (Lev. 10:10, 11; Deut. 33:10; Mal. 2:6 , 7), but that was not his main priority. Because God is a just but forgiving God, the priest could present his forgiveness to the people if they met God's conditions. The priest was usually a channel of forgiveness while the prophet was usually a channel of judgment. The people would have chosen to see a priest over a prophet any day.

Jesus is our great high priest. The Bible teaches, "He is able also to save them to the uttermost that come unto God by him, seeing he ever liveth to make intercession for them" (Heb. 7:25). As our high priest, Jesus is constantly interceding for us. He understands the problems we encounter in life, having experienced the same when he lived on earth. "For we have not an high priest which cannot be touched with the feeling of our infirmities, but was in all points tempted like as we are, yet without sin" (Heb. 4:15). The priesthood of Christ is superior to that of Aaron in that it was after the order of Melchizedek (Heb. 5:10).

The priesthood of Jesus is superior in that other priests have died, whereas Christ "ever liveth" (Heb. 7:25). His priesthood is more secure in that God swore with an oath concerning it (Heb. 7:21). The Old Testament priests could only offer typical offerings that pointed to a complete offering for sin yet future. As Jesus hung on Calvary, he offered the actual sacrifice for sin. "We are sanctified through the offering of the body of Jesus Christ once for all" (Heb. 10:10).

THE KINGSHIP OF CHRIST

When God finally allowed Israel to have a king, the earthly sovereign was responsible to represent God. The king was the leader of the nation and filled the third "anointed" office. Christians were persecuted in the first century when they taught the kingship of Christ (Acts 17:7). They recognized that Jesus alone must be the single supreme Ruler in their lives. This idea was offensive to Rome, who believed their Caesar was both god and king.

Jesus is king. The kingship of Christ is seen in his deity. Because he is God, he is also king. In heaven "they sing the song of Moses, the servant of God, and the song of the Lamb, saying, Great and marvelous are thy works, Lord God Almighty; just and true are thy ways, thou King of saints" (Rev. 15:3). The Romans considered their Caesar to be a god. Christians, on the other hand, recognized Jesus alone to be their king.

Jesus has a kingdom. Every king has a domain over which he rules. Jesus is no exception. Jesus said "My kingdom is not of this world" (John 18:36), but he never denied that he had a kingdom. It was the custom of the Romans to identify the crime of a condemned man on the cross upon which he died. Jesus was executed as "the King of the Jews" (John 19:19). His kingdom continues on earth today as his Word is preached (Acts 8:12; 14:22; Col. 1:13). When he returns to this earth, he will do so to establish his earthly kingdom. Revelation 20 describes his kingdom as a thousand-year reign of peace on the earth, often called the millennial kingdom.

Jesus has subjects. Christ is now a ruler to those who submit their lives to him. Someday, "At the name of Jesus every knee [shall] bow, of things in heaven, and things in earth, and things under the earth: And . . . every tongue should confess that Jesus Christ is Lord" (Phil. 2:10, 11). Today, those who receive Christ as Lord and Savior recognize the kingship of Christ in their lives. Jesus told a parable equating the Christian with a servant. He concluded, "So likewise ye, when ye shall have done all those things which are commanded you, say, We are unprofitable servants: we have done that which was our duty to do" (Luke 17:10).

One of the unique differences between the Christians of the New Testament and those of today is their attitude toward their relation with Christ. They saw him as a supreme ruler and themselves as slaves in comparison. Perhaps if we had a similar biblical conviction today, we would see similar biblical results.

CONCLUSION

One of the many titles of our Lord is that of Christ or Messiah. As God's anointed One, Jesus holds three offices. As the great prophet of God, he speaks to us for God. The wise Christian will heed what he says. Jesus is also our great high priest. As such he is constantly on duty in heaven, interceding on our behalf. Because of his work on Calvary, we too can have direct access to God in prayer. Finally, Jesus holds the office of king. As his subjects, we are responsible to serve him. Part of serving our king includes serving as a prophet, speaking to men on behalf of God, and as a priest, speaking to God on behalf of men.

DAILY READINGS

☐Monday: *Deuteronomy 18:9-22*   ☐Tuesday: *John 1:35-51*
☐Wednesday: *Acts 3:12-26*   ☐Thursday: *Hebrews 4:1-16*
☐Friday: *Hebrews 5:1-10*   ☐Saturday: *Hebrews 9:11-22*
☐Sunday: *Acts 17:1-10*

SIXTEEN
THE VIRGIN BIRTH

Behold, a virgin shall conceive, and bear a son, and shall call his name Immanuel. Isaiah 7:14

INTRODUCTION

At the beginning of this century, liberal theologians were denying the virgin birth of Jesus Christ. They were greatly influenced by the humanistic attitude to Christianity that manifested itself in an antisupernatural approach to the Scriptures. Other doctrines were denied, such as the verbal inspiration of Scriptures, the substitutionary atonement, the physical resurrection, and the bodily return of Jesus Christ at the end of this age. These important doctrines came to be called "the fundamentals of the faith."

Some theologians denied some of the fundamentals, but accepted others. Of the fundamentals, the inerrancy of Scripture and the virgin birth were usually the first doctrines to be denied. Liberal theologians, because of their aversion to the supernatural, tried to maintain that belief in the virgin birth was not really necessary.

In our day, artificial insemination creates the possibility of a woman experiencing birth without knowing a man in a sexual way. However, this is not true of virgin birth in the biblical sense, which involved a virgin giving birth to a child without the seed of a man. The virgin birth is the supernatural method that was used for the birth of Jesus Christ.

The virgin birth of Christ is not an independent doctrine which we can receive or reject without affecting our Christianity. It is one of the foundation stones of Christianity; our faith will crumble if it is removed. This doctrine is tied to biblical inerrancy, Christ's sinless character, the atonement, and other key doctrines of the Bible. If Jesus was not born of a virgin, he would be unable to save himself, because he would not be a sinless Savior. If we cannot accept the virgin birth of Christ, very little credibility remains in the Bible. Therefore, we must understand the virgin birth if we are going to understand our faith.

THE VIRGIN BIRTH IN PROPHECY

Several biblical authors believed and wrote of the virgin birth of Christ. If we choose to deny this doctrine, we would raise the issue of the honesty or credibility of some of the most prominent Bible writers. This is true in both the Old and New Testament. Some of these authors spoke prophetically of the virgin birth while others wrote after the fact.

Moses. When Moses quoted the words of God in Genesis 3:15, he became the first biblical writer to mention the coming of Christ. Referring to him as "the seed of the woman" might have been an allusion to a virgin birth. After Adam and Eve sinned in the Garden of Eden, God immediately judged their sin. Even in judgment, however, God demonstrated himself as a merciful God. He told the serpent, "I will put enmity between thee and the woman, and between thy seed and her seed; it shall bruise thy head, and thou shalt bruise his heel" (Gen. 3:15).

The introduction of a theological subject in Scripture is often an embryonic statement, sometimes called the Law of First Reference. The doctrine is there in "seed" form. When God introduced the prospect of salvation to Adam and Eve and the whole race, the implication of the virgin birth was alluded to in the reference to "her seed." If the coming Messiah was to have a normal physical birth, the "seed" would have come from a man. This reference in the beginning of

Scripture to a woman's "seed" implied that the coming Redeemer would not have a human father. God would be the father of his only begotten Son and a virgin would give birth to "her seed."

Isaiah. Probably the best known Old Testament verse referring to the virgin birth is found in Isaiah. God had instructed Isaiah to allow King Ahaz to ask God to perform a miracle. Ahaz, apparently apathetic to God and the divine message, refused to ask God for a sign. The Lord chose to give a sign to the king who had rejected it. "Therefore the Lord himself shall give you a sign; Behold, a virgin shall conceive, and bear a son, and shall call his name Immanuel" (Isa. 7:14). Some have commented this was an unfair sign because it was impossible for Ahaz to witness the virgin birth that occurred many years after his death. It must be remembered, however, that Ahaz had already rejected the sign before it was identified.

Some also argue that Isaiah did not mean a "virgin" but rather a "young maid" when he wrote this verse. Actually, the Hebrew word *almah* was translated either way. But the context suggests Isaiah was talking about a virgin. A non-virgin having a child would not be an extraordinary event but would be expected. The introduction of a miraculous sign implies the use of "virgin" rather than "young woman." A virgin and a young woman ready for marriage today are not always the same thing as it usually was in Old Testament times. Under Mosaic law, a young woman could be stoned if she was found pregnant out of wedlock. Birth control methods and therapeutic abortions were not available to cover up one's promiscuity in Bible times. Even if Isaiah was referring to a young woman ready for marriage, it is reasonable to assume she had not known a man. When the Septuagint, the Greek language version of the Old Testament, was translated, a Greek word was used that could mean only "virgin." Until recent times, it was generally assumed by translators that Isaiah here referred to a woman who had not known a man.

Not only is there a cultural and traditional reason for accepting the translation of the word "virgin," there is a biblical mandate. When Matthew wrote under the inspiration of the Holy Spirit, he cited this verse to demonstrate that Christ's birth was fulfilling Bible prophecy. In doing so, he followed the Septuagint translation and used the Greek word *parthenos,* which could only be translated "virgin." If he had so desired, he could have used another Greek word to identify a young woman, but this is not the word chosen by the Holy Spirit. Matthew noted, "Now all this was done, that it might be fulfilled which was spoken of the Lord by the prophet, saying, Behold a virgin shall be with child, and shall bring forth a son, and they shall call his name Emmanuel, which being interpreted is, God with us" (Matt. 1:22, 23).

THE VIRGIN BIRTH IN HISTORY

Three New Testament writers wrote historically of the virgin birth.

Matthew. Just as the virgin birth was implied at the beginning of the Old Testament, so it is fully revealed at the beginning of the New Testament. Matthew clearly believed Mary was a virgin until the birth of Christ. He cited Isaiah 7:14, identifying the birth of Christ as the fulfillment of Isaiah's prophecy (Matt. 1:22, 23). On two occasions in the first chapter, Matthew identifies the Holy Spirit as the source of Mary's son (Matt. 1:18, 20). In listing the genealogical data concerning Christ, Joseph is listed as the husband of Mary but not the father of Jesus. Even though this is an argument from silence, its omission is not accidental. Matthew records that Joseph married Mary knowing her condition. Then he clearly states, "And knew her not till she had brought forth her firstborn son; and called his name Jesus" (Matt. 1:25). Even in announcing the birth of Jesus, it was the birth of "her son" (v. 25), not "his son" or even "their son."

In Matthew's account of the birth of Christ, there are at least seven direct or indirect statements suggesting Jesus was born of a virgin. Since Matthew was one of the original twelve apostles, it is reasonable to assume that the doctrine of the virgin birth of Christ was one of the original parts of "the apostles' doctrine" taught to the members of the Jerusalem church (Acts 2:42).

Luke. Matthew's Gospel was written by a Jew primarily to a Jewish audience. The only other Gospel writer to emphasize the virgin birth of Christ was a Gentile writing primarily to a Gentile audience. It is particularly significant that Luke, a medical doctor, should be among the men that the Holy Spirit chose to comment on the doctrine of the virgin birth. Luke twice calls Mary a virgin. He tells of an angel sent by God "to a virgin espoused to a man whose name was Joseph, of the house of David; and the virgin's name was Mary" (Luke 1:27). When she learned she was to become a mother, "Then said Mary unto the angel, How shall this be, seeing I know not a man?" (Luke 1:34). Later, Luke listed the family tree of Mary, not Joseph. Here he identified Jesus as "being (as it was supposed) the son of Joseph" (Luke 3:23).

Luke also teaches the virgin birth by his careful phrases. He calls Jesus "the Son of the Highest" (Luke 1:32) and "the Son of God" (Luke 1:35), but never clearly identifies him as the son of Joseph.

Luke was both a medical doctor and a historian concerned with accuracy, "to write unto thee in order...That thou mightest know the certainty of those things, wherein thou hast been instructed" (Luke 1:3, 4). The virgin birth was not simply a rumor but rather an event investigated by a historian who was also a physician, after which the account was written under the inspiration of the Holy Spirit.

Paul. The third New Testament writer to support the doctrine of the virgin birth was the apostle Paul. Writing to the churches in the province of Galatia, he said, "But when the fulness of the time was come, God sent forth his Son, made of a woman, made under the law" (Gal. 4:4). The readers of Galatians were concerned with Old Testament law, so they would have been careful to list the genealogies from father to son. But Paul recognized the uniqueness of this birth. Jesus was "made of a woman," meaning more than a simple acknowledgment that Jesus had a mother. It suggests that Jesus had *only* a mother, a reasonable assumption when we realize that both Paul and Luke were closely related in the ministry and both accepted the virgin birth.

THE VIRGIN BIRTH IN THEOLOGY

At stake in the controversy surrounding the doctrine of the virgin birth of Christ are a number of other doctrines. If Jesus had a human father, he would have inherited a sin nature. In that case he would be unable to save himself, let alone be the sinless substitute for the sins of the world. With human parents, it would be impossible for him to be the Son of God.

FOUR STATEMENTS OF CHRIST'S SINLESSNESS	
Scripture	Truth
2 Cor. 5:2	Christ knew no sin
Heb. 4:15	Christ was without sin
1 Pet. 2:22	Christ did no sin
1 John 3:5	In Christ is no sin

Sinless character of Christ. If Jesus had a human father, he would have inherited the sin nature of Adam, the head of the human race. "Wherefore, as by one man sin entered into the world, and death by sin; and so death passed upon all men, for that all have sinned" (Rom. 5:12). It would only have taken one sin to make Jesus a sinner. Jesus was a man without a sin nature because he had a father without a sin nature. Jesus is the only begotten Son of the heavenly Father and was born of a virgin, being conceived by the Holy Spirit, hence he became flesh.

Jesus argued his divine origin with the Jewish leaders. He told them he came from the heavenly Father (John 8:38). The Jews answered Jesus that their father was Abraham (v. 39), to which he replied that they should be doing Abraham's works. Then in retaliation, the Jews made the innuendo, "we be not born of fornication" (John 8:41), implying that Jesus was born out of wedlock. From this, we gather that news of Mary's pregnancy before the wedding to Joseph was public knowledge. This gives added historical credibility to the virgin birth.

Word of salvation. When Paul referred to the virgin birth of Christ, he also identified a purpose in his coming, "to redeem them that were under the law, that we might receive the adoption of sons" (Gal. 4:5). God required a lamb "with-

out blemish" as a sacrifice for sin (Exod. 12:5). Jesus was un-
blemished in that he did not have a sin nature, and unspotted
in that he lived a sinless life. Because of this, Paul can say,
"For he [God] hath made him [Christ] to be sin for us, who
knew no sin" (2 Cor. 5:21).

Son of God. A man can only be the son of his father. This universal principle also applies to the Son of God. Jesus is called
"the Son of the Highest" (Luke 1:32) and "the Son of God"
(Luke 1:35). This could only have been true if Mary was a virgin when she conceived and gave birth to her son. Again our
salvation is dependent upon that. "For God so loved the
world, that he gave his only begotten Son, that whosoever believeth in him should not perish, but have everlasting life"
(John 3:16).

Inerrancy. A key battle among theologians today is over the
question of inerrancy. If the doctrine of the virgin birth is
false, then we have no confidence in the accuracy of anything else in Scripture. The following chart illustrates what
books we would question in our Bible if we denied the virgin
birth.

THE VIRGIN BIRTH AND INERRANCY		
Virgin Birth Taught	*Author*	*Writings*
1. Gen. 3:15	Moses	Genesis, Exodus, Leviticus, Numbers, Deuteronomy
2. Isa. 7:14	Isaiah	Isaiah
3. Matt. 1	Matthew	Matthew
4. Luke 1:3	Luke	Luke, Acts, (Hebrews?)
5. Gal. 4:4	Paul	Romans, 1 Corinthians, 2 Corinthians, Galatians, Ephesians, Philippians, Colossians, 1 Thessalonians, 2 Thessalonians, 1 Timothy, 2 Timothy, Titus, Philemon, (Hebrews?)
*22 or 23 of the 66 books of the Bible are unreliable if the virgin birth is unreliable.		

Supernatural power of God. When Mary was confronted with the announcement that she would give birth to the Son of God, she asked, "How shall this be, seeing I know not a man?" (Luke 1:34). She learned the answer to her question when the angel observed, "For with God nothing shall be impossible" (Luke 1:37). If the truth were known, the real reason some theologians deny the virgin birth of Christ is their unwillingness to recognize a supernatural God.

CONCLUSION

When we study the virgin birth of Christ, we are primarily concerned with Jesus. There was another person involved in this miraculous event—Mary. When Mary was presented with the opportunity to serve God in this way, she responded, "Behold the handmaid of the Lord; be it unto me according to thy word" (Luke 1:38). She responded in yielding her life to God despite the obvious problems it created. Her closest friends and relatives would assume she had been morally impure. Under the law, her fiancé could have had her put away for her unfaithfulness. Her dreams of marriage and "living happily ever after" could have been shattered, yet she yielded her life to God.

The lesson of the virgin birth stands as a challenge to us today. Later in life, Mary had not changed her attitude. When faced with the problem of no wine at the wedding in Cana, she turned to the servants and said, "Whatsoever he saith unto you, do it" (John 2:5). Mary's attitude of yieldedness brought blessing to the human race in the birth of Jesus Christ. Her continued yieldedness brought blessing to those at the feast. If she could give us advice today, it would be the same exhortation as Paul, "Present your bodies a living sacrifice...unto God" (Rom. 12:1).

DAILY READINGS

☐ Monday: *Luke 1:26-38*   ☐ Tuesday: *Luke 1:39-56*
☐ Wednesday: *Luke 2:1-20*   ☐ Thursday: *Matthew 1:1-25*
☐ Friday: *Isaiah 7:1-16*   ☐ Saturday: *Genesis 3:1-19*
☐ Sunday: *Galatians 3:25—4:7*

SEVENTEEN
HOW CHRIST BECAME A MAN

Who, being in the form of God, thought it not robbery to be equal with God, but made himself of no reputation, and took upon him the form of a servant, and was made in the likeness of men. Philippians 2:6, 7

INTRODUCTION

During the fall of 1775, a man who appeared to be a typical American farmer attempted to book a room in Baltimore's most fashionable hotel. Concerned about the hotel's reputation, the manager refused to rent the room. The man left and took a room in another hotel. Later, the manager learned he had refused a room to Thomas Jefferson, the Vice-president of the United States. Immediately he sent an invitation to Jefferson, asking him to return to his hotel as his guest. Jefferson's response was simple and to the point: "I value your good intentions highly, but if you have no place for an American farmer, you have no right giving hospitality to the Vice-president of the United States."

When Jesus came to live among men over nineteen hundred years ago, people did not recognize the One they met. Jesus is God, always was, and always will be. Yet it was God in the form of a man that was symbolically rejected by the innkeeper, and was later to be rejected, hated, and even crucified. When Jesus became a man he remained God. Still he was truly God during his earthly ministry. He voluntarily set aside what was rightfully his to become a man.

CHRIST EMPTIED HIMSELF

Definition. The term *kenosis* is a Greek word used in Philippians 2:7 to describe what happened when Christ became a man. The term is translated from "made himself of no reputation," which appears in the *King James Version* of the Bible. It is translated "He emptied himself" in the *New American Standard Version.* One theologian described it, "He stripped himself of the insignia of mystery."

For Christ, who was God before time began, to take on "the form of a servant" was indeed a humiliating experience. For ages theologians have faced the dilemma of interpreting this one word, *kenosis.* They cannot deny that "Christ emptied" himself, but "What was poured out?" is the question. Can Christ give away part of his deity and remain God? Can God be less than God? The answer is found in a threefold explanation. "Christ emptied himself" by (1) veiling his glory, (2) accepting the limitations of being a human, and (3) voluntarily giving up the independent use of his relative attributes.

Jesus was still God. Some argue that Jesus was not God during his life on earth. In explaining the *kenosis,* they say Jesus gave up his attributes. But that would make him less than God. Others claim he gave up the right to be worshiped, by emptying himself of the expression of the attributes. A third argument by some is that Jesus gave up the divine self-consciousness, meaning he had the attributes of God but did not know it. A problem exists if we say that Jesus could have given up any attributes. If he had, he would have ceased to be God.

One of the chief themes of the Gospel of John was to illustrate the deity of Christ. "But these are written, that ye might believe that Jesus is the Christ, the Son of God; and that believing ye might have life through his name" (John 20:31). John's use of the term "Son of God" refers to deity. Jesus was "the only begotten Son of God," which means he possessed the nature and character of his Father while on earth. He was God. John begins his Gospel by arguing, "In the beginning was the Word, and the Word was with God, and the Word was God" (John 1:1). Describing Jesus when he became a man, John wrote, "And the Word was made flesh, and dwelt among us, (and we beheld his glory, the glory as of the only begotten of the Father,) full of grace and truth" (John 1:14). Therefore, the *kenosis* was a self-emptying, not a self-extinction on the part of Christ.

WHAT IS THE SELF-EMPTYING?

Veiling his glory. Jesus hid his glory when he became a man in order to show his Father's glory. "No man hath seen God at any time; the only begotten Son, which is in the bosom of the Father, he hath declared him" (John 1:18). When Old Testament believers witnessed an appearance of Christ, they were often fearful for their lives. They knew that sinful man could not look upon God and live. The glory of God was also the judgment of God; the natural person who saw it died. When Moses spent forty days alone with God on Mount Sinai, it was necessary to cover his face when he came down because it reflected the glory of God. The people could not look upon God and live.

When John was on the Isle of Patmos, he too had a vision of Christ. When John saw Jesus in the full glory that was his from the beginning, John wrote, "And when I saw him, I fell at his feet as dead" (Rev. 1:17). When Paul had a similar vision of Christ, he was blinded with light from heaven (Acts 9:3-9). Later he wrote of being "caught up into paradise, and heard unspeakable words, which it is not lawful for a man to utter" (2 Cor. 12:4). When Isaiah saw the Lord in the temple, he cried out, "Woe is me . . ." (Isa. 6:1-8).

If Jesus had not veiled his preincarnate glory he could not have accomplished what he came to earth to do. It was necessary for Christ to hide his glory temporarily as he sought to save the souls of men. After the work of atonement was done, he could pray, "And now, O Father, glorify thou me with thine own self with the glory which I had with thee before the world was" (John 17:5).

Submitting to the limitations of humanity. As a result of the incarnation, Jesus became the God-man. He was at all times both God and man as he lived on earth. When Jesus became flesh, he voluntarily subjected himself to its limitation. Before his birth, heaven was his throne. Now in the flesh, Jesus was limited to the distance that a man could walk on the paths of Galilee. The Son of God who created water voluntarily lived in a body that got thirsty.

Jesus was born into this world as other humans (Luke 2:1-20), even though his conception was supernatural. As a child he developed as every human must develop. Jesus grew in mental, physical, spiritual, and social areas of life (Luke 2:52). He had the essential elements of human nature. He was body (Heb. 10:5), soul (John 12:27), and spirit (Mark 2:8). Jesus became hungry when he did not eat (Matt. 4:2). He became tired and asked the woman at the well for water to drink (John 4:6). Throughout his life on earth, Jesus was just as human as any one of us, subject to the same emotional experiences of sorrow, pain, and hurt which any man experiences.

The willingness of Jesus to limit himself to becoming a man gives us confidence that he understands the affairs of our lives. "For we have not an high priest who cannot be touched with the feelings of our infirmities; but was in all points tempted like as we are, yet without sin" (Heb. 4:15). Because he has experientially known the frustrations of humanity, we have a "God of all comfort" (2 Cor. 1:3) upon whom we can depend. While those who deny his deity believe they are honoring Jesus Christ in calling him a great man, the Bible says he emptied himself voluntarily by accepting the limitations of humanity. Yet at all times he remained God.

He surrendered the independent use of some attributes. Self-emptying took place also by the voluntary choice not to use certain of his attributes.

Perhaps the best expression of omnipotence is that of the miracles of God. Even though Jesus was known as a miracle worker, he performed those miracles through the power of the Holy Spirit (Matt. 12:28). He voluntarily laid aside his

THE COMPARATIVE ATTRIBUTES OF GOD	
Omniscience	Mark 13:32
Omnipresence	John 1:14
Omnipotence	John 11:41, 42

power to do them and relied on the Holy Spirit or the Father. On various occasions he made it clearly known he was doing the work of his Father. "Then answered Jesus, and said unto them, Verily, verily, I say unto you, The Son can do nothing of himself, but what he seeth the Father do: for what things soever he doeth, these also doeth the Son likewise" (John 5:19).

During his earthly life and ministry, Jesus was omniscient, but did not know the time of the second coming. He was omnipresent, but when he became flesh, he limited himself to being in one place at one time. He was omnipotent, yet he prayed to God to perform the raising of Lazarus from the dead. Jesus had not lost these attributes of God, but rather, in the process of emptying himself, he chose not to use his relative attributes.

WHY JESUS EMPTIED HIMSELF

From time to time we hear of someone who leaves a superior opportunity or job for less pay and what appears to be a lesser job. Often we are left wondering why that person acted as he did. There may be many reasons involved in such a decision. When we consider the willingness of Jesus to empty himself and become a man, we are left wondering why. We will never completely understand all that was involved in the mind of God, but there are several reasons identified in Scripture.

Love. The Love of God for us was certainly one of the chief motivating factors in the *kenosis.* The love of God is the foundation for every aspect of the gospel. Before Jesus came, he knew he would be rejected and die for the sins of the world. He told his disciples, "Greater love hath no man than this, that a man lay down his life for his friends" (John 15:13). Paul observed, "But God commendeth [demonstrated] his love toward us, in that, while we were yet sinners, Christ died for us" (Rom. 5:8). The apostle John reminds us, "Beloved, if God so loved us, we ought also to love one another" (1 John 4:11).

To reveal God. It seems ironic that Christ would have to empty himself of his original glory to reveal his glory, but that is apparently what happened. John twice recorded that Christ revealed the Father (John 1:14, 18; 14:7-11). If Jesus had not emptied himself, sinful man would not have been able to understand and witness that revelation. Jesus knew men could only understand so much. So God had to empty himself to become a man, so man might better understand God.

God reveals himself to us progressively. As we grow in our Christian lives, we grow in our understanding of the Bible and learn increasingly more about the God who loves us. Jesus recognized this principle when he emptied himself to reveal God.

Salvation. Jesus emptied himself to provide for our salvation. It was through one man the world was lost, so through one man the world would be saved. Paul explained this relationship between Adam and Christ in Romans 5:12-21.

ROMANS 5:12-21	
Adam	*Christ*
Sin entered upon all	Salvation provided for all
Death for all	Eternal life for all
Sin nature	New nature
Disobedience	Obedience
Sin abounded	Grace abounded
Imputed sin	Imputed righteousness

Example. Jesus emptied himself to demonstrate an example of how we ought to behave in our relationship with others. If you examine the context of the giving of the *kenosis*, it teaches the believers humility because of Christ's humility.

The Philippians were told to "Let this mind be in you, which was also in Christ Jesus" (Phil. 2:5). They were told to solve their social problems by following his example. Paul told the men in Ephesus to "love your wives, even as Christ also loved the church, and gave himself for it" (Eph. 5:25). Many times conflicts arise among Christians because an individual stands up for what he believes is rightfully his. Jesus was willing to empty himself of that which was rightfully his in order to accomplish the will of God in a more important matter.

CONCLUSION

C. T. Studd was a wealthy young man who had declared himself an atheist. When he studied the life of Christ, he came to the realization that Jesus was God. C. T. Studd trusted Christ as his personal Savior. He left his inheritance to serve as a missionary to China and later Africa, giving birth to one of the world's largest independent faith missions. The motto which ruled his life was, "If Jesus Christ be God and died for me, then no sacrifice is too great for me to give for Him."

As we consider the glory that Jesus left to come to earth and his willingness to empty himself of his rightful position, we are left wondering if there is anything so important in our lives that could not be set aside to serve him.

DAILY READINGS

☐Monday: *Philippians 2:1-11*   ☐Tuesday: *Hebrews 4:14—5:10*   ☐Wednesday: *Hebrews 2:9-18*   ☐Thursday: *John 17:1-13*   ☐Friday: *John 4:5-26*   ☐Saturday: *Mark 13:24-37*   ☐Sunday: *Matthew 17:1-13*

EIGHTEEN
THE PERFECTION OF CHRIST

And the Word was made flesh, and dwelt among us, (and we beheld his glory, the glory as of the only begotten of the Father,) full of grace and truth. John 1:14

INTRODUCTION

Daniel Webster was once asked how, as a Christian and educated man, he could understand that Christ was both God and man at the same time. "I cannot comprehend it," responded Webster. "If I could comprehend him, he would be no greater than myself. I feel that I need a superhuman Savior."

One of the most difficult doctrines to understand concerning Christ is the relationship of his divine and human nature. The Bible teaches that Jesus is both God and man. That does not mean he is half God and half man, nor does it mean he is God sometimes and man at other times. Jesus is God-man. The term is hyphenated to show Jesus is all God and all man at the same time.

Both sides of the nature of Christ are seen in the titles that describe him. Jesus is often called the Son of God in the Gospel of John, while he is called the Son of man in Luke, the latter denoting both humanity and deity. He is at all times 100 percent God in his nature, words, and actions. Yet at the same time he is 100 percent man. He left footprints in the sand as he walked on the shore of the Sea of Galilee. He needed rest and nourishment because he was human, but the winds and waves obeyed him. He was at all times and in every way the God-man—100 percent God and 100 percent man. This union of divine and human is one of the most difficult doctrines to understand, yet one which is foundational to Christianity.

THE INCARNATION

The thing that people usually remember about Christ is his birth, celebrated at Christmas. Many who are familiar with the events surrounding that birth, fail to understand that his conception in the virgin's womb represented the merging of God and man into one human body. John summarizes this miracle in one statement. "And the Word was made flesh, and dwelt among us" (John 1:14). When we use the term "incarnation," we are speaking of the miracle of God becoming man, yet remaining God.

The divine Word. This title of Christ, used only by the apostle John, implies his deity. A word is a medium of communication. When John called Jesus "the Word," he was implying that God communicated himself to man through the medium of Jesus Christ. The Word was the embodiment of a Person—showing to people what God was and what God revealed to them.

Some New Testament scholars claim John got the title "Word" for Jesus from Greek philosophy. Others argue he was thinking of the Hebrew idea of wisdom. They claim Christ is the personification of wisdom as described in Proverbs 5—8. But perhaps John was using the term "Word" as it was used literally in the Old Testament—"The Word of God." Since the term "Word" means expression or communication, John probably called Jesus the "Word of God" to reveal how God spoke over 1,200 times in the Old Testament. The Word of the Lord was the message or communication from God to men. Since Jesus was the personification of the written and spoken Word of the Lord, he is the revelation of the Lord. He is the incarnate Word of the Lord, just as the Bible is the inspired Word of the Lord.

The first eighteeen verses of the Gospel of John provide our fullest description of the Word. "In the beginning was the Word" (John 1:1), refers to eternity, not a specific point in time. The first thing we are told about the Word is that he pre-existed the creation and is therefore eternal. Second, we are told that at a point in time he has a personality: "The Word became flesh and dwelt among us" (John 1:14). Third, the Word was engaged in active personal communion with God. This is seen where the "Word was with God" (John 1:1), meaning Jesus was face to face with God. The fact that the Word and God are the same suggest both the plurality of the Godhead and deity of the Word (Christ)—"the Word was God" (John 1:1). Yet this verse cannot be translated "God was the Word," or "the Word was a God" as some religious cults suggest. To do so would ignore the rules of translating the Greek language. Groups such as the Jehovah's Witnesses try to translate the verse to show that Jesus was not "God" but "a God," but they are unable to find a single reputable Greek scholar to acknowledge the possibility of translating the verse "The Word was a God" or "God was the Word." To do so would deny the distinction between the Person of God the Father and the Person of Christ.

The next conclusion we may draw about the Word from this passage concerns the unity of the Father and Son. They are one together, two consciousnesses, yet one essence.

John also points out the Word was the avenue by which God expressed or revealed himself. "No man hath seen God at any time; the only begotten Son, which is in the bosom of the Father, he hath declared him" (John 1:18). The incarnate Word is the continuity of the preincarnate Word. Jesus is called the Word and the only begotten (John 1:14). These were used as stepping-stones to explain the nature of Jesus, the unique revelation of God.

A final and crucial observation concerning the Word may be made in this passage. "The Word was made flesh and dwelt among us" (John 1:14). The verb tense of "was made" denotes action in a point of time. The word "dwelt" means "to tabernacle." In the Old Testament, God's glory dwelt in the tabernacle. As Israel set up their tents in the wilderness around the tabernacle, the glory of God descended on the holy of holies. This meant God's presence dwelt with Israel. One commentator described the wilderness wanderings as "camping with God." As God dwelt with Israel by his glory cloud in the Old Testament, so God dwells in a human tabernacle with his people in the New Testament. The body of Jesus Christ is likened to a tent that was called glorious.

The Gospel writers record the glory of Jesus on the mount of transfiguration where his earthly body was bright and glorious: John observes, "And we beheld his glory, the glory as of the only begotten of the Father" (John 1:14).

JESUS THE WORD IN JOHN 1:18

1. He is eternal.
2. He is a Person.
3. He is face to face with God.
4. He is deity.
5. He is distinct from God.
6. He is one with the Father.
7. He is the expression of the Father.
8. He is a continuation of the preincarnate Word.
9. The glory of God is tabernacled in his body.

Jesus in human flesh. Not only was Jesus God, he was at the same time flesh. The term "flesh" speaks of his humanity. In the effort to combat the liberal denial of Christ's deity, conservative Christians have sometimes neglected his humanity. We need to realize that both aspects are true—Jesus was both God and man. And to perfectly understand Jesus, we must seek to understand the reality of his earthly body. As he climbed the mountains of Israel, he became tired and was subject to the limitations of humanity.

The birth of Jesus, though miraculous, was a human birth. Like any other child, he inherited his nature from his parents. His father was God, thus he has a divine nature. His mother was human, thus he has a human nature. (Jesus did not possess a sin nature because it was not a part of the original nature of man but was acquired with the first transgression.) Jesus had everything that is part of human nature. He identified with man in everything but sin. "For we have not an high priest which cannot be touched with the feeling of our infirmities; but was in all points tempted like as we are, yet without sin" (Heb. 4:15).

Jesus grew as a normal child would grow (Luke 2:52). He had the limitations of human nature. There were times when Jesus got hungry (Matt. 4:2) and, on at least one occasion, he had to stop his journey to rest. The primary reason why Jesus became human and endured the limitations of humanity was to help us. "For in that he himself both suffered being tempted, he is able to succour them that are tempted" (Heb. 2:18).

THE UNION OF NATURES

When we think of the dual nature of Christ, we must somehow not divide him into two parts as though he were a schizophrenic or was two persons in one body. Rather we must think of him as a unity; he is the God-man. His nature has been described a number of ways. At the Council of Chalcedon in A.D. 451, an ecumenical gathering called to settle some of the eastern church divisions, Jesus was described as having been "made known in two natures without confusion, without change, without division, without separation, the distinction of natures being by no means taken away by the union." In essence, when we examine the two natures of Christ orthodox doctrine forbids us either to divide the person or to confound the natures.

When the council said it could not divide the person it meant that Christ did not have two personalities (persons) but one. He did not have a perfect divine mind and a limited human mind—Christ had one mind. As humans we cannot understand it, but we can see it in the Gospels. As a person, Christ had one mind, one set of emotions, as well as one will.

Commenting on this union, the theologian Shedd wrote: "The two natures, or substances, constitute one personal subsistence. A common illustration employed by the Chalcedon and later fathers is, the union of the human soul and body in one person, and the union of heat and iron, neither of which loses its own properties."

The union of two natures in one Person. This union of the two natures of Christ is personal, meaning they merged in the Person of Christ. Common man is both material and nonmaterial, body and soul. Man's personality exists in his immaterial nature or intrinsic being. The nature is the real man and without it he would cease to exist. Jesus possessed both a divine nature (see Chapter 7) and a human nature (see Chapter 29). The union of the divine and human natures in Christ provided a personal Savior.

The union of two natures was complete. Jesus did not act as God on some occasions and man at other times. We do not say that he performed miracles as God and suffered on the cross as a man. What Jesus did, he did as a unity. He was at all times and in all ways the God-man. Divine and human qualities are both found in him, sometimes one more prominent than the other. When he cried, "I thirst," it was the human body that required water, but back of the cry was Christ dying in a body. When he later cried, "My God, my God, why hast thou forsaken me," it was deity talking to deity, yet Christ was using a human vehicle to express his prayer.

The union of two natures was permanent. Some have tried to understand the God-man by recognizing his work as God at times and his work as man at other times. The hypostatic union guarantees the constant presence of both the divine and human natures of Christ. The Bible teaches "Jesus Christ [is] the same yesterday, and today, and forever" (Heb. 13:8).

Christ had only one personality. This means he had only one mind, one set of emotions, and one will. As a person he had one self-determination and one self-perception. He possessed all the characteristics that would be true of only one personality. As we read the Gospels we see someone whose personality is consistent in his nature, words, and actions.

His union into two natures continued. When Christ took on human flesh in the incarnation, he did not give it up when he ascended back into heaven. Today we worship a Person who is both God and man. The physical body that was born in Bethlehem is now seated at the right hand of the throne. The Hebrews were told of Jesus, "But this man, because he continueth ever, hath an unchangeable priesthood" (Heb. 7:24). Jesus is the Man seated in glory. Paul reminded Timothy, "There is one God, and one mediator between God and men, the man, Christ Jesus" (1 Tim. 2:5). He reminded the Romans that their salvation was dependent upon the work of a man who had overcome the failings of the first man (Rom. 5:12-21). These Scriptures do not diminish the deity of Christ but rather recognize his humanity.

THE REASONS FOR THE INCARNATION

The Lord does not work indiscriminately without any purpose in mind. Everything has a purpose and is mandated by God's nature. This includes why the incarnation was necessary.

To confirm God's promises. "Now I say that Jesus Christ was a minister of the circumcision for the truth of God, to confirm the promises made unto the fathers" (Rom. 15:8). At least three hundred specific prophecies were fulfilled that could not have been realized if Jesus did not have a human body. Jesus said, "Think not that I am come to destroy the law, or the prophets: I am not come to destroy, but to fulfil" (Matt. 5:17). He kept the laws that were imposed on Israel, and what the Old Testament fathers could not do—keep the law—Jesus fulfilled in his human life.

To reveal the Father. From the beginning of time, God desired fellowship with his highest creation. In the garden, it was God's custom to walk with man. Later God dwelt in the tabernacle and, later still, the temple. When Jesus came, he was able to reveal the nature of God in human flesh. "No man hath seen God at any time; the only begotten Son, which is in the bosom of the Father, he hath declared him" (John 1:18).

To become a faithful high priest. Jesus could not today carry out his high priestly functions if he had not become a man.

"For every high priest taken from among men is ordained for men in things pertaining to God, that he may offer both gifts and sacrifices for sins" (Heb. 5:1). Because of that, Jesus is our great high priest. "Wherefore, he is able to save them to the uttermost that come unto God by him, seeing he ever liveth to make intercession for them" (Heb. 7:25).

To put away sin. A chief purpose in the incarnation was that Jesus could be born without sin, live without sin, and ultimately die for the sins of the world. When God clothed Adam and Eve with skins of an animal, he was symbolically covering their nakedness, as one day the sacrifice of a lamb would cover the spiritual sin of God's people. This sacrifice was predicted by Abraham, who told Isaac the day would come when "God will provide himself a lamb for a burnt offering" (Gen. 22:8). When John the Baptist saw Jesus, he recognized the prediction would soon be completed by calling Christ "the Lamb of God, which taketh away the sin of the world" (John 1:29).

To destroy the works of Satan. "For this purpose the Son of God was manifested, that he might destroy the works of the devil" (1 John 3:8). After Satan tempted Eve to sin, and she fell, God predicted that the seed of the woman (Christ) would crush Satan's head. Obviously, Christ had to be born of a woman to deliver the blow to Satan, so Jesus was born of Mary. When Jesus on the cross cried, "It is finished" (John 19:30), he was signaling the end of several things, among them the fact that victory over sin and Satan had been completed.

To provide an example. By becoming a man, Jesus was able to show men how they ought to live. The Christian is responsible to live a holy life. "He that saith he abideth in him ought himself also so to walk, even as he walked" (1 John 2:6). Peter exhorted his readers, "Christ...leaving us an example, that ye should follow his steps" (1 Peter 2:21). Over the years certain people have believed that Jesus came to earth for the sole purpose of being God's example of righteousness. In doing so, such people deny his work of redemption. In truth, his incarnation accomplished both purposes.

CONCLUSION

The incarnation tells us that Jesus was "tabernacled" in flesh. In a certain sense, that principle continues. Today, God still desires to live in a human tabernacle or temple. Christians are described as "temples of the Holy Ghost" (1 Cor. 6:19). Jesus taught his disciples "If a man love me, he will keep my words: and my Father will love him, and we will come unto him, and make our abode with him" (John 14:23). This word "abode" means "mansion." Christians are exhorted to make their heart a "mansion" in which God lives.

When someone visits in another person's home, he may be entertained in the living room. But when one visits a friend, he is told to make himself at home. He settles down and relaxes, treating the home as his own. Many Christians have invited Christ into their lives (Rev. 3:20) as a guest, but not a close friend. God desires to "make himself at home" in our bodies if we will let him. In the first step, the divine and human natures coexist in Christ, so now we must let the second step be completed in our lives.

DAILY READINGS

☐Monday: *John 1:1-18*   ☐Tuesday: *Romans 5:12-20*
☐Wednesday: *Romans 6:1-17*   ☐Thursday: *John 14:15-26*
☐Friday: *John 15:1-17*   ☐Saturday: *1 Corinthians 6:1-20*
☐Sunday: *Colossians 3:1-17*

NINETEEN
THE DEATH OF JESUS CHRIST

But God commendeth his love toward us in that, while we were yet sinners, Christ died for us. Romans 5:8

INTRODUCTION

The hill named Calvary outside of Jerusalem was well known as a place of execution. There Roman soldiers drove spikes through Jesus' hands and feet to nail him to the cross. As he hung on that cross, the soldiers and citizens continued their abuses. Looking down, Jesus saw his mother and a few close friends attending his execution. Finally he spoke. He did not condemn his executioners but forgave them. He did not pity himself but prayed for others.

Usually when men face death, they become increasingly concerned about themselves, but this Man arranged in his last hours for the continued care of his mother. Finally, in the darkness of that day, he cried out, "It is finished!" The first recorded speech of Jesus as a child was that he must be about his Father's business (Luke 2:49). Now he announced to the world he had completed his Father's business.

The death of Jesus Christ was unusual by any standard, but its uniqueness stands out in the realization that it included the physical suffering and death of God's Son. The heaven became dark at the death of Christ, reflecting the response of nature to an attack upon its Creator. This death of Christ had an unusual purpose. The cross is the doorway for all spiritual blessing. At the end of the world all men will be judged and the death and resurrection of Christ are the basis of entrance into heaven. Therefore, an understanding of the death of Christ will help us better appreciate what Christ did to accomplish our salvation.

Like a gigantic interstate cloverleaf, several doctrines intersect and merge in the death of Christ. First, the incarnation is evident in that Jesus the man yielded to the evil imagination of men, yet, the divine Son of God controlled the events according to the sovereign purpose of God. Next, the *kenosis* revealed Christ's veiled glory, his human limitations, and the fact that he had voluntarily given up his comparative attributes. In his death he destroyed the works of Satan. The justice and holiness of God was satisfied, plus the demands of the law were met, yet in the same action God exercised unlimited love to the sinner.

Only a few stood on the hill of Calvary: soldiers, a jeering mob, and a handful of faithful followers; yet everyone born of woman stood spiritually before the cross. The sins of eternity past were joined with those of the future, and all humans are measured by that event. Therefore we need to examine the human events that led up to the death of Christ. By understanding the historical background, we have a better basis for understanding the doctrinal significance of the atonement.

THE CHRONOLOGY OF THE DEATH OF CHRIST

Sometimes when we study Bible doctrine, we forget that our doctrine is based upon historical events. The doctrine of sin is founded on the actual event of Adam's sin. The doctrine of salvation is founded on the historical fact of the death and resurrection of Christ. Paul taught that Christ died (history) for our sins (theology) (1 Cor. 15:3).

The final meal. The night began with the celebration of the Passover and the eating of the Passover meal. As the disciples gathered with Jesus, he took it upon himself to wash his disciples' feet and teach them humility (John 13:1-20). As they ate, he announced his betrayal and made his last appeal to Judas Iscariot, the financial secretary of the group, who would betray him (John 13:21-29). That night Jesus introduced the ordinance of the Lord's Supper (Luke 22:17-20) and gave them the Upper Room discourse, which contained the embryonic teachings of the church age, including a life of love, fruitfulness, yet persecution. Right up to the end, Jesus was involved in the training of the twelve.

The final journey. Jesus left the upper room and walked with his disciples as a group for the last time. They headed for the Mount of Olives. This group which had traveled together for over three years had already begun to break up. Judas had gone to arrange for the soldiers to arrest Jesus. Together, those that remained made their way to a favorite spot for prayer. Perhaps it was seeing the vines climbing the side of a building that prompted Jesus to say, "I am the true vine" (John 15:1). With this observation he taught his disciples about the abiding life (John 15). Recognizing the sorrow they would soon experience, he told his disciples he was going to send the "Comforter" (John 16). Together they arrived in the garden to pray.

The garden prayers. Jesus prayed for many things. He prayed for the events he would soon be experiencing. He prayed for the accomplishment of the will of God in his life. He prayed for his disciples and those who would someday become his disciples. He prayed for those of us today who seek to live for him in our society. Finally, he prayed for himself. He understood the wrath of the cup of judgment he was to drink in death. "O my Father, if it be possible, let this cup pass from me: nevertheless, not as I will, but as thou wilt" (Matt. 26:39, 42, 44). When he finished, he woke his disciples to witness his arrest.

The arrest of Christ. As the soldiers and religious leaders accompanied Judas Iscariot to the garden, Jesus was waiting. Knowing what was happening, he called Judas his "friend" (Matt. 26:50). He was taken with force, despite the fact he offered no resistance. The only act on his part was to heal a ser-

vant's ear which had been cut off by one of his disciples
(John 18:1-12). Jesus willingly submitted to those he knew
had come to kill him. He was about his Father's business.

The trials. The night was filled with mock trials to humiliate
the Son of God. He appeared before the high priest, who had
judged him guilty before he was arrested. Then Jesus was
tried before the Sanhedrin (the ruling body of the Jews) that
had arranged his arrest. He was sent to Pilate, the Roman
military leader, who questioned Jesus and then sent him to
Herod. After interrogating Jesus, Herod returned Jesus to the
original Roman judge, Pilate. Being found innocent in a Roman court of law, the mob vote of the people suggested the
method of punishment. Before crucifixion, he was beaten by
the soldiers.

The crucifixion. Crucifixion was abhorred in the mind of
every Roman subject. Roman soldiers had learned from the
Phoenicians a very sadistic and painful way of executing
criminals. The very word "cross" would stimulate a repul-
sion by anyone who had witnessed this event.

Crucifixion usually began with a beating. A man would be
lashed with a whip which had bits of metal, bone, or stone at
the end of each thong. The whip, as it cut the back of the convicted man, would wrap around him. When it was raised to
be lowered again, it would tear the flesh. Often a condemned
man would faint from the pain. The second aspect of the crucifixion was the custom known as "bearing one's cross." The
written-out accusation would be tied about his neck and he
would be paraded to the place of execution. The shingle he
wore would then be nailed above him on his cross so that
those who witnessed the event knew his horrendous crime.
Jesus' crime was published in three languages and read,
"This is Jesus of Nazareth, the King of the Jews" (Matt. 27:37;
Mark 15:26; Luke 23:38; John 19:19).

The third aspect of crucifixion was agony leading to death.
A man was crucified in such a way that he could not easily
breathe. His arms and feet were fastened to the cross in such
a way that he had to push his body up to breathe. Every time
Jesus would breathe, he had to raise his body to gasp for air.

As he reached for air he would scrape the open wounds on his back up and down the rough wood of the cross. The Romans knew their craft. They could execute a man and let him suffer for as long as nine days until he died. And besides the physical suffering, there was the degrading humiliation.

When the soldiers came by to break Jesus' legs to speed up his death, they found a lifeless body. A spear thrust into his side produced blood and water. A friend of Jesus was granted permission to bury the body in his tomb. Jesus was anointed with spices and placed in the borrowed tomb. There he stayed for three days.

A key to understanding the death of Christ is to recognize the resurrection of Christ. The focus of Christianity is not a crucifix but rather an empty cross and an empty tomb. Christ died but lives today.

THE WORDS OF CHRIST ON THE CROSS

When we examine the nature of crucifixion, it would be understandable to expect irrational behavior, cursing, or self-justification from the mouth of the condemned man. Such was not the case with the death of Jesus. Seven times he spoke from the cross. These are known as the seven last words of Christ. They reflect his divine-human nature, that he was the God-man. These words reflect the purpose for which he came—the salvation of God. These seven sayings give insight into how Jesus faced the crucifixion.

The first word—forgiveness (Luke 23:34). His first words were a prayer of forgiveness: "Father, forgive them; for they know not what they do" (Luke 23:34). As Jesus was experiencing more pain than most of us could imagine, he was praying for those that caused his suffering. Here, Christ reveals the divine attribute of love for everyone, including those who evidenced the most hate toward him.

The second word—acceptance (Luke 23:43). In the midst of the crucifixion, one of the thieves being crucified with Jesus realized he was spiritually condemned also. Though he had earlier mocked Christ, he now asked for forgiveness. Jesus responded, "To day shalt thou be with me in paradise." God is bound by his nature to punish every sin, but in contrast, he also is bound by his nature to forgive all who repent and call for forgiveness.

The third word—human responsibility (John 19:26, 27). As he hung on the cross, Jesus saw his mother standing by the apostle John. Turning to them, "He saith unto his mother, Woman behold thy son." The care of parents was the responsibility of the firstborn. Since Jesus had lived a sinless life, in death he would not forget to honor his mother (Exod. 20:12).

The fourth word—separation (Matt. 27:46). When the sin of the world was placed upon Christ, the heavenly Father could not look on his Son because God cannot look on sin. Fulfilling prophecy, Jesus cried out, "My God, my God, why hast thou forsaken me?" (Ps. 22:1). Jesus, at that moment, experienced alienation from God. This is when he dealt with the sins of the world. Death does not mean to cease to exist. Death means "to separate," and in this cry Jesus reveals the fact that he was separated from God. Though Jesus was perfect, having never sinned, he experienced the consequence of sin—separation from God, which is the character of hell or punishment.

The fifth word—suffering (John 19:28). The fifth saying on the cross reflected the suffering of Jesus as he was crucified. "After this, Jesus knowing that all things were now accomplished, that the scripture might be fulfilled, saith, I thirst." Even his thirst was a fulfillment of Scripture (Ps. 22:15). As a crucified man reaches the human limit of suffering, he experiences intense pain. Jesus' cry of thirst reflects that he was not supernaturally exempt from the suffering normally experienced in crucifixion. Some may assume that Jesus did not suffer to the limit of physical endurance because he was God. But Jesus probably suffered more intense pain because he was not a hardened sinner but was a perfect human. Most Bible scholars believe Jesus cried for something to drink so that he would have strength to make his victorious benediction.

The sixth word—victory (John 19:30). "It is finished!" The sixth cry from the cross was the cry of the victor. Scholars actually suggest several interpretations of what was finished. First, "It is finished" means Christ had accomplished salvation for the human race. Second, the statement means he had bruised the head of the serpent (Gen. 3:15). Third, he had demonstrated the love of God (John 3:16), and fourth, he had satisfied the demands of God's holiness (Rom. 5:8). Fifth, Jesus had fulfilled the Old Testament prediction of a coming Messiah, and sixth, it meant the suffering of the past six hours was over. But the seventh meaning applied to every Jew—they no longer had to bring an animal sacrifice continually for their sins. He was the sacrifice for sin of which all the animal sacrifices were only the symbols. There is reason to believe that the expression, *tetelestac* in Greek, was the mark placed on a bill of sale which had the significance of "paid in full." Symbolically, the veil in the temple was rent from the top to bottom (from God to man) when Jesus cried, "It is finished!"

The seventh word—completion (Luke 23:46). The final word from the cross was a prayer of benediction. "And when Jesus had cried with a loud voice, he said, Father, into thy hands I commend my spirit: and having said thus, he gave up the ghost" Jesus had completed what he began to do. As Christ died, he committed his spirit to God. Because of the death of Christ, we can approach God with confidence that he is approachable. As Jesus committed his death to God, so we can commit our lives to him.

The words of Christ on the cross reflect the doctrine of his atonement for man.

THE CHARACTER OF THE DEATH OF CHRIST

The death of Christ was more than a fact of history. The events of these three days, his death and resurrection, are the central experience of biblical theology. Christ provided in his death the possibility of a salvation experience for any who would respond to his invitation.

HIS WORDS	SCRIPTURE	ACCOMPLISHMENTS OF CALVARY
1. Father, forgive them.	Luke 23:34	Forgiveness
2. Today thou shalt be with me.	Luke 23:43	Acceptance
3. Behold thy son.	John 19:26	Human responsibility
4. Why hast thou forsaken me?	Matt. 27:46	Separation from God
5. I thirst.	John 19:28	Suffering
6. It is finished.	John 19:30	Victory
7. Into thy hands I commend my spirit.	Luke 23:46	Completion

The death of Christ was foreshadowed in the Old Testament. When God wanted to save Israel from a judgment upon Egypt, he commanded the sacrifice of a lamb and the applying of the blood to the doorpost of the house. "And the blood shall be to you for a token upon the houses where ye are: and when I see the blood, I will pass over you, and the plague shall not be upon you to destroy you, when I smite the land of Egypt" (Exod. 12:13). God will save for eternity those who have trusted Christ "and have washed their robes, and made them white in the blood of the Lamb" (Rev. 7:14).

CONCLUSION

The message of the gospel is that "Christ died for our sins according to the scriptures; And that he was buried, and that he rose again the third day according to the scriptures" (1 Cor. 15:3, 4). That fact of history may become a part of our personal experience in theology as we trust Christ as our Savior. Often companies will offer special gifts with the purchase of their product. Usually a gift offer is for a limited time. Anyone who desires the gift of eternal life must realize that it is a limited-time offer, which ends at our death or when Christ returns.

Some people say a loving God would never send people to hell. Certainly God does not desire to punish anyone. "For God sent not his Son into the world to condemn the world;

but that the world through him might be saved" (John 3:17). God has made a limited-time offer available to all. If a person does not receive Christ, God cannot be held responsible for sending that person to hell. If a person does not accept that offer because he procrastinates or is negligent for other reasons, then he is guilty of passive rejection. Others are guilty of active rejection because they have chosen not to believe. Certainly a loving God does not want to send anyone to hell, but neither will he take them to heaven against their will.

DAILY READINGS

☐Monday: Mark 14:1-21   ☐Tuesday: Mark 14:22-42
☐Wednesday: Mark 14:43-65   ☐Thursday: Mark 14:66—15:15   ☐Friday: Mark 15:16-41   ☐Saturday: Mark 15:42—16:8   ☐Sunday: John 19:16-30

TWENTY
THE ATONEMENT

Being justified freely by his grace through the redemption that is in Christ Jesus: Whom God hath set forth to be a propitiation through faith in his blood, to declare his righteousness for the remission of sins that are past. Romans 3:24, 25

INTRODUCTION

Among the various religions of the world, Christianity stands unique in the doctrine of the atonement. No other religion or religious movement apart from Christianity can guarantee personal salvation to its followers. For the Christian, his relationship with God is not based upon his continuing works or efforts, but rather upon the finished work of Christ on the cross. This doctrine, called "the atonement," forms the heart of Christianity. Toward the end of his life, Thomas, Earl of Kinnoul, wrote of the atonement:

I have always considered the atonement to be characteristic of the gospel, as a system of religion. Strip it of that doctrine, and you reduce it to a scheme of morality, excellent indeed, and such as the world never saw; but to man, in the present state of his faculties, absolutely impracticable. The atonement of Christ, and the truths immediately connected with that fundamental principle, provide a remedy for all the wants and weak-

nesses of our nature. They who strive to remove those precious doctrines from the Word of God, do an irreparable injury to the grand and beautiful system of religion which it contains, as well as to the comforts and hopes of man. For my own part, I am now an old man, and have experienced the infirmities of advanced years. Of late, in the course of severe and dangerous illness, I have been repeatedly brought to the gates of death. My time in this world cannot now be long; but, with truth I can declare that, in the midst of all my part afflictions, my heart was supported and comforted by a firm reliance upon the merits and atonement of my Saviour; and now, in the prospect of entering upon an eternal world, this is the only foundation of my confidence and hope.

The Bible teaches that Jesus loved the world and died for it. This does not mean everyone will be saved. The universal scope of the gospel is possible because of the nature of Christ's death. The results of his death are called the atonement, and some have applied the word to mean "God at-one-ment with man." The word "atonement"—*kaphar* (Lev. 16:6)—in the Old Testament meant "to cover." "For it is not possible that the blood of bulls and of goats should take away sins" (Heb. 10:4). The atonement of the Old Testament only covered sins until the blood of Christ cleanses the sinner from sin's defilement. "Whom God hath set forth to be a propitiation through faith in his blood, to declare his righteousness for the remission of sins that are past" (Rom. 3:25).

However, modern use of the word "atonement" has a broad sense, including substitution, redemption, propitiation, and reconciliation. These four terms will be studied in their progressive nature so you can see the scope of the death of Christ.

THE SUBSTITUTE FOR ALL

The Bible teaches that the atonement was substitutionary in nature. In the Old Testament, God required the sacrifice of lambs and other types of animals as a substitute for the sins of the people. Each year on the day of Atonement the high priest would place his hands upon the head of two goats, identifying the nation with the animals. Symbolically, the animals bore the sins of Israel. One of the two goats was then offered in a sacrifice for the sins of the nation. The second goat was led out into the wilderness, illustrating how God had separated the sins of the people from himself. All this was typical of another "day of atonement" when Christ would die as our substitute.

In Washington D.C., a group of men and women meet as our representatives. In a democracy, where the people rule, these people are elected to office to represent us as our substitutes in the decision-making process of government. They do not represent Democrats, Republicans, or Independents, but all the people in their district. Even if we voted for the opposing candidate or failed to vote at all, our senator or representative is still our representative, acting on our behalf as our substitute.

Substitution for Christians. On the cross of Calvary, God placed our sin upon Christ and accepted him in our place as he provided for our atonement. "For he hath made him to be sin for us, who knew no sin; that we might be made the righteousness of God in him" (2 Cor. 5:21). Paul reminded the Romans "that, while we were yet sinners, Christ died for us" (Rom. 5:8). The Bible teaches that Christ was the Christian's substitute at Calvary.

The full meaning of the substitutionary death is understood by examining the two Greek words translated "for" as they are used in the phrase "Christ died for our sins." The first Greek word, *anti,* is usually translated "instead of," as "Christ died instead of us for our sins." The second preposition, *huper,* is sometimes used when the sufferings and death of Christ are spoken of "in behalf of" our sins.

Christ died (*anti*) for our sins is found in Matthew 20:28, and Mark 10:45. Christ died (*huper*) in my behalf is found in John 10:11, 15; 11:50; Romans 5:8; 8:32; 1 Corinthians 15:3; 2 Corinthians 5:14; Galatians 2:20; 3:13; Titus 2:4. The theologian Shedd makes a significant observation:

The... preposition (anti) excludes the idea of benefit or advantage, and specifies only the idea of substitution. The former (huper) *may include both ideas. Whenever the sacred writer would express both together and at once, he selects the preposition huper. In so doing, he teaches both that Christ died in the sinner's place, and for the sinner's benefit* (Dogmatic Theology, p. 382).

Substitute for the church. Christ also gave himself for the church. In doing so, he portrayed one aspect of a man's responsibility in the home. Paul told the Ephesian men, "Husbands, love your wives, even as Christ also loved the church, and gave himself for it" (Eph. 5:25). In one sense, the church is the corporate body of believers, and when Christ suffered for all, he suffered for the church.

Substitute adequate for every person. The blood of Jesus Christ was enough for the sins of every man. The Bible talks of seeing Jesus "who was made a little lower than the angels for the suffering of death, crowned with glory and honour, that he by the grace of God should taste death for every man" (Heb. 2:9). This word "taste" means to "partake fully; not just sip." There is not a man who has ever lived on the face of the earth who was beyond the hope of salvation. No man has to suffer for his own sins, because Jesus has already died in his place. In that sense, the Bible teaches that he died for everyone.

REDEMPTION

The word "redemption" means "to purchase." When Jesus died for our sins, he paid the price that satisfied the demands of God's holiness. The price of this redemption was the blood of Jesus (1 Pet. 1:18, 19). In explaining redemption to the Galatians, the apostle Paul used three different words which shed better light on our redemption.

Agorazo—"To purchase in the market." This term, used in Galatians 3:10, was a term used to describe the act of purchasing a slave in the marketplace. This word *agorazo* means Christ paid the redemption price of his blood which was sufficient to purchase every person in the market that was "sold under sin." But only for those who believe in Christ will his blood become efficient to save. Peter speaks of false teachers who surely are not saved because they ". . . privily shall bring in damnable heresies, even denying the Lord that bought them, and bring upon themselves swift destruction" (2 Pet. 2:1).

Ekagorazo—*"To purchase and take home."* The second word used by Paul is a variation of the first. *Ek* is added, which means "out." These slaves were purchased and brought out of the slave market. The master took the slave home with him. Christ paid the price with his blood and took us "slaves to sin," out of the marketplace, no longer for sale. Using this word for Christians, Paul writes, "Christ hath redeemed us from the curse of the law, being made a curse for us; for it is written, Cursed is every one that hangeth on a tree" (Gal. 3:13).

Lutroo—*"To purchase and give freedom."* Normally when a master purchased a slave, he required the slave to serve him. Occasionally an owner might buy the freedom of a slave. The master would pay the redemption price, but he would give the slave his liberty. Sometimes the slave was made a member of the family. The term *lutroo* used to describe this practice was also used by Paul to describe our redemption. Jesus came "that he might redeem us from all iniquity" (Titus 2:14). We have been purchased by Christ and in one sense we are slaves, but in another perspective, we have been elevated into the family. We have been given liberty to live as sons, not servants. With this gift comes a responsibility to use, not abuse, our liberty. "Stand fast therefore in the liberty wherewith Christ hath made us free, and be not entangled again with the yoke of bondage" (Gal. 5:1).

The substitutionary atonement of Christ's redemption was sufficient for all. Therefore, the message of redemption is that Jesus Christ has paid the price for all who receive it by faith. When an unsaved person appears before God in judgment, he will be judged on the basis of what he has believed concerning Christ. "He that believeth not is condemned already, because he hath not believed in the name of the only begotten Son of God" (John 3:18).

The Lamb's book of life will be opened and those whose names are written there will go into heaven (Rev. 20:12-15). Those who have not believed in Christ will be punished. No one is sent to hell for sin, but for unbelief.

SATISFACTION FOR ALL SIN

The third aspect of the work of Christ is satisfaction of the necessary judgment on sin. When Jesus died on the cross, he satisfied the justice and holiness of God. A biblical term meaning satisfaction is used to describe this aspect of the work of Christ. Since the law is an extension of the nature of God, Christ had to satisfy the demands of the law in his death.

The word "propitiation" (Rom. 3:25; 1 John 2:2, 4:10) is from *hilasterion*, "a place of propitiation," or the mercy seat. In the holy of holies in the tabernacle, the mercy seat was the covering on the ark of the covenant. The priest sprinkled blood on the mercy seat on the day of atonement, hence it was symbolically the judgment seat. This was the place where the justice of God was satisfied.

Satisfying God. Sin is offensive to God because it represents rebellion against himself and a rejection of who he is. As such, the sin of mankind could never be retracted or simply ignored. The nature of God is such that he could not forgive the sinner without a payment or propitiation of satisfaction. The only price worthy had to come from a sinless substitute, "And he is the propitiation for our sins: and not for ours only, but also for the sins of the whole world" (1 John 2:2). God did not save us because of any merit in ourselves but rather because of the merit of Christ our substitute.

The blood is important to God, not because it is blood but because it represents both life and death. When blood circulated from the heart, it represented life and when it was spilt, it represented death. In Old Testament times, God forbade the eating of blood that men might respect the sanctity of life (Gen. 9:4). When Jesus left the ordinance of the Lord's Supper with his disciples, he provided a symbol to remind all Christians of the sacrifice of his blood (1 Cor. 11:25). Paul asked a carnal church, "The cup of blessing which we bless, is it not the communion of the blood of Christ?" (1 Cor. 10:16). The blood therefore represents the perfect life of Christ given in death for sinners. At the first Passover, God instructed Moses, "And the blood shall be to you for a token upon the houses where ye are: and when I see the blood, I will pass over you, and the plague shall not be upon you to destroy you, when I smite the land of Egypt" (Exod. 12:13). The context of the first Passover suggests an Egyptian could have escaped the plague if he had spread the blood upon the doorposts of his house and a Jew would suffer the plague if he did not do as instructed. It was the blood, not the people themselves or anything they had done, that satisfied the justice and holiness of God.

Satisfying the law. While most Christians tend to think of the law as something evil, the New Testament teaches that "the law is holy, and the commandment holy, and just, and good" (Rom. 7:12). As such, the demands of the law needed to be satisfied because man had broken them in every part.

When Adam sinned in the Garden of Eden, he violated the "law of God" he had received. As the law is an extension of the nature of God, the head of the human race offended the moral nature of God. The law could not be ignored, overlooked, or changed any easier than God could be ignored, overlooked, or changed. The demand of all the law was upon every man, "For whosoever shall keep the whole law, and yet offend in one point, he is guilty of all" (James 2:10).

Jesus perfectly kept the law, hence he could say, "Think not I am come to destroy the law...but to fulfil" (Matt. 5:17). Therefore when he died on Calvary, he "abolished in his flesh the enmity, even the law of commandments contained in the ordinances; to make in himself of twain one new man, so making peace" (Eph. 2:15). In another place the propitiation of the law is described as, "Blotting out the handwriting of ordinances that was against us, which was contrary to us, and took it out of the way, nailing it to his cross" (Col. 2:14).

The demands of the justice of God have been met and the broken law no longer is a moral judge to condemn mankind. Christ has satisfied the justice of God and paid the penalty for broken law. Now, persons do not go to hell because God is angry at them or because they broke God's law. People go to hell because they have not received the provision of salvation.

RECONCILIATION FOR ALL

In this act of reconciliation, Christ brought all into a favorable light of God's mercy. On the cross, Christ was bringing together two enemies and making them friends. "To wit, that God was in Christ, reconciling the world unto himself, not imputing their trespasses unto them, and hath committed unto us the word of reconciliation" (2 Cor. 5:19). This work of reconciliation was accomplished by destroying the cause of the enmity between God and man and changing man himself.

Removing the enmity. Jesus came and died "that he might reconcile both unto God in one body by the cross, having slain the enmity thereby" (Eph. 2:16). That enmity which formed "the middle wall of partition between us" (Eph. 2:14) was the law (Eph. 2:15). Christ abolished this in his flesh when he died. The first step in bringing together two enemies is to remove the reason for the strife between them.

In Christ. The second step is for a mediator (1 Tim. 2:5) to present two enemies to each other in a positive light. Because of the cross, the unsaved man can meet God, not as a judge, but as a Savior. God looks at Christians as having been "crucified with Christ" (Gal. 2:20). When God saves a man, he saves him "in Christ." Essentially, Christ presents us to God as "savable sinners."

CONCLUSION

When Jesus died on the cross, he accomplished a work to insure salvation for all who believe on his name. As we understand the atonement and work of Christ on the cross, we come to appreciate more fully what Jesus did for each of us and the world. To say that "Christ died for all" or "for the world" must not be taken to mean that all are saved. Christ's atoning work provided the basis of our reconciliation and believing faith is the condition for receiving the benefits of his work on our belief. The fact that some die without Christ today is contrary to the will of God (2 Pet. 3:9). "Who will have all men to be saved, and to come unto the knowledge of the truth" (1 Tim. 2:4). When we understand the nature of the atonement, we should be active in spreading the gospel to everyone because God has "committed unto us the word of reconciliation" (2 Cor. 5:19).

DAILY READINGS

☐Monday: *Hebrews 9:1-15*   ☐Tuesday: *Romans 3:21-31*
☐Wednesday: *2 Corinthians 5:11-21*   ☐Thursday:
Galatians 3:13—4:5   ☐Friday: *1 John 1:5—2:6*
☐Saturday: *Hebrews 2:5-18*   ☐Sunday: *Romans 5:1-11*

TWENTY-ONE
THE RESURRECTION

And what is the exceeding greatness of his power to us-ward who believe, according to the working of his mighty power, which he wrought in Christ, when he raised him from the dead, and set him at his own right hand in the heavenly places.
Ephesians 1:19, 20

INTRODUCTION

Ever since the first official announcement of the resurrection of Christ, there has been a conspiracy to explain it away. The Roman guards at the tomb were instructed to report that the disciples stole the body of Jesus (Matt. 28:13). Since then, dozens of other alternative explanations of the resurrection have surfaced.

A number of years ago, Frank Morrison sought to write a book that would explain once and for all what really happened that first Easter. He was convinced he could shatter the faith of the most sincere believer. Assuming Jesus had not miraculously risen from the dead, Morrison set out to study the alternative explanations. As a lawyer, he gathered the evidence and possible interpretations. As he asked the question, "Who moved the stone?" his conclusions were somewhat different than anticipated.

Morrison realized the resurrection of Christ was not as unhistorical as he had imagined. He systematically eliminated the alternative explanations due to lack of supporting evidence or their conflict with the known facts of history. After a long search for an answer, Morrison published his manuscript as a Christian. Over the years, it has been known as one of the finest apologetics for the historicity of the resurrection of Christ.

The resurrection of Christ is the evident demonstration of victory over sin and the grave. It is the basis of new life in our Christianity. Inasmuch as the life of Christ is the "hinge" of history (all time is dated B.C., Before Christ, or A.D., *anno Domini*), then the resurrection of Christ is more than a historical fact. The resurrection is the basis for victorious Christian living and successful Christian service.

THE NATURE OF THE RESURRECTION

When the women arrived at the tomb on Easter morning, they discovered that the body of Jesus was missing. They did not fully understand what had happened. The resurrection involved much more than reviving the physical body of Jesus. The body and spirit that had separated at death once again were reunited. Jesus was now subjecting the powers of Satan, based upon the authority of the cross. Before his death, he was subjected to the limitation of humanity, but in his resurrected body he once again enjoyed access to heaven. Jesus applied the spiritual authority and position of his new life to all believers. So the issues concerning the resurrection of Christ are certainly much more than the mystery of a missing body.

Resurrection—Renewed life. There can be no denying that Jesus died on the cross. The Romans who were responsible for the actual execution of Christ were professionals. They had crucified more than one man before Jesus and crucified many after him. They understood when a man was dead, and they understood the nature of death because it was a part of their job. The holiday season was approaching so the Roman soldiers came to break the legs of Jesus and the two thieves so that they would die that day. But Jesus was already dead. "When they came to Jesus, and saw that he was dead already, they broke not his legs" (John 19:33). When the soldier pierced the side of Jesus, it was evident that the blood and water had begun to separate in his body (John 19:34). There is no doubt about the physical death of Christ.

Jesus had irritated the Jews when he predicted, "Destroy this temple, and in three days I will raise it up" (John 2:19). By this prophecy, Jesus was predicting both his resurrection and attributing the source of its power to himself. Jesus raised himself from the dead, but it was not his power alone. At Pentecost, Peter reminded his listeners that God the Father had a part in the resurrection. They had crucified Jesus, "whom God hath raised up, having loosed the pains of death: because it was not possible that he should be holden of it" (Acts 2:24). Finally, the Scriptures teach that the Holy Spirit had a part in the resurrection. "If the Spirit of him that raised up Jesus from the dead dwell in you, he that raised up Christ from the dead shall also quicken your mortal bodies by his Spirit that dwelleth in you" (Rom. 8:11).

Resurrection—Reunion of body and spirit. One of the controversial questions confronting medical doctors today is the method of determining death. Doctors once agreed that death occurs when a person's heart stops beating, but today medical technology has advanced to the point that a heart sometimes can be revived after it stops beating as during a heart attack. A heart that has stopped working can be supported by an electronic pacemaker, or even be replaced with the heart of another who is otherwise considered dead.

Other methods of determining the onset of death include the absence of brain activity, or cessation of bodily impulses. Medically, our definition of death may change a dozen or more times during our lifetime, but the biblical definition of death is always considered the separation of a person's body and spirit: "For as the body without the spirit is dead, so faith without works is dead also" (James 2:26). When Jesus died, "He bowed his head, and gave up the ghost" (John 19:30). At the resurrection of Christ, the body and spirit that were separated were once again reunited.

Resurrection—Subjecting the power of death. Death was never part of the original plan of God for man. Death only became a part of the human experience when Satan was successful in causing man to fall into sin. "Wherefore, as by one man sin entered into the world, and death by sin; and so death passed upon all men, for all have sinned" (Rom. 5:12). The resurrection of Jesus after he endured the experience of death is proof that believers will also be raised after they die and are buried in the grave.

In discussing the resurrection, Paul wrote, "Death is swallowed up in victory. O death, where is thy sting? O grave, where is thy victory?" (1 Cor. 15:54, 55). He recognized that Christ had gained a victory for believers over death in his resurrection. "Behold, I shew you a mystery; We shall not all sleep, but we shall all be changed, in a moment, in the twinkling of an eye, at the last trump: for the trumpet shall sound, and the dead shall be raised incorruptible, and we shall be changed. For this corruptible must put on incorruption, and this mortal must put on immortality" (1 Cor. 15:51-53).

When Jesus was crucified and died, some theologians teach that the devil thought he had gained a victory. Satan wanted to prohibit or destroy Christ (Gen. 3:15; Matt. 4:1-11). His part in "bruising the heel of Christ" (Gen. 3:15) was a necessary step to the resurrection of Christ, which would seal his own fate and cause his power to be subjected to Christ's authority. When Jesus conquered the grave, he did so for all who would some day have to die. In ignorance, Satan's activity in the crucifixion of Christ was actually helping Christ accomplish his work.

Resurrection—A new glory. When Jesus left heaven to come to earth, part of the *kenosis* experience was his voluntary setting aside of the glory in heaven, and assuming the limitations of a human body. He submitted himself to the plan and protection of the Father. Jesus told his disciples, "My meat is to do the will of him that sent me, and to finish his work" (John 4:34). When Jesus arose from the dead, he had finished the work of his father and was ready to receive his former glory. During the years he spent as a man on earth he was led by the Holy Spirit and accomplished the purpose of the Fa-

ther. After the resurrection Jesus received his former glory
and former position in heaven. But, because of his resurrection, Jesus has new responsibilities. He is now our intercessor before the Father (Heb. 7:25) and our advocate with the
Father (John 2:1). At his ascension, Jesus returned to the
glory that he gave up at the virgin birth. He did pray to receive "the glory which I had with thee before the world was"
(John 17:5), but he also is "the man in the glory" (Heb. 7:24).
He is the Lamb who is glorified in heaven (Rev. 5:7-14).

Resurrection—Spiritual life. The apostle Paul equated his own
spiritual experience with that of the resurrection life of
Christ, "I am crucified with Christ: nevertheless I live; yet
not I, but Christ liveth in me; and the life that I now live in
the flesh I live by the faith of the Son of God, who loved me
and gave himself for me" (Gal. 2:20). This was not a postcon-
version experience in the mind of Paul, but rather he saw
every Christian receiving the spiritual life of Christ at conversion. Being raised together with Christ resulted in a
change in the Christian's standing in the heavenlies, and
should result in a change in state on earth. "Therefore, we
are buried with him by baptism into death: that like as Christ
was raised up from the dead by the glory of the Father, even
so we also should walk in newness of life" (Rom. 6:4).

One benefit of the resurrection of Christ was the sharing of
spiritual life with believers. God is at work in our lives as
Christians "according to the working of his mighty power,
Which he wrought in Christ, when he raised him from the
dead" (Eph. 1:19, 20). The key to living the victorious Christian life is simply allowing God to live his life through the believer. The secret of successful Christianity is in applying the
truth of the union that exists between Christ and the believer.
The enthusiasm of New Testament Christianity is experienced when we understand our life has been placed into the
life of God.

Resurrection—A glorified body. Jesus arose from the dead
with a glorified body. This was the same body which he had
on earth, but it was now transformed. The wounds of the
nails in his hands and feet (Ps. 22:16) and the cut in his side

were still visible (John 20:25-29). This transformed body engaged in some of the same physical activity of any human body. He still breathed (John 20:22), talked (John 21:15), stood (John 21:4), ate (Luke 24:41-43) and walked (Luke 24:15). Yet, after his resurrection, the body of Jesus was also different. He was not always easily recognized by his disciples (Luke 24:31). He could pass through barred doors and windows and appear or disappear. There is no evidence that the resurrection body of Christ needed rest or sustenance to sustain itself. While he could eat, the Bible does not indicate that he had to do so. While this resurrection body of Jesus was the same as his preresurrection body, it was also uniquely transformed.

Perhaps the relationship that exists can be seen by contrasting an acorn and an oak. Both are the same in that the oak is the product of an acorn. No distinction can be made in terms of essence. Yet as the acorn dies and is buried, it springs to life as an oak. While the body of Christ is essentially the same before and after the resurrection, certain distinctives are noticeable as demonstrated in the following chart.

THE BELIEVERS' RESURRECTION BODY (1 Cor. 15:42-44)	
Sown	*Raised*
1. in corruption	1. in incorruption
2. in dishonor	2. in glory
3. in weakness	3. in power
4. a natural body	4. a spiritual body

THE RESULTS OF THE RESURRECTION

Jesus accomplished a number of things in his resurrection that affect our life. Essentially, the resurrection of Christ permitted Christ to apply the victories or accomplishments of the cross to the believer. But beyond the benefits of the cross, there are also the benefits of the resurrection that are applied to the believer. Jesus began a new dimension to his work and ministry. These various accomplishments affect our daily walk with Christ and our legal position in the heavenlies.

Giving eternal life. Every Christian has eternal life, this is why Jesus came (John 3:16). The basis for eternal life is the resurrection. "Jesus said,...I am the resurrection and the life; he that believeth in me, though he were dead, yet shall he live" (John 11:25). Again Paul stated, "The gift of God is eternal life through Jesus Christ our Lord" (Rom. 6:23). Jesus said, "He that heareth my word, and believeth on him that sent me, hath everlasting life, and shall not come into condemnation, but is passed from death unto life" (John 5:24).

Imparting power. Paul prayed that the Ephesian Christians would understand "what is the exceeding greatness of his power to us-ward who believe, according to the working of his mighty power, which he wrought in Christ, when he raised him from the dead" (Eph. 1:19, 20). If Christians understood and applied the resurrection and ascension of Christ, it would radically change much of the work done for God by them. Christians need not be defeated. The same power that raised Jesus from the dead works not only to save us but to assist us in our Christian life and service.

Manifesting justification. The Christian is justified by the substitution of Jesus Christ for sinners on Calvary. Some Christians have mistakenly thought they were justified by the resurrection. They base their view on the verse that reads in the King James, "Who was delivered for our offenses, and was raised again for our justification" (Rom. 4:25). The verse should be translated "raised because of our justification" (Rom. 4:25). We are "justified freely by his grace through the redemption that is in Christ Jesus" (Rom. 3:24). The substitution of Christ on Calvary was all that was needed for our justification, but that act was not accomplished in our life until we personally put our faith in Christ as Savior. This accomplishment of Calvary wins God's approval for us; the resurrection of Christ announces it to the world.

Providing our future resurrection. A major concern among Corinthian Christians was a misunderstanding of the resurrection. Some Christians did not realize that the resurrection also applied to them as Christians (1 Cor. 15:12). The Bible teaches that all the dead will someday be raised, the saved and the unsaved (Dan. 12:2). The fact that Jesus rose from the dead guarantees our glorious future resurrection from the dead, and the resurrection of those who have already died in Christ. "But now is Christ risen from the dead, and become the firstfruits of them that slept" (1 Cor. 15:20). Paul used this truth to comfort troubled Christians (1 Thess. 4:13-18). "For if we believe that Jesus died and rose again, even so them also which sleep in Jesus will God bring with him" (1 Thess. 4:14).

Union with Christ. At the resurrection and ascension of Christ, we received a standing in the heavenlies. This is due to the union that a Christian has with Christ. It is best seen in Jesus' illustration of the vine and branches. When you look at a vine as it climbs toward the sun, it is hard to tell where the vine ends and the branches begin. So it is with the Christian. As we live for Christ, it should be evident to an observer that he is accomplishing the will of God through us. Christ will indwell us (Gal. 2:20) to do the will of God. But also, we can do the will of God when we recognize our union with the resurrected Christ in the heavenlies.

OUR UNION WITH CHRIST	
1. Planted together	Romans 6:5
2. Made alive together	Colossians 2:13
	Ephesians 2:5
3. Raised together	Ephesians 2:6
4. Sit together	Ephesians 2:6
5. Workmen together	2 Corinthians 6:1
6. Live together	1 Thessalonians 5:10
7. Glorified together	Romans 8:17

Of course, there may exist some difference between our standing and state. We possess the life of Christ but we do not always allow Christ to live through us. The effective Christian life is a continual progress toward becoming more Christlike here on earth. The moment we are saved, we receive his perfection in heaven. But our life on earth is filled with striving to overcome temptation and to serve him faithfully. Like the apostle Paul, we realize we have not arrived spiritually but we are constantly pressing in the right direction (Phil. 3:11-14).

CONCLUSION

The thing that makes Christianity unique from other religions is the resurrection of Christ. The uniqueness is further identified with the reality of Christ living his resurrection life in the believer. The amazing truth is that the One who died now lives. And for the Christian to live with Christ, he must be yielded to God and allow Christ to live his life through him.

DAILY READINGS

☐Monday: *Matthew 28:1-20*   ☐Tuesday: *Mark 16:1-18*
☐Wednesday: *Luke 24:1-26*   ☐Thursday: *Luke 24:27-53*
☐Friday: *John 20:27-53*   ☐Saturday: *1 Corinthians 15:1-34*   ☐Sunday: *1 Corinthians 15:35-58*

TWENTY-TWO
THE ASCENSION OF CHRIST

And when he had spoken these things, while they beheld, he was taken up; and a cloud received him out of their sight. Acts 1:9

INTRODUCTION

The ascension of Christ occurred when Jesus met with his disciples, forty days after his suffering (Acts 1:3). During this time, called the postresurrection ministry, the Lord taught his disciples more fully concerning the ministry they were about to have. On the day of ascension, Jesus met with his disciples on the Mount of Olives, just outside the city of Jerusalem. There he reminded them once again of the spiritual power they would soon receive and repeated the commission to take the gospel to the whole world (Acts 1:8).

Jesus reminded them that they could never know some things, such as the time of his return, but there was one thing they could be certain of. "But ye shall receive power, after that the Holy Ghost is come upon you: and ye shall be witnesses unto me both in Jerusalem, and in all Judea, and in Samaria, and unto the uttermost part of the earth" (Acts 1:8).

When Jesus completed that command, it was as though he had given them their final orders. There was nothing else left to do. With the disciples watching, he ascended up into a cloud. Two angels stood by and reminded the disciples that Jesus would return to earth, in the same manner he had departed. Jesus left his disciples and entered the presence of his Father to begin his present ministry in heaven. Luke recorded this event in a single verse, "And when he had spoken these things, while they beheld, he was taken up; and a cloud received him out of their sight" (Acts 1:9).

The ascension of Christ is one of the important doctrines of Scripture, but, similar to the doctrine of the virgin birth, there are only a few but strategic passages devoted to the subject. The historical event of the ascension is recorded in Acts 1:1-12 and the writers of the New Testament epistles based much of their doctrine on the fact of this event.

THE NATURE OF THE ASCENSION

The disciples who witnessed the ascension of Christ probably did not completely understand what they were seeing. It involved more than his physical return to heaven. The ascension meant that Christ was returning to his former place of authority in heaven, he was reclaiming his former place of glory, and he was beginning a new ministry for believers in heaven. The technical aspects of the ascension are as follows:

The end of self-limitations. When Christ became a man, part of the kenosis experience involved the voluntary limitations of his comparative attributes. Jesus was still God and able to exercise any of those attributes according to his own will, but Jesus chose not to exercise his self-will but rather to do the will of his heavenly Father (John 4:34). At the resurrection, those self-limitations ended. This meant that, although Jesus was still the same omnipotent God who spoke the world into existence (John 1:3; Heb. 11:3), there was a time during his earthly life and ministry when he chose not to exercise that power (John 18:36, 37). Jesus was still the same omniscient God who alone understands all the intricacies of our immense universe. Yet he determined during his earthly ministry that there were some things he would choose not to know (Matt. 13:32). Jesus was still omnipresent, meaning he was everywhere present in the vast universe, yet for a brief period of his eternity he chose to limit himself to the confines of a human body (John 1:14). Christ no longer limits himself but exercises all his attributes to their full potential.

The glorification of Christ. From the beginning of time, Jesus had his own glory. That celestial glory was temporarily hidden during his earthly life. But on earth, John could say, "We beheld his glory, the glory as of the only begotten of the Father" (John 1:14). Perhaps John made reference to the glory when "Jesus was transfigured" (Matt. 17:2) on the mount of transfiguration. Some feel the earthly humanity was the perfect example of what every man should become, hence as a man, Jesus glorified God. As Jesus approached the cross, he prayed, "And now, O Father, glorify thou me with thine own self with the glory which I had with thee before the world was" (John 17:5). When Jesus hung on the cross, he looked forward to the glorification of himself and the joy of that time (Heb. 12:2). At the resurrection of Christ, Jesus was glorified. "Wherefore God also hath highly exalted him, and given him a name which is above every name" (Phil. 2:9). Where the previous glory of Christ in heaven was dependent upon his person, this added dimension of glory is based upon his completed work.

It is interesting to contrast the postresurrection appearances of Christ and the postascension revelations. In the former instances, Christ had sufficiently veiled his glory to the point that he was often not recognized, such as with the disciples at Emmaus (Luke 24:16, 31), or Mary Magdalene who also did not recognize him (John 20:14). His person was witnessed by John, Paul, and Stephen. There was no doubt in their minds that they were in the presence of deity. The difference between John's meeting with Christ in John 21 and Revelation 1 was the glorification of Christ that he received at his ascension.

The exaltation of Christ. Closely related to his glorification was the exaltation of Christ to his new position of authority. David, in a messianic psalm, prophesied concerning this exaltation of Christ when he wrote, "The Lord said unto my

Lord, Sit thou at my right hand, until I make thine enemies thy footstool" (Ps. 110:1). Peter quoted this psalm in his message on the day of Pentecost in his discussion of the resurrection. He concluded by pointing out the Lordship of Jesus Christ. "Therefore let all the house of Israel know assuredly, that God hath made that same Jesus, whom ye have crucified, both Lord and Christ" (Acts 2:36). The apostle Paul also cited the resurrection and ascension of Christ as his exaltation. "Wherefore, God also hath highly exalted him, and given him a name which is above every name" (Phil. 2:9). Jesus is the object of worship by those around his throne. They cry out, "Worthy is the Lamb" (Rev. 5:12).

The entrance of humanity into heaven. Paul noted, "To be absent from the body [is] to be present with the Lord" (2 Cor. 5:8). This entrance into heaven is only possible because "the forerunner is for us entered, even Jesus" (Heb. 6:20). Jesus was the first man to enter heaven with a glorified body. At his ascension, he became "the man in the glory" (Heb. 7:24).

The beginning of a new ministry. When Jesus ascended into heaven, he was not entering retirement. He simply added a new task to his job description. He had finished his task of dying for the salvation of the world (John 19:30) but now he lives for the saved as their intercessor and advocate. In his position, Jesus is continually interceding for Christians as they are tempted to sin (Heb. 7:25). He gives them grace to keep from sinning. If, on occasion, they should yield to temptation and sin, Jesus becomes their advocate before God (John 2:1). As such, Christ forgives the sin based on his sacrifice and restores the Christian after he sins. (For a further discussion of the present ministry of Christ, see Chapter 23.)

THE RESULTS OF THE ASCENSION OF CHRIST

Everything Jesus accomplished had an impact on the life of the believer. As a result of the ascension of Christ, Christians have a number of benefits for a fulfilled life and successful service. The following chart identifies some of the results of the ascension of Christ.

THE RESULTS OF THE ASCENSION OF CHRIST	
1. The sending of the Holy Spirit	John 16:7
2. The giving of spiritual gifts	Ephesians 4:8
3. The imparting of spiritual power	Acts 1:8
4. The preparation of a heavenly home	John 14:3
5. The standing of the believer	Romans 8:29

The sending of the Holy Spirit. If Christ did not ascend to heaven, we would not have the ministry of the Holy Spirit for the church. Jesus taught that both the Father (John 14:26) and he himself (John 15:20) would send the "Comforter." This could not be accomplished during his earthly ministry. Jesus said, "Nevertheless, I tell you the truth; it is expedient for you that I go away: for if I go not away, the Comforter will not come unto you; but if I depart, I will send him unto you" (John 16:7). This promise was again made by Jesus on the last recorded meeting with his disciples on the last day of his ascension (Acts 1:5). Less than ten days later, the Holy Spirit came in mighty power upon the disciples (Acts 2:1-4). Today the Holy Spirit lives in every Christian (1 Cor. 6:19) and helps them live for God (Gal. 5:25).

The giving of spiritual gifts. When a person is saved, he not only receives the Holy Spirit, he also receives his spiritual gift(s) (1 Cor. 12:11; 1 Pet. 4:10). A spiritual gift is an ability to serve God, given initially by Christ. "When he ascended up on high, he led captivity captive, and gave gifts unto men" (Eph. 4:8). After a Christian is saved he must discover his gift(s) (1 Cor. 12:1, 32) and develop those gifts for better service. The Bible contains three lists of gifts (Rom. 12; 1 Cor. 12; Eph. 4). Certain special abilities were given by God to the apostles as signs to verify their preaching, as mentioned in the last chapter of Mark's Gospel. These were considered by most scholars to have been temporary, and given primarily as signs to unbelieving Jews (1 Cor. 1:22). The Bible instructs the Christian to seek "earnestly the best gifts" (1 Cor. 12:31). Everyone should seek to use their gift or gifts to glorify God. There may be other gifts that God gives to people that are not specifically identified in Scripture. The exact number of the gifts is not uniformly accepted by all Bible scholars, since the reference to spiritual gifts in Ephesians 4, for example, appears to refer to the positions certain gifted people fill in the church and not necessarily to the gift or gifts themselves. For example, a pastor might have the gifts of teaching, exhortation, wisdom, and faith.

The imparting of spiritual power. A third benefit of the ascension of Christ was the giving of spiritual power to his disciples. Jesus taught his disciples to "tarry ye in the city of Jerusalem, until ye be endued with power from on high" (Luke 24:49). On the day of Pentecost, the disciples received this spiritual power to witness. The power was continuously present in their lives as they continued to be filled with the Holy Spirit. This spiritual power is available to every believer today in the same power God used in the resurrection and ascension of Christ (Eph. 1:19, 20). By yielding to God (Rom. 12:1) and being filled with the Holy Spirit (Eph. 5:18), we will be better able both to witness and to live our lives for God.

The preparation of a heavenly home. A fourth result of the ascension of Christ involves the preparation of heaven for Christians. Jesus said, "In my Father's house are many mansions: if it were not so, I would have told you. I go to prepare a place for you" (John 14:2). When Jesus ascended to his Father's house, we must assume he began preparing those dwelling places. Had there been no ascension, there would be no place prepared for those who trust Christ as Savior.

The standing of the believer. When Jesus ascended to his Father, those who trust Christ as Savior ascended with him. God "hath raised us up together, and made us sit together in heavenly places in Christ Jesus" (Eph. 2:6). As Jesus was exalted at his ascension, so the Christian is raised up and stands before God because of the ascension of Christ. This is an application of the union every believer has with Christ.

The following list is drawn from *Finding Your Spiritual Gifts* by Tim Blanchard:

THE GIFTS OF THE SPIRIT

1.	Prophecy (preaching)	Rom. 12:6	Ability to speak forth God's truth.
2.	Teaching	Rom. 12:7	Ability to help others grasp truth.
3.	Knowledge	1 Cor. 12:8	Ability to know by observation (sight) and experience.
4.	Wisdom	1 Cor. 12:8	Ability to make discerning application of truth to practical questions.
5.	Exhortation	Rom. 12:8	Ability to exhort and comfort.
6.	Faith	1 Cor. 12:9	Special ability of vision and foresight; boldness in claiming God's promises.
7.	Discerning of spirits	1 Cor. 12:10	Ability to judge the true spiritual level and integrity of others.
8.	Helps	1 Cor. 12:28	Ability and grace to seize opportunities of service.
9.	Serving (ministry)	Rom. 12:7	Derived from the word translated "deacon." Ability to give special personal service rendered out of love for God.
10.	Administration (government)	1 Cor. 12:28	Wisdom, decisiveness; ability to give guidance to others.
11.	Ruling	Rom. 12:8	Confidence, desire, and skills to lead others.
12.	Mercy	Rom. 12:8	Compassion for those physically and spiritually suffering.
13.	Giving	Rom. 12:8	Motivated to share with others who are in need.

The preparation of the throne. Jesus, the King of kings, is currently seated on his throne in heaven, preparing the millennial throne for the years that he will rule on earth. The angel Gabriel told Mary before the birth of Christ, "He shall be great, and shall be called the Son of the Highest: and the Lord God shall give unto him the throne of his father David" (Luke 1:32). John was told concerning the ascended Christ, "The Lion of the tribe of Juda, the Root of David, hath prevailed to open the book, and to loose the seven seals thereof" (Rev. 5:5). Most Bible commentators agree that the book or scroll is the title deed to the world. When the seven seals are broken and the scroll is opened, the announcement is made: "The kingdoms of this world are become the kingdoms of our Lord, and of his Christ, and he shall reign forever and ever" (Rev. 11:15). This is the end of the tribulation and the beginning of the millennial kingdom.

CONCLUSION

After his postresurrection ministry, Jesus ascended to his Father, leaving Christians behind to love and serve him. We were identified with Christ in his ascension, and as a result have a legal standing of perfection in the heavenlies. This makes it imperative that we demonstrate Christlikeness in our daily life that is as consistent as possible with our standing in heaven. The angels asked the disciples who witnessed the ascension, "Why stand ye gazing up into heaven? this same Jesus, who is taken up from you into heaven, shall so come in like manner as ye have seen him go into heaven" (Acts 1:11). In expectancy of his return, we need to live for Jesus as he makes intercession on our behalf.

DAILY READINGS

☐Monday: *Acts 1:1-11*   ☐Tuesday: *Ephesians 4:7-16*
☐Wednesday: *Philippians 2:1-11*   ☐Thursday:
1 Corinthians 12:1-18   ☐Friday: *1 Corinthians 12:19-31*
☐Saturday: *Romans 12:1-16*   ☐Sunday: *John 14:1-12*

TWENTY-THREE
THE PRESENT MINISTRY
OF JESUS CHRIST

Wherefore he is able also to save them to the uttermost that come unto God by him, seeing he ever liveth to make intercession for them. Hebrews 7:25

INTRODUCTION

Many people are confused about the present-day ministry of Jesus Christ to Christians. They believe in a "shift-worker" concept of God. They believe God the Father had the early morning shift, from creation to the birth of Christ. Therefore, the Father is the God of the Old Testament. They believe the afternoon shift was filled by God the Son in his earthly life and ministry. They feel Christ has finished his job and is resting on the throne in heaven. Finally, they think we are living in the evening shift and as we approach the final hours of human history, it is the Holy Spirit who works this shift. As easy as this idea is to accept in the mind of many Christians, it is not an accurate portrayal of the biblical teaching concerning the Trinity.

The Bible teaches there is one God in three distinct persons, each possessing the total attributes of God and each working together throughout history to accomplish the work of God. The Bible teaches that God the Father, the Son, and the Holy Spirit were involved in creation, the judgment of

Old Testament civilizations, the birth, life, death, and resurrection of Christ, the New Testament church, and, still future, the return of Christ to establish his kingdom.

As we have already seen in our study of the person and work of Christ, he had an existence and ministry before his birth in Bethlehem. We also know he is coming again someday, to call away his own and will later establish his kingdom on earth. It should not be surprising, then, to learn that Jesus is currently engaged in a special ministry for believers.

The Bible calls Jesus both our intercessor (Heb. 7:25) and our advocate (1 John 2:1). While some do not distinguish between these two works, a distinction does exist. As our intercessor, Jesus represents us before the throne to give grace so that we may gain victory over temptation. It would be ideal if Christians were all victorious over temptation. Unfortunately, that is not the case. When we do sin, as Christians, Jesus is our advocate, restoring us to fellowship with God. These two words summarize much of the present ministry of Christ. Understanding the present ministry of Christ will help us live consistently and confidently for him.

THE INTERCESSION OF CHRIST

A concerned mother will take great care concerning the health of her children. She will reflect that concern by practicing both preventive and curative medicine. She will prevent her children from eating the wrong kinds of foods, or stop them from playing in dangerous places, or keep them inside when it is cold outside unless they wear warm clothing. A loving mother will carefully plan a family menu and provide her children with supplementary vitamins whenever she feels it is necessary. Many times her preventive steps are far more effective than treatment for some sickness.

The intercessory work of Christ is similar to preventive medicine for the Christian. While in one sense we may use the term "intercession" to identify all of the present work of mediation in heaven, the biblical use of the term more specifically relates to the work of Christ on behalf of the believer's weakness and temptation. As a lawyer may often make calls on behalf of his client, so Christ is continually interceding to the Father on our behalf. "Wherefore he is able also to save them to the uttermost that come unto God by him, seeing he ever liveth to make intercession for them" (Heb. 7:25). Several things characterize this ministry of Christ.

Continual intercession. Effective intercession is not a once-and-for-all event, but a continuing event. In our world, intercessory prayer is a ministry of praying for the needs of others as long as the needs exist. Yet Christ is not described as praying, but he personally is our intercessor. "He ever *liveth* to make intercession for them" (Heb. 7:25, italics mine). Since Christ lives forever and will not change, we can expect him to be our continual intercessor for us. Paul asked, "Who is he that condemneth? It is Christ that died, yea rather, that is risen again, who is even at the right hand of God, who also maketh intercession for us" (Rom. 8:34).

Active intercession. Many parents will teach their children to pray at bedtime for others but it is often in maturity that those same Christians pray actively for others. The intercessory prayers of Christ are not just a recitation of an old familiar prayer list, but an expression of the heart of God. Jesus was "moved with compassion" (Matt. 9:36) when he asked his disciples to intercede for the world. "Pray ye therefore the Lord of the harvest, that he will send forth labourers into his harvest" (Matt. 9:38). It is significant that his intercessory prayer for us is also motivated by love. As Jesus prays for us he also becomes actively involved in helping us.

Christ has given us the Holy Spirit to help us in our Christian lives. This was one of the first items on his prayer list. Jesus told his disciples, "I will pray the Father and he shall give you another Comforter, that he may abide with you forever" (John 14:16). Christ wants to give us the best in every part of our life. Paul asked, "What shall we then say to these things? If God be for us, who can be against us? He that spared not his own Son, but delivered him up for us all, how shall he not with him also freely give us all things?" (Rom. 8:31, 32).

Specific intercession. We should rejoice that the prayers of Jesus for us are not as general as some Christians' prayers for others. There are certain matters in which Jesus will specifically intercede. He alone understands us, even better than we may understand ourselves. In addition to the specific needs and weaknesses in our own lives, there are a number of specific prayer requests on the "Prayer List of Jesus." Some of these are listed in the following chart. The Scripture references help us better understand what Jesus wants God to do in our lives.

THE PRAYER LIST OF JESUS FOR ME

1. The giving of the Comforter—John 16:16
2. The security of the believer—John 17:11
3. The unity of believers—John 17:11, 21
4. The joy of the Lord—John 17:13
5. Protection from evil—John 17:15
6. The sanctification of the believer—John 17:17
7. Success in evangelism—John 17:21
8. Maturity (perfection)—John 17:23
9. Fellowship with Christ in heaven—John 17:24

Preventive intercession. A fourth characteristic of Jesus' intercession or prayer is that it is preventive in design. God does not delight in our failure. Some seem to feel that God delights in judging us and punishing us for our sin (1 Sam. 15:22). The ministry of Christ as our intercessor works in cooperation with the work of the Holy Spirit and Scripture to prevent us from sinning. As long as we are in the flesh we are subject to sin, but sinlessness should still be the aim of every Christian. David said, "Thy word have I hid in mine heart that I might not sin against thee" (Ps. 119:11). This promise is one of the Old Testament foundations. John writes in his first epistle, "My little children, these things write I unto you, that ye sin not" (1 John 2:1). As we attempt to gain victory over temptation in our lives on earth, we have an intercessor in heaven who understands the nature of temptation experientially and interprets for us. "For we have not an high priest which cannot be touched with the feeling of our infirmities; but was in all points tempted like as we are, yet without sin" (Heb. 4:15).

Effective intercession. "The effectual, fervent prayer of a righteous man availeth much" (James 5:16). We seek to apply this promise in our own prayer life, but it can also be applied to the prayer life of Christ. The apostle Paul described righteousness as an attribute of Christ, because he is the source of all righteousness (Rom. 5:17-21). Certainly if our prayers are guaranteed to be effectual if we live righteously, then we may be certain God will respond to the intercession of his righteous Son.

Every Christian sins because he was born with a sinful nature (Ps. 51:5; 1 John 1:8), because of the temptation of Satan (1 Pet. 5:8), because of the influence of this world (Eph. 2:2, 3), but most of all because of the lust within him (1 John 2:15, 16). Christ intercedes for the believer lest he sin, but when he sins. . . Jesus is his advocate.

WHEN A CHRISTIAN SINS, HE...

1. Yields to his own lusts—James 1:14, 15
2. Fails to appropriate his new nature—Rom. 6:7
3. Fails to appropriate the Scriptures' influence—Ps. 119:11
4. Fails to appropriate the Fathers' will—James 5:16
5. Fails to appropriate the prayer of Christ—Heb. 7:25
6. Fails to appropriate the work of the Holy Spirit—Rom. 8:9
7. Fails to appropriate the influence of other Christians—Heb. 10:24, 25

JESUS CHRIST, OUR ADVOCATE

However we may wish to rationalize it, when a Christian sins, the creature is actively rebelling against his Creator, despite all God has done to prevent him from sinning. It would be understandable if God chose to punish us as we deserved, but the Lord chooses rather to show mercy. Although it is ideal that the Christian break the habit of sin, John gives the sinning Christian the following consolation, "If any man sin, we have an advocate with the Father, Jesus Christ the righteous" (1 John 2:1). An "advocate" is a legal term denoting a lawyer who represents his client before a court of law. When applied to the present ministry of Christ, it speaks of his work for sinning believers to restore them to fellowship. His work as an advocate is based upon the sufficiency of the blood of Christ for all sin, past, present, and future.

Lost fellowship. When a person receives Christ, he is saved eternally. Nothing can separate him from the love of God (Rom. 8:38, 39). Even if he denied Christ, Christ remains faithful (2 Tim. 2:13). Although our union with Christ is secure, our fellowship with God is dependent upon our daily walk with him. As long as we attempt to do what is right, i.e., "walk in the light, as he is in the light" (1 John 1:7), our fellowship is secure, and any sin committed unknowingly is cleansed. "And the blood of Jesus Christ his Son cleanseth us" (1 John 1:7). It is when we step out of line and do sin that we break our fellowship with God. As long as we are consciously aware of sin that exists between ourselves and God, there is a barrier that God will not cross. Our salvation remains secure, but the quality of our Christian life suffers because we are out of fellowship with him.

Restored fellowship. "If we confess our sins, he is faithful and just to forgive us our sins, and to cleanse us from all unrighteousness" (1 John 1:9). We should never cease to be amazed how much God desires to fellowship with us. Sin is an insult to the nature of God, and when a Christian commits such an act, he is choosing his own way and actively opposing God. The fact that God tolerates our sin is evidence of the depth of the love of God. There is nothing on the part of God that will prevent the restoration of fellowship. We must simply be willing to admit and turn from our sins and he will forgive (1 John 1:9).

Propitiation. Fellowship can be restored only because Jesus "is the propitiation for our sins, and not for ours only, but also for the sins of the whole world" (1 John 2:2). The term "propitiation" means "satisfaction." When we sin, the holiness of God is offended. To be restored to his fellowship, the holiness of God is satisfied by the blood of Christ. The cost involved in providing salvation for a lost world was the person of Christ and his shed blood (Rom. 3:24). This payment was necessary to satisfy the righteousness of a holy God. Only in this way could it be possible for God to forgive sins and still be righteous. The blood of Christ is sufficient to save the entire world from all their sins (1 John 2:2). This makes possible restored fellowship even when we sin against God.

Confession. A lawyer is only as good as the information given him by the client. Sometimes the client may fail to follow his lawyer's advice or forget to tell him something that is necessary for the trial. Christ, our advocate, knows already about our sins. The root meaning of "confess..." is "to say the same thing," or to agree. We must agree with Christ concerning our sins in order to find forgiveness (1 John 1:9).

If the Advocate is going to restore our fellowship with God, we must confess our sins—totally. If we are unwilling to do that, we prevent the work of our Advocate in heaven.

Confession involves acknowledging our error and agreeing with God as to its sinful nature. When we are prepared to admit our responsibility in sin, Jesus pleads our case before God on the basis of the payment he has already made for our sin (1 John 2:2). God "is faithful and just to forgive us our sins, and to cleanse us from all unrighteousness" (1 John 1:9).

Jesus used the social custom of the day of footwashing to illustrate this principle of continually cleansing the Christian. Before the disciples came to the meeting place for the Passover, they had no doubt washed in a public bath completely, including their feet. In walking along the dusty streets of Jerusalem to the upper room, their feet got dusty. When we are saved, we are cleansed from all sin (parallel to an entire bath), but as we walk in the world our feet often get dirty. It is not necessary that we seek a total cleansing again (getting saved again), as Peter suggested (John 13:9), but rather that we confess known sin in order to be cleansed (John 13:10).

CONCLUSION

There is no good reason for the Christian to fail. Jesus is our intercessor, praying for our success as Christians. If we should fail to live up to that expectation, he is also our advocate and will represent us before God. It is needful for us to regularly evaluate our life to determine the degree to which we are allowing Christ to minister to us today.

DAILY READINGS

☐Monday: *Hebrews 7:11-28*   ☐Tuesday: *Psalm 23*
☐Wednesday: *1 John 1:5—2:2*   ☐Thursday: *Luke 22:31-46*
☐Friday: *John 17:1-26*   ☐Saturday: *Romans 8:28-39*
☐Sunday: *2 Timothy 2:11-18*

PART FIVE

UNDERSTANDING THE DOCTRINE OF THE HOLY SPIRIT

TWENTY-FOUR
THE PERSON OF
THE HOLY SPIRIT

But ye are not in the flesh, but in the Spirit, if so be that the Spirit of God dwell in you. Now if any man have not the Spirit of Christ, he is none of his. Romans 8:9

INTRODUCTION

When the French explorers first discovered Niagara Falls, they listened intently to the Indian legends about its formation. The Indians believed the Falls were created by a large snake which had coiled itself in the midst of the river. The Frenchmen observed annually as the Indian tribe chose the most beautiful young girl in the tribe and placed her in a highly decorated canoe. Each year the tribe sent the canoe with a girl sacrifice to drift over the Falls so the snake god would not leave the river and attack the tribe.

As roads were built to the area, Niagara Falls became better known, resulting in a popular tourist center. Local businessmen and international corporations together recognized a new way to tap the resources of this natural wonder. Soon it became the "Honeymoon Capital of the World," a bustling center of tourism.

During the twentieth century, electrical engineers discovered a means of tapping the resources of Niagara Falls to produce hydroelectric power. A large generating plant was built and water was channeled from the upper rapids through machines to produce electricity. Today, much of southwestern Ontario and western New York State is supplied with hydroelectric power from the Niagara Falls Generating Station.

As we look at contemporary attitudes about the Holy Spirit, we can see a parallel in the history of attitudes concerning Niagara Falls. Some people today have a mystical idea about the Holy Spirit, such as the Indians who worshiped the nonexistent snake god. Others appreciate the Holy Spirit, but, like tourists to the Falls, they are only spectators. A few have a biblical understanding of the Holy Spirit, realizing the power of God is available through the full resources of the Holy Spirit.

THE PERSON OF THE HOLY SPIRIT

Much confusion exists today concerning the Person of the Holy Spirit. His personality is denied by both liberal theologians and extreme religious cults. Some liberals will acknowledge he is portrayed as a person, but claim the Scripture is communicating a myth. Radical cults like the Jehovah's Witnesses deny his personality, referring to him as simply an influence. Because of the comparatively little teaching about the Holy Spirit that has been done over the years, there are some good Christians who do not realize that the Holy Spirit is a Person.

The Holy Spirit has the attributes of a person. The Holy Spirit is the Third Person of the Trinity—equal with the Father and Son in essence. Since one of the major aspects of God's nature is that he is a person, it follows that the Holy Spirit is a person.

The apostle Paul noted the intellectual ability of the Holy Spirit when he asked, "What man knoweth the things of man save the spirit of man which is in him? Even so the things of God knoweth no man, but the Spirit of God" (1 Cor. 2:11). The rational capacity of the Holy Spirit was expanded to include wisdom and communication when Paul's prayer request for the Ephesians included "That the God of our Lord

Jesus Christ, the Father of glory, may give unto you the spirit of wisdom and revelation in the knowledge of him" (Eph. 1:17).

The emotional ability of the Holy Spirit is evident in the word of the apostle, "the love of the Holy Spirit" (Rom. 15:30). One of the problems associated with emotions is the possibility of being grieved by someone who is loved. The Bible warns Christians, "Grieve not the Holy Spirit of God" (Eph. 4:30). Isaiah cited an example of how Israel "rebelled, and vexed his Holy Spirit" (Isa. 63:10). The Holy Spirit has the ability to respond emotionally to the ideas and experiences he encounters.

The Holy Spirit also has the ability of will and the ability to exercise it. By his own choice, the Holy Spirit accomplishes a number of specific acts, such as giving spiritual gifts. "But all these worketh that one and the selfsame Spirit, dividing to every man severally as he will" (1 Cor. 12:11).

The Holy Spirit performs the actions of a person. The Holy Spirit does a number of things only a person can do. It should be noted that the Holy Spirit is not a Person because he does those things attributable to personality, but rather does the actions of the personality because he is a person. Consider the following chart to see how the Holy Spirit does those things which only a person can do.

THE ACTS OF THE PERSON OF THE HOLY SPIRIT	
1. He teaches	John 14:26
2. He testifies	John 15:26
3. He guides	Rom. 8:14
4. He speaks	1 Cor. 2:13
5. He enlightens	John 16:13
6. He strives	Gen. 6:3
7. He commands	Acts 8:28
8. He intercedes	Rom. 8:26
9. He sends workers	Acts 13:4
10. He calls	Rev. 22:17
11. He comforts	John 16:7
12. He works	1 Cor. 12:11

The above actions cannot be accomplished by a mere influence or force. Only a rational, emotional, and active person could do all that the Scriptures teach the Holy Spirit accomplishes.

The Holy Spirit was addressed as a person. The New Testament clearly shows the early Christians recognized and affirmed the Holy Spirit as a Person. Peter obeyed the Holy Spirit when he was commanded to go to Cornelius's household (Acts 10:19). Philip followed the leading of the Holy Spirit in his ministry also (Acts 8:39). Against his better judgment, Ananias came to Saul, obeying what the Holy Spirit had revealed to him (Acts 9:10-17). Paul and Silas were constantly led by the Holy Spirit in their ministry (Acts 16:7-10).

The Bible also records the story of two disciples who attempted to lie to the Holy Spirit (Acts 5:3). At his trial, Stephen addressed the Sanhedrin, saying, "Ye stiffnecked and uncircumcised in heart and ears, ye do always resist the Holy Ghost: as your fathers did, so do ye" (Acts 7:51). Jesus also warned about blaspheming the Holy Spirit (Matt. 12:31), and the Bible also warns of the consequences of insulting the Holy Spirit. "Of how much sorer punishment, suppose ye, shall he be thought worthy, who hath trodden under foot the Son of God, and hath counted the blood of the covenant, with which he was sanctified, an unholy thing, and hath done despite unto the Spirit of grace?" (Heb. 10:29). Is it any wonder the writer concludes, "It is a fearful thing to fall into the hands of the living God" (Heb. 10:31)? This would not be so if we had a proper reverence for the Person of the Holy Spirit as did David (Ps. 51:11).

Association of persons. A fourth scriptural illustration of the Holy Spirit as a person is seen in the references to the Trinity. Jesus commanded his disciples to "teach all nations, baptizing them in the name of the Father, and of the Son, and of the Holy Ghost" (Matt. 28:19). Jesus acknowledged three distinct Persons of the Trinity but recognized their unity in a simple name. In our understanding of the Trinity, we realize that what is true of God is true of each part of the Trinity of God.

God the Father is a personal God interested in us (John 3:16; 1 John 3:1). God the Son is also shown as a personal God interested in us (John 13:1). If the teaching of Scripture were unclear concerning the personality of the Holy Spirit, his association with other members of the Trinity of God as an equal indicates that he too is a person.

THE DEITY OF THE HOLY SPIRIT

Not only is the Holy Spirit a person, he is also God. As God, he is worthy of our worship and obedience. His deity is demonstrated in part by the names of God which are attributed to him. It is further understood through a correct understanding of the Trinity. The Bible ascribed the attributes of deity to the Holy Spirit and, finally, the Holy Spirit accomplishes that which only God can do.

Names. When God identifies his name in Scripture, it is not without meaning. The first mention of the Holy Spirit in Scripture identifies him clearly as God. "And the *Spirit of God* moved upon the face of the waters" (Gen. 1:2). Early in the history of civilization, the rebellion of man grieved God. "And the Lord said, *My Spirit* shall not always strive with man" (Gen. 6:3).

The most common name for the third Person of the Trinity is "Holy Spirit." While not a strong proof, this name associates him with deity because holiness is a reflection of his attributes, while "Spirit" is a reflection of his nature. His deity is also implied by the titles "Comforter" (John 16:7; 2 Cor. 1:3), "Spirit of Truth" (John 16:13), and "Holy One" (1 John 2:20). Most of the names ascribed to the Holy Spirit in Scripture either relate him directly to deity, as "the Spirit of the Lord God" (Isa. 61:1), or to some attribute of God, such as "the eternal Spirit" (Heb. 9:14) or "the spirit of judgment and...the spirit of burning" (Isa. 4:4).

Trinity. When we speak of the Trinity of God, we are speaking of one God in three distinct persons, each being God. The Holy Spirit is a part of the Trinity and is therefore God. Peter asked Ananias, "Why hath Satan filled thine heart to lie to the Holy Ghost?" (Acts 5:3) and charged, "Thou hast not lied unto men, but unto God" (Acts 5:4). Later Peter charged Sapphira with involvement in the conspiracy "to tempt the Spirit of the Lord" (Acts 5:9). No one challenged Peter in his interchange of titles identifying the Holy Spirit as God.

Further evidence that the early church recognized the deity of the Holy Spirit is evidenced in the equal recognition given him in the Pauline benediction: "The grace of the Lord Jesus Christ, and the love of God, and the communion of the Holy Ghost, be with you all" (2 Cor. 13:14). Jesus gave equal recognition to the Holy Spirit with the other two members of the Trinity in the baptismal formula of the New Testament (Matt. 28:19). The teaching of Jesus, Peter, and Paul formed the basis of the doctrine taught and believed in the early church and each of these recognized the deity of the Holy Spirit.

Even in the Old Testament, where the Trinity is not as clearly taught as in the New Testament, the Holy Spirit is identified as God. Jeremiah revealed that the new covenant came from the "Lord [Jchovah]" (Jer. 31:31), but the writer to the Hebrews identified the same as from "the Holy Ghost" (Heb. 10:15). Apparently the name Yahweh was used sometimes in the Old Testament to identify the Holy Spirit. The same thing seems to have happened in Isaiah's life. Isaiah "heard the voice of the Lord" (Isa. 6:8ff.). John identified the one on the throne as Christ (John 12:41), but Paul identified the voice as "the Holy Ghost" (Acts 28:25ff.).

Attributes. Both the absolute and comparative attributes of God are possessed by the Holy Spirit. His holiness and justice are identified in his titles "Holy" (Ps. 51:11) and "Spirit of judgment" (Isa. 4:4). The apostle Paul spoke of "the love of the Spirit" (Rom. 15:30). The goodness of the Holy Spirit is seen in Psalm 143:10. Jesus identified the Holy Spirit as a good gift from God (Luke 11:13).

The comparative attributes of God, omniscience, omnipotence, and omnipresence, are also attributed to the Holy Spirit. His omnipotence is seen in his ability to accomplish

what could not be otherwise accomplished. Zerubbabel recognized the work of God was done "Not by might, nor by
power, but by my spirit, saith the Lord of hosts" (Zech. 4:6).
David recognized the omnipresence of the Holy Spirit when
he asked, "Whither shall I go from thy spirit? or whither shall
I flee from thy presence?" (Ps. 139:7). Paul taught that the
Scriptures could not be understood without the aid of the
omniscient Spirit of God (1 Cor. 2:10-16). The degree of the
omniscience of the Holy Spirit is seen in the statement "the
foolishness of God is wiser than men" (1 Cor. 1:25).

Work. The Holy Spirit accomplishes the work of God, demonstrating his deity. At creation, "the Spirit of God moved upon
the face of the waters" (Gen. 1:2; also Job 26:13; 33:4; Ps.
104:30). The Holy Spirit is also active in the work of regeneration. "Jesus answered, Verily, verily, I say unto thee, Except
a man be born of water and of the Spirit, he cannot enter into
the kingdom of God" (John 3:5). Both Peter and Paul saw the
Holy Spirit involved in the work of sanctification and spoke
of the "sanctification of the Spirit" (1 Pet. 1:2; 2 Thess. 2:13).

The Holy Spirit was involved in much of the work of God
during the life and ministry of Christ. As we saw earlier, he
was involved in the virgin birth of Christ (Luke 1:35). The
ministry of Christ began with the descent of the Holy Spirit
upon him (Matt. 3:16) and continued by the presence of the
Holy Spirit on him (Luke 4:14, 15). He was "declared to be
the Son of God with power, according to the spirit of holiness, by the resurrection from the dead" (Rom. 1:4). Even as
Christ prays for us in heaven today (Heb. 7:25), so "the Spirit
itself maketh intercession for us with groanings which cannot be uttered" (Rom. 8:26).

An additional work of the Holy Spirit relates to the Scriptures. The Scriptures were written by "holy men of God
[who] spake as they were moved by the Holy Ghost" (2 Pet.
1:21). As men wrote the Word of God, they did so as the Holy
Spirit guided them and gave them the message from God, so
they made no mistakes (John 16:13). The Holy Spirit who inspired Scripture uses Scripture today to "reprove the world
of sin, and of righteousness, and of judgment" (John 16:8).

For the Christian, the Holy Spirit has a ministry whereby he helps us understand the Bible. "Now we have received, not the spirit of the world, but the spirit which is of God; that we might know the things that are freely given to us of God" (1 Cor. 2:12).

CONCLUSION

Paul told the Romans, "For as many as are led by the Spirit of God, they are the sons of God" (Rom. 8:14). A characteristic of a Christian's life should be his willingness to follow the leading of the Holy Spirit (Gal. 5:25). Because he is a person, the Holy Spirit is able to lead, guide, and direct in our lives. Because he is God, he has a supernatural ability to help us overcome our temptations and successfully serve the Lord. Because he is a person, the Holy Spirit can be followed. Because he is God, he must be followed.

DAILY READINGS

☐Monday: John 14:15-31   ☐Tuesday: John 16:1-15
☐Wednesday: Romans 8:1-17   ☐Thursday: Romans 8:18-39   ☐Friday: Acts 5:1-11   ☐Saturday: Galatians 4:17-32   ☐Sunday: Acts 15:13-29

TWENTY-FIVE
THE PRESENT MINISTRY
OF THE HOLY SPIRIT

For as many as are led by the Spirit of God, they are the sons of God. Romans 8:14

INTRODUCTION

The Holy Spirit has many ministries. Before a person is saved, the Holy Spirit convicts of sin and brings the person to Jesus Christ. At salvation, the Holy Spirit works in the person's heart to regenerate the sinner and to give a new nature so that the believer experiences a new life. The Holy Spirit also indwells those who yield to God. The Spirit works through the Christian by means of spiritual gifts to produce the fruit of the Spirit. The Holy Spirit also works in the believers' behalf in heaven. He gives the Christian a new standing in Christ and seals a guarantee of eternal life. The Holy Spirit lives in every Christian and his presence becomes the channel through which God makes the Christian holy and spiritual.

Those who seek the filling of the Holy Spirit will receive power for Christian service. Dwight L. Moody had such an experience of the fullness of the Holy Spirit and saw God use him to accomplish more than he had previously done. "One day in New York—what a day! I cannot describe it! I seldom refer to it! It is almost too sacred to name! I can only say God revealed Himself to me! I had such an experience of love that I had to ask Him to stay His hand! I went to preaching again. The sermons were no different. I did not present any new truth. Yet hundreds were converted. I would not be back where I was before that blessed experience if you would give me Glasgow!"

We should study the biblical principles of how God works and examine the great men in our heritage so we can have the same power today. The Holy Spirit that used Peter on the day of Pentecost and Moody in the last century, is the same Holy Spirit that will work in us today. God's will for us may not be as an evangelist like Dwight L. Moody. But for whatever task, and however mundane, God desires that we yield ourselves to him (Rom. 6:13) so that he can use us fully.

As we come to study the present ministry of the Holy Spirit, we must remember that there are many false teachings regarding his ministry. Some teach that a Christian's sin nature can be eliminated by the baptism of the Holy Spirit. Others teach that speaking in tongues by the power of the Holy Spirit is a gift to be universally sought. A systematic study of the present ministry of the Holy Spirit will ground the believer in truth, and if this is done well, he will not become involved in contemporary false teachings and practices.

THE HOLY SPIRIT IN THE WORLD

The Holy Spirit is active in the world today. Though at times we may wonder if anything is going right and we may think the world is in total chaos, things are never as bad as they would be if the Holy Spirit were removed from the world. The Holy Spirit is working in reproving the world so people will become Christians, and he is restraining the power of sin in the world.

Reproof. Concerning the Holy Spirit, Jesus taught, "And when he is come, he will reprove the world of sin, and of righteousness, and of judgment" (John 16:8). The Holy Spirit today is actively reproving, or convicting, in the world. The terms "reprove," "convict," and "illuminate" all have similar meanings. These terms speak of the work of the Holy Spirit in setting forth the truth and causing a person to see it as such. Jesus identified at least three areas in which the Holy Spirit could convict a person in the world. This does not necessarily mean a person will respond positively to the gospel and accept the truth, but that the Holy Spirit will cause a person to see the truth.

The Holy Spirit will convict of sin. The sin which keeps people out of heaven is unbelief. "He that believeth on him is not condemned: but he that believeth not is condemned already, because he hath not believed in the name of the only begotten Son of God" (John 3:18). Of course, all sin can be forgiven but sin is not forgiven apart from faith. "But without faith it is impossible to please him; for he that cometh to God must believe that he is, and that he is a rewarder of them that diligently seek him" (Heb. 11:6). When a man violates the law of God, he has attacked the character of God. The Holy Spirit convicts "of sin, because they believe not on me [Jesus]" (John 16:9).

The Holy Spirit convicts concerning righteousness. When Paul described the process in which an individual or society degenerates into gross immorality, he identified the starting point of the downward cycle as "unrighteousness of men, who hold the truth in unrighteousness" (Rom. 1:18). When Jesus spoke of righteousness, he was not referring to the good works or moral codes of men. He was speaking of the righteousness of God.

When Jesus was among men, he stood as an example and reflection of the righteousness of God. His sinless life convicted men who saw him of their own unrighteousness. When the religious leaders of Jerusalem brought a woman caught in the act of adultery, Jesus responded, "He that is without sin among you, let him first cast a stone at her" (John 8:7). That statement brought conviction to the accusers (John 8:9).

Now that Jesus has returned to heaven, the Holy Spirit convicts "of righteousness, because I [Jesus] go to my Father, and ye see me no more" (John 16:10). It is the Holy Spirit who today causes men to see themselves in relation to the righteousness of God. When that occurs, like Isaiah, men see

themselves as "[men] of unclean lips, and dwell in the midst
of a people of unclean lips; for [our] eyes have seen the King,
the Lord of hosts" (Isa. 6:5).

The Holy Spirit convicts today in terms of "judgment,
because the prince of this world is judged" (John 16:11).
When Jesus died on the cross, one of his last statements was,
"It is finished" (John 19:30). That victorious pronunciation
marked the sealing of a victory in a battle which began in the
Garden of Eden. At the fall of man, God promised one who
would win the battle over the serpent and his seed (Gen.
3:15). This struggle continued through the years and
continues today. When Jesus was about to leave his disciples
for the cross, he said, "Be of good cheer; I have overcome the
world" (John 16:33). Though the struggle between God and
the devil has continued since then, the victory is secure. The
Holy Spirit causes men to see that the devil has been judged
and their sin will also be judged if they continue in it.

Oftentimes it is our tendency to classify certain sins as
more evil than other sins. Depending upon cultural values,
some sins may be more acceptable than others in the world,
but all sin is repulsive to God. The sins we may choose to
identify in our soul-winning efforts may not be committed by
all people. For example, not everyone lies, cheats, steals, or
hates, but everyone apart from Christ is guilty of the sin of
unbelief and unrighteousness. The Holy Spirit convicts men
of the sins of which they are guilty and "causes them to see"
that their sin already has been judged. In this way he shows
men their need of a Savior and draws them to the place of
salvation.

Restraint. A second major ministry of the Holy Spirit in the
world today is that of restraint. The discouraging reports of
increasing crime in our cities may make it hard to believe,
but things are not as bad today as they could be.

On the day of Pentecost, the age of the Holy Spirit was
instituted and will remain until Christ returns. During this
period of time, his presence prevents the complete
corruption of the world. Sometimes a Christian can have a
similar effect on the unsaved with whom he works. When the
Christian is not there, the non-Christian may enjoy off-color
stories or curse when speaking, but when the Christian is

there, the non-Christian does not feel comfortable in his sin. A man began attending church and was saved in a matter of days after a preacher of the gospel saw him driving a beer truck and waved at him. As God can use our presence to restrain others in their sinful life-style, so the Holy Spirit restrains the devil and the fallen angels of hell in their efforts to totally corrupt the world.

THE HOLY SPIRIT IN SALVATION

The moment a person is saved, a number of things take place in his life. He is born again, indwelt by the Holy Spirit, baptized by the Holy Spirit into the body of Christ, sealed with the Spirit, and a host of other things almost too numerous to list. Much of this is accomplished by the Holy Spirit. Many times a person will not be totally aware of all that takes place when he is saved until years later, but these things happen the moment he trusts Christ as personal Savior.

Regeneration. The Greek work translated "regeneration" is used only once in the Bible as it relates to this ministry of the Holy Spirit. "Not by works of righteousness which we have done, but according to his mercy he saved us, by the washing of regeneration, and renewing of the Holy Ghost" (Titus 3:5). Jesus told Nicodemus, "Except a man be born of water and of the Spirit, he cannot enter into the kingdom of God" (John 3:5). Regeneration is that work of the Spirit of God whereby men are given God's life and God's nature and made a part of the family of God. Occurring at the moment of conversion, it lasts a lifetime and for eternity to follow. Jesus said, "He that heareth my word, and believeth on him that sent me, hath everlasting life, and shall not come into condemnation, but is passed from death unto life" (John 5:24). This passing "from death unto life" is perhaps the chief feature of regeneration.

Indwelling. One of the purposes of God since the beginning was to dwell with man and enjoy fellowship with him. In the Garden of Eden, God would come to walk with Adam and talk with him. After the fall, God spoke with various men to enjoy their fellowship. When men failed to live for God even after the Flood, God established a unique relation with the heads of the patriarchal families. Later on Mount Sinai, he gave Moses the plans for the tabernacle which served as "the dwelling place of God's glory." When the tabernacle was replaced with a temple, the glory of the Lord moved into that place where men could meet their God. During the life of Christ, God's desire to dwell with men was fulfilled when "the Word was made flesh, and dwelt among us" (John 1:14). Today, God dwells by his Holy Spirit in the bodies of those who have been redeemed.

"Know ye not that your body is the temple of the Holy Ghost which is in you, which ye have of God, and ye are not your own?" (1 Cor. 6:19). Our human bodies have become temples to house the Holy Spirit. A realization of this truth will assist us in our efforts to properly care for our physical bodies. It will also help to keep us spiritually pure and clean. Within the context of the apostle's question, he is discussing morality. Even if a man had no concern about engaging in immoral activity, the thought of involving "the temple of God" in such a practice should help prevent the progress of sin. When we realize we are never alone but that the Holy Spirit is always with us, even present inside, we will be more cautious in our efforts to live for God.

Baptism. John the Baptist, after witnessing the descent of the Holy Spirit as a dove at the baptism of Jesus, recorded these words: "He that sent me to baptize with water, the same said unto me, Upon whom thou shalt see the Spirit descending, and remaining on him, the same is he which baptizeth with the Holy Ghost" (John 1:33).

Later Jesus promised his disciples, "Ye shall be baptized with the Holy Ghost not many days from now" (Acts 1:5). On the day of Pentecost, the disciples had a number of experiences involving the Holy Spirit, including the baptism of the Holy Spirit. Some Christians today have confused some of the facts recorded in Acts 2 and, as a result, they do not fully realize what the Holy Spirit did for them at their conversion. A key to clearing up this confusion is to understand the difference between the terms "baptism" and "fullness."

Baptism means to immerse or totally surround something. Fullness, on the other hand, refers to placing something within another. It can carry with it the idea of control. On the day of Pentecost, the group in the upper room were both baptized and filled with the Holy Spirit. At conversion the person is baptized or placed into Jesus Christ, "For by one spirit are we all baptized into one body" (1 Cor. 12:13). Then there is the filling of the Spirit which Paul commands for Christians. "But be filled with the Spirit" (Eph. 5:18). The baptism of the Spirit is our new position in Jesus Christ and the filling of the Spirit is his power working through us in Christian service.

Sealing. The Bible also teaches that Christians are sealed by the Holy Spirit. "Ye were sealed with that Holy Spirit of promise, who is the earnest of our inheritance until the redemption of the purchased possession" (Eph. 1:13, 14).

When a man and woman agree to marry, it is customary in our culture for the man to give the woman an engagement ring as a symbol of his commitment to her. Paul was drawing on a similar custom of the first century to explain this aspect of the ministry of the Holy Spirit in salvation. When we are born again, we immediately become heirs to all God has promised us. God gives us the Holy Spirit as a down payment of his commitment to someday give us all the other things he has promised. By way of application, it is important that we "grieve not the Holy Spirit of God, by whom [we] are sealed unto the day of redemption" (Eph. 4:30).

THE HOLY SPIRIT IN THE CHRISTIAN LIFE

The ministry of the Holy Spirit in our lives does not end at conversion, but continues beyond. He fills Christians as they yield to him and allow him to control their lives. He also sheds light on the Scripture, helping the Christian to learn better the things of God.

Fullness. Paul commanded the Ephesian Christians: "And be not drunk with wine, wherein is excess; but be filled with the Spirit" (Eph. 5:18). God has given men and women the opportunity to be continually filled with the Holy Spirit for effective service. Rather than allowing alcohol to control the mind of the Christian, it is God's desire that his Holy Spirit be in control. As we establish our fellowship with God through confession of sins (1 John 1:9) and yield to him (Rom. 6:13), we can be filled with the Holy Spirit as commanded in Scriptures.

Some sincere Christians today seek spectacular signs to accompany the fullness of the Holy Spirit in their life. Actually, the Bible does not teach these should be expected today. The Holy Spirit's fullness within us is primarily to produce the fruit of the Spirit (Gal. 5:22, 23). The evidence in the Book of Acts of the fullness of the Holy Spirit promised by Jesus was power to witness (Acts 1:8). On some occasions (but not every occasion) when Christians were filled with the Holy Spirit sometimes the building shook (Acts 4:31), sometimes they spoke in tongues (Acts 10:44-46), but always the gospel was preached and people were saved. These occasional outward occurrences were often tools God used at that time to accomplish the main objective of witnessing. These outward signs were similar to the purpose that miracles had in the early church, they were an objective authority for the message of God. But when God provided the full revelation of the Word of God as the authoritative message, the outward signs or authorities passed off the scene.

Illumination. Jesus promised, "When he, the Spirit of truth, is come, he will guide you into all truth" (John 16:13). While part of that promise relates primarily to the apostles who recorded Scripture by the inspiration of the Holy Spirit, it also has application to Christians today as the Holy Spirit illuminates Scripture today. The Holy Spirit has a present-day ministry in the life of a Christian, "that we might know the things that are freely given to us of God" (1 Cor. 2:12).

CONCLUSION

The Holy Spirit is still at work today. He is working to bring the unsaved to Christ. When they accept the invitation of the gospel, the Holy Spirit works to accomplish the salvation of that individual. Even after that experience, he is eager to teach us biblical truth and to lead us each step of the way. Only as we yield our rights to him is he able to fill us and use us as effectively as he desires. This is a constant challenge for each of us as we must be constantly filled with the Holy Spirit. This is not simply a convenience, but rather a command.

THE HOLY SPIRIT AND YOU		
Preconversion	*Conversion*	*Postconversion*
1. Reproof/Convict (John 16:7-10)	1. Regeneration (Titus 3:5)	1. Fullness (Eph. 5:18)
2. Restraint (2 Thess. 2:7)	2. Indwelling (1 Cor. 6:19)	2. Illumination (1 Cor. 2:12)
	3. Baptism (1 Cor. 12:13)	3. Fruit of the Spirit (Gal. 5:22, 23)
	4. Sealing (Eph. 4:30)	

DAILY READINGS

☐Monday: *Acts 2:1-13*   ☐Tuesday: *Joel 2:28-32*
☐Wednesday: *Acts 4:23-37*   ☐Thursday: *Acts 6:1-15*
☐Friday: *Acts 7:51-60*   ☐Saturday: *Acts 10:1-22*
☐Sunday: *Acts 10:24-48*

THE MINISTRY OF THE HOLY SPIRIT

Work	Scripture	Significance	How to Receive	Necessity	Feature
Regeneration	John 3:3-8 2 Cor. 5:17 Titus 3:5	rebirth sons of God	believing and receiving Christ	for eternal life	passes from death to life
Indwelling	John 14:10-17 John 7:37-39 1 Cor. 6:19, 20 1 John 4:12-15	Christ abides with us forever	believing and receiving Christ	for Spirit to work in the believer's character	secures the believer of being the son of God
Filling	Gal. 5:16 Eph. 5:18	power for service and Christian character	seeking, yielding, and confession	for victorious Christian service	life of dedication, prayer, Bible study, confession
Sealing	2 Cor. 1:22 Eph. 1:13 Eph. 4:30	the Holy Spirit guarantees the "contents" of the one he seals	automatic at salvation	for eternal security	assurance of everlasting life
Illumination	John 16:13 1 Cor. 2:12 1 John 2:27	to know the things of God in Scripture	as the Holy Spirit removes the blindness of a Christian	for understanding the Bible	guide us into all truth
Reproves	John 16:7-11	convicts the world of sin	Holy Spirit works upon Scripture to reveal sin, righteousness, and judgment	draws men to Christ	convicts sin, convinces of righteousness, judgment
Restraint	1 Thess. 2:3-10	works against sin in the world	God's mercy to people in this age	restrains the world from utter corruption	when restraint is removed so are the believers

PART SIX

THE DOCTRINE OF MAN

TWENTY-SIX
THE NATURE OF MAN

What is man, that thou art mindful of him? and the son of man, that thou visitest him? Psalm 8:4

INTRODUCTION

Both children and philosophers ask the question, "What is man?" The young boy asks the question because he wants to know what he will be like when he grows up. The philosopher asks the question because it is one of the major areas of his study. The psalmist asked, "What is man?" because he wanted to instruct his readers concerning the relationship of man to God. The psalmist answers his question by stating that man who is created in the image of God should be "mindful of him" (Ps. 8:4). Then the psalmist notes, "Thou hast made him a little lower than the angels, and hast crowned him with glory and honour" (Ps. 8:5).

Man is unique in all of creation. The Bible tells us man was created by God out of the dust of the earth (Gen. 2:7). Contrary to the hypothesis of the evolutionist, man did not come from a carbon molecule. Man is unique from animal life in that God created him a living soul and body; man thinks, feels, wills, and has self-perception and self-determination. Man is creative because he is made in the image of God the Creator. He is a reflection of God in his nature, yet because, by his own choice, man sinned, he became scarred, and the image of God was marred within him. But even after the Fall, man has an immaterial nature.

Today, man is a living soul and a living body, joined inextricably together so that both material and immaterial permanently affect the other. Man is a physical body, but he is higher than animal so that there can be no intermingling of blood, sperm, or transplanted organs. Physical man was created differently, and the difference is the soul he possesses.

THE MATERIAL PART OF MAN

Man has a body that is composed of the basic elements found in the physical universe, specifically those found in the dust of the ground from which he was created. Though it is possible for a skilled craftsman to carve the physical form of man out of a rock, and the most advanced medical technician to assemble the elements that compose a body, neither can make his creation live. Life, either material or immaterial, cannot be duplicated by man. The apostle Paul teaches there is a distinction between bodies (1 Cor. 15:39-41), and the seed that produces one kind of body will not produce a body for a different realm (1 Cor. 15:38).

DISTINCTION BETWEEN VARIOUS CREATED BODIES (1 Cor. 15:38)	
1. Human body	1 Cor. 15:39
2. Body of a beast	1 Cor. 15:39
3. Body of a fish	1 Cor. 15:39
4. Body of a bird	1 Cor. 15:39
5. Celestial bodies	1 Cor. 15:41
6. Terrestrial bodies	1 Cor. 15:40

Created body. Man was created by God on the sixth day of creation and is the grand climax of all God had accomplished in that week of miracles. The greatest aspect of man is the joining of material and immaterial, "And the Lord God formed man of the dust of the ground, and breathed into his nostrils the breath of life; and man became a living soul" (Gen. 2:7). If we were to stand before Michelangelo's David we might be moved by the high quality of its craftsmanship. How much more impressed ought we to be with God who can create not just a replica of himself, but inhabit the same body from birth through old age with a soul.

Our formation by natural birth is no less noteworthy than Adam's formation from the dust. With David we need to say, "I will praise thee; for I am fearfully and wonderfully made: marvellous are thy works; and that my soul knoweth right well" (Ps. 139:14).

Physical body. The body is not the total man; the body is only the temporary dwelling place of man. The apostle Paul discussed the various physical bodies in our world (see chart). He recognized that each body had a different purpose: "to every seed his own body. All flesh is not the same flesh: there is one kind of flesh of men, another flesh of beast, . . . another of birds. There are celestial bodies, and bodies terrestrial" (1 Cor. 15:38-40).

Body of death. Someone has observed, "From the moment we are born, we begin to die." Death was not part of the original creation of God. The philosopher called death "obscene," and he was right. Death is not natural to man; it is abnormal. Man was created to live, not die. However, death is the result of the judgment on sin. God warned Adam in the garden, "But of the tree of the knowledge of good and evil, thou shalt not eat of it: for in the day that thou eatest thereof thou shalt surely die" (Gen. 2:17). Paul recognized that death was a part of the human experience as a result of the Fall. "Wherefore, as by one man sin entered into the world, and death by sin, and so death passed upon all men, for all have sinned" (Rom. 5:12). In his struggle with the influence of sin at work in his physical life, he cried out, "Who shall deliver me from the body of this death?" (Rom. 7:24).

Body of sin. Our bodies die as a consequence of sin. Since the fall of Adam, everyone of us was born with a body that will die because of sin. As Adam was head of the race, his sin was transferred to every person. "For as by one man's disobedience many were made sinners" (Rom. 5:19). The only sinless man born of a woman was Jesus. Because he was sinless, he could become the substitute for lost sinners.

Body of humiliation. Most would agree that their physical body is not what it should be. Each year, millions of people engage in jogging and other physical fitness and recreational programs to increase the effectiveness of their bodies. Almost everyone is unsatisfied with the performance level of his body, wishing he could lose weight or occasionally gain some weight, wishing he were as agile as he was when he was younger, or as coordinated as he will be when he gets older. Not only are our bodies not what they should be, the Bible tells us they are not what they could be.

The apostle Paul identified Jesus Christ as his Savior and the one "Who shall change our vile body [literally "body of humiliation"], that it may be fashioned like unto his glorious body, according to the working by which he is able to subdue all things unto himself" (Phil. 3:21). It may be dangerous to draw too many specific conclusions from this single verse regarding our resurrection bodies, except to say they will be vastly improved over the ones we currently possess. Our present bodies are something less than God intended in creation, but our bodies will be much more useful and glorious.

Disciplined body. The evidence and consequence of sin in our physical bodies is no reason to continue some of our harmful practices. As a Christian, "Your body is the temple of the Holy Ghost, which is in you" (1 Cor 6:19). Since God lives in our bodies, we need to take greater care of them. Paul suggests a second reason for disciplining the body, that it may be more useful in the service of God. "But I keep under my body, and bring it into subjection: lest that by any means, when I have preached to others, I myself should be a castaway" (1 Cor. 9:27). This verse tells us that we should make the body serve the inner man, rather than the reverse. Many Christians have adopted a "luxurious life-style" and actually harm their bodies by not providing them with proper nutrition or opportunity for exercise. The opposite is also practiced by some through asceticism and physical abuse. It is conceivable that a Christian may harm his body by violating the basic principles of health and care. Other Christians may harm their souls by allowing the luxuries of the body to starve the effectiveness of their service for God. The key is to discipline the body.

THE IMMATERIAL PART OF MAN

Theologians often debate the question of whether man is a two-part being (dichotomy) or a three-part being (trichotomy). Some verses seem to teach that man consists only of a body and soul, while others apparently teach a third aspect to man, the spirit. Sometimes the Bible seems to use the terms "soul" and "spirit" interchangeably, yet at other times a distinction between the two is more clearly made. Part of the problem is solved when we study the verses more closely and realize there are actually two ways to look at man. When we consider the nature or makeup of man, he is a two-part being. He consists of both material (the body) and the immaterial (the soul). In activity or function, however, the body, soul, and spirit of man each has a function. The distinction and similarity of the soul and spirit can be seen in a biblical discussion of the Word of God.

"For the word of God is quick, and powerful, and sharper than any twoedged sword, piercing even to the dividing asunder of soul and spirit, and of the joints and marrow, and is a discerner of the thoughts and intents of the heart" (Heb. 4:12). The writer makes an interesting parallel. The joints and marrow are different in function, yet both are similar in that they are part of the bone structure of man. Thoughts and interests are also two distinct mental activities, yet they are similar in that they are activities of the mind. So the soul and spirit are distinct in function yet both are similar in immaterial composition. The writer is drawing five distinctions between things we may class together because of their similarity.

Soul. The Bible makes a clear distinction between the body and soul (Isa. 10:18). The term is used in the Bible to identify something that cannot be defined materially. The soul is that part of us that is life. At the creation of Adam, God "breathed into his nostrils the breath of life; and man became a living soul" (Gen. 2:7). Man did not have a soul but he became a soul, and the life-principle was the breath (Hebrew ruah: spirit) of God. As a result, we say when man no longer has breath that he is dead. When Rachel died in childbirth, the Bible described it "as her soul was in departing, (for she died)" (Gen. 35:18). In the Old Testament, the word "soul" is used to speak of the whole person (Song of Sol. 1:7).

Spirit. A further consideration of the immaterial side of man will reveal additional aspects of truth in examining the spirit of man. The term "spirit" is sometimes used in Scripture to speak of the mind (Gen. 8:1) or breath (1 Thess. 2:8).

That part of man which survives death is called the "spirit" in the Bible. When Stephen was stoned to death, the Bible identifies his spirit as departing the body when his life ended. "And they stoned Stephen, calling upon God, and saying, Lord Jesus, receive my spirit" (Acts 7:59). This principle is seen in the biblical definition of death. "For as the body without the spirit is dead, so faith without works is dead also" (James 2:28).

Relationship between the soul and spirit. The "soul" and "spirit" sometimes appear to be used interchangeably in Scripture (Gen. 41:8, and Ps. 42:6; John 12:27 and 13:21), because they both refer to the life-principle. We do not say man is a spirit, but that he has a spirit. On the other hand, we say man is a soul. The soul seems to be related to man's earthly life while the spirit relates to man's heavenly life. The knowledge of God is received by man's spirit (1 Cor. 2:2-16) and interprets it for the total man. It is this spirit in man that is related to the higher things in man. The spirit of man is definitely related to the conversion experience. The apostle Paul acknowledged "The Spirit itself [the Holy Spirit] beareth witness with our spirit, that we are the children of God" (Rom. 8:16).

Man is a unity. Man is the spiritual link between the life of God and the physical life of this planet. Man is a twofold being, possessing a dual nature in unity; a dual nature because he is spiritual and he is physical. At times these two natures seem separate but they operate as one. Man has one personality, but possesses two natures that interact on each other. First, man's physical body is regulated by the material universe—he must eat, sleep, breathe, and live in dependence upon the earth. Man's body is an essential part of his constitution, so much so that he would not be man without a body. But in the second place, man is immaterial. This is the life of God that entered man when God breathed into him and he became a living soul. Man became immortal and will live forever because God, his source, is eternal. Since man was made in the image of God who created all things, man has creative abilities, to rule the physical earth.

Man with his dual nature is a unity. The material receives direction by the immaterial, and man's spiritual nature grows in harmony with physical well-being. God created man as a well-balanced unity. Those who harm their body sear their personality.

Sin entered God's perfect world as a foreign element and violated divine law. As a result, man was ruined spiritually and will die physically. God's purpose was thwarted and man's constitution was affected. The only thing that can restore his spiritual condition is the grace of God through the message of the gospel. Man's spiritual rebirth also guarantees for him a resurrected body that will again be made like his Maker.

CONCLUSION

God made man unique from all else he created in that man consists both of the material and immaterial. Both of these aspects of man were divinely created but later scarred by sin. As the creation of God, they must be appreciated and respected for what they are. The influence of sin on our body and soul may be lessened when we discipline ourselves to work with the Holy Spirit. What we are physically is not only a result of the creation and Fall of man, but what we build upon the foundation that is given to us. What we shall be physically in the next life is a product of what God will do for us and in us.

DAILY READINGS

□Monday: *Psalm 8*   □Tuesday: *1 Corinthians 15:35-50*
□Wednesday: *Psalm 42*   □Thursday: *Matthew 5:1-12*
□Friday: *Philippians 2:1-5*   □Saturday: *Philippians 2:1-8*
□Sunday: *1 Corinthians 2:2-16*

TWENTY-SEVEN
THE FREEDOM OF MAN

And God said, Let us make man in our image, after our likeness: and let them have dominion over the fish of the sea, and over the fowl of the air, and over the cattle, and over all the earth, and over every creeping thing that creepeth upon the earth. Genesis 1:26

INTRODUCTION

Freedom is a thirst born in the heart of man, for history has shown that slaves will rebel and even die for freedom. The inalienable drive of man is for freedom—political, social, religious, and intellectual. When a person is in bondage, lacking any of these freedoms, he is not living according to God's expectations.

A famous man once cried, "Born free, but everywhere men are in chains." Rousseau's statement referred to law and government, but could have a broader application to spiritual liberty. Why do some rebel for their freedom, and why do others fight for the freedom of slaves? Because freedom first existed in the heart of God and man was created free because he was created in the image of God and with the nature of God. "God said, Let us make man in our image, after our likeness." Freedom for man means he has the power of spontaneous self-determination. The Westminster Confession reads: "God has indued the will of man with that natural liberty that is neither forced, nor by any absolute necessity of nature determined, to good or evil." The freedom of man cannot be understood apart from understanding how man was created in the image and likeness of God. And with man's freedom, he was given dominion over the animal and vegetable realm of creation.

While it is natural for people to seek their God-given liberty, the history of political revolutions demonstrates that they often replace one restrictive government with another usually more totalitarian than the former. Man would be far more successful in attaining greater personal liberty if he sought to reestablish the original image and likeness of God in his heart, rather than making his priority the search for political freedom. When God created man in his image and likeness, man was given freedom, with one limitation, and that was he was personally responsible to God alone. Man failed the test that centered on his freedom by rebelling against God. Immediately upon the entrance of sin into the human race, the liberties of man were restricted. Someday, the original image and likeness of God may be again personified in our nature and we will enjoy eternal freedom in heaven.

THE CREATED IMAGE AND LIKENESS

One of the principles by which God governs his universe is the law "like begets like," as seen in the verse "after his kind" (Gen. 1:12, 21, 24, 25). God created various forms of animal and plant life, commanding them to reproduce themselves after their own kind. When God created man he continued the same principle. God highlighted his creation with a representation and analogy of himself (Gen. 1:26). In a very real sense, man was not just another catalog selection of possible life forms in the mind of God, but rather, man is a representation of God himself. This is what Luke communicated when he called "Adam, the son of God" (Luke 3:38).

The image of God. The word "image" appears only thirty-four times in the Old Testament and twenty-three times in the New. The expression "image of God" is used primarily in reference to man, but it is also used to speak of idols, statues, and portraits. An image is a representation or replica of one person or thing by another. When Jesus asked his listeners whose "image" was on the coin (Matt. 22:20), they all understood him. When one looks at an image in the mirror, he sees an optical counterpart of himself. An image is something that is similar, with the same properties, but not necessarily identical.

THE USE OF "IMAGE" IN SCRIPTURE
1. Of man in the image of God—1 Cor. 11:7
2. Of Christ in the image of God—2 Cor. 4:4
3. Of man in the image of Christ—Rom. 8:20
4. Of idols as images of God—Rom. 1:23

The likeness of God. While some theologians do not distinguish between the terms "image" and "likeness," we think that words are important in Scripture and there is a distinction between them. The term "likeness" is used throughout Scripture in the sense of comparison or analogy. In our English language we may use the word "like" to make comparisons, as a child may look or act like his parent. A scene in one city may look like a similar scene in another city.

This idea of comparison is seen in the way Bible translators have translated the word in the original language. It is translated "likeness" twenty-two times, and also on occasion translated "fashion," "manner," "similitude," "like," "like as," "shape," and "made like to." The following chart identifies three truths in the New Testament concerning likeness.

THE USE OF "LIKENESS" IN THE NEW TESTAMENT
1. Of Adam's sin—Rom. 5:14
2. Of the death, burial, and resurrection of Christ—Rom. 6:5
3. Of Christ in human flesh—Phil. 2:7

The freedom of man. The best way to describe the original freedom of man at creation would be "freedom minus one"— he was free to do everything except that he could not eat of the fruit of certain trees in the garden. The idea of unlimited freedom is a misnomer. If everyone was completely free to accomplish his own desire, without any restrictions, he could not maintain his liberty because of his incomplete wisdom, power, or self-restraint. At creation, Adam was given the fewest restrictions possible. For his positive restrictions, man was placed in a garden and commanded to keep it (Gen. 2:15). He was told to name the animals (Gen. 2:19). Because man was created in the image and likeness of God, he was also given dominion over the rest of creation (Gen. 1:26). Man was given only one negative restriction, "And the Lord God commanded the man, saying, Of every tree of the garden thou mayest freely eat: But of the tree of the knowledge of good and evil, thou shalt not eat of it; for in the day that thou eatest thereof thou shalt surely die" (Gen. 2:16, 17).

The only other direction God gave man was to reproduce and fill the earth (Gen. 1:28). This is as close to "unlimited freedom" as anyone can have. Always, when man accepts personal liberty, he accepts personal responsibility. Adam had liberty to eat of the garden, but he also had responsibility to care for it. He was given both the responsibility of naming the animals and also dominion over them. This balance of personal liberty and responsibility was perfectly characterized in Adam before the Fall.

THE LOSS IN THE FALL

With the introduction of sin into the human race, the image and likeness of God was marred. While the image of God in man was not totally destroyed, there are some apparent marks remaining in every man, but not the same as Adam knew.

Man did not lose God's image completely when he sinned. When God prohibited one human from murdering another human, the basis was that man is made in the image of God (Gen. 9:6), and that prohibition continues to this day.

God hates the sin of idolatry so much that the first commandment prohibits worship of any other God and the second commandment prohibits idolatry. Why do these prohibitions receive more priority than prohibitions against moral sins? Because in worshiping idols, man becomes "a little god." Just as God makes man in his image, so man in turn makes an idol (the word "idol" means image) in his image. Then, instead of trying to get the idol to worship man, the human falls on his face to the "image." This is repulsive to God because he wants man to worship him.

Since man would not become like God, nor worship him, Christ was made in the "likeness of men" (Phil. 2:7). To remedy man's failure, Christ, "the image of the invisible God" (Col. 1:15), took human flesh and personified the image and likeness expected of Adam. In doing so, Christ made it possible for man to one day assume the image of God. There are at least three aspects to the image and likeness of God that were lost in the Fall of man.

Spiritual likeness. When man was created, he was created in innocence. He did not have an inner desire to rebel against God or to be disobedient to God's commands. Man learned to rebel experientially. Man was given freedom to obey the commands of God, therefore, it is reasonable to assume God was aware of the possibility of sin and rebellion. In the garden, the serpent promised Adam and Eve the possibility of gaining further knowledge to make them even more like God. "For God doth know that in the day ye eat thereof, then your eyes shall be opened, and ye shall be as gods [literally, God], knowing good and evil" (Gen. 3:5). With the violation of the law of God by Adam, sin entered the human race. The serpent was only half right. Adam and Eve were aware of the knowledge of sin experientially and all the consequences of it (Gen 3:10). They did not become more like God. In their innocence, they were spiritually alive. Now, the existence of a sin nature so hinders spiritual likeness with God that man's former fellowship with God cannot be regained apart from justification. "For as by one man's disobedience many were made sinners, so by the obedience of one shall many be made righteous" (Rom. 5:19). The means of being made right with God is the application of the work of Christ to our lives by faith. "Therefore, being justified by faith, we have peace with God through our Lord Jesus Christ" (Rom. 5:1).

Character likeness. A second aspect of the likeness of God that we lost in the Fall was our character likeness. Before the

Fall, man was inclined to perform the will of God. We have no way of knowing how long Adam and Eve remained in the garden before they sinned, except that it must have included at least the day of creation and the Sabbath day of rest. It may be that several other days were also involved. Adam was given various responsibilities before the Fall, and as we consider what he did compared with our present responsibilities, we begin to understand how his character was changed. Before the Fall, man reflected the character of God; he had holiness, although it was "unconfirmed holiness."

In the incarnation, God became like man, that men might become like God. The apostle Paul acknowledged that our nature would be transformed like Christ. "For whom he did foreknow, he also did predestinate to be conformed to the image of his Son, that he might be the firstborn among many brethren" (Rom. 8:29). Paul later challenged the Romans in the same epistle, "And be not conformed to this world: but be ye transformed by the renewing of your mind, that ye may prove what is that good, and acceptable, and perfect, will of God" (Rom. 12:2). We can regain a character like God through sanctification. Unlike the new birth, this is not an instantaneous experience but rather a continual process in the Christian life. But then one day the process will be completed, "We shall be like him, for we shall see him as he is" (1 John 3:2).

Physical likeness. No one is certain what Jesus looked like physically after his resurrection, but if we knew, we would have some idea of what Adam may have been like and what we shall be like someday. The one physical attribute that was lost at the Fall was eternal physical life on this earth. God promised, "In the day that thou eatest thereof thou shalt surely die" (Gen. 2:17). Since sin entered the human race, we have been plagued with death (Rom. 5:12). We must live with the sting of death until the return of Christ. At that time, "In a moment, in the twinkling of an eye, at the last trump: for the trumpet shall sound, and the dead shall be raised incorruptible, and we shall be changed. For this corruptible must put on incorruption, and this mortal must put on immortality" (1 Cor. 15:52, 53). Then we shall be like Jesus, restored in the original image and likeness of God.

THE LOST LIKENESS OF GOD		
Likeness	*Regained through*	*How*
1. Spiritual likeness	Justification	Instantaneous experience at conversion
2. Character likeness	Sanctification	Continuous process in the Christian life
3. Physical likeness to Christ	Glorification	Instantaneous experience at the resurrection or rapture

PRACTICAL APPLICATION OF FREEDOM

Freedom means we are responsible for where we spend eternity. The Bible teaches that man is totally depraved. That means that every part of his life is infected with sin, which, like cancer, has influenced the five senses, the bodily functions, the walk, speech, and thought processes of man. Depravity means every aspect of man is influenced by sin and as a result all are condemned. Total depravity means there is nothing a person can do to save himself or gain merit before God.

But total depravity does not mean that every person is outwardly as sinful as he could be. Some live "moral" lives, while others live evil lives, but such persons, who have rejected salvation, gain no merit before God.

Total depravity does not mean that a person cannot respond to the gospel. "Total depravity" does not mean total inability. The doctrine of freedom teaches that every person in whom the Holy Spirit brings enlightenment has the freedom to receive Jesus Christ and be saved. God offers salvation to all because of what Christ did. God will judge all who do not respond to the Holy Spirit's urging to receive Jesus Christ by faith.

Freedom means we are responsible for our daily lives. Wrong ideas about human responsibilities keep many believers from growing in Jesus Christ. Some blame their lack of joy or spirituality on someone else, while others just sit in a spiritual rocking chair, waiting for God to do all the work in their lives. The Bible teaches that freedom coincides with responsibility. A Christian is responsible to read the Scripture and claim the blessings of God. The Christian is responsible to witness, to be a responsible person (whether single or married), and to provide for his earthly needs. Man has the freedom to accept his responsibility to grow in Christ. But freedom to others is followed by failure because they reject their spiritual resources of God. And those who make unwise choices for their lives will be judged when they stand before Christ.

Freedom unlocks vast possibilities. Man is the greatest potential on earth. He has been given the freedom to subdue the whole earthly creation within the bounds God sets, as we see exercised at the tower of Babel (Gen. 10). We have seen man walk on the moon and split the atom. Man, the magnificent creation of God, is reflective of God the Creator. Man's freedom is his greatest attribute, but when he makes himself equal with God, or even tries to supplant God as man did at Babel, then his freedom leads to the bondage of ignorance and sin.

Freedom should be reflected in government. History has witnessed every type of slavery possible. People have been mental, physical, emotional, and religious slaves. But every time one person enslaves another, the basic drive for freedom is rekindled in the heart of the slave, because a person must have liberty, an attribute he gets from God.

CONCLUSION

The apostle John recognized that some day every Christian would again realize the image and likeness of God in his life. He also realized that that hope should affect the way we live. "And every man that hath this hope in him purifieth himself, even as he is pure" (1 John 3:3). If we know Jesus Christ as our personal Savior, some day we will be like him for eternity (1 John 3:2). If this is so, we need to be seeking continuously to become more like Jesus today. "But we all, with open face beholding as in a glass the glory of the Lord, are changed into the same image from glory to glory, even as by the Spirit of the Lord" (2 Cor. 3:18).

DAILY READINGS

☐Monday: *Genesis 1:24-31*   ☐Tuesday: *Romans 8:18-30*
☐Wednesday: *1 Corinthians 11:1-16*   ☐Thursday: *Philippians 2:5-12*   ☐Friday: *Genesis 5:1, 2; 9:1-7*
☐Saturday: *Romans 12:1-16*   ☐Sunday: *1 John 2:28-3:3*

TWENTY-EIGHT
THE PERSONALITY OF MAN

Keep thy heart with all diligence; for out of it are the issues of life. Proverbs 4:23

INTRODUCTION

When Professor Higgins first discovered crude Lisa Doolittle on a London street, he was convinced that she could fit into England's high society with proper education. He recognized that the real person within is not dependent upon outward appearances, mannerisms, and dialects. Though the story of *My Fair Lady* was fictional, it demonstrated the ability of a person to overcome insurmountable obstacles, to accomplish preconceived dreams.

A person has the power to accumulate knowledge, then interpret it, and draw conclusions that make the thinking man more independent than when the process began. A person is independent to draw insight, foresight, and hindsight, he can abstract an idea into principles, formulas, theories, or judgments. Hence, a person can be educated, not just trained as an animal.

A person can recognize, remember, and recall words, then interpret them in an hitherto unusual manner so that he creates, invents, or composes. A person can raise himself above his teachers or his previous level of attainment. A person can create beauty, harmony, or passion through pictures, music, literature, or the arts. A person can determine a goal and pursue it. He can use fire, or create tools for his work. A person has an innate sense of right and wrong, so that he suffers agony of conscience when his conscience is violated by others or himself. A person wonders about life after death, and is inquisitive for explanations of the causes of life that he cannot understand.

The inner person is so important that it becomes the criterion by which God judges each one. Saul had failed to be faithful to God as king of Israel and had to be replaced. The Lord sent Samuel to Bethlehem to anoint one of the sons of Jesse to the task but gave the aging judge some special instructions. "But the Lord said unto Samuel, Look not on his countenance, or on the height of his stature; because I have refused him: for the Lord seeth not as man seeth; for man looketh on the outward appearance, but the Lord looketh on the heart" (1 Sam. 16:7). In this verse the heart does not mean the physical organ but the inner man, specifically, the person. As the sons of Jesse passed before Samuel, it was David, the most unlikely, who was named as heir to the throne. While personnel managers today may be concerned with appearance, dress, health, and other matters when hiring employees, God's approval depends upon his evaluation of the inner man.

Understanding the heart or inner man is crucial in light of the contemporary study of the makeup of man. The Bible is not a psychology textbook, but when it speaks to this subject, it is authoritative. What the Bible has to say about the heart of man sheds light on the psychological makeup and functions of man.

In the Old Testament the term "heart" is used essentially to refer to a physical organ. It is the center of the circulatory system that distributes the blood of the body. The term "heart" is never used in the New Testament to denote the whole physical man, but it was a natural transition to bring the term "heart" into the spiritual world. The New Testament sees the heart figuratively as the center of the person or spiritual life. In every instance but one, the term "heart" in the New Testament signifies the inner man; the seat of intel-

lect, emotions, will, and moral consciousness. The heart is
the personality which has that extraordinary ability to perceive oneself. We say it is the seat of conscious life. Whether
viewed in one aspect or as a whole, the heart is pictured as
the fountainhead of life.

Key to understanding the personality of man is understanding what the Bible teaches about the heart. The heart is
the central seat and organ of man's conscious life in its
moral, intellectual, volitional, and emotional aspects. The
normal child is born with these embryonic abilities. Naturally, none of these areas are fully developed but, with the gift
of life, God also gives the responsibility to develop the infant
into a mature adult.

THE INTELLECT OF MAN

The word "brain" is not used in Scripture, although its intellectual function is surely there. The word "heart" is the immaterial term that conveys the intellectual activities of man.
The brain is the physical organ through which this phenomenon operates.

A number of specific intellectual activities are identified as
belonging to the heart. The absence of one or more of these
activities or even the severe limitation of any of these, as in
the case of a retarded individual, does not make a person less
of a person. Each person has some intellectual ability to a
greater or lesser degree than another. The tremendous intellectual capacity is part of God's design for the uniqueness of
every individual because man is created in the image of God
who has all wisdom. The following chart identifies some of
these intellectual activities ascribed to the heart in Scriptures.

THE INTELLECTUAL ACTIVITIES OF THE HEART	
1. Thinking	Heb. 8:10
2. Planning	Heb. 4:12
3. Memory	Luke 2:19
4. Perception	Matt. 13:14
5. Reasoning	Mark 2:8

Thinking. Thinking is a mental process by which we evaluate and interpret what we have seen, heard, experienced, or otherwise learned. When Paul promised the Philippians, "The peace of God, which passeth all understanding, shall keep your hearts and minds through Christ Jesus" (Phil. 4:7), he attached a key list of eight attributes by which they were to evaluate the content of their thinking (Phil. 4:8). God promised in the new covenant, "I will put my law in their inward parts, and write it in their hearts" (Jer. 31:33; cf. Heb. 8:10). The writer of Hebrews also ascribed thought patterns to the heart (Heb. 4:12).

Planning. The ability to plan grows out of dreams and desires, and at other times out of necessity or self-preservation. Planning is one of the greatest abilities of man because it involves the immaterial man. Planning involves the ability to develop a strategy by which to accomplish the perceived goals that may arise from emotions, self-perception, or self-preservation. Since plans would be useless unless man had ability to decide to carry them out, they are based on the total inner man. It is again the writer to the Hebrews who teaches us the heart is the instrument for planning: "For the word of God is quick. . . and is a discerner of the thoughts and intents of the heart" (Heb. 4:12).

Memory. The ability to recall the past is an intellectual activity springing from the intellect or heart. A number of unusual things occurred at the birth of Christ. While most people only observed them, "Mary kept all these things, and pondered them in her heart" (Luke 2:19). Memory is a reconsideration of a matter on a more personal and perhaps more practical level after it has occurred. David identified the heart in connection with Scripture memory. "Thy word have I hid in mine heart, that I might not sin against thee" (Ps. 119:11). When we obey the command to meditate on the Scriptures (Josh. 1:8), we are reflecting on a portion of Scripture seeking to apply it in various ways to different parts of our life. This is an activity of the heart of man.

Perception. Sometimes we will meet a special person who sees many things we fail to see. We may listen to a lecture, but when that special person listens to the same things, he picks up much more than we do. We may be looking across a meadow and see little but grass while the one standing next to us sees a groundhog, some birds, or a stick trapped in the creek. This ability to see and understand is called perception. Perception is the power to discern or interpret what we hear, see, or read, to see the connection between things. The lack of perception by religious leaders who listened to Jesus was a result of a darkened heart (Matt. 13:14).

Reasoning. Finally, the ability to weigh the evidence and make a rational and reasonable decision is an intellectual activity of the heart. When Jesus forgave the sins of a sick man, some listeners responded by thinking he was doing wrong. They knew that only God could forgive sins and therefore they reasoned that Jesus must be a blasphemer: "And immediately when Jesus perceived in his spirit that they so reasoned within themselves, he said unto them, Why reason ye these things in your hearts?" (Mark 2:8). Jesus was not critical here of the reasoning process but rather recognized it, and their ability to reason became the basis by which he condemned them. The ability to reason is a God-given ability. Used properly, God is glorified, but used falsely, man harms himself.

THE EMOTIONS

Often we speak of the heart as the emotional seat of man. When two people fall in love, they might say, "I love you with all my heart." A valentine heart is the symbol of persons who are emotionally involved. Most people have no problem understanding the use of the word "heart" to reflect the emotional part of man.

Man is an emotional being and these emotions spring from the heart. When Jesus said, "Thou shalt love the Lord thy God with all thy heart" (Matt. 22:37), he identified the source of love, and later identified the opposite—hate—as springing from the heart (Matt. 15:19). When he said, "Let not your heart be troubled" (John 14:1), he recognized fear as an emotion of the heart. In the same conversation with his disciples Jesus observed, "And ye now, therefore, have sorrow; but I

will see you again, and your heart shall rejoice, and your joy
no man taketh from you" (John 16:22, also v. 6). The Bible
identifies several emotions springing from the heart.

THE EMOTIONS			
Love	Matt. 22:37	Hate	Matt. 15:19
Confidence	John 14:1	Fear	John 14:27
Joy	John 16:6	Sorrow	John 16:16
Peace	Phil. 4:7	Frustration	Ps. 131
Unity & gladness	Acts 2:46	Division & strife	1 Cor. 1:10; 3:3

THE VOLITIONAL PERSONALITY OF MAN

God has given each one a will, the ability to make decisions.
But the free will never operates alone. God has given man the
responsibility to use his intellect to examine the alternatives
of life and then the will can choose the direction of life. Also,
God has given man emotions to enrich his life and these
sometimes control his will, while at other times the will dom-
inates both intellect and feelings. God gives men intellect,
emotions, and will to determine the direction and quality of
life. Our conversion, sanctification, and relationships with
others can all be determined in part by the way these act
upon one another. But in this section we shall examine the
will or volitional aspect of man, the final ability that makes
the decisions that gives meaning to life.

Conversion. The most important decision anyone will ever
make concerns his eternal salvation. God does not force anyone to believe in him because the Lord wants the free expression of a person's trust. Jesus Christ extends an invitation to
eternal life in the form of a choice. "Verily, verily, I say unto
you, He that heareth my word, and believeth on him that sent
me, hath everlasting life, and shall not come into condemnation; but is passed from death unto life" (John 5:24). Even the
last chapter of the Bible contains an invitation to respond to
the gospel. "And the Spirit and the bride say, Come.... And
let him that is athirst come. And whosoever will, let him take
the water of life freely" (Rev. 22:17).

When the Holy Spirit is at work in a person, and the person responds to the invitation of the gospel by faith and is saved, he has responded from the heart. The person knows he is lost and he knows the gospel (intellect), then he is convicted of his sin and in love reaches out to God (emotions); this leads to a decision of salvation (will). The Bible places the process of belief in the heart (Rom. 10:9), but the soul is saved. Children go through this process when they are told to pray, "Come into my heart, Lord Jesus." Paul rejoiced in the conversion of the Romans by identifying the will in the heart, "that whereas ye were once the servants of sin, ye have obeyed from the heart that form of doctrine which was delivered you" (Rom. 6:17).

Growth in Christ. We must serve God as Christians the same way we are saved, by faith from the heart. If we are desirous of pleasing God, we must remember that "without faith it is impossible to please him: for he that cometh to God must believe that he is, and that he is a rewarder of them that diligently seek him" (Heb. 11:6). Instructing the Corinthians, Paul reminded them that a decision to give to God came from the heart. "Every man according as he purposeth in his heart, so let him give; not grudgingly, or of necessity: for God loveth a cheerful giver" (2 Cor. 9:7).

Interpersonal relations. Paul told the Ephesians how a Spirit-filled Christian ought to behave. Part of those instructions included obedience to masters on the part of servants, "in singleness of your heart, as unto Christ" (Eph. 6:5). This obedience was obviously tied to their intellectual ability, since he used logic to appeal to their will: "doing the will of God from the heart" (Eph. 6:6). The total personality of man is operative in each act of thinking, willing, and feeling. The one cannot be considered without the other, for man is a unity, as is God, in whose image he was created.

MORAL AWARENESS

The last aspect of our definition of the heart is moral awareness. Deep within man there is a consciousness of God and an idea of what is required of him by God. John wrote, "That was the true Light, which lighteth every man that cometh into the world" (John 1:9). By this he implied the light of God shines within every person. Paul recognized this phenomenon among heathen, "which shew the work of the law written in their hearts, their conscience also bearing witness, and their thoughts the mean while accusing or else excusing one another" (Rom. 2:15). The conscience of man dwells in the heart, acting as a moral regulator regarding right or wrong.

As missionaries travel to foreign cultures, they are often accused of westernizing primitive peoples. Actually the most primitive tribes are highly civilized in their own way. They have a social structure we usually do not acknowledge since it differs from our own. Their society has usually determined certain acts as socially acceptable and others worthy of punishment. This is the moral code upon which society makes laws. Even among primitive tribes that appear amoral, missionaries have found traces of moral absolutes reflected in their laws (Rom. 2:1). These are all evidences of "the works of the law written in their hearts" (Rom. 2:15), so that they have some sense of what God requires of them.

The idea implied in the word "conscience" is "a knowing with oneself." Since memory and thinking operate as a function of the heart, it is the apparent location for the conscience. The heart/personality is the place where God communicates to the individual. However, it is possible for man continually to reject the message of his conscience and render it inoperative (1 Tim. 4:2). An incapacitated consciousness of God is called a seared conscience.

CONCLUSION

The moment we entered this world as babes, we were fully equipped with a personality. Of course, that personality needed to be developed and polished, and skills had to be acquired, such as walking and thinking, before we could accomplish much. Often Christians fail to realize that God has made them unique for a unique purpose. Because we all are made in the image of God, we are unique persons with all the properties of personality. God made us this way for his glory

(Rev. 4:11) and will use us as we become available to him. We can respond to God through our intellect, emotion, and will; plus we can improve those areas of our personalities which need improving. But in contrast, we can reject God and go our own way. Also, we can misuse our abilities and allow them to degenerate. Because God has given us a choice, we can make our lives what we choose to become.

DAILY READINGS

☐Monday: 1 Samuel 16:1-13   ☐Tuesday: Philippians 4:1-9
☐Wednesday: Mark 7:14-23   ☐Thursday: Proverbs 12:1-28
☐Friday: Proverbs 23:1-35   ☐Saturday: Proverbs 4:20-5:2
☐Sunday: Matthew 15:10-20

TWENTY-NINE
THE FALL OF MAN

Wherefore, as by one man sin entered into the world, and death by sin; and so death passed upon all men, for all have sinned. Romans 5:12

INTRODUCTION

One of the most tragic days in the history of the world was when sin was introduced to humanity. Before that day, the creation was approved, as God saw that "it was very good" (Gen. 1:31). God had planted a beautiful garden, or park, with Adam and Eve the sole human residents who lived in harmonious community with nature, God, and each other. But one day all of that changed.

Satan entered the garden to tempt man to rebel against the stipulations given by God. Satan did not appear as a sinister character but rather as something with which both Adam and Eve were familiar, a serpent. In his own cunning way, Satan conversed with Eve, causing her to compromise her loyalty to God. He began by making God's demands sound extreme and then seeking to show Eve how harmless it was to eat the fruit. When she ate and shared it with Adam, the evil purpose of Satan had been accomplished.

Satan began by placing doubt in the woman's mind concerning the word of God and then brought her to the point of outright disobedience. When Eve began to entertain the thought that perhaps God was somewhat extreme and perhaps God did not understand what was best for her, she opened the door of her mind to the lie of Satan. That moment of weakness resulted in the fall of all mankind, with all its consequences.

Understanding the nature of the Fall of man is imperative to appreciate our salvation and to live the Christian life. As we realize what Christ has done in overcoming the consequences of the Fall, we will appreciate our relationship with God even more. By realizing how man fell in the beginning, we can better combat temptation when it comes in our own lives.

THE CAUSE OF THE FALL

When God began to question Adam and Eve concerning their sin (Gen. 3:11-13), they passed off the responsibility to someone else. Adam blamed Eve; she in turn blamed the serpent. But the Bible teaches that man sinned, fully aware of his actions. "Adam was not deceived" (1 Tim. 2:14). Thus the entire race fell because he deliberately chose by an act of his own will to disobey God and fulfill his own desires instead. Those desires were encouraged by the temptation of Satan, who provided the occasion for the entrance of sin into the world.

Today, temptation is one of the chief functions of Satan and his demons. Though all people are tempted differently according to their own weaknesses, Satan's temptations followed certain patterns. John spoke of temptation in three categories when he wrote, "For all that is in the world, the lust of the flesh, the lust of the eyes, and the pride of life, is not of the Father, but is of the world" (1 John 2:16). If we were to look objectively at our own lives, we would find that all temptation that causes us to sin comes from one of these three sources. Satan has a devious strategy that has been successful for evil purposes, so he has not changed it. When he tempted Adam and Eve in the garden, he appealed to all three sources of temptation. He used the same strategy when he tempted Christ. Throughout the pages of Scripture we find those who have fallen into sin as a result of one kind of temptation or another. If Jesus "was in all points tempted like as we are" (Heb. 4:15), then we can assume that we will also be tempted in one or more of these areas.

The lust of the flesh. The word "lust" means desire, so the first area of temptation had to do with the desires of the body. Satan appealed to the lust of the flesh to cause Eve to partake of the forbidden fruit. It was not until "the woman saw that the tree was good for food" (Gen. 3:6), that she ate and gave to her husband. Satan took something good, what appeared to be harmless fruit, and used it to appeal to the human desire to eat. Neither the fruit nor the desire to eat was inherently evil. Adam and Eve sinned when they disobeyed the clear command of God. Our parents violated the one prohibition: "Thou shalt not eat of it" (Gen. 2:17). Satan appealed to the same desire for food when Jesus was hungry after a forty-day fast by saying, "If thou be the Son of God, command that these stones be made bread" (Matt. 4:3). While it would not have been wrong for Jesus to eat when he was hungry, it would have been wrong for him to abuse his power to succumb to the temptation of Satan. We are tempted to sin in the same manner. Satan will try to get us to satisfy the desires of our bodies in the wrong manner. As an illustration, the physical desire for sex is a human trait that is not evil until it is satisfied in the wrong manner.

The lust of the eyes. The second area of temptation that motivated Eve to eat the fruit was "that it was pleasant to the eyes" (Gen. 3:6). A second characteristic of humanity is to have dreams or desires. Man constantly seeks to improve his surroundings and himself. Man's desire for excellence and advancement is reflective of his Creator, in whose image he was created. Therefore, the appearance of the fruit appealed to Eve's desire to have something she did not possess. Just as the lust of the flesh is not evil in itself, so it is not sinful to desire things. But sin entered the human race when man's desire was contrary to the command of God. Satan was not successful when he attempted to appeal to the "lust of the eyes" as he tempted Jesus. "Again, the devil taketh him up into an exceeding high mountain, and sheweth him all the kingdoms of the world, and the glory of them" (Matt. 4:8). Satan thought that the sight of the kingdoms would cause Jesus to yield; Jesus used the Word of God to combat temptation. Unlike Eve, Jesus could not be persuaded to doubt the integrity of the Word of God.

The pride of life. The third temptation was an appeal to the basic self-worth, self-acceptance, and self-preservation of man. Man was created as an independent/dependent being. He was created separate from God, yet an autonomous being who is dependent on God. God in his wisdom gave man the ability to protect, preserve, and perpetuate himself. Satan appeals to the basic self-interest of humanity by showing Eve a tree to be desired to make one wise. "She took of the fruit thereof, and did eat, and gave also unto her husband with her; and he did eat" (Gen. 3:6).

It seems almost ironic that Satan was able to use man's interest in self-improvement to destroy everything man desired. Again, Satan was not successful in tempting Christ. Satan quoted a psalm out of context to challenge Christ to perform an unnecessary spectacular miracle (Matt. 4:6). This direct attack on the character of Christ was to induce him to act from motives of self-interest outside the will of God. Jesus did not listen to Satan's attack. While it may have been easier to allow his angels to protect him, Jesus would ultimately and conclusively prove his deity while redeeming lost humanity through his death, burial, and resurrection. Again he was able to use Scripture to combat the devil.

HOW SATAN TEMPTED		
Strategy	*Eve* (Gen. 3:6)	*Christ* (Matt 4:1-11)
1. Lust of flesh	1. Good for food	1. Stones for bread
2. Lust of eyes	2. Pleasant to eyes	2. Glory of kingdoms
3. Pride of life	3. Desired to make one wise	3. Prove his deity with a miracle

The fact that Christ overcame temptation while our first parents gave in to it can be directly attributed to Christ's reliance on the Scriptures. Eve had indicated willingness to doubt the direct command of God. Jesus, in contrast, rested his entire defense on Scripture. To answer each temptation, he stated, "It is written" (Matt. 4:4, 7, 10).

THE CONSEQUENCES OF THE FALL

The fall of man represents far more than just the sin of one man and woman. When one throws a rock in a quiet pond, the initial splash is followed by a continuous sequence of ripples. Likewise, the Fall of man influenced the entire world and in turn affects us today. When Adam and Eve disobeyed, God judged their sin. They immediately experienced the full force of God's judgment. After they died, the consequences of their Fall have rippled throughout the human race.

Immediate results of sin. Because of the widespread involvement of various beings, many were immediately judged. These included the serpent, man, woman, and the earth itself.

When Satan tempted Eve, he was embodied in a serpent. He did not form himself like a serpent nor take on qualities of a serpent but a serpent was used as a vehicle for the tempter. Satan used an actual serpent, so God cursed the serpent for his active part in the temptation. "And the Lord God said unto the serpent, Because thou hast done this, thou art cursed above all cattle, and above every beast of the field; upon thy belly shalt thou go, and dust shalt thou eat all the days of thy life" (Gen. 3:14). The actual physical form of the serpent was changed as a consequence of the Fall. We cannot ignore the fact that most people have an unusual fear of snakes, even those that are nonpoisonous.

God also judged Adam for his sin. God introduced a new emotion into his experience—sorrow (Gen. 3:17). He was to continue to have dominion over the ground, but now he would till a cursed ground. His labor would be multiplied and he would find himself working harder and producing less. Physical death also was introduced into the human experience. "In the sweat of thy face shalt thou eat bread, till thou return unto the ground; for out of it wast thou taken: for dust thou art, and unto dust shalt thou return" (Gen. 3:19). Apparently Adam also lost the complete dominion he earlier possessed over the animals (Rom. 8:18). Man would still rule the beasts of the earth, but with far more difficulty. Some animals would attack and kill man, other animals would resist him, and still other animals would be too dumb to heed man's direction.

Eve also was cursed for her part in the Fall. "Unto the woman he said, I will greatly multiple thy sorrow and thy conception; in sorrow thou shalt bring forth children; and thy desire shall be to thy husband, and he shall rule over you" (Gen. 3:16). Eve in particular, and women in general, live with two results of the Fall. First, they would have a natural inclination to their husband which would in some occasions lead to conception. And, second, they would have increased pain in childbirth.

Long-range results of the Fall. Adam, the federal head of the human race, was also the seminal head. The word seminal implies that all life existed in Adam and that everyone existed embryonically or existed in seed within the head of the human race. Today we trace our ancestry back to Adam. We were all in the loins of Adam when he sinned, just as Levi "was yet in the loins of his father, when Melchizedec met him" (Heb. 7:10). In that sense, every member of the human race played a part in the Fall of man. When Adam sinned, we were actually sinning with him. The language of Romans 5:12 explains that we participated in Adam's sin: "As by one man sin entered the world...for that all have sinned." This includes the federal headship of Adam over the human race. In this aspect, Adam's vote for our sin is similar in comparison to a congressman who might represent us in the legislature and by his vote obligate us for certain indebtedness. It also implies we were present with him as he voted. Therefore, it is consistent that the race experiences the consequences of the Fall.

Because of the Fall, every man received a sin nature at birth. It is now more natural for man to sin than not to sin.

That sin nature results in physical death for the human race born into condemnation. The sin of Adam has infected the nature of the entire race.

Every influence that Adam passed on to humanity, Christ overcame for the race. Because there is a sin nature in every man, Christ offers a new nature to those who experience his salvation (2 Cor. 5:17). His death is a substitute for ours and through the cross the repentant sinners receive new life. Jesus claimed "that they might have life, and that they might have it more abundantly" (John 10:10). While the race is "condemned already" (John 3:18) because of Adam's sin, "There is therefore now no condemnation to them which are in Christ Jesus" (Rom. 8:1). Jesus Christ came as the last Adam (1 Cor. 15:45) to lead a new race of those who were born again into his kingdom (John 1:13; 3:3). Writing to the Romans, the apostle Paul outlined something of a comparison between Adam and Christ and their respective "races."

ROMANS 5:12-21	
Adam	*Christ*
1. Sin entered	1. Grace entered
2. Offense transferred	2. Free gift offered
3. Condemnation	3. Justification
4. Death reigns	4. Righteousness reigns
5. Disobedience	5. Obedience
6. Makes men sinners	6. Makes men righteous
7. Sin abounds	7. Grace abounds
8. Death	8. Eternal life

Sin, and all the accompanying consequences of sin, entered the human race as a result of the historic Fall of Adam in the garden of Eden. It was in another garden many years later that a group of women found an empty tomb, to learn Jesus had risen from the dead (Matt. 28:6). That accomplishment demonstrated the ability of Jesus to undo all that Adam had bound up and to provide much more than a return to Adam's innocence. The listing of Christ's accomplishments by Paul to the Romans represents only a portion of all Jesus did on the cross. God is now able to provide men with personal salvation (Heb. 7:25) and an eternal home in heaven (John 14:3). Someday the consequences of the Fall will be completely overcome and done away with. The final chapters of the Bible describe for us a world which represents a vivid parallel with the world God gave man before the Fall (cf. Gen. 1, 2 with Rev. 21, 22). Those who know Christ as Savior can look forward to a day when the Fall of man will no longer affect our lives.

CONCLUSION

That day is not yet here. We still live in a world in which the devil is engaged in tempting us to evil. We must learn to gain victory over temptation as Jesus did. Peter warns, "Be sober, be vigilant; because your adversary the devil, as a roaring lion, walketh about, seeking whom he may devour" (1 Pet. 5:8).

DAILY READINGS

☐Monday: *Romans 5:12-21*   ☐Tuesday: *Genesis 3:1-13*
☐Wednesday: *Genesis 3:14-24*   ☐Thursday: *Genesis 4:1-15*
☐Friday: *Genesis 4:16-26*   ☐Saturday: *Genesis 6:1-8*
☐Sunday: *1 Timothy 2:1-15*

THIRTY
THE NATURE OF SIN

For all have sinned, and come short of the glory of God.
Romans 3:23

INTRODUCTION

Sin has become so much a part of the human experience that most people take it for granted today. When a small boy steals cookies out of the cookie jar, most people consider him cute. But in reality he is manifesting his sinful nature. The crime about which we read in the local newspapers is evidence of sin in the world. We laugh at jokes about sin, somehow ignoring the reality of sin in our lives. Perhaps the contemporary attitude toward sin is best revealed in the terms we use to describe it.

However, not everyone has shared a flippant attitude toward sin. The famous evangelist Billy Sunday was described as a sin-hating preacher. His attitude was reflected in his sermon, "I'm against sin. I'll kick it as long as I've got a foot. I'll fight it as long as I've got a fist. I'll butt it as long as I've got a head. I'll bite it as long as I've got a tooth. When I'm old and fistless and footless and toothless, I'll gum it till I go home to glory and it goes home to perdition."

Sin is not an illusion, nor is it simply a pervasive and impersonal influence in life. People sin in deed, thought, or desire. Sin can be defined as an act or an attitude. We are all sinners because we are born in sin. Our immoral state demonstrates itself in our life through wrong attitudes and evil actions. Basically, sin is anything that is opposed to the character and will of God as revealed in his Word. The apostle Paul identified three basic kinds of sin: personal sin, the sin nature, and imputed sin. Therefore, to understand sin, we need to realize how all three stand in opposition to the nature of God.

KIND OF SIN	FACT OF SIN	PENALTY	TRANS-MISSION	REMEDY
Personal	Rom. 3:23	Loss of fellowship	None	Redemption
Sin nature	Ps. 51:5	Spiritual death	From parent to child	New nature
Imputed sin	Rom. 5:12	Physical death	From Adam to us	Imputed righteousness

PERSONAL SIN

When we compare our lives with others, we usually find a difference in the degree or number of personal sins we commit. Probably we would choose to compare ourselves with someone much worse so we might appear better. But the Bible makes it clear that "there is no difference: For all have sinned, and coming short of the glory of God" (Rom. 3:22, 23). This may seem broad, but it is also accurate. No one other than Christ has lived on earth without committing personal sin, and most have engaged in far more than one sin.

A personal sin may be a sin of commission or a sin of omission. When we choose to do something that is prohibited, we have committed a sin of commission. We commit a sin of omission when we fail to do what is required of us. If we were caught speeding on the highway, the police officer would ask to see our driver's license. As he is preparing the summons, he may notice the license has expired. Perhaps we forgot or just did not get around to renewing it. The officer would give two summons for two different types of violations. We have broken the speed law (sin of commission) and failed to renew the license (sin of omission).

Personal sin may also express itself in an act or attitude. Jesus recognized that a man's desire determines his actions. He said, "from within, out of the heart of men, proceed evil thoughts, adulteries, fornications, murders,. . . All these evil things come from within, and defile the man" (Mark 7:21, 23). Jesus applied this principle by stating that lusting after women was only a different degree of the sin of adultery (Matt. 5:27, 28) and being angry with our brother was the same kind of sin as murder (Matt. 5:21, 22). These attitudes, if allowed to harbor and grow within the mind, will lead to the outward acts of sin. Every time we perform an act, good or bad, we are usually acting out a previous thought.

When we commit acts of sin, God breaks fellowship with us. The psalmist acknowledged, "If I regard iniquity in my heart, the Lord will not hear me" (Ps. 66:18). John told the Christians in the church at Ephesus, "if we say that we have fellowship with him, and walk in darkness, we lie, and do not the truth" (1 John 1:6). That broken fellowship with God can only be restored as we confess our sins and ask God's forgiveness. "If we confess our sins, he is faithful and just to forgive us our sins, and to cleanse us from all unrighteousness" (1 John 1:9). For one who does not know Christ as Savior, forgiveness of sins comes when he places saving faith in Jesus, "In whom we have redemption through his blood, the forgiveness of sins, according to the riches of his grace" (Eph. 1:7). Personal sins are identified in a variety of ways in Scripture.

Falling short. Sin is sometimes portrayed in the Bible as "coming short of the glory of God" (Rom. 3:23). God has a holy standard of perfection that he expects everyone to meet. When we fail to meet God's standard and we are not what we should be, we have sinned. The Greek word *hustereo* means "to fall short of God's Word" or literally "to miss the mark." When an arrow does not hit the target, it falls short. When we do not perfectly keep God's law, we sin. "Be ye therefore perfect, even as your Father which is in heaven is perfect"

(Matt. 5:48). At another place, James described the sin of falling short, "Therefore to him that knoweth to do good, and doeth it not, to him it is sin" (James 4:17).

The degree by which we miss the standard is not important. We do not win first prize if we are second in a race, just as sinning once is not being perfect. Both have fallen short. Two men try to jump a river that is sixteen feet wide. One man jumped five feet and the next man jumped fifteen feet, but both fell short of the goal. Even if you try to keep God's law and sinned only once, you are as much a sinner as the one who violates God's law at will (James 2:10).

Going astray. When we wander away from that which is right, we sin. Isaiah drew a parallel between wandering sheep and ourselves as sinners. "All we like sheep have gone astray; we have turned every one to his own way; and the Lord hath laid on him the iniquity of us all" (Isa. 53:6). Part of our personal sin for which Jesus died involves straying from the law of God.

Transgression. A third expression for sin in the Bible is "transgression." This word carries the idea of overstepping the law (Ps. 51:1; Luke 15:29). Paul described a certain kind of rebellious Jew, calling him "a breaker of the law" (Rom. 2:25). Often we find ourselves guilty of a double standard. That which we might permit in our own life, we criticize in the lives of others. We may fall into the trap of boasting in some good thing we are doing, when at the same time we are transgressing another law of God. "Thou that makest thy boast of the law, through breaking the law dishonourest thou God" (Rom. 2:23).

Trespass. A fourth kind of personal sin is the trespass. When a hunter passes a "No Trespassing" sign and crosses a field not belonging to him, he may be arrested and charged with trespassing. When we trespass as sinners, we have pushed our own will into the area of divine authority. The apostle Paul recognized that God was also able to deal with this aspect of personal sin. Writing the Ephesians, he commented, "And you hath he quickened, who were dead in trespasses and sins" (Eph. 2:1). "Doing our own thing" rather than the will of God in our life is sin.

THE SIN NATURE

The word "sin" appears in the Bible in both the singular and the plural. When we read "sins" we are reading about personal sins. When the word "sin" appears in the singular, it is usually speaking of the sin nature of man. Every person is born with a sin nature. John wrote, "If we say that we have no sin [nature], we deceive ourselves, and the truth is not in us" (1 John 1:8). Paul observed that the Ephesians "were by nature the children of wrath, even as others" (Eph. 2:3). David recognized the sin nature of his own soul when he wrote, "Behold, I was shaped in iniquity; and in sin did my mother conceive me" (Ps. 51:5). This nature is universal and manifests itself to varying degrees in individuals and societies. Of an earlier society it was said, "Every imagination of the thoughts of his heart was only evil continually" (Gen. 6:5). That society was eventually destroyed in the Flood.

The sin nature affects the personality. The sin nature affects various aspects of personality. Paul observed that the sin nature could negatively influence man's mind. "And even as they did not like to retain God in their knowledge, God gave them over to a reprobate mind, to do those things which are not convenient" (Rom. 1:28). The sin nature is partially responsible for blinding man's mind and understanding so that he cannot perceive spiritual things (Eph. 5:12).

The conscience and will of some people are also affected by the sin nature. Paul identified some who had departed from the faith: "Speaking lies in hypocrisy, having their conscience seared with a hot iron" (1 Tim. 4:2). The conscience is a moral regulator to inform man of his falling from that which is right (Rom. 2:15). But the conscience can become so corrupted by sin that it is of little or no value in determining moral direction.

Even though man is born with a nature to sin, God has given him a conscience to point him to righteousness. When man gives in to his sinful nature and follows the lust of his heart, he will be judged for rejecting the witness of his conscience. "For the wrath of God is revealed from heaven against all ungodliness and unrighteousness of men, who hold the truth in unrighteousness" (Rom. 1:18).

There are at least two reasons that justify God's judging the heathen. First, the Bible teaches that every man has a conscience which initially directs man toward God. Paul described it as "the work of the law written in their hearts" (Rom. 2:15). Secondly, God has clearly revealed himself to men in nature (Rom. 1:20). "The heavens declare the glory of God; and the firmament sheweth his handywork" (Ps. 19:1). When God judges a man for his sin, that man has already rejected the twofold revelation of God. Jesus observed another consequence of the sin nature in the religious leaders of his day. It had affected their wills. "And ye will not come to me, that ye might have life" (John 5:40). These men who sought to study the Scriptures were so affected by sin that they were unable to respond to God when they met him.

The sin nature influences us to sin. Most people may be willing to acknowledge that they are sinners because they sin. But the Bible teaches the reverse. We sin because we are sinners. It is our sin nature which results in our committing sins (Rom. 5:12). We are all "conceived in sin" (Ps. 51:5). Therefore the sin nature, when it surfaces, results in personal sin. We are all guilty and deserving of a twofold judgment upon sin. But God is willing to forgive personal sin, so he deals adequately with our sin nature.

The sin nature has been judged. The Bible teaches, "Knowing this, that our old man [was] crucified with him" (Rom. 6:6). When Christ died, he condemned the old man to death. Our old man is dead (v. 7), and we are exhorted to reckon it dead. But our sin nature continues to operate within us. The old nature was "judged" when Christ died. Until Christ returns we must live in the strength of the new man to overcome the sinful desires arising from the sin nature still at work in us. We can't eradicate our sin nature but we can use the Christian means of allowing the Holy Spirit to control us so that we don't give in to temptation.

IMPUTED SIN

In the third area, all men are sinners because of imputed sin. The meaning of imputation is "to ascribe to" or "reckon over." It is similar to a charge that is added to a credit card account when it is used. When we speak of imputed sin, we are talking about the sin of Adam being charged to our account. Adam was the seminal and the federal head. We were all in Adam when he sinned. God is justified in imputing the sin of Adam to our account. By imputation of sin we mean not the arbitrary charging to a man the sin for which he is not naturally responsible, but reckoning to a man the guilt which he deserves and which belongs to him. Imputation of sin is charged to all because they are connected with the race. Adam was more than our representative. Since we were in Adam, we sinned when he sinned. As a result it was charged against our account. "As by one man sin entered into the world . . . for that all have sinned" (Rom. 5:12). Because of imputation, "Death passed upon all men" (Rom. 5:12).

Imputed sin results in physical death. Again Paul restated the truth concerning this penalty: "By one man's offense death reigned" (Rom. 5:17). The fact that all will die is evidence enough that all have been included in Adam's sin (Rom. 5:12). Some may argue that this appears unjust of God to judge men for sins committed when they were not personally conscious. This charge may be due to a misunderstanding of imputation. First, Adam's sin in the garden was a personal sin. Second, it resulted in passing on to all children a depraved sin nature. And third, the penalty of Adam was imputed to everyone.

God not only imputes the sin of Adam to the race, he offers to do the same with the righteousness of Christ. "That as sin hath reigned unto death, even so might grace reign through righteousness unto eternal life by Jesus Christ, our Lord" (Rom. 5:21). When God imputes the righteousness of Christ to our account, he makes our record as good (or as perfect) as Jesus Christ's. Imputed righteousness is the only remedy for man's imputed sin. Therefore we see that for every expression of sin, God has provided a remedy that perfectly satisfies the penalty.

CONCLUSION

Sin is simply disobedience to God. However, we have seen that every person is a sinner for three reasons. Sin brings hideous results and not only affects our relationship with God but also with other people. But, most of all, sin will destroy the natural process of every man if not checked. If we do allow God to work in our lives to combat sin, we can, by the Holy Spirit's indwelling power, begin to combat its influence on us. In one of the earlier books of the Bible, God said, "Ye shall be holy; for I the Lord your God am holy" (Lev. 19:2).

As we focus our attention on God and strive to live a holy life, we will have no difficulty identifying sin in our lives. Once we are aware of sin, we need to claim God's victory. "Neither yield ye your members as instruments of unrighteousness unto sin: but yield yourselves unto God, as those that are alive from the dead, and your members as instruments of righteousness unto God" (Rom. 6:13).

DAILY READINGS

□Monday: *Romans 1:18-32*   □Tuesday: *Romans 2:1-16*   □Wednesday: *Romans 2:17-29*   □Thursday: *Romans 3:1-23*   □Friday: *Mark 7:14-23*   □Saturday: *Psalm 36*   □Sunday: *Psalm 14*

PART SEVEN

UNDERSTANDING THE DOCTRINE OF SALVATION

THIRTY-ONE
CONVERSION AND REGENERATION

But God be thanked, that ye were the servants of sin, but ye have obeyed from the heart that form of doctrine which was delivered you. Romans 6:17

INTRODUCTION

A young apprentice was converted in a New England church and later indicated he felt called to the ministry. As was the custom of that day, the pastor decided to check with others to determine the genuineness of the young man's conversion. He went to the boy's employer first to talk with him about it. The employer pointed to a chain hanging on the wall and asked, "Do you see that chain? That chain was forged for him. I was obliged to chain him to the bench to keep him at work. He was the worst boy I had in the establishment. I could not trust him out of my sight, but now, he is completely changed. He is one of my best apprentices. I would trust him with untold gold."

The religious experience the Bible describes as conversion results in a change in the life-style of the convert. As a young woman was attempting to join Spurgeon's church in London one day, she was asked, "What makes you think you have become a Christian?" Not understanding the related Bible doctrines of conversion and regeneration, she simply responded, "Because now I sweep under the doormat!" During the Welsh Revival among the coal miners of that land, the change in the lives of the men was so dramatic, the animals in the mines refused to obey them. The miners had formerly cursed them and abused them to make them work; the animals were not trained to respond to kind language. As the caterpillar emerges from a cocoon a beautiful butterfly, so the person who experiences conversion emerges a "new creature" (1 Cor. 5:17).

Two biblical terms are used to describe this experience, depending upon the perspective of the context. When viewed in terms of man's role in salvation, the term used is "conversion." When considered from God's perspective, the Bible describes it as "regeneration." These two terms are discussed in this chapter. When we understand them and all they represent, we will better appreciate our salvation. Then as we seek to reach others for Christ, we can anticipate a similar change in their lives.

DEFINITION OF REGENERATION

Regeneration is the work of God through the Holy Spirit of placing in one who has been given the gift of faith a new nature which is capable of doing the will of God. The regenerated person is capable of doing the "righteous things" required by God. Regeneration results in more than eternal life, it makes possible our sanctification. Regeneration is the result of that experience which is called being born again. "Therefore, if any man be in Christ he is a new creature; old things are passed away; behold, all things are become new" (2 Cor. 5:17).

Regeneration is an act of God. Only God can save a soul. Jonah recognized that "salvation is of the Lord" (Jonah 2:9). Salvation is called the "gift of God" (Rom. 6:23; Eph. 2:8). No one is able to forgive sin and save a soul but God (Mark 2:7).

But it is not enough to think of salvation as only a legal act whereby God erases our sins from the legal record. Salvation results in a living, dynamic experience. One of the greatest promises given by God is, "Whosoever believeth on him...[has] everlasting life" (John 3:16). The new life of a Christian is more than endless duration. A Christian receives a new quality of life the moment he receives Christ (John 3:36; 4:14; 7:37-39).

Regeneration produces spiritual life. Every person has a living body and soul, and at regeneration the spirit is made alive. Writing to the Ephesians, Paul said, "And you hath he quickened [made alive] who were dead in trespasses and sins" (Eph. 2:1). Jesus said, "I am come that they might have life, and...have it more abundantly" (John 10:10).

Much has been said in recent years about being born again. This expression was used by Jesus to explain regeneration to Nicodemus. The term *anothen,* translated "born again," can also be rendered: "born from above." A person needs a spiritual rebirth because he is spiritually dead. When Adam was created, he was a living soul (Gen. 2:7), which meant he was living both spiritually and physically. God warned, "For in the day that thou eatest thereof thou shalt surely die" (Gen. 2:17). Adam disobeyed God and ate the fruit, but lived 930 years (Gen. 5:5). Adam died spiritually the day he ate the fruit, even though he lived over 900 years physically. As a result everyone is born into the world spiritually dead (Eph. 2:1) because of trespasses and sins. But when a person receives Jesus Christ he receives spiritual life—this is eternal life (John 5:24).

When a person is born again (John 1:12, 13), the indwelling presence of Jesus Christ comes into his life. Christ is the spiritual life of the new believer. But regeneration is more than the presence of Christ. Christ promised the Father would also indwell the believer. "We will come unto him and make our abode with him" (John 14:23). Finally, the Holy Spirit also indwells the Christian, and his presence is the guarantee of new life, "by his Spirit that dwelleth in you" (Rom. 8:11). Hence, when a person is regenerated he receives the life of God because he is indwelt with the presence of God. One of the great devotional classics of sixteenth-century England discusses this very theme, *The Life of God in the Soul of Man.*

When Jesus told his disciples, "I am the vine, ye are the branches" (John 15:5), he was illustrating the unique relationship into which every believer enters at the moment of conversion. He becomes one with Christ. Paul often wrote of being "in Christ" and "Christ in you." Both statements are the result of an act that occurred at the moment of salvation. Many people are saved and pray, "Come into my heart, Lord Jesus." Every saved individual has become one with Christ in a unique manner. This is a part of the work of God in regeneration.

New nature. When a person receives Jesus Christ he becomes a new creation, but this does not mean the sin nature is eliminated or is upgraded. Paul recognized the continuance of the sin nature when he stated the Ephesians had put off "concerning the former conversation the old man" (Eph. 5:22). He wanted them to recognize that the act of crucifying the old nature took place at Calvary (Rom. 6:6). The sinful nature was not eliminated, only condemned. Paul also recognized the struggle he had with the continuing sin nature. He wrote, "The evil which I would not, that I do" (Rom. 7:19). He also recognized his continuing inability to perform righteousness, "for the good I would that I do not" (Rom. 7:19). While on earth a Christian will struggle with the desires of his old nature. But in regeneration he receives a new nature with new power and new attitudes. Now it is the duty of a Christian to allow his new nature to direct his life. To do this the Christian must "control" his old nature (Rom. 13:14), and allow the power of the new nature to overcome the old life.

New creation—transformation. Paul used this expression when he told the Corinthians, "If any man be in Christ, he is a new creature; old things are passed away, behold all things are become new" (1 Cor. 5:17). God works in the life of an individual not just to improve him but to totally transform him. Paul also described the results of regeneration as a "new man." He notes, "that ye put on the new man, which after God is created in righteousness and true holiness" (Eph. 4:24).

The usual testimony of regeneration is the changed lives of those who have been delivered from the power of sin. The Bible teaches that no person is beyond hope. Paul reminded the

Corinthians of their past lives: "Know ye not that the unrighteous shall not inherit the kingdom of God? Be not deceived: neither fornicators, nor idolaters, nor adulterers, . . . nor covetous, nor drunkards, nor revilers, nor extortioners shall inherit the kingdom of God" (1 Cor. 6:9, 10). The very next verse explains their transformation, "and such were some of you: but ye are washed, but ye are sanctified, but ye are justified in the name of the Lord Jesus, and by the Spirit of God" (1 Cor. 6:11). What Paul was saying was that the church of Corinth had members who had formerly been unfaithful, idol worshipers, homosexuals, thieves, drunks, terrorists, and extortioners, but their lives had been changed by God. The power for that transformation is regeneration.

Before Zacchaeus met Jesus, his unethical financial practice was a way of life. When he met the Savior, he immediately wanted to restore what was taken unethically.

Levi (or Matthew, as he was also known) was, like Zacchaeus, a self-centered tax collector interested primarily in his own prosperity at the expense of others. When he met Jesus, he sponsored a gathering of his colleagues to introduce them to the Messiah.

Two boys were preparing their wagon for the Easter parade at Sunday school when their pastor walked by. They had spent many hours making a beautiful cross complete with ribbons and bows. "Boys," the pastor explained, "you've got it all wrong. The cross upon which Jesus died was ugly and despised but yours is beautiful."

One of the boys looked to his pastor and said, "I thought you said Jesus never touched anything and left it the same."

When Jesus meets a life, a change takes place that only God can perform. Sometimes the change is very dramatic. A man who has been an alcoholic for years may lose his desire for drink the moment he is saved. For another, the change in his life may be slow and gradual, almost unnoticeable without careful observation.

DEFINITION OF CONVERSION

The human side of regeneration is conversion. Many people have different ideas about conversion. Fortunately, we are not bound to the ideas and opinions of others. The Bible describes the doctrine of conversion by written explanations of what we can expect and a detailed example of how people come to know God in the Scriptures.

The apostle Paul described the conversion experience of the Romans when he wrote, "Ye have obeyed from the heart that form of doctrine which was delivered you" (Rom. 6:17). Conversion does not involve learning a catechism or knowing the doctrine of Christ. It embraces the total person, which means conversion is related to all three powers of man: the intellect, the emotions, and the will. A person must know certain things to experience conversion, but a knowledge of these facts alone will not save him. Conversion also involves the emotions, but it is far more than an emotional experience. Conversion is not complete until an act of the will has taken place, but even an act of our will is not enough to save if it is done in ignorance or without a heart desire.

The intellect. The conversion of a man to Christ is different from a conversion to another religion or commercial product. Though many have tried, conversion cannot be passed off as a mere psychological phenomenon.

To be saved, a person must know the gospel. There is only one gospel (Gal. 1:9) but it contains two sides of the same truth. Just as a door has two sides, so the gospel is propositional and personal truth. The gospel is *propositional truth* which means it is a formula that is accurate. The gospel is the account of the death of Christ for our sins, his burial and resurrection from the dead on the third day (1 Cor. 15:1-4). Only Jesus could provide for us salvation. "But God commendeth his love toward us, in that, while we were yet sinners, Christ died for us" (Rom. 5:8).

A second aspect of this gospel is *personal truth*. When Paul came to Corinth to preach his gospel he "determined not to know anything among you, save Jesus Christ, and him crucified" (1 Cor. 2:2). The gospel is not complete in its presentation until it focuses attention on the Person of Christ. Jesus said, "As Moses lifted up the serpent in the wilderness, even so must the Son of man be lifted up: That whosoever believeth in him should not perish, but have eternal life" (John 3:14, 15). If a person does not trust in Christ, that person is not saved. It is important that we know both the content (doctrine) and the Person (Jesus Christ) of the gospel to be converted.

Knowing the propositional truth of salvation is knowing God's plan of salvation. If one wishes to become a chess master, he must learn the rules of the game and discipline himself to play by them. If one wishes to be a Christian, he must follow God's plan. This is sometimes called the Roman Road of Salvation since the verses that are often used to lead a person to Christ are found in the Book of Romans.

The first step in this plan is to *know your need.* The Bible says, "There is none righteous, no, not one" (Rom. 3:10). This does not mean there is nothing good in man but rather that none of us is as righteous as God himself. God has a perfect standard of holiness required for entrance into heaven. Unfortunately, "All have sinned, and come short of the glory of God" (Rom. 3:23). It makes little difference how good we are. We are not good enough. If a marathon runner attempts to set an Olympic record, it makes little difference if he misses by five seconds or five hours. He has missed the standard he had set for himself. Even if we were "almost perfect," we still fall short of God's holy standard of perfection.

The second step is to *know the penalty.* The Bible says, "The wages of sin is death" (Rom. 6:23). This refers to both physical and spiritual death. Physical death occurs upon the separation of the body and spirit of man (James 2:26). Spiritual death occurs when one is eternally separated from God. John wrote of a future point in time when "death and hell were cast into the lake of fire. This is the second death" (Rev. 20:14).

A third step in God's plan of salvation is to *know the provision.* This provision is found in the gospel. "While we were yet sinners, Christ died for us" (Rom. 5:8). Because we could not pay the price for our sins, Jesus did. Today he provides salvation as a free gift to all who will take it (Rom. 6:23). Jesus provided what we could not provide for ourselves. That provision gives us the option to receive or reject God's gift of eternal life.

A person can know the above three steps in this plan and never be saved. He must personally respond. "That if thou shalt confess with thy mouth the Lord Jesus, and shalt believe in thine heart that God hath raised him from the dead, thou shalt be saved" (Rom. 10:9). Jesus traveled through Israel and offered salvation to his own people, but he was rejected. "But as many as received him, to them gave he power to become the sons of God, even to them that believe on his name" (John 1:12). You must *know how to respond* to the gospel and respond to be saved.

The emotions. Many religious groups place too much emphasis on a person's emotions and create what is known as a "psychological conversion" to their particular religious sect. In reaction to this, some conservative Christians have attempted to deny their emotions completely. Neither emphasis is correct. God made man complete with an emotional capacity. If kept in proper perspective, our emotions lead to a healthy conversion. The abuse of emotions by some radicals should not cause us to abandon that which is good. A person will be emotionally affected by his conversion by either a cause or an effect experience.

The apostle Paul rejoiced "not that ye were made sorry but that ye sorrowed to repentance: for ye were made sorry after a godly manner. . . . For godly sorrow worketh repentance to salvation not to be repented of: but the sorrow of the world worketh death" (2 Cor. 7:9, 10). Paul recognized there were two kinds of emotional reactions to the gospel: "godly sorrow" and "sorrow of the world." There is a place for "godly sorrow" in our lives that leads to further spiritual insight. The "sorrow of the world" is remorse for getting caught, not sorrow for the act committed.

Sometimes God will allow a person to experience guilt so he can understand and appreciate forgiveness of sins. Often God must use our emotions to cause us to respond to the gospel. On other occasions, God will use our emotional reaction so he can better deal with us after salvation. When Philip preached the gospel in Samaria and many people were saved, the Bible records "there was great joy in that city" (Acts 8:8). The apostle Paul expected his converts to continue to respond emotionally to God. He told the Philippians, "Rejoice in the Lord always: and again I say, Rejoice" (Phil. 4:4). It is all right to get excited about our relationship with Christ.

Each of us has a different way of expressing emotions depending upon age, sex, background, and a host of other unique experiences that make us who we are. Sometimes we tend to think the person who shouts and jumps for joy or a person who cries loudly is more emotionally involved in a situation than the person who sits apparently oblivious to what is happening around him. A person is not more or less saved depending upon the volume of his emotional outbursts, but when we are converted, it will affect our emotions.

The will. God created man with a will to choose to respond or reject the work of God in his life. In order to be converted, a person must respond. This does not mean we save ourselves. "For by grace are ye saved through faith; and that not of yourselves: it is the gift of God: Not of works, lest any man should boast" (Eph. 2:8, 9). While "Salvation is of the Lord" (John 2:9) and we do not earn our salvation, God does tell us to receive it (John 1:12).

Some churches baptize, teaching that baptism saves a person. But baptism should not be equated with salvation. Baptism could be defined as "salvation symbolized." When a Christian is baptized, he is illustrating a twofold symbol. First, it is a symbol of redemption, how Christ died for his sins, was buried, and on the third day rose again from the dead (Rom. 6:4; 1 Cor. 15:1-4). Second, baptism is a symbol of regeneration. The candidate being baptized is saying he has personally trusted Christ as Savior and a supernatural change has taken place in his life (Gal. 2:20).

THE WILL AND CONVERSION	
1. Trust in	Prov. 3:4
2. Repent	Acts 2:38
3. Believe	Acts 16:31
4. Receive	John 1:12
5. Be born again	John 3:7
6. Call	Rom. 10:13
7. Confess	Rom. 10:9

THE BASIS OF REGENERATION AND CONVERSION

The instrument of salvation. The Bible plays a significant role in an individual's salvation. Just as a workman uses tools to get his job done, so God uses the Bible as a tool to deposit spiritual life into a new believer. We are "born again, not of corruptible seed, but of incorruptible, by the word of God, which liveth and abideth forever" (1 Pet. 1:23). The Bible convicts of sin (John 16:9-11), gives a new nature (2 Pet. 1:4), and becomes the basis of spiritual power to overcome sin (Ps. 119:9, 11). The Bible contains an interesting promise concerning its power. "So shall my word be that goeth forth out of my mouth: it shall not return unto me void, but it shall accomplish that which I please, and it shall prosper in the thing whereto I sent it" (Isa. 55:11).

When we are seeking to reach the lost for Christ, we would do well to remember the power of the Word of God and use it. People are not saved because of intellectual arguments, but because the Holy Spirit uses the Scripture to point out needs and to convict of sin. We should learn to work with God in winning souls.

The agent of salvation. The Holy Spirit is the Person who grants eternal life to the repentant sinner. He is the divine workman who regenerates the individual. He works in the heart to convict the sinner of sin, then he draws the sinner to the Savior. Next the Holy Spirit effects the work that Paul describes, "Put on the new man which is renewed in knowledge after the image of him that created him" (Col. 2:10). Paul described it further, "the Spirit of God dwell in you" (Rom. 8:9). After the Spirit is in our hearts, he witnesses our conversion. "The Spirit itself beareth witness with our spirit, that we are the children of God" (Rom. 8:14).

CONCLUSION

God is in the life-changing business. He takes the broken pieces of our lives and makes new vessels. Someone has said God takes the canvas of our life when the colors are running and blurring, then paints a masterpiece. As powerful as God is, he chooses to limit his power to what the Christian will allow him to do.

God could save everyone today, but he will not save anyone who will not let him do so. We need to come by faith and allow God to perform the work of regeneration in us. We then need to continue to cooperate with God as he perfects that change in us.

DAILY READINGS

☐Monday: *John 3:1-16*   ☐ Tuesday: *John 10:1-10*
☐Wednesday: *2 Corinthians 5:11-21*   ☐Thursday:
1 Corinthians 6:1-11   ☐ Friday: *Acts 8:1-8*   ☐ Saturday:
Acts 16:16-34   ☐Sunday: *John 4:5-30*

THIRTY-TWO
OUR POSITION

Therefore if any man be in Christ, he is a new creature: old things are passed away; behold, all things are become new.
2 Corinthians 5:17

INTRODUCTION

The moment a person is born again, many things happen to him that will enable him to live for God. Unfortunately, most Christians are ignorant of the position they enjoy. Many find themselves struggling to accomplish God's will for their lives without tapping into all the resources God has provided. We believe we will someday enjoy eternity with Jesus in heaven, but we fail to remember God has already provided us with that heavenly treasury. Perhaps as we better understand our position in Christ, we will find the heavenly blessings of Christ more within the realm of possibility.

ENTERING OUR POSITION

Each of us can be transformed by understanding our position with God. First, we must understand how to enter this new position. The doorway to our new position is justification by faith (Rom. 5:1). Our new position is not an experience based on feeling. We are now to be considered as sons of God with all the privileges of living in the heavenlies. This position involves our legal standing before God, not our struggles of everyday life.

The Christian life has a heavenly standing and an earthly state. By justification, we have a legal standing by which we are declared righteous before God, and, on the basis of this judicial act, the Christian enjoys the life and peace of God. He no longer has to worry about offending God; God is pleased with him because of justification. God has graciously accepted the Christian into his family. By faith the Christian "acts" on the account that is once and for all settled in heaven.

Abraham. Abraham is the first person in the Bible described as having been justified by faith (Gen. 15:6). This is not saying he was the first person to become a child of God. When God made a promise to Abraham, he accepted it as possible and trusted in God as though the results were actual although it would be thirteen years before God would fulfill the promise. Abraham's act of believing resulted in a declaration by God that Abraham was justified.

The Bible testifies of Abraham, "He staggered not at the promise of God through unbelief; but was strong in faith, giving glory to God; And being fully persuaded that, what he had promised, he was able also to perform" (Rom. 4:20, 21). The secret to Abraham's faith was his conviction that God would do what he had promised.

God promised that Abraham would have a son. Abraham "considered his own body now dead" (Rom. 4:19), yet he trusted the promise that God would give him a son. The Bible says Abraham "believed, even God, who quickeneth the dead" (Rom. 4:17). As a result of this belief, Abraham was justified.

We must look beyond our inner faith to its object—God. We must understand the commands and promises of the Bible. Then when we understand what God has promised, we can claim those promises. Faith is simply accepting what God has promised in the Bible and acting upon it.

Righteousness. Justification is an act whereby God declares a person righteous when that man trusts Christ. Hence, the Bible teaches that justification establishes a legal relationship between God and man. Justification declares men perfect in God's sight, and results in man's elevation to a new position in the heavenlies (Eph. 2:6).

Justification and righteousness are linked in Scripture, in that both come from the same word (*dikaios* means "righteous" and *dikaioo* means "to justify"). When we express saving faith in God, God enters "righteous and perfect" to our record in heaven. This is the act of justification. Since justification and righteousness represent words of common origin, these can be distinguished by noting that God is the source, declaring us righteous; and man is the recipient, being declared righteous.

Our record and Christ's. Two things happen at salvation. Our sin is transferred to Jesus Christ. He became our sinbearer and took our punishment. Christ died for us (John 1:29), giving his life a ransom for many (Matt. 20:20). Second, the perfection of Jesus Christ is credited to our account. We become, as far as the record is concerned, as perfect as the Son of God. When asked why we should be allowed in heaven, our answer is simple: "I am declared to be as perfect as Jesus Christ." In the act of justification, we are declared as righteous as God's Son. "For God hath made him to be sin for us . . . that we might be made the righteousness of God in him" (2 Cor. 5:21). Both sides of the transaction are mentioned in that verse.

If someone is convicted of a criminal offense, he stands guilty before the law. His record will show he was guilty. But if he is charged with an offense, and the judge dismisses the case against him, he is not considered guilty. His record has no mark or violation against it. "Acquittal" means that the record indicates that the accused did not commit the crime. Our justification before God is as one who has been acquitted.

The second part to justification declares that we have a perfect record before God. This same declaration is made of us when we are justified by faith. We are clothed in the righteousness of Jesus Christ; we have the merit of someone else.

Position. Justification is an act whereby our legal position in heaven is changed. Being declared justified is similar to the act whereby a government declares that an alien is a citizen. The moment the person is pronounced a citizen, nothing happens to him physically. His thought processes remain the same, as does his personality and pattern of speech. The only actual change is his legal standing. But as he becomes aware of the benefits of being a citizen, he may shout, cry, or break out into a grin. The emotional reaction has no organic connection to his changed legal status, but surely there is a cognitive relationship with his new advantages. In the same way, justification changes our legal papers in heaven; we become children of God. In response to this new relationship we may cry, rejoice, or worship God in silent gratitude.

STATE AND STANDING

Even though we are justified immediately upon our salvation, it often takes time before we begin to experience the changes that have taken place in our lives. While we stand justified before God in heaven, we have, because of our new nature, struggles with the sin nature here on earth, a problem each of us faces as we attempt to "work out our salvation."

Perhaps the best way to tie together a man's legal position in heaven and his daily walk on earth is Habakkuk 2:4, "The just shall live by his faith." This verse changed Martin Luther's life. As a Roman Catholic priest he tried to work his way to heaven. But his life was changed when he realized that Christ had done it all. The apostle Paul used this verse to combat legalistic Judaizers that influenced the churches in the province of Galatia (Gal. 3:11) and it became the foundational text of his entire theology (Rom. 1:17). In Romans 6, the apostle uses four words to aid us in applying this truth to our Christian life.

Know. Three times Paul reminded these Christians of what they knew was true (Rom. 6:3, 6, 9). He realized our actions were the result of certain attitudes and they could only be produced when they were built on an accurate intellectual basis. The key truth Paul wanted the Romans to know was their identification with Christ. "Know ye not, that so many of us as were baptized into Jesus Christ were baptized into his death?" (Rom. 6:3). Because of this a Christian should have victory over sin. "Knowing this, that our old man *has been* crucified with him" (Rom. 6:6 italics added). If we know the old man has received the death penalty on the cross, then we do not have to allow Satan to tempt and condemn us. Knowledge of our co-crucifixion with Christ is the basis of our victory over sin.

At the heart of this passage Paul reminded the Christian that he has been "planted together" (Rom. 6:5) with Christ in death. This phrase introduces what has become known as "the seven togethers." In each occurrence, we are identified with Christ in the heavenlies. Our perfection in Christ then becomes the basis for our daily victory.

THE SEVEN TOGETHERS

1. Planted together in death—Rom. 6:5
2. Quickened (made alive) together—Eph. 2:5; Col. 2:13
3. Raised together—Eph. 2:6 (placed in a new position)
4. Set together—Eph. 2:6 (continuing in a new position)
5. Workmen together with him—2 Cor. 6:1
6. Live together with him— 1 Thess. 5:10
7. Glorified together (future)—Rom. 8:17

Reckon. The second word Paul used is "reckon," which carries the idea of "be counting on" or "be relying upon." "Likewise reckon ye also yourselves to be dead indeed unto sin, but alive unto God through Jesus Christ our Lord" (Rom. 6:11). Part of the key to harmonizing our exalted standing in heaven with our state on earth is to rely upon what we know to be true and to act accordingly.

Yield. The third important word used is "yield." Based on what we know and how we have reckoned, we should surrender our lives on this earth to the designs of heaven. "Yield yourselves unto God, as those that are alive from the dead, and your members as instruments of righteousness unto God" (Rom. 6:13). Yieldedness involves giving God the "right of way" to every aspect of our lives. It is impossible for a Christian desiring to serve God consistently to divide the sacred and secular in his life.

Obey. Obedience is the natural implication of recognizing the lordship of Christ in our lives. The one who is the Lord of our lives is the one we obey (Rom. 6:16, 17). When a Christian refuses to do the will of God, he is denying the lordship of Christ in that area of his life.

The moment we are saved, we are risen with Christ into a new position and a new standing with God. But we still have human natures with sinful desires. Many times our walk with God will be inconsistent with standing before God, yet as we apply these four verbs daily, those inconsistencies will decline in number.

SANCTIFICATION IN STATE AND STANDING

The word "sanctification" is used in the Bible to identify that person, institution, act, or thing set apart by God as holy. The confusion over sanctification is that many groups have wrongly defined "sanctify" to mean "eradicate the sin nature," or to gain a position where it is no longer possible to sin. Those who hold this position call it "entire sanctification." In both the Old and New Testament, the Hebrew and Greek words for both "holy" and "sanctify" mean "to set apart to God." When sanctification is used of things, it does not mean that a vessel or piece of furniture has moral qualities (only God is holy). It means they are set apart for God.

Sanctification for the Christian is past, present, and future. Paul reminded the Philippians that "he which hath begun a good work in you will perform it until the day of Jesus Christ" (Phil. 1:6). Our practical sanctification is a continual process beginning with conversion and finally being accomplished at the coming of Christ.

Positional sanctification. Positional sanctification is the relationship with God which we enter by faith in Jesus Christ. What God made holy by redemption, remains holy. Positional sanctification applies to our completed standing in heaven. The moment a person is saved, he becomes a "new creature" (2 Cor. 5:17). His position is changed from an alien (Gal. 2:12) to a citizen (Heb. 11:13-16). In the books of heaven he is set apart as holy, having obtained the righteousness of Christ (Rom. 3:25). The rest of his Christian life is an attempt to apply that truth to his practical level of living.

Progressive sanctification. This is called experimental or practical sanctification. It involves the struggles of victory and defeat of the Christian in this present life. But God continues to work in the life of every Christian (Phil. 1:6) to change him into the image of his Son (Rom. 8:29). The various circumstances and experiences we encounter in our life are the result of God's work in us (Rom. 8:28). We need to cooperate with God in living under the discipline of the Word of God which is given for our direction and spiritual growth (2 Tim. 3:17). As we grow and mature "in Christ" it will become more natural for us to practice the godly habits God desires that we develop.

Prospective sanctification. This is consummational sanctification, for God will not complete the process until we arrive in heaven. Then our position and our walk will be harmonious. That day is soon coming when "we shall be like him [Jesus]; for we shall see him as he is" (1 John 3:2). At the coming of Christ, all the limitations we now experience will be removed, allowing us instantly to be transformed into holiness (1 Cor. 13:10-12). The Christian today can only anticipate that future day by striving to make needed changes in their life as revealed in the Word of God (Phil. 2:12).

THREE STEPS OF SANCTIFICATION			
Position	Positional sanctification	I was sanctified	Heb. 3:1
Experience	Progressive sanctification	I am being sanctified	1 Thess. 5:28
Consummation	Prospective sanctification	I shall be sanctified	1 John 3:2

CONCLUSION

If we know Jesus Christ as our personal Savior, we have entered into a unique relationship with God. As far as God is concerned, we possess the righteousness of Christ. Hence we are perfect in his sight. We are entitled to all the privileges of one who is a child of God.

DAILY READINGS
☐Monday: *John 15:1-16*   ☐Tuesday: *Romans 6:1-23*
☐Wednesday: *Romans 5:1-11*   ☐Thursday: *Romans 4:1-25*
☐Friday: *Colossians 3:1-27*   ☐Saturday: *Ephesians 5:22-33*
☐Sunday: *1 Peter 2:1-10*

PART EIGHT

UNDERSTANDING THE DOCTRINE OF ANGELS

THIRTY-THREE
THE NATURE OF ANGELS

And I saw another mighty angel come down from heaven, clothed with a cloud: and a rainbow was upon his head, and his face was as it were the sun, and his feet like pillars of fire.
Revelation 10:1

INTRODUCTION

Christian parents usually tell their children, from an early age, stories about angels. But they often fail to teach the correct doctrine of the angels. The Bible does not describe every appearance of angels as a fair-skinned man dressed in white robes with two large wings. In fact, many times angels appeared to man without being recognized as angels. Neither does the Bible picture them sitting on clouds in neatly organized choirs or playing harps. In contrast, the primary function of angels is to deliver messages for God, encouraging and ministering to the needs of people, and opposing the work of Satan and his demons. The word "angel" in Greek means "messenger," implying both their nature and duty. Not only have angels been used greatly of God in the past, but they also have a ministry in the world today. Jesus, Paul, and the apostles wrote frequently about angels. The Bible teaches that in the years to come, we will spend eternity with the angels and at some future point, be engaged in judging them.

As we study the doctrine of angels, a number of benefits can be derived. First, when we realize they constantly observe our Christian lives (1 Cor. 4:9; 11:10; Eph. 3:10), we will improve our conduct. Then, when we understand their protection of us, we will be encouraged by God's care for us (Heb. 1:7). Then, as we consider the tremendous strength and authority of the angels in contrast with the unnoticed tasks they are called upon to perform, we cannot help but learn a lesson in humility. Finally, the example of their unceasing service ought to motivate us to more consistent service for God.

THE DESCRIPTION OF ANGELS

There are many terms used in the Bible to describe angels: *host, creatures, throne, dominions, principalities, powers, sons of God,* and the *angel of his presence.* The phrase "the angel of the Lord" usually implies the presence of deity in angelic form (Gen. 16:1-13; 22:11-16; 31:11-13; Exod. 3:2-4; Judg. 6:12-16). Most interpret the phrase "the angel of the Lord" as Christ and call this appearance a "Christophany." However, the phrase in Luke 1:11 and Acts 12:7, 23 is not a description of deity.

Created beings. When were the angels created? Obviously before the beginning of the earth, because angels watched the magnificent drama of creation. God asked the question, "Where wast thou when I laid the foundations of the earth?" (Job 38:4). The narrative goes on to indicate, "When the morning stars sang together, and all the sons of God shouted for joy" (Job 38:7). The angels were rejoicing as God created the world.

The record of the creation of angels appears in the first verse of the Bible: "In the beginning God created the heaven(s) and the earth" (Gen. 1:1, plural added). In the Hebrew language, the plural form of "heavens" reveals that God created the whole of heaven, composed of all its innumerable separate parts. The heavens included not only the stars but the present abode of God, plus the angelic beings. Angels were the first created beings and later, while the earth was being created, they admired God's beauty, orderliness, and power. Since one task of angels is to give glory to God, they sang and shouted during the creation.

Even though the Father and the Holy Spirit were active in the creation of angels, Jesus Christ is identified as their Creator. "For by him were all things created, that are in heaven, and that are in earth, visible and invisible, whether they be thrones, or dominions, or principalities, or powers: all things were created by him, and for him" (Col. 1:16). The terms *thrones, dominions, principalities* and *powers* are all terms used in the Bible to describe angels. David urged the angels to praise the Lord because they were created (Ps. 148:2-5).

Incorporeal beings. Though angels have appeared to men in physical form, they are essentially spirit beings. Since they are without physical bodies, they are spirits. David recognized and blessed the Lord "Who maketh his angels spirits; and his ministers a flaming fire" (Ps. 104:4).

Even though angels are spirits, they have the ability to become visible in the semblance of a human body (Gen. 19:1; Exod. 3:2; Judg. 2:1; Matt. 1:20; Luke 1:26; John 20:12). Angels are always referred to as being masculine, but without specific reference to gender.

David reflected on the nature of man and observed, "For thou hast made him a little lower than the angels, and hast crowned him with glory and honour" (Ps. 8:5). In the hierarchy of heaven, angels are above man, yet they are listed below Christ. "Being so much better than the angels, as he hath by inheritance obtained a more excellent name than they" (Heb. 1:4).

Holy beings. All angels were originally created holy to praise God and to serve him. Perhaps the best known phrase that came from the mouth of angels is, "Holy, holy, holy, is the Lord of hosts" (Isa. 6:3). The word "host" means "angels," hence God is the Lord of the angels. Again the angels were fulfilling their task when they sang, "Worthy is the Lamb" (Rev. 5:12). They were created holy because their message of praise is holy. But there was a group of "angels who kept not their first estate, but left their own habitation" (Jude 6). Some

theologians believe that some of these fallen angels are demons who now serve Satan, while those who didn't fall are
holy angels, who serve the Lord God. Even these demons
were originally created in a state of holiness. Another group
of the fallen angels are "chained under darkness," awaiting
the judgment of God (2 Pet. 2:4; Jude 6). But the holy angels
that did not sin are in fellowship with God and can look upon
him. Jesus warned his disciples not to abuse children because their angels are in the presence of God. "Take heed
that ye despise not one of these little ones; for I say unto you,
That in heaven their angels do always behold the face of my
Father which is in heaven" (Matt. 18:10). The fact that angels
are in fellowship with God and remain in his presence implies their holiness. If they did not flee from the presence of
God, he would judge the sin he finds in them.

Personal beings. Angels are similar to God and man in that
they have a personality, which is intellect, emotion, and will.
Having personality or being a person gives the angel the
power of self-perception and self-direction. God created angels with intellectual ability. They are identified as wise
(2 Sam. 14:20). Throughout the Scriptures, angels are portrayed in the obedient service of God, thus demonstrating the
existence of a will. The angel who showed John the Revelation would not allow John to worship him. "Then saith he
unto me, See thou do it not: for I am thy fellowservant, and of
thy brethren, the prophets, and of them who keep the sayings
of this book: Worship God" (Rev. 22:9).

Today, the will of angels to choose evil has apparently been
preempted by God because they choose not to follow Satan.
Today, angels are surrendered to God and cannot choose evil.
When the Scriptures indicate that "the angels desire to look
into" the glories of salvation (1 Pet. 1:12), it is an indication
of their emotions and the interaction of their will—obviously
a reflection of personality.

The personality of angels is further demonstrated in the
work of communication with God and men. On several occasions an angel was sent by God to an individual to communicate a special message from God. To accomplish that task, he
possessed the powers of speech that involved word recognition, memory, and rational ability to form sentences. Angels

have the ability to discern (used to answer questions), wisdom, and basic knowledge regarding life on earth and the plan of God. These are all elements of personality.

Deathless beings. When God created angels, he did not plan for their death; as a matter of fact, death is inconsistent with the nature of God and cannot be a part of his original purpose. Jesus taught we would someday be "deathless" like angels. "Neither can they die any more: for they are equal unto the angels" (Luke 20:36). Death is an experience of the human race because of the entrance of sin into the world (Rom. 5:12). Angels were created in a state of holiness. When Satan rebelled against God, they chose to follow God, therefore they have no sin that leads to death. Hell was created for those angels that rebelled against God and someday they will be eternally consigned there. John noted that "the devil that deceived them was cast into the lake of fire and brimstone" (Rev. 20:10). Jesus described it as "everlasting fire, prepared for the devil and his angels" (Matt. 25:41).

Unseen beings. Angels are unseen until they choose to appear for some special purpose. They seemed to have manifested themselves at certain times in Bible history more than others. They were frequent visitors during the period from Abraham to Moses, then primarily around the life of Christ. They were said to be present when the world was created. They appeared when circumstances on earth changed and God needed to give specific "messages" to his people about new covenants or different responsibilities. Because they don't appear frequently as persons in bright apparel does not mean they have no ministry today, for they constantly minister to "them who shall be heirs of salvation" (Heb. 1:14). In their work they are not perceived, but perhaps work through people, or perhaps they appear as a person. "Be not forgetful to entertain strangers: for thereby some have entertained angels unawares" (Heb. 13:2).

THE CHARACTER OF ANGELS

The names of individuals often reveal their character. Much of what we know about God is a result of his self-revelation through his names. God also gave names to his angels to reveal something about their character. Only three angels are named in Scripture but the Bible indicates the significance of those names in contrast with the name of Jesus. "He [Jesus] hath by inheritance obtained a more excellent name than they [angels]" (Heb. 1:4). The following chart demonstrates the superior meaning of the name Jesus over the angelic names.

A MORE EXCELLENT NAME	
Name	*Meaning*
1. Jesus ("Savior")	He shall save his people from their sins (Matt. 1:21)
2. Lucifer	"Bearer of light"
3. Gabriel	"Man of God"
4. Michael	"Who is like the Lord?"

Lucifer. Lucifer is thought to be the original name for the devil. This name reflects not the present character of Satan but his original created purpose and character. Lucifer originally possessed a high place in heaven (Isa. 14:12), perhaps the highest above all angels, but was cast down because of his desire to rise above God (Isa. 14:14). His name means "bearer of light," reflecting his purpose, to bear the light of God. By bearing light, angels are messengers of God. Hence, Lucifer should have been a "light bearer" to Jesus himself who is "the true Light, which lighteth every man that cometh into the world" (John 1:9).

Gabriel. Gabriel is the messenger angel of God. Gabriel is usually sent from God to man with a special message. The name Gabriel means "man of God"; his character trait is strength. Again, the name of Jesus surpasses the name of Gabriel. Whereas Gabriel is the "man of God," Jesus is "God."

APPEARANCES OF GABRIEL		
Appearance	*To Whom*	*Scripture Reference*
1st	Daniel	Dan. 8:16; 9:21, 26
2nd	Zacharias	Luke 1:11, 19
3rd	Mary	Luke 1:26, 27
4th	Joseph	Matt. 1:20
5th	Joseph again	Matt. 2:13, 19
6th	Jesus in Gethsemane	Luke 22:43
7th	The apostles in prison	Acts 5:19
8th	Philip	Acts 8:26
9th	Peter	Acts 12:7
10th	Herod	Acts 12:23
11th	Paul	Acts 27:23
12th	John	Rev. 22:8

Michael. The third angel named in Scripture is the most powerful. Michael is usually related to Israel and the resurrection (Dan. 10:13; 12:1, 2; 1 Thess. 4:19). He is described as the archangel (Jude 9), meaning he is the highest in the order of angels. His name means "who is like the Lord?" The name Michael emphasizes his godly character. Once again this angelic name falls short of the Lord Jesus Christ.

APPEARANCES OF MICHAEL		
Appearance	*To Whom*	*Scripture Reference*
1st	Daniel	Dan. 10:13, 21; 12:1
2nd	Satan on earth	Jude 9
3rd	Satan in heaven	Rev. 12:7

Cherubim. This special group of angels guard the holiness of God from the sinfulness of man. After Adam and Eve sinned, a cherub guarded the gate to Eden. Two likenesses of these angels were placed on the ark of the covenant in the tabernacle (Exod. 25:18-22), and later in the temple (1 Kings 6:23-29).

These statues stood symbolically in protection of the presence of God. Finally, John describes four angels (living creatures) that guarded the throne of God in heaven. "And round about the throne, were four beasts [living creatures] full of eyes before and behind. And the first beast was like a lion, and the second beast like a calf, and the third beast had a face as a man, and the fourth beast was like a flying eagle. And the four beasts had each of them six wings about him; and they were full of eyes within: and they rest not day and night, saying, Holy, holy, holy, Lord God Almighty, which was, and is, and is to come" (Rev. 4:6-8).

Seraphim. Literally, the word "seraphim" means "burners." Like the cherubim, they are concerned with the holiness of God (Isa. 6:3). Inasmuch as the seraph cleansed Isaiah with a live coal from the altar (Isa. 6:6, 7), this order of angels relates to sacrifice and cleansing. In contrast, the cherubim deal with judgment.

THE ATTRIBUTES OF ANGELS

Angels were especially created by God to serve him. To adequately represent God, they were given great strength and superior intelligence. Since God requires "all things be done decently and in order" (1 Cor. 14:40), angels are a highly organized company. They are described as "a multitude of heavenly host" (Luke 2:13).

The apostle John fell at the feet of one angel to worship him (Rev. 22:8). John was certainly aware the worship of angels was not permitted by Scripture, even though it was practiced by some early sects within Christianity (Col. 2:18). We are therefore led to believe that John was so overwhelmed with all the angel had done and shown him that for the moment he looked upon him as God, perhaps even an incarnation of Jesus.

Strength. The power of angels is so vast that humans cannot comprehend it. The angels were given great power yet they are not omnipotent. The apostle Paul calls them "mighty angels" (2 Thess. 1:7). The power of a single angel was demonstrated in part on the resurrection morning. "And, behold, there was a great earthquake; for the angel of the Lord descended from heaven and came and rolled back the stone from the door, and sat upon it" (Matt. 28:2). First, in an act of authority, the angel broke the Roman seal which was an immediate challenge to the sixteen armed guards at the tomb. But in an act of strength, the angel rolled a massive stone away from the tomb. Isaiah records an instance where God sent an angel to kill one hundred and eighty-five thousand Assyrian soldiers during a single night (Isa. 37:36).

As we consider these two accomplishments by single angels, we must observe with David "his angels, that excel in strength, that do his commandments, hearkening unto the voice of his word" (Ps. 103:20). While we recognize that angels are powerful, we also realize that omnipotence is never ascribed to them. There can only be one omnipotent One, and that is God. If another omnipotent being existed in the universe, by definition God would not be God.

Intelligence. Earlier we saw how angels had rational ability as an aspect of their personality. Jesus predicted his return, but qualified those who knew the time, "But of that day and hour knoweth no man, no, not the angels of heaven, but my Father only" (Matt. 24:36). Most obviously, Jesus was teaching that the intelligence of angels was limited. There definitely are some things angels do not know, so they do not possess the omniscience of God. In the phrase "no, not the angels" Jesus was teaching that the angels were more intelligent than man. Jesus is listing the priority of intelligence from man who is knowledgeable, to angels who are more knowledgeable, to God who is omniscient in all things. The intelligence of the angels lies somewhere between that of men and God. They were created intelligent beings. But their wisdom is not static. They have continued to learn since their creation (Eph. 3:10). It should also be remembered that the learning capacity of angels has not been corrupted with sin as in the case with man (Rom. 1:21).

Order. Jesus told those who arrested him, "Thinkest thou that I cannot now pray to my Father, and he shall presently give me more than twelve legions of angels?" (Matt. 26:53). The writer to the Hebrews called them "an innumerable company of angels" (Heb. 12:22). The apostle John counted in excess of 2 million angels in heaven (Rev. 5:11), but this would not include about one-third of the angels that fell when Satan was cast out of heaven. If there is a guardian angel for each person on earth (Matt. 18:10; Acts 12:15), then the number exceeds at least 4 billion, but less if only saints have guardian angels (Heb. 1:14). A group this large could not function efficiently without an organization. Various groups of angels are identified in Scripture in relation to specific spheres of ministry. Michael the archangel is apparently the leader among the holy angels.

CONCLUSION

Just as we often find ourselves doing meaningful tasks for God, so the angels have the same desire and serve the same function. If we think that God is not using us as greatly as we desire, we can learn from the angels. The lowest angels far surpass all that we are or could accomplish, yet they are satisfied listening to the voice of God and obeying it (Ps. 103:20). Our service to Christ should be no different. Jesus said, "So likewise ye, when ye shall have done all those things which are commanded you, say, We are unprofitable servants; we have done that which was our duty to do" (Luke 17:10).

DAILY READINGS

☐Monday: *Judges 13:9-21*   ☐Tuesday: *Matthew 2:1-20*   ☐Wednesday: *Exodus 25:18-22*   ☐Thursday: *Colossians 2:8-23*   ☐Friday: *Genesis 19:1-13*   ☐Saturday: *Revelation 4:1-11*   ☐Sunday: *Luke 1:30—2:14*

THIRTY-FOUR
THE WORKS OF ANGELS

Are they not all ministering spirits, sent forth to minister for them who shall be heirs of salvation? Hebrews 1:14

INTRODUCTION

It is not often that a seminary dean can be challenged by a four-year-old to review his theology, but it happened while this chapter was being written. My father-in-law passed away, and it fell to me to explain the death of her great-grandfather to my granddaughter. Mr. Forbes was a fine Christian and had served Christ for many years. Though he remained a layman all his life, he had served diligently with the Gideons International, then as a staff worker at a Bible institute. Though we were saddened at his loss, we were happy that his suffering was ended.

I told my granddaughter by long distance phone, "Great-grandpa has gone to heaven." Her response was immediate, "Did the angels take him?" Since she is being raised in a Christian home, immediately I thought, "Where did this little four-year-old get that idea?" Of course someone taught her properly, for one of the duties of angels is described as: "And it came to pass, that the beggar died, and was carried by the angels into Abraham's bosom" (Luke 16:22).

Understanding the works of angels is not just a bunch of

stories with no relevance to contemporary life. The works of angels affect the daily life of each one of us. Their work should be studied by every Christian, not just by theologians in the seminaries. Even four-year-old children have begun to think about the work of angels as it may affect their lives.

THE GENERAL WORKS OF ANGELS

God has in the past used angels to accomplish a number of tasks. They were involved in delivering the revelation of the Word of God. At times, God has sent angels to protect his people. Men have been encouraged and motivated to greatness by angels. They have also been used of God both to free captured men and to strengthen men in their service for God. When God has had to judge sin, often he has sent his angels to execute his judgment. Beyond these specific duties, angels have been the messengers of God to men on a number of occasions.

Angelic transportation at death. The Bible teaches that "to be absent from the body [is] to be present with the Lord" (2 Cor. 5:8). Apparently we are taken instantaneously to heaven at death. God uses angels to transport the souls of the saved to the presence of God. Luke recorded a story that Jesus told about the death of two men, one who went to a place of eternal paradise, the other to the place of eternal punishment. "And it came to pass, that the beggar died, and was carried by the angels into Abraham's bosom" (Luke 16:22). Though this is the only reference to this phase of the works of angels, there is no indication that anything beyond the norm happened here or that anything less than the norm can be expected today. Since every Christian has a guardian angel, it is assumed that that angel accomplishes his final duty, which is to deliver the soul of the departed saint into the presence of God.

Angelic revelation. God has used a variety of ways to make his revelation known to man (Heb. 1:1); angels are just one means of delivering his revelation. After recording the Revelation of Jesus Christ and seeing the new heavens and new earth, John spoke of "the angel which showed me these things" (Rev. 22:8). Ezekiel described his vision of the cherubim in the first chapter of his prophecy. Also, the angel of God was sent on three occasions surrounding the birth of Christ to reveal something that God was about to do. First he appeared to the priest Zacharias, to tell him of the coming birth of his son, John (Luke 1:11). About six months later, "Gabriel was sent from God unto a city of Galilee, named Nazareth, To a virgin espoused to a man whose name was Joseph, of the house of David; and the virgin's name was Mary" (Luke 1:26, 27). It was probably about five or six months later, after announcing the birth of Christ to Mary, "the angel of the Lord appeared unto him in a dream, saying, Joseph, thou son of David, fear not to take unto thee Mary, thy wife: for that which is conceived in her is of the Holy Ghost" (Matt. 1:20). God also used an angel to reveal the birth of Samson to the barren wife of Manoah (Judg. 13:3) and later to teach the parents of Samson how to raise their son (Judg. 13:9-21). In this role, the angels characterize the meaning of their name by delivering a message from God.

Angelic protection. Before God destroyed the cities of Sodom and Gomorrah, he sent two angels to warn Lot and his family to flee the city (Gen. 19:12, 13). During the evening, the safety of Lot's family and his guests was threatened by the men of the city. The two angel visitors protected Lot and themselves when they "smote the men that were at the door of the house with blindness, both small and great: so that they wearied themselves to find the door" (Gen. 19:11). After Daniel had spent the night in a den of lions, he was able to report to the king, "My God hath sent his angel, and hath shut the lions' mouths, that they have not hurt me, forasmuch as before him innocence was found in me" (Dan. 6:22). David, too, had learned throughout his experience as both shepherd and soldier that "the angel of the Lord encampeth round about those that fear him, and delivereth them" (Ps. 34:7).

Today, there are guardian angels to give physical protection to the people of God. Children are described as having "their angels" (Matt. 18:10) and the Christians described the knocking at their door by Peter, "It is his angel" (Acts 12:15).

Protection begins early in life and continues throughout life. The guardian angels "do always behold the face of my Father which is in heaven" (Matt. 18:20), implying that God, who knows what danger faces us, can send our angel immediately to help us. This protection seems to extend to physical help. Our spiritual help comes from the indwelling Christ and the Holy Spirit. We should avail ourselves of the filling of the Holy Spirit and the presence of Christ to keep us from temptation and sin. Even though it is an argument from silence, there is not one verse that suggests we should pray to angels for help. We pray to the Father and he sends angels.

Angelic emancipation. Angels not only protect people from trouble, they also on occasion provide for their deliverance. Very early in the church in Jerusalem, the Sadducees arrested the apostles and threw them into prison. "But the angel of the Lord by night opened the prison doors, and brought them forth" (Acts 5:19). It must have infuriated the Sadducees, who denied the theological existence of angels, that God should send an angel to release their prisoners. On another occasion, while the church prayed for Peter, who was in prison awaiting his execution, God sent an angel to release him from his jail cell (Acts 12:7). This was quite different from the occasion when Peter attempted to prevent the arrest of Jesus with a sword, and Jesus said, "Thinkest thou that I cannot now pray to my Father, and he shall presently give me more than twelve legions of angels?" (Matt. 26:53).

Angelic provision. When Elijah ran from Jezebel in fear of his life, he was discouraged and tired. God sent an angel to prepare a meal while he slept. Then he was encouraged to eat. The nature of this food provided by the angel was such that "he arose, and did eat and drink, and went in the strength of that meat forty days and forty nights unto Horeb, the mount of God" (1 Kings 19:8).

After Jesus had fasted forty days in the wilderness and the devil had failed in his attempt to cause Jesus to sin, "Then the devil leaveth him, and, behold, angels came and ministered unto him" (Matt. 4:11). Part of that ministry of angels to Jesus may have included providing nourishment and physical sustenance.

Angelic encouragement. God has sent angels to encourage servants of God who were discouraged. The Book of Revelation was written in part to encourage those being persecuted by the Roman authorities. The reader is reminded in the final book of the Bible that God is still on the throne, no matter how bad things may appear. When the angel of the Lord appeared to Gideon (Judg. 16:12), he was a discouraged young man. After the angel commissioned him, Gideon was used of God to remove the idols from his father's house and deliver Israel from the Midianites.

Angelic administration. Because God is holy, his nature demands that he judge sin. On several occasions, God used his angels to administer justice, and one angel in particular to judge sin—the angel of death. When David numbered the people of Israel, God decided to judge it as sin. "So the Lord sent a pestilence upon Israel from the morning even to the time appointed: and there died of the people, from Dan even to Beer-sheba, seventy thousand men. And when the angel stretched out his hand upon Jerusalem to destroy it, the Lord repented of the evil, and said to the angel that destroyed the people, It is enough: stay now thine hand" (2 Sam. 24:15-18). There is coming at least one more occasion when God will use angels to administer judgment. "The Son of man shall send forth his angels, and they shall gather out of his kingdom all things that offend, and them who do iniquity, And shall cast them into a furnace of fire" (Matt. 13:41, 42).

THE SPECIFIC WORKS OF ANGELS

The Bible describes more specifically some of the works of angels. Angels served God throughout the life of Christ, at times prepared to do more than they were called on to perform. In some aspects of their work in relationship to the work of Christ, the angels were waiting for service. Currently, much of the work of angels in this age affects the church and various political states. Even the lost are not exempt from the work of angels today.

Angels and Christ. From the prediction of his birth through the judgments by Christ at his return, the angels are engaged in working with Jesus. Not only did they predict his birth to Mary (Luke 1:30) and Joseph (Matt. 1:20), they were on hand at that historic birth to announce it to the shepherds (Luke 2:10). When Herod heard about the Messiah's birth and planned to destroy Jesus, God warned Joseph and Mary through angels to go to Egypt (Matt. 2:19). The angels ministered to Jesus at the beginning of his public ministry in the wilderness (Matt. 4:11) and at the end in the garden of Gethsemane (Luke 22:43). They were on hand to defend Jesus during his arrest if he should have asked for them (Matt. 26:53), and one was present to roll back the stone on the resurrection morning (Matt. 28:2). Two angels were the first to officially announce Jesus' resurrection to the world (Matt. 28:6). They were nearby at the ascension of Christ into heaven and predicted his second coming (Acts 1:11). Jesus taught he would return accompanied by his angels (Matt. 25:31). At the judgment of Christ, angels will be on hand to carry out the judgment pronounced by Christ (Matt. 13:39, 40).

ANGELS IN THE MINISTRY OF CHRIST

1. Predicted his birth—Luke 1:30-33
2. Announced his birth—Luke 2:10-14
3. Warned his parents of Herod's plot—Matt. 2:19, 20
4. Ministry after the temptation—Matt. 4:11
5. Ministry before the betrayal—Luke 22:43
6. On call at the arrest of Jesus—Matt. 26:53
7. Rolled back the stone from the tomb—Matt. 28:2
8. First announcement of the resurrection—Matt. 28:6
9. Ascension of Christ—Acts 1:11
10. Return of Christ—Matt. 25:31
11. Execute the judgment of Christ—Matt. 13:39, 40

Angels and the church. Much of the general works of angels discussed in the first section of this chapter relates specifically to the church and its members. The Bible tells us that angels may attend the services of the church as spectators of church worship, order, and ministry. The angels are present to observe and presumably report to God concerning the order in our corporate worship (1 Cor. 11:10; Eph. 3:10; 1 Tim.

5:21). Some commentators suggest that the Book of Hebrews may have referred to angels: "Wherefore, seeing we also are compassed about with so great a cloud of witnesses, let us lay aside every weight, and the sin which doth so easily beset us, and let us run with patience the race that is set before us" (Heb. 12:1). If the witnesses that observed the race of Christians were angels, Christians would be motivated by their observation.

Angels and the nations. The prophet Daniel wrote of a time when Michael the archangel would help protect the nation Israel. "And at that time shall Michael stand up, the great prince which standeth for the children of thy people: and there shall be a time of trouble, such as never was since there was a nation even to that same time; and at that time thy people shall be delivered, everyone that shall be found written in the book" (Dan. 12:1). As Israel passes through the Great Tribulation, they will have a national guardian angel.

Angels and the lost. In many instances when angels appeared to men, one of the first things they said was, "Fear not." Obviously, the lost should fear angels because they are sometimes used as agents of judgment. God used an angel to kill Herod when he accepted the worship of the people. "And immediately the angel of the Lord smote him because he gave not God the glory; and he was eaten of worms, and gave up the ghost" (Acts 12:23). God may also do the same thing today. He will use angels to warn of the judgment of the world at Armageddon (Rev. 19:17) as he did in Sodom (Gen. 18:12, 13). They will also be involved in gathering and casting the lost into their assigned place of punishment at the end of the age (Matt. 13:39, 40).

CONCLUSION

Yes, Tammy was right. The angels did take Great-grandpa to heaven. This little four-year-old theologian has a better understanding of the theology of angels than many who know more facts but have never been able to relate them to their own lives. Also, like other children in the world, Tammy has a guardian angel in heaven who constantly has access to God the Father (Matt. 18:10). But the work of angels goes far beyond these two incidents. Every day angels are at work helping us accomplish God's will for our life. Their presence and assistance ought to lead us to do far more for Jesus than we have ever done before.

DAILY READINGS

☐Monday: *Genesis 16:1-13*   ☐Tuesday: *1 Kings 6:23-29*   ☐Wednesday: *Genesis 22:1-14*   ☐Thursday: *2 Samuel 24:1-18*   ☐Friday: *Matthew 18:1-10*   ☐Saturday: *Isaiah 6:1-13*   ☐Sunday: *Hebrews 12:1-22*

PART NINE

UNDERSTANDING THE DOCTRINE OF SATAN

THIRTY-FIVE
THE NATURE OF SATAN

How art thou fallen from heaven, O Lucifer, son of the morning! how art thou cut down to the ground, who didst weaken the nations! Isaiah 14:12

INTRODUCTION

Week after week a man stood up to pray at his church's prayer meeting. Typically, he closed his prayer with the phrase "and clean all the cobwebs out of my life." After listening to this man's continual request, the night came when a friend petitioned, "Lord, kill the spider instead!"

How often do we find ourselves dealing with "cobwebs" while ignoring the "spider" in our lives? Our main adversary is greater than a spider; it is Satan. Just as soldiers going into battle are instructed about their enemy, so we need to know about our enemy. The problem is that we live in a culture filled with fairy tales or false information about the devil. If we were to ask a dozen different people what they thought about the devil, we may get a dozen different answers.

During the Middle Ages, people enjoyed religious plays for entertainment. Over the years the devil was played by one dressed in a red suit with horns and a pitchfork. Even today people think the devil is evil-looking. When portrayed in movies, he has a sinister appearance.

Because of the recent increasing interest in the occult, movies have made Satan a box office attraction. Also, we see a growing cult of Satan worshipers. People are prepared to give Satan control over their lives to a greater or lesser degree. The interest and influence of Satan is growing from such simple things as a Ouija board or astrological chart, to witches' covens and stores that sell artifacts that relate to satanism.

Another group denies the existence of Satan completely. Someone noted that the Christian Science church takes the d out of devil, making it evil. Also, certain factions of liberal Christianity deny the supernatural aspect of the devil, while others recognize the existence of Satan but deny his power. Since secrecy is one of the characteristics of Satan, it is understandable why so many Christians are deceived concerning his nature and work. Satan has blinded them about it. He is most effective when he keeps himself hidden from public sight.

THE PERSONALITY OF SATAN

The devil is a real person. Originally, he was created as one of God's angels, possessing all the attributes of angels. Even after his rebellion and fall, Satan remained a person. He is identified in Scripture by personal pronouns and he is involved in various activities belonging only to persons. Those who deny the existence of a personal devil have no biblical basis upon which to base their conclusions.

God does not deny the personality of Satan. When Satan appeared with the angels, "The Lord said unto Satan, hast thou considered my servant Job...?" (Job 1:8, italics added). Later in the story, the Bible notes, "Satan came also among them to present himself before the Lord" (Job 2:1, italics added). In Zechariah's vision of the high priest's meeting with Satan, "The Lord said unto Satan, the Lord rebuke thee, O Satan; even the Lord that hath chosen Jerusalem rebuke thee" (Zech. 3:2, italics added). When tempted by Satan, Jesus five times used personal pronouns in his conversation with Satan (Matt. 4:7, 10).

Satan demonstrates intellectual ability, emotions, and an active will. His intelligence is reflected in his ability to memorize Scripture. When he tempted Jesus (Matt. 4:6), he cited an obscure verse out of context (Ps. 91:11, 12) to give authority to his temptation. His superior intellect is further demonstrated by his ability to organize in excess of 100 million angels under him. The Bible also portrays the devil's temptations in terms like "wiles" (Eph. 6:11), "depths" (Rev. 2:24), and "devices" (2 Cor. 2:11).

Jesus warned Peter of the emotional side of Satan when he told him, "Satan hath desired to have you, that he may sift you as wheat" (Luke 22:31). James identified fear as part of the emotional experience of all fallen angels (James 2:19). They also have the sensation of pain, because they will someday "be tormented day and night for ever and ever" (Rev. 20:10).

It is the will of Satan that best characterizes Satan. Isaiah cited the fall of Satan coming as a result of his attempt to take the place of God in heaven. Satan revealed his selfish nature in the exclamation "I will" five times (Isa. 14:12-15). The apostle Paul also identified pride as the sin of Satan (1 Tim. 3:6).

Satan is identified as performing acts normally ascribed to persons. Satan had the power of word selection and use as he tempted both Eve (Gen. 3:1-6) and Jesus (Matt. 4:1-11). He is currently accusing the brethren "before our God day and night" (Rev. 12:10). On at least two occasions, Satan is engaged in battle (Rev. 17:17; 20:8, 9). When Moses appeared before Pharaoh, Satan demonstrated limited power to perform some miracles when he turned the Egyptian magicians' rods into serpents (Exod. 7:12).

THE ORIGIN OF SATAN

God could not have created anything evil. Originally, man was created in the image and likeness of God but fell into sin when Adam exercised his will in rebellion against God. Satan also was originally created as a being with the power of personality and the freedom of choice. He was an angel with apparent honor and leadership in heaven. When Satan's pride blinded him and led him to exercise his will in rebellion against God, he was cast out of heaven (Isa. 14:12-15).

THE FALL OF SATAN (Isa. 14:12-15)	
I will. . .	*Take God's place*
Ascend into heaven	Acts 1:9-11
Exalt my throne	Rev. 22:1
Govern heaven	Isa. 2:1-4
Ascend above the heights	Phil. 2:9
Be like the Most High	Gen. 14:19, 22
"Yet thou shalt be brought down to hell, to the sides of the pit."	

Ascend into heaven. The ultimate desire of Satan was to take God's place. Lucifer's first attempt involved his ascent into the abode of God. The Bible identifies three heavens. The first heaven is the sky surrounding our planet, the atmosphere. The second heaven is the stellar heaven which is apparently the abode of angels. The third heaven is the dwelling place of God. When Lucifer determined to ascend into heaven, he sought to move into the third heaven, the dwelling place of God. Satan wanted to ascend above the position and place where he was created and assume the place of his Creator.

Exalt his throne. Satan sought authority over the other angels. Satan wanted to be exalted above the stars. The term "star" is often used in the Bible to identify angels (Rev. 1:20; 12:4). Some commentators believe Satan ruled the angels as an archangel along with Michael and Gabriel. If this were the case, Satan then sought to expand his sphere of authority over Michael and Gabriel and those angels they ruled. This would make Satan the ultimate authority in heaven, perhaps taking the place of God over the angels. If this trinity of archangels exited before the Fall, it may explain why a third of the angels fell with Satan (Rev. 12:4).

Govern heaven. Satan desired to "sit also upon the mount of the congregation, in the sides of the north" (Isa. 14:13). The phrase "mount of the congregation" is an expression relating to ruling in the kingdom of God (Isa. 2:1-4). Lucifer seemed to be saying, "I want a share in the kingdom." The problem was he wanted God's share. The "north side" is a term relating to God's presence in Scripture (Ps. 75:6, 7). During the millennial reign of Christ, Christ will rule this earth from the north (Ps. 48:2).

Ascend above the heights. There can be no question that Satan was prepared to attempt a coup in heaven. His desire was not simply to get closer to God but to surpass God. "I will ascend above the heights of the clouds" (Isa. 14:14). Clouds are often used to refer to the glory of God. In fact, 100 of the 150 uses of the word "cloud" in the *King James Version* have to do with divine glory. Satan sought glory for himself that surpassed the glory of God. Paul revealed the ultimate desire of Satan when he wrote, "who opposeth and exalteth himself above all that is called God, or that is worshipped, so that he as God sitteth in the temple of God, shewing himself that he is God" (2 Thess. 2:4).

Be like the Most High. When Abraham paid his tithes to Melchizedek, this priest "blessed him and said, Blessed be Abram of the most high God, possessor of heaven and earth" (Gen. 14:19). "The Most High" (*El Elyom*) means the possessor of heaven and earth, exercising divine authority in both spheres. When Jesus appeared to his disciples in Galilee after his death, he said, "All power is given unto me in heaven and in earth" (Matt. 28:18). Satan sought the authority of God for himself. By becoming the most high, Satan would be the possessor of heaven and earth. By ascending into heaven, he would rule angels and ultimately enjoy a messianic rule.

This attempt to be like God is similar to Satan's strategy today. All of Satan's plans in the universe are counterfeit to God's plans. One of the chief works of Satan today is imitating Christianity. He attempts to counterfeit all that God performs (see Chapter 36). The Christian needs to be certain he is not tricked into accepting a satanic counterfeit of God's best for his life.

THE CHARACTER OF SATAN

The Bible describes the character of Satan in three ways. First, certain names or titles are ascribed to him which reflect his true nature. Second, his character describes his behavior. In the third place, Satan is described through his nature.

Names of Satan. Just as God uses his own names to reveal who he is and what is his nature, so God has revealed the nature of Satan through his name. Over thirty different names or titles are given to this sinful fallen angel.

THE NAMES AND TITLES OF SATAN	
1. Satan—Job 1:6	17. Prince of the power of the air—Eph. 2:2
2. Devil—Rev. 12:7	
3. Apollyon—Rev. 9:11	18. Prince of this world—John 14:30
4. Beelzebub—Matt. 12:27	
5. Belial—2 Cor. 6:15	19. God of this age—2 Cor. 4:4
6. Old serpent—Rev. 20:2	20. Dragon—Rev. 12:9
7. Adversary—1 Pet. 5:8	21. Beast out of the bottomless pit—Rev. 11:7
8. Anointed cherub—Ezek. 28	
9. Deceiver of the whole world—Rev. 12:9	22. Accuser of the brethren—Rev. 12:10
10. Evil one—John 17:15	23. Angel of the bottomless pit—Matt. 4:1
11. Leviathan—Isa. 27:1	24. Angel of light—Matt. 4:1
12. Lucifer—Isa. 14:12	25. Enemy—Matt. 13:39
13. Murderer—John 8:44	26. Father of lies—John 8:44
14. Roaring lion—1 Pet. 5:8	27. Liar—John 8:44
15. Son of the morning—Isa. 14:12	28. Prince of demons—Matt. 9:34
16. Wicked one—John 3:12	29. Man of sin—2 Thess. 2:3
	30. Thief—John 10:10

Satan's subtle character. The Bible makes no effort to hide the craftiness of Satan. When false teachers and false apostles appeared in the church at Corinth, Paul wrote, "And no marvel; for Satan himself is transformed into an angel of light" (2 Cor. 11:14). The apostle acknowledged one of his purposes in writing a second epistle to the Corinthians was "lest Satan should get an advantage of us; for we are not ignorant of his devices" (2 Cor. 2:11). He further recognized the cunning and subtle character of Satan when he advised the Ephesians to "put on the whole armour of God, that ye may be able to stand against the wiles of the devil" (Eph. 6:11).

Nature of Satan. It is the nature of a man that causes him to act as he does. The same principle exists as we try to better understand Satan. John identified the devil as the originator and chief practitioner of sin (1 John 3:8). He further described Satan as "that wicked one" (1 John 5:18). Jesus called Satan a liar (John 8:44) and thief (John 10:10). The evil acts of Satan are a natural expression of his evil nature. "The thief cometh not, but for to steal, and to kill, and to destroy" (John 10:10). The apostle Paul recognized the destructive nature of Satan when he wrote, "The god of this world hath blinded the minds of them which believe not, lest the light of the glorious gospel of Christ, who is the image of God, should shine unto them" (2 Cor. 4:4).

CONCLUSION

The Bible teaches the existence of a personal devil, the author of sin, who tries to destroy the work of God today. When Christians see evidences of sin all around them, they need to think soberly of their enemy, recognizing the existence of a person seeking their destruction. Peter warns us even today, "Be sober, be vigilant; because your adversary the devil, as a roaring lion, walketh about, seeking whom he may devour" (1 Pet. 5:8). Apart from total dependence upon God, we cannot win the victory over the devil.

DAILY READINGS

☐Monday: *John 8:30-51*   ☐Tuesday: *Revelation 9:1-12*
☐Wednesday: *Job 1:1-22*   ☐Thursday: *Job 2:1-10*
☐Friday: *Zechariah 3:1-10*   ☐Saturday: *Ezekiel 28:1-19*
☐Sunday: *Isaiah 14:1-17*

THIRTY-SIX
THE WORKS OF SATAN

Be sober, be vigilant; because your adversary the devil, as a roaring lion, walketh about, seeking whom he may devour.
1 Peter 5:8

INTRODUCTION

Years ago, an artist painted a portrait of the devil playing chess. The devil had challenged a young chess player. If he could win, the young man would be eternally free from the influence of evil. If he lost, the devil would possess his soul.

The picture showed the determination of the devil to win. Chess experts who saw the picture realized in just four short moves the young man was in trouble. The picture visualizes torment in the face of the man as the devil is moving his queen to announce checkmate. The young man has his hand over his rook, amazed and disheartened at what appears to be his ultimate loss.

For years the picture hung in a Cincinnati art gallery, illustrating the power of the devil over the affairs of men. As the viewers passed the portrait, they saw the hopelessness of the young man's situation. Some of the world's finest chess players stood amazed at the artist's brilliance at chess and the application to life.

Finally, one person who studied the picture was convinced someone could beat the devil in a chess game. An aging chess master, Paul Murphy, was brought from New Orleans to view the picture. A crowd gathered to see if he could solve the dilemma in the portrait. He sat attempting various moves, only to see the futility of those attempts. Then suddenly his eyes lit up as he realized there was an unthought-of combination, which not only saved the young man's king, but placed the devil in checkmate. The people shouted, "Young man, make that move. That's the move!"

Many Christians feel they must give up in defeat when it comes to doing battle with the devil. The Bible, on the other hand, claims, "Greater is he that is in you, than he that is in the world" (1 John 4:4).

All of Satan's works are against God. At times he actively opposes the work or plan of God. On other occasions, he simply imitates God so as to draw Christians away from the simple plan of God.

OPPOSITION TO GOD

Jesus portrayed the devil in one of his parables as the enemy of God (Matt. 13:39). As such, the devil is constantly opposing God and all God does. That opposition portrayed itself in his attempt to destroy the messianic line. Then he sought to destroy the race God sought to redeem. When God chose a people of his own, the nation Israel, Satan unreservedly sought their destruction. Throughout the life of Christ, Satan sought to distract the Savior from his mission. As God works through the church today, so Satan is opposed to the work of God there.

Messianic line. As soon as God in his righteousness began to judge sin, God also in his mercy promised a Redeemer. "And I will put enmity between thee and the woman, and between thy seed and her seed; it shall bruise thy head, and thou shalt bruise his heel" (Gen. 3:15). With the birth of Abel, the devil began his opposition. Satan worked in Cain to kill his brother Abel. With Abel dead, the line would be broken and the Messiah could never be born. He did not realize that God would replace Abel with Seth (Gen. 4:25). Every attempt to destroy the godly line by extinction or by sexual contamination was an attempt by Satan to destroy the coming Messiah. Even in a small way, the dangers to David the shepherd boy carried out Satan's plot. David was twice attacked by wild beasts. Satan may have felt David's great sin with Bathsheba would prevent God from using him to be the father of the Messiah, but in contrast, it was that very relationship God chose to use (Matt. 1:6).

Human race. God created man in his image and likeness to have fellowship with God and have dominion over the earth. When Satan approached Eve in the garden, he promised Eve not only that she would not die (Gen. 3:4) but that eating the fruit would lead to her experiencing life on a higher plane (Gen. 3:5). With the entrance of sin into the race, Satan knew God would have to judge them as he had been previously judged. When Satan saw that God was offering to redeem the world, he sought to contaminate the human race by leading them into grievous sins (Gen. 6:5). God did judge most of them for their sin, but eight, Noah and his family, were kept safe in the ark (Gen. 7:13).

Israel. From the time of the call of Abraham, the devil has been the enemy of the Jew. God had told Abraham, "Look now toward heaven, and tell [count] the stars, if thou be able to number them: and he said unto him, So shall thy seed be" (Gen. 15:5). After the nation went to Egypt and began to grow as God had promised, Satan moved Pharaoh to command the destruction of all male children (Exod. 1:16). Later, Satan used the personal animosity of Haman toward Mordecai to plan the first systematic genocide of the Jews. The Book of Esther records this attempt and Haman's ultimate defeat (Esther 3:6; 7:9, 10). Satan has continued to raise up anti-Semitic leaders who have unsuccessfully attempted to exterminate the Jews.

Christ. With the birth of Christ, Satan used Herod to plan the murder of all children of Jesus' age (Matt. 2:16). After forty days in the wilderness, Satan himself tempted Jesus in an attempt to destroy the ministry of Christ before it began (Matt. 4:1-11). He used the forces of nature to try to destroy Christ before he could redeem the world (Mark 4:35-41). On occasion, Satan used both Peter (Matt. 16:23) and Judas (John 13:27) to attempt to thwart Christ from his purpose. Even in the final hours before his death, Satan attempted to convince Christ to bypass the cross. Even after Christ died and was buried, Satan inspired the Jewish leaders to appoint a guard and seal the tomb in a feeble effort to prevent the resurrection.

Church. Jesus said, "I will build my church, and the gates of hell shall not prevail against it" (Matt. 16:18). From the first mention of the church in Scripture, Jesus taught that it would be in opposition to Satan. The picture of gates is not that of a church struggling to hold out against the incredible opposition of the near-overwhelming forces of hell, but rather that of an aggressive church smashing down the strongholds of the devil as he attempts feebly to keep the dynamic church from winning people to Christ.

As we read the Book of Acts, we see this principle at work. Opposition toward the church stimulated the church to more aggressive outreach. Throughout history, Satan has actively opposed the work of the church. But the lesson of history is clear. The blood of the martyrs has ever been the seed of the church. Under the most severe opposition of the devil, God has worked best to glorify himself. His church has not only survived the opposition of the devil, it has survived it victoriously.

THE IMITATOR

The old adage goes, "If you can't beat them, join them." In one respect, this also reflects one aspect of the work of Satan, that of imitation. The devil is the master counterfeiter of all that pertains to evil. The following chart contrasts the works of God and the devil's attempts to reproduce them.

Imitation. From the very beginning, it has been Satan's desire to be like God (Isa. 14:14). In his present work, Satan is attempting to duplicate the works of God. Almost everything God has established, Satan has duplicated. There even exists today a satanic "bible" and church of Satan.

THE COUNTERFEITS OF SATAN	
1. Jesus is the Son of God—Ps. 2:1	1. Satan is the God of this world—Eph. 2:2; 2 Thess. 2:3
2. Trinity—Matt. 28:20	2. Tri-unity—Rev. 20:10
3. Mystery of godliness— 1 Tim. 3:16	3. Mystery of iniquity— 2 Thess. 2:7
4. Children of God—John 1:12	4. Children of Satan— John 8:44
5. God's mark on his servants—Rev. 7:3	5. Satan's mark of the beast—Rev. 13:16
6. Miracles of Christ— Matt. 4:23	6. Miracles of Satan— 2 Thess. 2:9
7. Christ the true Light— John 1:7	7. Angel of light—2 Cor. 11:14
8. Christ appoints apostles—Matt. 10:1	8. Satan appoints apostles— 2 Cor. 11:13

Infiltration. "Satan himself is transformed into an angel of light" (2 Cor. 11:14) so he can infiltrate the people of Christ and affect the work of God. Jesus claimed that some who called themselves Christians would not be permitted entrance into heaven because they do not possess a personal relationship with Christ (Matt. 7:23). By the end of the first century, Satan was clearly trying to control the church of Jesus Christ from both the outside (Rev. 2:13) and the inside (Jude 4). The apostle Paul had warned the Ephesian pastors that Satan would attempt to destroy the church by sending into the church evil men who would attempt to corrupt good men (Acts 20:29, 30).

DESTRUCTION

A third aspect of the works of Satan is to corrupt all that God has created, thereby destroying it. But Satan's work is in contrast to the work of Christ. "The thief cometh not, but for to steal, and to kill, and to destroy: I am come that they might have life, and that they might have it more abundantly" (John 10:10). Jesus helps, while Satan hinders our efforts to live for God.

Deceiving the nations. Some of Satan's destructive energies are directed against the nations of this world. When Jesus returns, Satan will be sealed in a pit "that he should deceive the nations no more" (Rev. 20:3). This happens during the millennial rule of Christ. Currently, though, Satan has freedom to perform his deceptive work among the nations. In the future, Satan will convince the nations to support his cause in the battle of Armageddon, where he will lead the nations to their ultimate destruction.

Deceiving the unsaved. Satan is aggressively keeping the unsaved from understanding the gospel. Paul explained to the Corinthians, "The god of this world hath blinded the minds of them which believe not, lest the light of the glorious gospel of Christ, who is the image of God, should shine unto them" (2 Cor. 4:4). Not content with blinding the unsaved so that they cannot understand the gospel, he also has another strategy. "Then cometh the devil, and taketh away the word out of their hearts, lest they should believe and be saved" (Luke 8:12). The Book of Acts records one account after another where the devil used men to oppose the progress of the gospel. Satan's strategy is simple. If he can prevent men from hearing the gospel and understanding what Christ offers them, then men will be content to go their own way. The Bible warns, "There is a way that seemeth right unto a man, but the end thereof are the ways of death" (Prov. 16:25).

Defeating the saved. Merely to defeat a Christian must be the most frustrating aspect of Satan's work, for he cannot destroy the child of God. Satan will use the lust of the flesh, the lust of the eyes, and the pride of life to attack Christians (1 John 2:15, 16). Satan will attack them directly or indirectly. If Satan cannot get a Christian to fall into the pollution of sin, he will push the believer beyond the will of God into legalism or fanaticism. On occasion a Christian may stumble, but the Bible teaches that "a just man falleth seven times, and riseth up again" (Prov. 24:16). The Christian is not able to defeat the devil in himself but is victorious only as he allows the power of Christ to live in him. "Ye are of God, little children, and have overcome them: because greater is he that is in you, than he that is in the world" (1 John 4:4). But remember, the fact that Satan cannot ultimately destroy us does not mean he will not tempt us.

Satan has successfully tempted Christians to lie to God in the past (Acts 5:3). He is called the "accuser of the brethren" (Rev. 12:10). He seeks to hinder Christians in their work for God (1 Thess. 2:18) and to defeat them in their Christian walk (Eph. 6:12). Satan tempted one Christian to engage in immorality in Corinth (1 Cor. 5:1). He attempted to destroy the Corinthian church, first by sowing tares of dissension (Matt. 13:38, 39) among the believers (1 Cor. 3:1-7). Also, Satan will attempt to destroy a church by sending in unsaved members and leaders (2 Cor. 11:5, 13-15). If internal opposition fails, Satan will attack the church through external persecution against Christians (Rev. 2:10). However, none of Satan's attempts to destroy the Christian need be successful; we have been promised the victory over Satan (2 Cor. 2:14).

HOW TO OVERCOME SATAN

It should be more natural for us to defeat Satan than the reverse. God has revealed certain principles in his Word that can protect the Christian against defeat. But more than insulating against evil, these principles should make the Christian victorious. The Bible clearly states, "There hath no temptation taken you but such as is common to man: but God is faithful, who will not suffer you to be tempted above that ye are able; but will with the temptation also make a way to escape, that ye may be able to bear it" (1 Cor. 10:13). That "way to escape" is found by applying biblical principles to each temptation.

The principle of respect. Too often Christians rely on fleshly strength to deliver them from Satan. Though Jesus is greater than the devil (1 John 4:4), we must still have a healthy respect for our enemy. A good football team, if they become overconfident, may lose to a lesser team. Overconfidence will cause a team to play carelessly, allowing the opposition to do things they could not otherwise accomplish. So if a

Christian does not realize that Satan possesses the attributes and abilities of angelic beings, he will allow Satan to gain victories where he could not otherwise do so. Even Michael, the archangel, was not prepared to confront Satan except in the name of the Lord (Jude 9). How much more should we be afraid of the power of Satan!

The principle of removal. It has often been said that one bad apple will spoil the whole barrel. This principle also applies to a confrontation with the devil. A wise Christian should evaluate his life and avoid those areas where he is most likely to be tempted. Paul reminds us to "abstain from all appearance of evil" (1 Thess. 5:22). When Joseph found himself tempted by Potiphar's wife, "he left his garment in her hand, and fled, and got him out" (Gen. 39:12). Paul also applied this principle in reverse to false teachers, meaning that not only should we remove ourselves from evil, we should remove its influence from our lives. "A man that is an heretick after the first and second admonition reject" (Titus 3:10). By separating ourselves from the source of the temptation both morally and geographically, we can gain a temporary victory over the devil. The word "temporary" is used because no one is ever immune from temptation till death. But in this life, remember, "An ounce of prevention is worth a pound of cure."

The principle of resistance. A Christian is disobedient to God if he passively entertains Satan or his influence. "Submit yourselves therefore to God. Resist the devil, and he will flee from you" (James 4:7). It is possible for the Christian to send the devil running in defeat by taking definite action. The apostle Peter advised the believer that he should not give in to Satan, but "resist steadfastly in the faith" (1 Pet. 5:9). We would not be defeated if we would quote the name of Jesus Christ and refuse to listen to Satan's temptation. When Jesus was tempted, he gained the victory by using the Scriptures to resist the devil (Matt. 4:1-11).

The principle of readiness. The Boy Scouts have a motto, "Be prepared." That principle is the watchword of the tempted Christian. "Watch ye and pray, lest ye enter into temptation"

(Mark 14:38). Paul advised the Ephesians, "Put on the whole armour of God, that ye may be able to stand against the wiles of the devil" (Eph. 6:11). The prepared Christian will recognize his weak areas and strengthen them. David assured us that memorizing Scripture will help keep us from sin (Ps. 119:1, 11). One who is serious about gaining victory over some besetting sin should concentrate on memorizing several verses of Scripture that deal with the particular area of weakness in his life. Also, he should be certain he is fully equipped to meet the devil in battle.

PROTECTION AGAINST THE DEVIL (Eph. 6:13-17)
1. Girdle (belt) of truth 2. Breastplate of righteousness 3. Shoes of the preparation of the gospel 4. Shield of faith 5. Helmet of salvation 6. Sword of the Spirit

CONCLUSION

There is a personal devil actively working to defeat every Christian in the world today. His influence is certain to affect our lives. The works of the devil need not overcome the saint. By exercising our faith in God and obeying his Word, we can gain the victory over the devil.

DAILY READINGS

☐Monday: *Genesis 3:1-19*   ☐Tuesday: *Genesis 6:1-8*
☐Wednesday: *Revelation 12:1-17*   ☐Thursday: *Matthew 4:1-11*   ☐Friday: *2 Thessalonians 2:1-17*   ☐Saturday: *2 Corinthians 11:1-15*   ☐Sunday: *Ephesians 6:10-20*

PART TEN

UNDERSTANDING THE DOCTRINE OF DEMONS

THIRTY-SEVEN
DEMONS

Now the Spirit speaketh expressly, that in the latter times some shall depart from the faith, giving heed to seducing spirits, and doctrines of devils. 1 Timothy 4:1

INTRODUCTION

The existence of a personal devil and demons is less and less being considered a fairy tale or a superstition. Our society reminds us that demons are real and at work. Some people worship demons, while others engage regularly in other practices of the occult relating to demon activity. Popular music and songs have been increasingly addressed to occult themes. As a result, the existence of evil and the accompanying demonic beings is not generally rejected by the unsaved in today's world.

Understanding demons is especially important for the Christian. The Bible makes it clear that we are engaged in a spiritual warfare (Eph. 6:12). As we seek to win the battle, it is to our best advantage to understand not only Satan but his messengers. But a word of caution is in order. It is good to know about demons but we should not be consumed with learning about them.

The Bible is God's revelation to aid us as we search for truth and our attempt to live for God (Deut. 29:29; 2 Tim.

3:15-17). It is our only reliable authority on the subject of demons. Some Christians affect their thinking negatively by engaging in excessive study of occult literature. Not only does
this fail to provide accurate and reliable information about
the devil and demons, it is a direct violation of the command
of God (Deut. 18:9). The Bible contains all the "intelligence
information" we need about demons to engage in battle with
them and emerge successful.

THE ORIGIN OF DEMONS

Two Greek words are translated similarly in the New Testament but their meanings are slightly different. The word *di-
abolos* is translated "devil" and refers to the devil himself.
Another word, *diamon,* is usually translated "devils" in the
King James Version but might be better translated "demons."
The Bible makes a very real distinction between a single
devil and many demons. Whenever we read of "devils" in
the Bible, we are reading about demons. It appears most
likely that demons are fallen angels who rebelled against God
in heaven and were cast out of the presence of God. As such,
what things are true about the nature of good angels are also
true of demons. When it comes to identifying demons, the
question that should be asked is "Where do demons come
from?" At least four suggestions have been made to help explain the origin of demons.

Spirits of the dead. One contemporary idea relating to the ori-
gins of demons claims they are the spirits of the evil dead.
This is the underlying assumption of much of the popular occult literature. It is not a new idea at all, for it was the explanation of some Greek philosophers years before Christ. The
early age of this theory does not however make it any more
believable. It stands in direct conflict with biblical teaching.
The Bible teaches that the souls of the evil dead go to "hades"
(Luke 16:23). They will remain there until the end of the millennial reign of Christ on this earth. Only then are they
brought before God to be judged (Rev. 20:11). Then they are
cast into eternal punishment: "And death and hell [hades]
were cast into the lake of fire. This is the second death" (Rev.
20:14).

Children of angels. Some have suggested that demons are the result of the union of angels and women as described: "There were giants in the earth in those days; and also after that, when the sons of God came in unto the daughters of men, and they bore children to them, the same became mighty men who were of old, men of renown" (Gen. 6:4). Some suggest that this verse describes sexual relations between angels and women, since the expression "sons of God" is used elsewhere in the Old Testament to identify angels. Even if this interpretation is correct, it is extremely unlikely that such a union produced demons. Some have suggested the "giants" could be an expression of the political or military might of these men. Others believe it could refer to the results of genetic tampering in a pre-Flood society. But there is no scriptural evidence to prove that the result of the union of humans and angels were demons.

Pre-Adamic spirits. One explanation, called the "gap theory," presupposes that the world is several million years old. According to this theory, God created a perfect world and society, as recorded in the first verse of the Bible but, for one reason or another, God had to destroy it before the situation as described in Genesis 1:2. This theory allowed for a society which existed for millions of years, thus harmonizing the contemporary views of the age of the world with the Bible account of creation. The spirits of those who lived before Adam, still inhabiting the earth are the demons, according to those who hold this view. But before we can conclude that demons are the disembodied spirits of a pre-Adamic race, we must first prove the existence of such a race. Once again, most biblical evidence is against such a theory, since Adam, for instance, was called the first man.

Fallen angels. Most conservative scholars believe that demons are fallen or evil angels. When Jesus described hell, he called it "everlasting fire, prepared for the devil and his angels" (Matt. 25:41). John described the fall of Satan in a highly symbolic fashion, noting that the devil took a third of the angels in heaven with him. "And his tail drew the third part of the stars of heaven, and did cast them to the earth: and the dragon stood before the woman who was ready to be

delivered, for to devour her child as soon as it was born"
(Rev. 12:4). This has led some to conclude that Satan was one
of three angels responsible, with Gabriel and Michael, to lead
other angels. When Satan fell, a third of the angels over
which he had supervision may have followed him in rebellion against God.

THE DESCRIPTION OF DEMONS

Demons are real beings, probably fallen angels. If this is true,
whatever is known of the nature of angels is also true of demons. They are nonmaterial, because all angels are spirit beings. As good angels are the messengers of God to carry out
his works, so demons are the emissaries of Satan to carry out
his diabolical plans. Like angels, demons possess tremendous intellectual ability. Apparently they have personalities
that inspire emotions and will. The 2,000 demons exercised
desire when they inhabited the swine that were drowned in
the sea. Demons have tremendous power at their disposal.

Spirit nature. All angels are spirit beings. Describing the evening of a busy day in the life of Christ, Matthew wrote,
"When the even was come, they brought unto him many that
were possessed with devils, and he cast out the spirits with
his word, and healed all that were sick" (Matt. 8:16). There
are times when these spirits can indwell a human. Demons
can also take on other physical forms. John "saw three unclean spirits [demons] like frogs come out of the mouth of the
dragon, and out of the mouth of the beast, and out of the
mouth of the false prophet" (Rev. 16:13). Revelation 9 describes the release of many demons from the bottomless pit
during the Great Tribulation. John described their physical
form and appearance as distinct yet similar to that of locusts
and scorpions.

Intellectual nature. Many Christians live with the deluded
idea that demons are ignorant servants of the devil. This is
totally contrary to every biblical indication of their intellectual capabilities. Even if they had been created ignorant, today they would possess a great deal of knowledge because

they have been observing and retaining knowledge since their creation. They were able to clearly identify the Person and deity of Christ during his earthly ministry (Mark 1:24; 5:6). Also, they possess a limited understanding of some aspects of their future (Matt. 8:29). While they possess enough facts to believe intellectually in God, their moral state prohibits their possessing saving faith (James 2:19). The apostle Paul credited demons with enough intellectual ability to design and propagate the various false doctrines of different religious sects (1 Tim. 4:1-3).

Moral nature. The chief difference between angels of God and demons lies in their moral nature. Demons are reprobates and evil. Apparently they have no opportunity of repentance or salvation. They are perpetually immoral because of their rebellion against God. The sin was serious enough in the mind of God so that hell and everlasting fire were created for Satan and demons (Matt. 25:41). Their nature is described by the adjective "unclean" (Matt. 10:1; Mark 1:27; Acts 8:7). Peter described demons as "the angels that sinned" (2 Pet. 2:4). A major part of the work of demons today is to propagate evil, teach false doctrine, and recruit others to rebel against God.

Power. It would be a serious mistake to underestimate the power of demons. Because angels in general are called "mighty" (Rev. 10:1), we may assume demons are also mighty. The final book of the Bible describes demons performing many unusual feats during the Tribulation. Even a person possessed by demons in the New Testament was described as having tremendous strength (Mark 5:3, 4). Actually it was the power of the demons working through him. The Christian that believes he can "wrestle" with demons without "taking on the whole armour of God" is seriously deluded (Eph. 6:10-18).

DESTINY OF DEMONS

When Jesus encountered a demon-possessed man during his earthly ministry, the demons asked, "Art thou come hither to

torment us before the time?" (Matt. 8:29). Demons understand something of their eternal destiny. The phrase "the
time" could mean that they feared premature expulsion from
the man, but it probably means premature judgment into
hell. The destiny of demons can be summarized in three
phases of confinement.

Present confinement. Some demons are currently confined.
John described the release of some of these demons in Revelation 9 during the Great Tribulation, when they will come
from the bottomless pit to afflict the people. Jude identified
another group of demons whom God "hath reserved in everlasting chains under darkness into the judgment of the great
day" (Jude 6). Apparently the crime of these angels was so
horrendous that they will never again experience any degree
of liberty (2 Pet. 2:4).

Millennial confinement. During the Great Tribulation, there
"are the spirits of devils, working miracles, which go forth
unto the kings of the earth and of the whole world, to gather
them to the battle of that great day of God Almighty" (Rev.
16:14). As demons are in part responsible for the battle of Armageddon, it is reasonable to expect they would be prevented from making war during the millennial reign of
Christ. While their millennial destiny is not specifically identified in the Bible, most commentators would agree that they
would be confined with Satan their leader in the bottomless
pit (Rev. 20:3). They certainly are not active during Christ's
reign on the earth.

Eternal confinement. One of the key thoughts to keep in mind
when attempting to understand hell is to remember it was
never the will of God that anyone should go there (1 Pet. 3:9).
When confronted with that truth, the obvious question is,
"Why did God create hell in the first place?" The answer to
that question is found in Matthew 25:41. Hell was "prepared
for the devil and his angels." A man will only go to hell by
choice, his choice as expressed by his rejection of Christ. Demons are apparently aware that someday they will be eternally confined to the lake of fire (Matt. 8:29).

CONCLUSION

Demons are a part of today's world. These fallen angels have rebelled against God. Even though they have a similar nature to good angels, their evil nature is permanent and irrevocable. Just as good angels assist the Christian today, demons will strive to hinder the Christian. "We wrestle not against flesh and blood, but against principalities, against powers, against the rulers of the darkness of this world, against spiritual wickedness in high places. Wherefore, take unto you the whole armour of God, that ye may be able to withstand in the evil day, and having done all, to stand" (Eph. 6:12, 13).

DAILY READINGS

☐Monday: *Matthew 8:1-17*   ☐Tuesday: *Matthew 8:18-34*
☐Wednesday: *Matthew 10:1-15*   ☐Thursday: *Matthew 17:1-21*   ☐Friday: *Matthew 25:31-46*   ☐Saturday: *Matthew 12:14-30*   ☐Sunday: *Jude*

THIRTY-EIGHT
DEMON ACTIVITY

For we wrestle not against flesh and blood, but against principalities, against powers, against the rulers of the darkness of this world, against spiritual wickedness in high places. Ephesians 6:12

INTRODUCTION

Several years ago, an author produced a best-selling book dealing with the works of Satan and his demons. The book was heavily documented with evidence of demon activity in our contemporary society. One of the surprising facts brought out by the author was that demons are worshiped. Beyond that it is evident that demons are at work today not only in primitive and superstitious societies, but also among the upper echelons of highly civilized Western Europe and North America. From astrology to witches and their sciences, the author concluded *Satan Is Alive and Well on Planet Earth.*

Everything God created performs a function. Even after sin has infected the creation of God, everything still has a purpose, so that God works his will indirectly. Not recognizing this principle, many Christians picture demons with their red suits, horns, and pitchforks sitting around a party table celebrating the progress of sin in the world. C. S. Lewis may have been more accurate in his fictional account of *The Screwtape Letters* as he described the efforts of one demon in hindering a person in his walk with God.

Demons are certainly busy today. Despite the clear instructions of the Word of God, some Christians are engaged in occult practices. Oftentimes a person may not be fully aware of what he is doing. Unsaved individuals involved in such activities leave themselves open to the dangerous possibility of demon possession. Those who have studied the biblical doctrine of demons and are aware of contemporary trends in society share this conclusion.

Understanding the works of demons is important to every Christian who desires to live for God. The Christian who knows and is able to recognize demonic activity around him will be better able to engage in spiritual battle for God.

THE WORK OF DEMONS

Several activities are identified in the Bible in which demons may be involved. Sometimes they are responsible for physical disease or mental suffering. While not all mental disorders are demonic in origin, some apparently are. Demons are also credited with tempting people to engage in immoral practices. They are the originators and propagators of the false doctrines taught by heretical religious groups. The Bible also teaches that some people were possessed by demons. Demons are committed to evil, yet God will use them to accomplish his plan during the end of the world.

Physical disease. There are many reasons why a person may experience physical illness. Sometimes it is the result of God's judgment for sin (1 Cor. 11:30). On other occasions the same sickness may come as a result of breaking some health law and exposing oneself to germs or viruses. It may come from God as his means of ending a person's life in a natural way. On other occasions, demons may be the reason a person experiences physical suffering.

Several specific physical afflictions are attributed to demons in the Bible. Jesus cast a demon out of a dumb man who immediately began to speak (Matt. 9:32, 33). On another occasion, a blind man began to see when the demon was cast out of him (Matt. 12:22). Job was afflicted physically with boils covering his body, the result of satanic activity (Job 2:1-10). Demons may have been the messengers that carried out Satan's commands to smite Job. Of course, afflictions are not always symptoms of demon activity, but demons are capable of and do occasionally cause physical pain and suffering.

Mental disease. Various forms of mental diseases can also be related to demons. In at least two cases of demon possession treated by Jesus during his ministry, the demons had so affected the minds of the victims to cause abnormal behavior. One man lived among tombs and created a disturbance day and night (Mark 5:4, 5). A young boy possessed with a demon involuntarily went into an apparent convulsion when he encountered the presence of Jesus (Luke 9:37-42). In both instances, the victims engaged in some form of self-destruction and physical mutilation of the body. After the demon was cast out of the person, the apparent mental problem disappeared.

Moral impurity. For the Christian, our final moral code of ethics is the Bible. Those who oppose God would also oppose the morality of the Bible. Demons are instrumental in leading both the saved and unsaved into moral compromise. One of the often-used names for demons in the Bible is "unclean spirit," an appropriate name, as they tarnish everything they influence. When Israel left Egypt, God gave them the land of Canaan. One of the reasons God wanted them in a separate land was that the heathen nations had given themselves over to unclean spirits and had become corrupted (Lev. 18; Deut. 18).

False doctrine. Paul discussed one main work of demons when he warned young Timothy of conditions "in the latter times." "Now the Spirit speaketh expressly, that in the latter times some shall depart from the faith, giving heed to seducing spirits, and doctrines of devils (1 Tim. 4:1). Demons are the source of many organized doctrines of the false cults. Even in the early church, there were false apostles (Rev. 2:2) and false doctrines (Rev. 2:14) that had to be opposed. The Bible teaches the coming of an antichrist during the Great Tribulation but, by the end of the first century, John wrote, "Little children, it is the last time: and as ye have heard that antichrist shall come, even now are there many antichrists; whereby we know that it is the last time" (1 John 2:18). The word "anti" had a twofold designation; first it meant "against" Christ, but the secondary meaning was the most evident, it meant "in substitution for," or "instead of," Christ. The existence of "antichrist" leaders throughout the church age is the result of demon activity. Their main activity is to foster a "substitute religion" in place of Christ and his doctrine.

Spiritual battle. One of the chief difficulties of living for God today is not the social pressures or inconvenience of life; it is the spiritual battle in which we are engaged. Our enemies are demons. Paul observed, "We wrestle not against flesh and blood, but against principalities, against powers, against the rulers of the darkness of this world, against spiritual wickedness in high places" (Eph. 6:12). The phrase "principalities...powers...rulers of the darkness of this world, against spiritual wickedness" refers to demons and their activities. Part of the work of demons, particularly as it relates to the Christian life, is doing battle with Christians on the spiritual level. This condition is the reason behind the apostolic imperative, "Put on the whole armour of God, that ye may be able to stand against the wiles of the devil" (Eph. 6:11). Without spiritual help from God, the Christian is unable to win the battle against demons.

Demon possession. "Demon possession" is not a biblical expression, yet the idea of demon control is more than simply a carry-over of ancient superstitions. Demon possession, as we understand it, occurs when God permits demons to possess a person and control his mind or body. On many occasions demon possession resulted in mental derangement. In most cases recorded in Scripture, the person possessed was apparently responsible for being possessed.

There is much confusion about demon possession. The following will give some guidance. Demon possession is the culmination of a volitional rejection of God and a volitional acceptance of Satan and his demons. A person does not become possessed by demons on a casual basis.

Demon possession is the opposite of the filling of the Spirit. Just as some Christians are more effective when filled with the Holy Spirit, so some unbelievers have greater demonic power as a result of their demonic possession. The same word is used of the Holy Spirit controlling in Ephesians 5:18 as Satan's control of Ananias and Sapphira (Acts 5:3). Demon possession and demon activity is more commonly recognized among heathen societies. However, there is increasing evidence of demonic activity in our Western society because of its waning Christian influence. As our nation turns from God and more people worship Satan and demons, there will be more evidence of demon activity in our society.

Many have conjectured about whether or not demons can "possess" or "influence" believers. Since the Bible is silent concerning Christians being "possessed," it has much to say concerning demons' possible influence on us and of our need to be aware of their desire to adversely affect our walk with God.

The will of God. It must be frustrating to demons after they had accomplished some evil scheme to later find out that they were carrying out the will of God. Satan did not realize what God wanted to do in Job's life when he caused him physical suffering. Also, God used "an evil spirit" to accomplish his will in the life of Saul, Israel's first king (1 Sam. 16:14). On another occasion, God used "a lying spirit" to deceive the false prophets of an evil king (1 Kings 22:22, 23). At the end of the Great Tribulation, demons will be used by God to gather the nations of the world to battlefields of Armageddon (Rev. 9:16). God is able to use even demons to accomplish his will.

THE WORSHIP OF DEMONS

When Israel finally prepared to enter the Promised Land, God definitely instructed Israel regarding their relationship to the occult religions of Canaan. "When thou art come into the land which the Lord thy God giveth thee, thou shalt not learn to do after the abominations of those nations" (Deut. 18:9). Despite the obvious implication that Christians should not be engaged in occult practices, some church youth gatherings have played around with such things as astrology, Ouija boards, and other games that have some relationship to "the spirits." One who recognizes biblical authority will seek to rid his life of any occult influences.

Divination. Divination was one of the specific practices named by Moses in his prohibition on occult worship (Deut. 18:10). Often this practice included the killing of a chicken or some small animal, and on occasions to observe its liver to determine the state of affairs and direction of the immediate future (Ezek. 21:21). Essentially divination is an illegitimate means of determining the will of God. This would apply to other variations of divination including palmistry, and tea-leaf reading. The Christian desiring to know the will of God should consult the Scriptures, not the stars (Ps. 119:9).

Necromancy. A second occult practice of today was also banned by God. "Necromancy" is an effort to communicate with and interrogate the dead. As the Bible teaches the dead are unable to communicate with the living (Luke 15:27-31), it only stands to reason that those who claim to have this ability are lying or are themselves deceived. In either case, the necromancer was considered an abomination unto the Lord (Deut. 18:11, 12).

Magic. The use of magic formulas and incantations was also forbidden. Today it is popular to distinguish between white and black magic, but leading biblical scholars agree that both forms of magic find their source and strength in demon power. Those who practice magic are under certain limits as to what they can accomplish (Dan. 4:7). Even when it appears that magicians are able to duplicate the power of God, they still fall short of what God is able to accomplish (Exod. 7:11, 12).

Sorcery. Closely related to magic is sorcery. Magic usually relates to accomplishing specific acts—such as rods becoming serpents—whereas sorcery relates more closely with calling upon demons to create situations around people. Thus the enchanter or sorcerer is one who uses incantations or omens. Their practices may have also included the use of mood-changing or psychedelic drugs. This has led some Bible scholars to denounce the use of such drugs because they are used as part of occult worship.

Witchcraft. Around the world today, there exists a growing number of those who call themselves witches. Witchcraft is directly opposed to God (Deut. 18:10). When Saul became the first king of Israel, one of his first acts was to ban the practice of witchcraft from the kingdom (1 Sam. 28:9). The witch is one who makes use of magic and sorcery to accomplish the will of demons.

Astrology. Perhaps the most popular form of occult practiced today is astrology. Contemporary astrology is really a combination of astrological cults practiced in Babylon, Egypt, and Canaan. In Canaan, astrology centered around the bull. The worship of the golden calf, child sacrifices to Molech, and Baal worship were all part of Canaanite astrology. The Old Testament is very clear to prohibit God's people from involvement there. In Egypt, God challenged the astrological gods of Egypt in sending ten plagues which directly attacked the authority of those gods. The highest of the Egyptian gods was Ra, the sun god. Three days of darkness was a direct indictment against the religion of Egypt.

CONCLUSION

There are many other forms of demon worship today, but the Christian has no authority to engage in any of them. Those who are practicing in the occult need to follow the Ephesian example of denouncing their involvement with demons. Apparently, some Ephesian believers were "dabbling" in the occult until an attempted exorcism backfired in their town. Then "many that believed came, and confessed, and shewed their deeds (Acts 19:18). The result of such action led to a revival in which many occult books were destroyed and the church experienced revival. Perhaps a similar abandonment of the occult will produce similar results today. In any case, every Christian needs to be properly equipped to do battle with demons.

DAILY READINGS

☐Monday: *Acts 19:11-22*   ☐Tuesday: *Ephesians 6:10-20*   ☐Wednesday: *Deuteronomy 18:9-22*   ☐Thursday: *Leviticus 20:1-27*   ☐Friday: *1 Samuel 28:7-25*   ☐Saturday: *Revelation 13:1-18*   ☐Sunday: *Revelation 17:1-18*

PART ELEVEN

UNDERSTANDING THE DOCTRINE OF THE CHURCH

THIRTY-NINE
THE NATURE
OF THE CHURCH

And I say also unto thee, that thou art Peter, and upon this rock I will build my church, and the gates of hell shall not prevail against it. Matthew 16:18

INTRODUCTION

The word "church" has come to mean a number of different things. Sometimes people say they "attend church" when they join a group of people in worshiping God. When they decide to go to the church, they make their way to a building. A young man who feels God's call upon his life may be ordained by the Evangelical Free Church, which means he is identified with a particular denomination. If we ask a person to which church he belongs, he might acknowledge he belongs to the First Presbyterian Church, which means a particular local assembly of people. When a young girl accepted Christ she was told how she was now spiritually related to everyone in the Church, which meant the universal Body of Christ. When we think of the many ways we use the word "church," it is understandable why there is so much confusion surrounding this doctrine.

Three divinely established institutions are the family, the state, and the church. Each has a unique purpose and God has chosen to work in specific ways through these institutions. If one of these does not function according to biblical patterns, its purposes are frustrated. When the church is not doing its job, God's most effective tool for evangelism and edification is blunted. This is not because of an arbitrary decision by God, but he has chosen to limit himself to the effectiveness of the strategy of these institutions.

Differing philosophies concerning the nature of the local church tend to be a divisive issue today. Inasmuch as we live in a pluralistic society, people conceive of their own needs and ideas for the church. Each person from a different background devises a different concept of what the church should be. The pages of the New Testament should be carefully studied to determine the biblical makeup of the local church.

A church is not a building, nor is it just any gathering of Christians, simply because those assembled call themselves a church. Whenever we think of the term "church," we should concern ourselves with the people and their purpose for assembling in the name of the Lord.

The first step in understanding the church is to determine its nature. Not only is the word "church" used in a variety of ways, but there are several important facts to understand concerning the etymology of the word. In the original language the word *ekklesia*, usually translated "church" in the Scriptures, occurs over a hundred times. It comes from the Greek words meaning "out" and "call." The church is a group of people who are "called out."

On some occasions when the word "church" was used it referred to a guild (Acts 19:32, 39, 41). Sometimes it referred to a general gathering (Acts 7:38), in this case Israel, the "church in the wilderness." At least once, the word was used in reference to the synagogue (Matt. 18:17).

Most other appearances of the word are translated "church," and are used in two ways. We read frequently of local assemblies as "the church of Christ" (Rom. 16:16), "the churches of God" (1 Cor. 11:16; 1 Thess. 2:14), and "the church in Corinth" (1 Cor. 2:1).

In other places (Eph. 1:22; 3:10, 21; 5:23-32) we read not of "churches" but of one Church, the Church, used in a general way as speaking of all the people of God as the Lord used the term: "Upon this rock I will build my church; and the gates of hell shall not prevail against it" (Matt. 16:18). Many refer to the church (the local assembly) and the Church (the universal Body of Christ). Most of our discussion in this section will deal with the local, visible church.

A local church is more than a gathering of Christians. It must assemble for the right purpose and have the right authority. It must reproduce itself and have the right organization. And, finally, it must have God's seal on its existence which gives credibility to its ministry.

A church is an assembly of born-again believers in whom Christ dwells by the Holy Spirit, an assembly that exists for the glory of God, under the discipline of the Word of God, and spiritually prepared to carry out the Great Commission. Its credibility is evident through the manifestation of spiritual gifts to nurture and reproduce itself. When a group of Christians is characterized by these distinctives, it is a church in the biblical sense of the word.

ASSEMBLY OF BAPTIZED BELIEVERS

Many groups use the generic name "church," but they do not fit the characteristics of the New Testament. The first part of the definition relates to members and how they got into the church. First, the members had to be believers; second, they were baptized; then they chose to assemble together. This pattern is clearly established in the Book of Acts.

Assembly. The word *ekklesia* means "called-out ones" and was used by the Greeks to identify a special group of people, such as a town meeting (Acts 19:32). In the New Testament, it came to refer to those God had called out to himself. Peter wrote, "Ye are a chosen generation, a royal priesthood, an holy nation, a peculiar people, that ye should show forth the praises of him who hath called you out of darkness into his marvelous light" (1 Pet. 2:9). The first characteristic of the New Testament church is that it is a group of people that assemble together with the Lord and for his purpose.

Believers. The Bible holds up the standard of a regenerate church membership but even then recognizes that some only profess salvation and become members who do not possess eternal life. Only those who know Jesus Christ personally should belong to his church. Because God worked through the apostles in the church at Jerusalem, a divine respect and reverence became evident among the community. "And of the rest [dared] no man join himself to them: but the people magnified them. And believers were the more added to the Lord, multitudes both of men and women" (Acts 5:13, 14). Even though the people of the city did not themselves desire to join the church, they admired the members of the church. Only believers were members of that church.

Baptized. On the day of Pentecost, Peter and the other apostles preached to Jews from around the world in their native tongues. Many were saved as they responded to the gospel preached that day. "Then they that gladly received his word were baptized: and the same day there were added unto them about three thousand souls" (Acts 2:41). Baptism is the first step after salvation. Members of the New Testament church were baptized soon after conversion. The New Testament gives no illustration of an unbaptized Christian except the thief on the cross, and his yieldedness to Christ indicates he would have been baptized if given the opportunity. While baptism has no merit in securing salvation, this act of obedience is a "badge of discipleship" in which a believer publicly identifies with Christ and his church.

THE BODY OF CHRIST

The church is more than an organization, it is an organism. The life of the church is the very life of Christ himself. Paul recognized the presence of Christ in the church when he called it "the body of Christ" on a number of occasions (1 Cor. 12:27; Eph. 1:23). Jesus observed the uniqueness of the church when he predicted, "For where two or three are gathered together in my name, there am I in the midst of them" (Matt. 18:20). Paul spoke also of Christ being the head of the Body (Eph. 4:15). While these truths are spoken of the universal body, what is true of the whole should be true of each individual part, each local church. In the same way, individuals are a part of the universal body by the Holy Spirit's work of joining us to the Body of Christ: "For by one Spirit are we all baptized into one body, whether we be Jews or Gentiles... and have been all made to drink into one Spirit. For the body is not one member but many" (1 Cor. 12:13, 14).

BIBLICAL DISCIPLINE

A New Testament church will place itself under the direction of the Word of God. When the church takes itself out from under the Scripture by disobeying it, that church no longer meets the biblical standards of being a church.

Doctrinal purity. One of the first characteristics of the church in Jerusalem was that "they continued steadfastly in the apostles' doctrine" (Acts 2:42). When church problems threatened to cut into the time the apostles needed for the ministry of the Word, an alternative solution to the problem was proposed (Acts 6:2, 3). A biblical theology was characteristic of New Testament churches (Acts 17:11).

Right practice. The Bible is not just a collection of theological truths. It is a practical manual written "that the man of God may be perfect, throughly furnished unto all good works" (2 Tim. 3:17). The apostles taught doctrinal content to the early Christians but also applied it to life. What we believe, when applied to life, does affect the way we live. Being under the discipline of the Word of God will involve both positive and negative discipline. The Scriptures on one occasion called on the church to remove any of its members for some problem in that person's life (1 Cor. 5). That is negative discipline. Just as a parent disciplines in the home to correct the child and help him grow, so the discipline of the Word of God must be applied in the church.

ORGANIZED

God is a God of order and organization. That is obvious as you consider the immense universe around us which was created by God. That is also obvious when you look closely at the church in the New Testament. While some may suggest there was no organization in the early church, the Bible tells us members were added (Acts 2:41), job descriptions were present (1 Tim. 3), votes were conducted to expel immoral members (1 Cor. 5:4), and votes were taken to elect church officers (Acts 6:5; 14:23). The church also organized a missionary team and sent them out (Acts 13:27). There may even have been some "order of service" in the early church. Paul advised, "Let all things be done decently and in order" (1 Cor. 14:40). To accomplish this task, the Holy Spirit endows certain ones with the gifts of government and leadership (Rom. 12:8; 1 Cor 12:28). The church is organized and equipped to carry out its purpose, which is the Great Commission.

Purpose. The early church gives us insights into what the church was intended to accomplish. The first believers "continued stedfastly in the apostles' doctrine and fellowship, and in breaking of bread, and in prayers" (Acts 2:42). "Continuing in the apostles' doctrine" implies that there was a teaching ministry going on. The church was also to be a place of fellowship, meaning more than coffee and cookies in the church gym after the evening service. Fellowship occurs when Christians involve themselves constructively in the lives of other believers.

Mission. The mission of the church is set forth in the Great Commission: "Go ye therefore, and teach all nations, baptizing them. . . . Teaching them to observe all things, whatsoever I have commanded you" (Matt. 28:19, 20). In another place Christ commanded: "Go ye into all the world, and preach the gospel to every living creature" (Mark 16:15). In yet another place Christ said "that repentance and remission of sins should be preached in his name among all nations, beginning at Jerusalem" (Luke 24:47). At his ascension Jesus told his disciples, "Ye shall be witnesses unto me both in Jerusalem, and in all Judea, and in Samaria, and unto the uttermost part of the earth" (Acts 1:8).

The pattern of evangelism was established by the first church. "And daily in the temple, and in every house, they ceased not to teach and preach Jesus Christ" (Acts 5:42). As those early Christians believed everyone without Christ was lost, they felt the need to present the gospel to everyone. Before long their critics accused them of having saturated their town with the gospel (Acts 5:28). Later others recognized their influence upon the world (Acts 17:10).

ORDINANCES

God has given the church two symbolic rituals to increase our understanding of our relationship to Jesus Christ. Paul wrote to the Corinthians, "Now I praise you, brethren, that ye. . . keep the ordinances [traditions], as I delivered them to you" (1 Cor. 11:2). Part of the traditions was clearly the Lord's Supper but it probably included also the meaning of baptism (Rom. 6).

Baptism. The first ordinance of the church is baptism. It was practiced by the church with every believer, as far as we know. As people were baptized, they were symbolically identifying with the church (Acts 2:41) and their Savior (Rom. 6:3-7; Gal. 2:20). Usually baptism was an evidence to their friends and neighbors that they were serious in their decision to follow Christ. It became known as a "badge of discipleship."

Lord's Supper. On Jesus' final night with his disciples, he observed the Passover and ate the Passover meal. After dinner, he gathered his disciples around to initiate the second ordinance of the church. The Lord's Supper is practiced by a church as a constant reminder of Christ's death on Calvary. "For as often as ye eat this bread, and drink this cup, ye do show the Lord's death till he come" (1 Cor. 11:26). The observance of this ordinance also provides an opportunity for self-examination (1 Cor. 11:28). God provided this ordinance as one means whereby he could keep his church pure and separated from the world.

SPIRITUAL GIFTS

The Scriptures teach that every Christian has a spiritual gift. Some gifts are given specifically to the church in the form of gifted leaders (Eph. 4:11) but all gifts can be used in the church for the building up of the Body of Christ (1 Cor. 12:13-28). God provides the spiritual leadership in a group to make it a church. When an organization ceases to have spiritual leadership, it ceases to function as a church. It is important that every Christian determine his spiritual gift and exercise it in the ministry of the local church (see chart in Chapter 22).

CONCLUSION

Jesus promised, "I will build my church" (Matt. 16:18). It is an institution that he organized, so we must carefully study its nature to determine if we are building our churches to fulfill the pattern begun by Christ. Today the church is still near to the heart of God, "Even as Christ also loved the church, and gave himself for it" (Eph. 5:25). Because of its priority, every Christian needs to belong to and involve himself in the ministry of a good church. If God has promised to bless his church, then those who desire the blessing of God upon their service need to serve him through a church.

DAILY READINGS

☐Monday: *Acts 17:1-15*   ☐Tuesday: *Matthew 18:15-35*
☐Wednesday: *2 Timothy 3:15—4:8*   ☐Thursday: *John 4:5-26*
☐Friday: *1 John 1:1-10*   ☐Saturday: *1 John 2:1-17*
☐Sunday: *1 John 2:17—3:3*

FORTY
CHURCH MEMBERSHIP

Not forsaking the assembling of ourselves together, as the manner of some is, but exhorting one another: and so much the more, as ye see the day approaching. Hebrews 10:25

INTRODUCTION

In the communist state of Rumania, citizens are discouraged from attending church. Many church attenders have been arrested, fined, and even imprisoned for their faithfulness. All of this is accomplished legally under the provisions of Law Number 153/190, Article 1-D, forbidding Rumanian citizens from "coming together to play cards, drink alcohol, or waste time." Even though the national constitution guarantees the religious liberty of its citizens, communist leaders are able to prosecute Christians for "wasting time" by attending the services of their church. If such a law were enforced in the free world, there may be many Sunday morning attenders who could be found guilty of wasting time because they do not properly use the church service.

Church membership and attendance has lost its meaning to many. Perhaps some have taken it for granted; others have become so involved in interdenominational work that they minimize the Christian's obligation to a church. Also, some minimize their relationship to their church because of false teaching or lack of teaching.

Every Christian should be a member of and be involved in a local church for many reasons. Some people leave one home and move across the country to a new home, but never transfer their church allegiance. They are careful to change their address, their phone number, their job, and even their life-style to a certain extent, but their church membership remains in the old church. In doing so, they are ignoring the ministry of God to them personally, their ministry to a group of believers in a new location, and their ministry to a new community. Also, the Christian who is not a member of a local church robs himself of a major part of his Christian experience. Every Christian needs to learn how to become a member of a good church and to do so.

THE BENEFITS OF THE CHURCH

God has established three institutions on earth through which he performs and accomplishes his will: the family, the government, and the church. He established the family as the basic social unit of society. Governments were established by God (Rom. 13:1) to rule corporate society and protect the people of those states. The church was established by Christ (Matt. 16:18) to accomplish God's redemptive purposes in the race. The church preaches the eternal message of God's love for the world (John 3:16), supplies workers to accomplish the harvest (John 4:35), fulfills the obligation to teach doctrine and the biblical principles needed for a successful Christian life. And, finally, the church is an instrument to keep Christians consistent in the faith.

Entrusted with the message. The church is entrusted by God with the story of his love for mankind and his desire to save them. The history of the Bible shows that it was organized groups of Christians that collected the gospels and epistles and gave the Bible to both Christians and the lost. In spite of the tremendous opposition to it, the Bible has survived these many years, usually preserved by the church. Jesus said, "And I will give unto thee the keys of the kingdom of heaven: and whatsoever thou shalt bind on earth shall be bound in heaven: and whatsoever thou shalt loose on earth shall be loosed in heaven" (Matt. 16:19). The "keys" is the message of redemption that was revealed to man from God by the apostles and prophets (Eph. 2:29). It is this message that looses man from sin; when it is rejected, man is bound in his sin. This promise, given to Peter, was tied to Jesus' promise to "build my church" (Matt. 16:18). This authority was later given to all the disciples in the upper room (John 20:23). This group represented the church in its embryonic form. This did not give the church or leaders of the church authority to forgive sin, but rather acknowledged that only as the church was faithful in the proclamation of the gospel could people enjoy the assurance of salvation. As the church faithfully preached and taught the Scripture, people heard and believed the gospel. If a church is not a witnessing church, it is as if it were locking the door to heaven, forbidding the members of their community the gift of eternal life.

An *assembly of workers*. Jesus told his disciples, "Pray ye, therefore, the Lord of the harvest, that he will send forth labourers into his harvest" (Matt. 9:38). It is the desire of Christ that Christians be engaged in his work. One of the reasons God established the church was to assemble his workers into a team that could get the job of evangelism done. Some people think pastors, teachers, and evangelists are responsible for doing the work of God. While they are the leaders in the church, in another sense *we* are "full-time Christian workers." We should all live for God at all times and serve him also at all times. The Book of Acts records that everyone, not just the apostles, were engaged in evangelism. When the persecution in Jerusalem resulted in the death of Stephen, the Christians were scattered into other towns and cities. Only the apostles remained in Jerusalem (Acts 8:1). As Christians and the apostles had been evangelizing Jerusalem, the practice of evangelism continued in their new towns. The Bible says, "Therefore, they that were scattered abroad went everywhere preaching the word" (Acts 8:4). God still has a work to be done. The gospel story of the death and resurrection of Christ is the catalyst that draws the church together and is the power that sends it out to serve him. God gave the Great Commission and the responsibility to win souls to his church.

A place of Christ-centered education. The third benefit of the church from God's point of view is to provide an educational institution to train Christians concerning the things of God. Part of Christ's commission to the church included: "Teaching them to observe all things whatsoever I have commanded you" (Matt. 28:20). When Barnabas went to Antioch to establish the church, he got Saul from Tarsus and "he brought him unto Antioch. And it came to pass, that for a whole year they assembled themselves with the church, and taught much people" (Acts 11:26). The first church to be labeled "Christian" was a church that was characterized by training people.

The Berean church was identified for its nobility. "These were more noble than those in Thessalonica, in that they received the word with all readiness of mind, and searched the scriptures daily, whether those things were so" (Acts 17:11). Bible study and teaching characterized the ministry of the apostles and the early church. The gift of teaching is one of the abilities that God gives to his pastors who lead the church (Eph. 4:11).

A place to build up believers. Because instability is so characteristic of our lives, God established the church to help us live more consistently. We often quote the first part of Hebrews 10:25 when we exhort others to church attendance but neglect the latter part of the verse and the purpose of church attendance. The complete verse reads, "Not forsaking the assembling of ourselves together, as the manner of some is, but exhorting one another: and so much the more, as ye see the day approaching" (Heb. 10:25). The reason we assemble together is to exhort each other to keep on serving the Lord. The writer of Hebrews introduces this challenge by touching on the real problem, "Let us hold fast the profession of our faith without wavering" (Heb. 10:23). Many people will walk down the church aisle to be saved but comparatively few may be living for God six months or a year later. Those that are baptized and become faithfully involved in the church

are more likely to "hold fast." We need others' encouragement to live for God which we receive in a church. The
church is God's way of providing stability in our lives.

WHY CHURCH MEMBERSHIP?

Many churches do not keep a formal church roll, so we
should ask the question, "Why should there be church membership?" Even those churches that do not have a formal list
of members usually have a recognized group that are accepted in the body. These churches have either written or un-
written standards by which they accept those who share
common values and principles.

The church in the New Testament was called upon to take
corporate action such as sending out missionaries (Acts
13:3), or denying fellowship to a sinning brother (1 Cor. 5:1-
7). If a group acted together, they must have known who was
included in their fellowship and they must have had standards that became the basis to excommunicate those who did
not live up to them.

The church corporately is told to keep pure doctrine (Titus
1:9; Col. 1:23; Jude 3). They carried out this exhortation by
identifying those who denied the faith (1 Tim. 5:8). The end
result was, "A man that is an heretick after the first and
second admonition reject" (Titus 3:10). The New Testament
implies that there was a listing or roster of the Christians.
The term "numbered" was used to describe the Christians in
the church at Jerusalem, indicating a census of both total
count and inclusion of names. The church is described as a
"number of names together" (Acts 1:15; also see Acts 2:41,
47; 4:4; 5:14; 6:1, 7).

God accomplishes much through his church. Since God
loves people and most of what he does is for the welfare of
those he created, he uses the church to accomplish that purpose. These are several good reasons why joining a church is
among the important requirements for a successful Christian
life.

Joining a church gives evidence of our association with God.
God wants the world to know who his people are and that
they have identified themselves with him. When a Christian

is baptized, he is telling the world a number of things; among these is that he is now identified with Christ. As he is baptized, he is saying, "I am crucified with Christ: nevertheless I live; yet not I, but Christ liveth in me: and the life which I now live in the flesh I live by the faith of the Son of God, who loved me, and gave himself for me" (Gal. 2:20).

When we are saved, we are identified with the body of Christ on the cross in the vicarious-substitutionary atonement. By the Spirit's baptism, we are placed into his body. Therefore, when we are baptized, we are symbolically fulfilling the meaning by being joined to his Body (the Church). By joining a local church we are telling the world in another way that we belong to Christ's Body, both in heaven and on earth.

Joining a church places us under the ministry of the Word of God. Joining a church places us under the influence of the Word of God. Of course, this is not true if the church we attend does not believe and preach the Bible. In that case, it is important that we find a good Bible-believing church for ourselves and our family, where we can study the Bible together. The following chart lists some of the values you lose out on when you are not learning more of the Bible in church.

RESULTS OF KNOWING THE BIBLE	
1. Spiritual growth	1 Pet. 2:2
2. Victory over sin	Ps. 119:105
3. Answered prayer	John 15:5
4. Christian character	1 Cor. 3:23
5. Stronger faith	Rom. 10:13

When we join a church we pledge ourselves to Christ and his Word. This commitment will help keep us faithful to him. Also, if a church will preach and teach the whole counsel of God (Bible content, doctrine, and life expectations) a Christian will grow to maturity. Those who do not regularly attend church will not grow as consistently because there are gaps in their biblical education.

Joining a church causes us to grow through fellowship. Fellowship with believers in a local church will help us grow spiritually. By "fellowship" we are talking about much more than having coffee together after church. Fellowship occurs when Christian experiences with God are exchanged in an atmosphere of love and respect. Fellowship means giving and taking, not just selfishly absorbing from others like a spiritual sponge. Everyone must communicate himself to others and, in the act of fellowship, learn and be strengthened by others. Fellowship involves letting others see us as we really are. At times, this involves confessing our faults (James 5:16). We hinder fellowship when we refuse to acknowledge our weaknesses to others. When we recognize our shortcomings, we become more dependent upon God. In essence, we cannot live for God by ourselves. We need the reciprocal fellowship of others. An important biblical principle to remember is that we become like those with whom we fellowship.

Joining a church fulfills the New Testament example. Almost every Christian in the New Testament was part of a local assembly. Obviously the thief on the cross was not included, but his yielded spirit to Christ indicates he would have followed the admonition of his Lord. Also, the Ethiopian eunuch was baptized, but there was not a church where he was converted. Even in his case, there is a strong tradition that the eunuch returned to his native Ethiopia with the message of the gospel to found what is now known as the Coptic Church. The pattern of the New Testament Christian's experience was established on the day of Pentecost. "Then they that gladly received his word were baptized: and the same day there were added unto them three thousand souls" (Acts 2:41). The next verse revealed their continual commitment to Christ: "And they continued stedfastly in the apostles' doctrine and fellowship" (Acts 2:42).

CRITERIA FOR CHURCH MEMBERSHIP

We should belong to a church close to where we live. This better enables a church to watch over us. Because many who band together are more effective than one by himself, our testimony will be more influential for God when we identify with a group of believers in our town. Working with other Christians for a common goal will increase our effectiveness for God. Others will be able to pray for us and help us in some cases do what we cannot do by ourselves. There are four conditions on which members shall be received into a church: belief, baptism, doctrine, and morals.

Profession of faith. The ideal church is made up entirely of regenerate members. Since we never are absolutely sure that a person is saved, candidates are taken into the church upon their profession of faith. Even Paul was not sure about some Corinthians: "Examine yourselves, whether ye be in the faith" (2 Cor. 13:5). Some who professed salvation later left the fellowship of Christians (1 John 2:19). Since only God can determine the reality of a person's faith, a church accepts members who follow Paul's instruction to "confess with [their] mouth the Lord Jesus, and...believe in [their] heart" (Rom. 10:9).

It wasn't as popular to join a church in New Testament times as it sometimes is today. Because God judged the sin of Christians, "no man [would] join himself to them" (Acts 5:13). Because of this judgment, it may have been easier to determine who was a Christian. As the church in Jerusalem grew, the unsaved did not want to be identified with the church but "the believers were the more added to the Lord, multitudes both of men and women" (Acts 5:14).

Baptism. The question is asked, "Why be baptized to join a local church?" First, because of the example of the early Christians. Those who believed were baptized (Acts 2:41). Second, all who professed faith were considered members of the local church where they served, and all who were baptized were considered part of the local body of Christ. Since, all who professed Christ were baptized and considered a part of the fellowship, there was a strong tie between baptism and church membership. The third reason is the symbol which baptism gives of the identification in the death, burial, and resurrection, of being with Christ (Rom. 6:4, 5). Therefore, a

Christian should give testimony by being placed in water as a sign of being identified in the death and resurrection of Christ.

In the Bible narrative, all of those who professed faith were baptized before they were added to the church. Just as Spirit baptism places us in the body of Christ (1 Cor. 12:13), so water baptism identifies us with the local body, the church.

Knowledge and agreement with doctrine. There was no written doctrinal statement required for identification with an assembly during the New Testament as far as we can tell. Yet, the necessity of doctrinal purity is self-evident. In the early church the power and reality of the message of Jesus Christ swept the world. Whereas unbelievers might have doubted the message, Christians experienced the assurance of the indwelling Christ individually (Gal. 2:20) and corporately (Matt. 18:20). Immediately after conversion, a new Christian was taught "the apostles' doctrine" (Acts 2:42). Any who rejected the gospel was rejected by the church (Titus 3:10). While no verse can be found to demand conformity to scriptural teaching for church membership, it can be argued that any cause (doctrinal heresy) that was serious enough to expel a person from the church is also a biblical ground to deny him church membership in the first place.

Moral conformity. Jesus said, "Ye are the salt of the earth: but if the salt have lost his savour, wherewith shall it be salted?" (Matt. 5:13). The church ought to represent God's standard of morality in the life of its members. While the New Testament church did not give a moral prescription for new members, it was generally accepted that those who had repented of their sins were expected to live for God (1 Cor. 6:9-11). Obviously, a person cannot become perfect at conversion, but he should turn from all known sin in his life. As he grows in biblical knowledge, he will become aware of other sins from which he will also turn. Since we never become perfect in this life, let us ask the question, "How much moral conformity is required for church membership?" A person must repent of those sins that he knows and must meet the minimum standard of the Christians in his new local assembly. There is no prescription in Scripture that gives the standard to join a church, but any sin that would be serious enough to cause expulsion from a church, would be serious enough to keep a person from joining its fellowship.

CONCLUSION

God established the church to help carry out his plan of redemption. If we are not members of a church in our town, we are preventing God from both blessing us as he desires and from using us to our fullest potential in his service. While some practice "free-lance Christianity" by faithfully attending several churches, such persons rob themselves of spiritual growth. If we are not faithfully involved as a member of a good church in our area, that is something we need to remedy.

DAILY READINGS

☐Monday: *Acts 2:37-47*   ☐Tuesday: *Acts 3:12—4:4*
☐Wednesday: *Acts 4:5-22*   ☐Thursday: *Acts 4:23-37*
☐Friday: *Acts 5:1-16*   ☐Saturday: *Acts 5:17-32*
☐Sunday: *Acts 5:33-42*

FORTY-ONE
THE AIMS OF
THE CHURCH

Go ye therefore, and teach all nations, baptizing them in the name of the Father, and of the Son, and of the Holy Ghost: Teaching them to observe all things whatsoever I have commanded you: and, lo, I am with you alway, even unto the end of the world. Amen. Matthew 28:19, 20

INTRODUCTION

Every institution can only justify its existence as it accomplishes its objectives. The aims of an organization give it a sense of direction and determine its course of action. What is true of a commercial institution is also true of the divine institution of the church.

There are many forms of the local church. Some are centered around liturgy. Others are centered around evangelistic preaching, while other churches resemble a Bible College classroom. There is room for variety, but all churches have been given a set of goals to give them direction and purpose. There should be no confusion about the "marching orders" given by Jesus Christ. "And Jesus came and spake unto them, saying, All power is given unto me in heaven and in earth. Go ye therefore, and teach all nations, baptizing them in the name of the Father, and of the Son, and of the Holy Ghost: Teaching them to observe all things whatsoever I have commanded you: and, lo, I am with you alway, even unto the end of the world" (Matt. 28:18-20).

The Great Commission is many times applied to foreign missions but often neglected at home. But God has only one strategy since he returned to heaven, and that works in every place at all times. The controlling purpose of the local church is to make disciples. Those who are evangelized are then to be baptized, which is a testimony of their identification with Christ. The final phrase of this simple command is to educate those disciples to effective Christian service. The Commission to the church is a unit; the Christian cannot choose one aspect and neglect the others. The Great Commission is a single command involving three steps, evangelism, baptism, and education.

EVANGELISM

The Greek word for "go" (Matt. 28:19) is a participle which means "while you are going," but it has the force of an imperative when it appears with an imperative, as "teach." Christ assumed the disciples would be in the act of going into all the world with the gospel. The word "teach" is an imperative, which is a command to obey. Actually, the word translated "teach" in the *King James* is the verb form of "discipline" which means "to make disciples." Making disciples is more than getting decisions; we are commanded to make people into followers of Jesus Christ. "Making disciples" means to lead them to be born again, then baptized, and finally taught in the Christian faith. "Make disciples" is an imperative that demands the full attention of every New Testament church. At least six elements are involved in the biblical idea of disciple-making.

Vision. We must know what we want to do if we will accomplish our task. "He that ploweth should plow in hope; and that he that thresheth in hope should be partaker of his hope" (1 Cor. 9:10). Vision is essential to keep a church heading in the proper path. The vision must begin with the pastor and he must share it with the congregation. In the Old Testament, one of the titles of the man of God was "seer" (1 Sam. 9:9). He was the one who saw first, saw most, and saw farthest. The man of God who leads the church today must see a "vision," not some "psychic phenomenon," but a clear goal of the purpose of the church to win people to Jesus Christ, to get them baptized, and to teach them the Word of God. As Jesus was engaged in his ministry, he saw the multitudes (Matt. 9:35, 36). That vision motivated him to deeper concern to do the work of God.

A second aspect of vision involves the ability of the man of God to realize his calling and to have an inner confidence of what God is going to do through him. This personal vision accounts for some of the success in the apostle Paul's ministry. The Lord told Ananias concerning Saul of Tarsus, "I will shew him how great things he must suffer for my name's sake" (Acts 9:16). Later, when Paul was starting the church at Corinth, God appeared to Paul in a vision to assure him he was still going to use him in that city to reach many people (Acts 18:9-11).

A final dimension is a vision of God. With the physical eye it is impossible to see God (John 1:18), yet it is possible to have a correct vision concerning his person and nature. Such was the experience of Isaiah as he received direction for his ministry (Isa. 6:1-13). We cannot have a correct vision of God without a correct understanding of Scripture because the Bible alone contains the correct doctrine of God. The first step in accomplishing the aims of the church is to ask God for a vision concerning the lost, concerning the work, and concerning God himself.

Compassion. A second element of evangelism is compassion. When Jesus "saw the multitudes, he was moved with compassion on them" (Matt. 9:36). The word "compassion" comes from a Latin term meaning "to suffer with." Compassion is the ability to share in the emotional experiences of others. It is love translated into action.

During the days when Dwight L. Moody conducted a Sunday school in Chicago, one small boy traveled halfway across the city to attend. When asked why he would go so far to attend Mr. Moody's Sunday school, the boy responded, "Because they love a fella over there." People will be drawn to the Lord by the love of a Christian. Jude wrote, "And of some have compassion, making a difference" (Jude 22).

Reaching. A third dimension of biblical evangelism is reaching. To reach means simply to use every available means to make contact with people and motivate them to give the gospel an honest hearing. It is not just enough to hand a gospel tract to the unsaved and assume we have done our duty in evangelism. We have not completely given out the gospel until we have urged the person to respond. The apostle Paul described the doctrine of reaching people, "To the weak became I as weak, that I might gain [reach] the weak: I am made all things to all men, that I might by all means save some" (1 Cor. 9:22). "Reaching" did not involve the compromise of biblical convictions but rather the application of common sense to preaching the gospel.

Testimony. The word "testimony" or "witness" also sheds light on the nature of biblical evangelism. Every Christian is to be a witness for Christ (Acts 1:8). In a court of law, a witness is called upon to give testimony to his experience, not his opinion or his judgment. In the same manner, Christians are called upon to give testimony concerning what they have seen, heard, and experienced in Jesus Christ. Sometimes this can take the form of a nonverbal testimony.

We witness for Christ by our godly living. The lame man healed outside the temple by Peter and John was a nonverbal testimony of what God can do in a life (Acts 4:14). The same was true in the experience of Lazarus after his resurrection (John 12:11). But we should go beyond a nonverbal testimony, and give a vocal witness for Christ. The apostles acknowledged, "We cannot but speak the things which we have seen and heard" (Acts 4:20). Testimony is an effective tool of evangelism because people cannot deny living evidence of the truth.

Preaching. Preaching is an important part of evangelism. Mark records Jesus' commission, "Go ye into all the world, and preach the gospel to every creature" (Mark 16:15). Christ's last command became the first concern of the scattered church. "Therefore they that were scattered abroad went everywhere preaching the word" (Acts 8:4). Preaching is not just giving a biblical speech in the church's pulpit. When we share Jesus Christ with a lost person, we are technically preaching. Preaching is communicating the gospel in an understandable manner and motivating that person to respond. Preaching is giving biblical content with persuasion so you convince the person to become a Christian. Preaching the gospel is essentially the same whether addressing a large crowd or talking with an individual.

Persuasion. Persuasion is the final aspect of biblical evangelism. This involves a conscious attempt to motivate the lost to accept Jesus Christ as Savior. We should have an urgency in pressing the claims of Christ upon the lives of the unsaved. The Christian is urged to "go out into the highways and hedges, and compel them to come in, that my house may be filled" (Luke 14:23). The burden of the lost was a strong motivating factor in the ministry of the apostle Paul (Rom. 10:1-3). Because of this urgency, he testified, "We persuade men" (2 Cor. 5:11).

BAPTISM

Disciple-making is the primary imperative of a local church and part of that command includes baptism. Baptism, in this context, involves more than placing a person in water. The true meaning of baptism is identifying the person with Christ. First the Christian is identified with Christ as he died, was buried, and then rose again from the dead. "Therefore we are buried with him by baptism into death: that like as Christ was raised up from the dead by the glory of the Father, even so we also should walk in newness of life. For if we have been planted together in the likeness of his death, we shall be also in the likeness of his resurrection" (Rom. 6:4, 5). Only after a person is saved (which means he has been identified with the death and resurrection of Christ) can he, with any significance, partake of water baptism. Just as we are identified with the Body of Christ in his death on the cross, so we should be identified with the Body of Christ in baptism. Paul identified "the church, which is his body" (Eph. 1:22, 23). Again the church is called his body (1 Cor. 12:25). Water baptism is an act of identifying the convert also with a local body of believers, since the church is an organized assembly (body) of believers with the responsibility of evangelizing the unsaved, educating Christians, worshiping God, and administering the ordinances. Identifying with the church carries with it a fourfold obligation.

Bible discipline. When a believer identifies with the church, he places himself under the discipline of the Word of God. The preaching or prophesying of the Word of God includes "edification, and exhortation, and comfort" (1 Cor. 14:3). For most people, placing themselves under the discipline of the Word of God will involve regular attendance at the preaching services and participation in some kind of consistent Bible study, such as Sunday school. Every church should have some kind of Christian education program that has a systematic, comprehensive, and complete coverage of Bible content, doctrine, and life expectation.

Gifts. Another reason people identify with the church is to develop their spiritual gifts. The Holy Spirit has given spiritual gifts to every Christian (1 Cor. 12:11). These gifts were given for the benefit of the church as a whole (1 Cor. 12:14-27). As every believer has a spiritual gift (1 Cor. 7:7), it is important that they all identify with a church where they can exercise that gift in ministry.

Worship. A purpose of the New Testament church is to glorify God and help every believer worship God (Luke 24:52, 53; John 4:23, 24; Acts 2:47). Worship is not an option but an obligation. It is giving to God the worth due him. Worship is not concerned with the needs of man. It is concerned with magnifying God. Since God wants worship from man individually and corporately (John 4:23, 24), it remains the duty of the church to worship him together.

Fellowship. The church is also a place of fellowship. The gospel unites believers of various backgrounds in Christ, thus providing a basis upon which fellowship can occur (Gal. 3:27, 28). Biblical fellowship involves a caring for the needs and concerns of one another. The *koinonia* is a part of the New Testament Christian experience in the church.

EDUCATION

The final phase of the Great Commission is teaching, or education. Just as Jesus taught his disciples (Matt. 5:2), so we, in making disciples, are responsible to teach our converts all that we have learned from the Lord (Matt. 28:20). This process has been called "reproducing reproducers." Those we teach should in turn teach others also (2 Tim. 2:2). Education is never an end in itself but rather a means to an end, which is the mature believer (Eph. 4:11, 12). A balanced educational program in the church will provide training in four areas.

Bible content. The apostle Paul reminded the Ephesian elders, "I have not shunned to declare unto you all the counsel of God" (Acts 20:27). The aim of every church is for the believer to know the doctrines contained in the Bible. A knowledge of Bible doctrine will produce several benefits in the life of the believer.

THE BENEFITS OF KNOWING DOCTRINE
1. Protection from sin (Ps. 119:9-11)
2. Growth in the Christian faith
3. Understanding God's purpose for life
4. More effective ministry for God

Training. Whereas teaching usually includes content, training puts into practice what is taught through theory. However, both teaching and training must be present for a well-balanced ministry. The aim of the church is to train Christians to be able adequately and faithfully to carry out their responsibility both inside and outside the church.

Attitudes. The attitude a person has toward the Christian life will reflect the quality of his walk with God. The ultimate aim of education (beyond content and skills) is the communication of biblical values and attitudes in accordance with the standards of Scripture. Proper attitudes will be based upon a person's knowledge of the Bible, but a good knowledge of the Bible does not necessarily guarantee biblical attitudes.

Growth to maturity. The final goal of Christian education in the church is to produce spiritual growth, "for the perfecting [maturing] of the saints, for the work of the ministry, for the edifying of the body of Christ" (Eph. 4:12). Christians will grow to spiritual maturity through proper application of the Scriptures (1 Cor. 2:10-14). A biblical education recognizes the work of the Holy Spirit through the human teacher as the path to spirituality (John 14:26). However, in the final analysis, spiritual maturity, Christlikeness, is the final step in the process of disciple-making.

CONCLUSION

The church of Jesus Christ has clear-cut biblical aims. But many churches ignore its clear-cut objectives and, as a result, they fail. It is the responsibility of a church to evangelize the lost, identify new converts with the church and train them in effective Christian service. Only as the church fulfills its objectives does it justify its existence.

DAILY READINGS

☐ Monday: *Matthew 28:1-20*   ☐ Tuesday: *Matthew 9:35—10:7*
☐ Wednesday: *Acts 1:1-11*   ☐ Thursday: *Mark 16:9-20*
☐ Friday: *Luke 14:15-24*   ☐ Saturday: *Acts 5:17-42*
☐ Sunday: *Acts 17:1-9*

FORTY-TWO
CHURCH LEADERSHIP

This is a true saying, If a man desire the office of a bishop, he desireth a good work. 1 Timothy 3:1

INTRODUCTION

Without leaders, an organization usually lacks direction and initiative to move forward. As a result, while a group may feel they are holding their own, they may be actually sliding backward when the situation is closely evaluated. Since the task of the church is great, a leader is demanded to organize, direct, and help the church accomplish its goal.

As we come to better understand pastoral and deacon leadership, we will be better prepared to let our church go forward. Many conservative churches today place unnecessary restraints upon church leaders. It is true no one should be allowed to lead the church indiscriminately without guidelines or controls. Biblical guidelines for leadership give the proper freedom and also give the proper restraints.

The church, like any other organization, needs human leaders. Even in the early stages of church history, the church was organized through human instrumentality. Initially, "the twelve" (Acts 1:26) gave leadership to establishing the church. As the church grew, the needs of the ministry demanded the appointment of seven men to serve as deacons

(Acts 6:1-7). By the time the church at Jerusalem hosted the Jerusalem Conference, James seemed to have been considered the chief elder or spokesman of that church (Acts 15:2, 13). In other references to church leadership it is difficult to tell if any one of the elders was considered the chief among them. By the time the apostle Paul traveled to start churches in the various cities of Asia Minor and Europe, it was generally recognized that two leadership offices were to be established in the church, bishops (overseers) and deacons (Phil. 1:1; 1 Tim. 3:1, 8). Since the growth and strength of a church reflects the stature of its leader, we should study their biblical qualifications, first to understand their role and next to understand the strength and directions of our own church.

ELDERS (PASTORS)

Every church is led by Christ if it is a New Testament church. "He is the head of the body, the church: who is the beginning, the firstborn from the dead; that in all things he might have the preeminence" (Col. 1:18). When the church no longer obeys the Word of God, the presence of Christ leaves a church and Christ is no longer the ruler of the church. We may call the organization a "church," but it is not, according to the biblical use of the term.

The final seat of authority in church government is best stated in terms of viewpoint. The congregations were charged to choose spiritual leaders. After that, the believers were charged to obey those who had the rule over them (Acts 15:2-4; 1 Tim. 5:17). The apostle Paul encouraged the Philippian believers to continue in and strengthen their unity as a church (Phil. 2:1, 2) and pleaded with the Corinthians that they do everything within their power to correct and prevent divisions in their church (1 Cor. 1:10). Because the Holy Spirit works through believers, he is able to freely lead a church when the members are yielded to his direction.

The pastor, who fulfills in today's church the role of the New Testament elder or bishop (overseer), is responsible before God for the spiritual welfare of the church (Acts 20:28). At the return of Christ, he will judge and reward the pastors (elders) according to their faithfulness in leading the church to accomplish the will of God (1 Pet. 5:4). In one sense, everything a church is and does is an extension of the pastor's personal ministry. So much is this true, that the prophet identifies the similarity between the leader and his followers, "As with the people, so with the priest" (Isa. 24:2).

The office of the pastor is identified by various titles in different denominations. He is called Reverend, Pastor, Preacher, Bishop, Minister, Elder, Doctor, or some other title. It is sometimes awkward for a person of one church to address the pastor of another faith because of uncertainty of how to address him. This problem has been complicated throughout church history where terms have been applied to the office in one culture only to remain after the culture has changed. The Roman Catholic Church uses the title of bishop to apply to a man who supervises many churches in a large area, whereas the New Testament applies it to the leader or leaders of one church.

At least seven different terms are used to identify men that filled the office of pastor in New Testament churches. Each of these words contributes toward a fuller understanding of the nature of the pastor's office.

Elder. The first term (Greek: *presbuteros*) used especially in the Jerusalem church was "elder" (Acts 11:30). The term "elder" appears over twenty additional times in the New Testament. It was brought over from the Old Testament synagogue of those who were respected for their maturity and wisdom. The Book of Proverbs gives admonition to heed those who can make wise decisions. While chronological age was certainly a consideration in identifying a man as an elder, the real emphasis is on wisdom and spiritual maturity. It is not advisable to place a young convert, even if he is saved late in life, in a position of leadership without his first being given the opportunity to gain spiritual maturity. In listing the qualifications of a pastor, the apostle Paul warned, "Not a novice, lest being lifted up with pride he fall into the condemnation of the devil" (1 Tim. 3:6).

The term "elder," when speaking of his function in the church, is always used in the plural (Acts 20:17; Titus 1:5; James 5:14; 1 Pet. 5:1), supporting the idea of a plurality of elders in a single local church. In churches today we have senior ministers, youth pastors, ministers of music, and directors of Christian education, all considered pastors. Even in the New Testament where many elders existed in one church, there sometimes appears to be a hierarchy of elders. There were many elders in the church of Jerusalem, but James was their spokesman. There were many elders at the Ephesian church (Acts 20:17), but Jesus addressed his comments to the angel (messenger) of that church (Rev. 2:1). Presumably this one was recognized by others as the spokesman.

Bishop. The term "bishop" (Greek: *episkopos*) is also used to describe the office of pastor and the man who fills it. The term is translated "overseer" in Acts 20:28 and is used four other times as "bishop" (Phil. 1:1; 1 Tim. 3:2; Titus 1:7; 1 Pet. 2:25). In one instance the reference is to Christ (1 Pet. 2:25). The emphasis of bishop seems to be "one who takes the oversight of a church," or the office of manager, superintendent, or chief executive officer of the church. Again, the term is always in the plural except where the qualifications of a bishop are given (1 Tim. 3:2). It is largely an administrative term used to identify the work of these church leaders. Whereas the term "elder" implied the character of the pastor, the term "bishop" describes the nature of his ministry.

Pastor. Probably the term "pastor" (shepherd) is the most common title used today by conservative Christians to identify their church leader. However, the term "pastor" except for one instance, is used always in the New Testament to refer to Christ. It is used to describe the ministry of shepherding and feeding the flock. It is not used in the Bible to describe a man in office, but only his ministry (Eph. 4:11; 1 Pet. 5:2). As the shepherd of the flock is responsible for the care of the sheep, so the pastor is responsible for the care of his flock (Acts 20:29; 1 Pet. 5:3).

First, the elder/shepherd is instructed to "take heed, therefore, unto yourselves, and to all the flock" (Acts 20:28). This makes a pastor responsible to watch over others to meet their needs. Sometimes a church member will become discouraged or backslidden. A pastor is the one who is responsible to see that this person is strengthened so he remains faithful or comes back into fellowship with the Lord.

Three times Jesus reminded Peter of his pastoral shepherding responsibility to feed the flock (John 21:15, 16, 17). This refers to his teaching ministry. To better accomplish this task, many pastors give leadership to such programs as Sunday school, youth clubs, or Bible study groups. Even when a pastor has delegated his ministry in part to others, he remains responsible before God for the feeding of the flock (Acts 20:28). This is why a pastor should be involved in the selection of the curriculum used in his Sunday school and why teachers should cooperate with him. In a very real sense, the Sunday school teacher is an undershepherd of that part of the flock to which he is assigned.

Pastors should also protect their flocks. The apostle Paul recognized that "grievous wolves" would come from the outside and gain control in the church if the flock was not carefully guarded (Acts 20:29). Sometimes, good men in the church may change and thus become dangerous to the security of the church (Acts 20:30). In both cases, the chief responsibility of protecting the flock falls on the pastors. Many times pastors may be misunderstood when they insist upon certain spiritual standards or certain emphases in special music or guest preachers. Actually, they may be attempting to protect those Christians who do not understand the total ministry that may be best for the church.

Most conservative churches use the term "pastor" to identify their church leader for cultural reasons. Often, the pastor who is a recent graduate is younger than his deacons, so the title "elder" seems inappropriate. The term "bishop" has come to refer to ecclesiastical hierarchy, thus becoming unsuitable for popular use in referring to pastors of the local church.

The terms "elder" and "bishop" are used interchangeably in Titus 1:5-7 and Acts 20:17-28, implying that these are two functions of the same office. A person grows into becoming an elder, but learns how to function as a bishop.

NAMING THE PASTOR		
	Acts 20:17-31	*1 Pet. 5:1-4*
Elder	20:17	5:1
Bishop	20:28 (overseers)	5:2 (taking oversight)
Pastor	20:28 (to feed)	5:2 (feed the flock)

Preacher. The term "preacher" implies a public proclamation of the gospel. Noah was the first to preach (1 Pet. 2:5), although Enoch's prophesying may also have involved preaching (Jude 14). Preaching is often defined as "the communication of the Word of God with persuasion through the personality." The pastor is the man God has called to proclaim his message in the church. In preaching, the pastor seeks to accomplish those things. "But he that prophesieth speaketh unto men to edification, and exhortation, and comfort" (1 Cor. 14:3).

Teacher. The teaching ministry is referred to some ninety-seven times in the New Testament. The pastor was given the dual gift of "shepherding/teaching." In referring to the gifts of ministry, Paul said: "And he gave some,...pastors and teachers" (Eph. 4:11). The use of the conjunction between these two terms and not the rest suggests that pastors also had the gift of teaching. This gift was exercised in the church from its beginning (Acts 2:42). Note, Jesus had left his disciples with a "teaching commission" (Matt. 28:19, 20). Their obedient response is seen in the biblical record. "And daily in the temple, and in every house, they ceased not to teach and preach Jesus Christ" (Acts 5:42).

Servant. The term *doulos,* usually translated "servant" in our Bibles, might better be translated "slave." Usually the term is used to refer to deacons, but it is also used in connection with pastors (1 Pet. 2:16; 5:3). Pastors are to be servants of the congregation. A pastor must keep sensitive to the poor, downtrodden, and underprivileged in the flock if he is to remain effective. As a slave of God he is the servant of the church because the assembly is indwelt by Christ and is his body. Jesus used the slave-master relationship to illustrate our duty to him. "So likewise ye, when ye shall have done all those things which are commanded you, say, We are unprofitable servants: we have done that which was our duty to do" (Luke 17:10).

Steward. A pastor is also to be a steward, who was a slave with the responsibility of overseeing other slaves in the master's house or field. A steward is one who manages what belongs to someone else. The pastor is a steward of the gospel (1 Pet. 4:10) and the church (Titus 1:7). His chief responsibility was identified by the apostle Paul: "Moreover, it is required in stewards, that a man be found faithful" (1 Cor. 4:2).

DEACONS

The second officer of the church is the deacon. The word "deacon" comes from one of the Greek words for servant or minister. This slave was also described as one who pulled the oars on a lower deck of the ship to keep the ship moving. Most people think that deacons were implied with the appointment of the first committee of men to care for an aspect of the church to free the apostles for the more important responsibility of prayer and the ministry of the Word (Acts 6:1-4). The deacons are a serving office. There is no "job description" for a servant; he does what he is commanded or what is necessary. Therefore, there is no itemized list of duties that deacons are to perform in the church. The suggestion is that deacons are to serve in whatever way best helps the church to minister. However, the nature of their qualifications gives insight into their duties.

Qualifications. The office of deacon is not without its standards. Two passages in particular identify more than a dozen standards for deacons (Acts 6:3-8; 1 Tim. 3:8-13). When a church selects its deacons, it should give careful consideration to each man's character. Too often churches have appointed men to this office simply because they were successful businessmen in the community. Actually, the qualifications for deacon are as high as those for bishop. After Paul lists the standards of a pastor, he uses the phrase "likewise the deacons" (1 Tim. 3:3). The term "likewise" implies that the deacon should be as qualified as the pastor. The only differences between elders and deacons are the spiritual gifts of the pastor and his calling from God to his office.

QUALIFICATIONS OF DEACONS (1 Tim. 3:8-13; Acts 6:1-8)	
1. Blameless	1 Tim. 3:10
2. Husband of one wife of good character	1 Tim. 3:11, 12
3. Grave	1 Tim. 3:8
4. Not double-tongued	1 Tim. 3:8
5. Not given to much wine	1 Tim. 3:8
6. Not greedy for money	1 Tim. 3:8
7. Pure conscience	1 Tim. 3:9
8. Proven ability	1 Tim. 3:10
9. Good ruler in the house	1 Tim. 3:12
10. Good reputation (honest report)	Acts 6:3
11. Filled with the Holy Spirit	Acts 6:3
12. Full of wisdom	Acts 6:3
13. Full of faith	Acts 6:8
14. Full of power	Acts 6:8

Function. While there is no specific biblical listing of the duties of deacons, there are some suggestions in the New Testament of the things deacons can do. The first deacons engaged in routine labors in the church. By assuming responsibility for food distribution, they left the apostles free to engage in the ministry of prayer and preaching (Acts 6:4). Although the word "deacon" does not occur in Acts 6, these seven men performed jobs that were later done by deacons.

Another area of ministry for deacons includes promoting harmony between various groups in the church. When the widows were arguing (Acts 6:1), the deacons did the job that solved the problem of contention in the church.

Wisdom is listed as one of the qualifications of deacons (Acts 6:3), indicating one of their functions. Pastors should seek the counsel and cooperation of others in guiding the church in its programs of worship, education, and evangelism. The deacons may be an advisory committee to assist the pastor in this ministry. Sometimes in the absence of pastors, the deacons may have to serve as the spiritual leadership of the church. There are several examples of deacons (ministers) having responsibility for spiritual ministry (Col. 1:7; 1 Thess. 3:2).

CONCLUSION

God is a God of order, requiring us to serve him in an orderly manner (1 Cor. 14:40). He has appointed offices in his church to assist the orderly function of the church. When these chosen and appointed ones—pastors, teachers, elders, bishops, deacons, ministers, as they are described in the New Testament—work together to accomplish God's will in leading the church, God is able to bless his church as he desires. It is important that every Christian support and follow his church leaders (Heb. 13:7, 17).

DAILY READINGS

☐Monday: *1 Timothy 3:1-16*   ☐Tuesday: *Titus 1:1-16*
☐Wednesday: *Acts 6:1-8*   ☐Thursday: *John 21:1-17*
☐Friday: *Acts 20:17-38*   ☐Saturday: *1 Peter 5:1-11*
☐Sunday: *Hebrews 13:7-17*

FORTY-THREE
CHURCH GOVERNMENT

Let all things be done decently and in order. 1 Corinthians 14:40

INTRODUCTION

Some who are saved in aggressively evangelistic churches become unhappy with the way the church is being run. They charge that the pastor is a dictator. When the pastor "controls" the church, it is not a biblical church. But on the other extreme is a church controlled by a board. Usually a board-controlled church does not have financial troubles, but it is not aggressively moving forward. As a matter of fact, when a board controls the church, there is usually a great amount of criticism among the congregation about the way the church is being run.

Then there is the third extreme which is pure democracy. The congregation attempts to run the church by group decision and consensus. Sometimes this third extreme takes the form of group dynamics so that the church as a democratic body makes all the decisions, but makes them on the basis of understanding, without evidence of a congregational vote. On other occasions, this third abuse takes the form of "protracted business meetings." The church votes on every bill and every small administrative decision. Obviously, this extreme in church government slows down the progress until the church cannot function. Therefore, the obvious question arises, "What is the proper church government?"

When a local congregation organizes itself properly, it is better prepared to carry out its objectives which are (1) making disciples, (2) baptizing them, and (3) teaching them all things. Also, when a church is properly organized, the people have a basis for a unified assembly, rather than the organization becoming a reason for criticism and faction. Finally, good government will make it possible for every person to grow into maturity. This chapter attempts to present a biblical approach to church government that will bring glory to God.

Christians believe the Bible alone is the final rule for all matters of faith and practice. This practice is more than individual godly living. It also includes the practical organization and administration of the church that will help believers grow into holiness. Therefore, we must look for principles for church government in the Bible, not in church tradition or contemporary management seminars. Some churches fail because they are too much influenced by a traditional denomination. Other churches fail because members try to run the church like they run their businesses. There appears to be at least three models of church government, all of which are claimed by their proponents as having biblical basis. To understand them, let us first look at the historic way churches have organized their congregations. Each of these three forms of church government provides some benefits. But there are also liabilities in each of the three. After examining these three forms of church government, we will see how they fit together into God's pattern for a local church.

THREE TYPES OF CHURCH GOVERNMENT		
CONGREGATIONAL *Baptistic* concensus leadership; by the people	*REPRESENTATIVE* *Presbyterian* led by a committee	*EPISCOPAL* *Anglican/Episcopal* led by an appointed leader

EPISCOPAL GOVERNMENT

Methodists, Episcopalians, and other denominations follow this style of church government. Basically, the authority of the church is centered in a person or position. Those who practice this government believe God has empowered certain leadership positions. The authority of God was centered in prophets, priests, and kings in the Old Testament. They teach the New Testament places this power in pastors, bishops, and elders (all biblical titles). Episcopal government is often paralleled with the idea of a monarchy.

One of the titles for the leader of the church is the Greek word *episkopos*. From this word we get the title "bishop," or those who rule. The other Greek word, *presbuteros*, translated "elder," also represents a church leader and is the same person as a bishop (Titus 1:5-7). This person is also the pastor or minister of a church.

The office of elder or bishop was a ruling office. "Let the elders that rule well be counted worthy of double honour, especially they who labour in the word and doctrine" (1 Tim. 5:17). This verse makes it clear that the elder or pastor of a church is worthy of salary. In the context of the verse, the elder is recognized for both ruling and preaching. Therefore, we are saying that the pastor who preaches should also rule, but they are to "rule well." However, the term "rule" does not mean to dictate or control. It means to exercise leadership by example, by interpreting biblical principles, by vision, and by spiritual service.

Also, the pastor was to lead the church, according to his job description. "One that ruleth well his own house, having his children in subjection with all gravity; (For if a man know not how to rule his own house, how shall he take care of the church of God?)" (1 Tim. 3:4, 5). One of the qualifications of the bishop in the New Testament churches was that he must be able to take care of a wife and lead his children to obey God. If he can lead his home, the Bible says he has met one of the qualifications to "take care of the church of God" (v. 5).

Peter provided several guidelines for the elders of the churches. "The elders which are among you I exhort, who am also an elder, and a witness of the sufferings of Christ, and also a partaker of the glory that shall be revealed: Feed the flock of God which is among you, taking the oversight thereof, not by constraint, but willingly; not for filthy lucre, but of the ready mind" (1 Pet. 5:1, 2). Part of their leadership included "feeding the flock." No doubt Peter was thinking of his meeting with Jesus on the shore of the Sea of Galilee when three times he was challenged to "feed the flock" (John 21:15-17).

A second part of an elder's job included "taking oversight." Peter is careful to emphasize that the pastor does not have dictatorial rights: "Neither as being lords over God's heritage, but being ensamples to the flock" (1 Pet. 5:3). The elders were challenged to lead the congregation for the right reasons. There are other verses that relate to pastoral leadership (1 Cor. 16:16; 1 Thess. 5:12; Heb. 13:7, 17). The following are advantages of the "gifted man" approach to church government.

Gifted leader. The key to effective leadership and production in the work of God is the character and style of the leader or leaders. At the ascension of Christ he "gave gifts unto men" (Eph. 4:8). Although each of us is able to serve God in a different way, we have each received those gifts from the same Holy Spirit. "But all these worketh that one and the selfsame Spirit, dividing to every man severally as he will" (1 Cor. 12:11). For a listing of the particular gifts of the Holy Spirit, see the chart in Chapter 22.

When God gives a person a gift, he expects that person to use his gift to his best ability. When a person is faithful in his biblical stewardship (1 Cor. 4:2), God will give more gifts and the ability to use them to a greater degree (1 Cor. 12:31). It is reasonable to expect that gifted people of God will arise to lead great works to the glory of God.

Example. One of the chief strengths of the Episcopal form of church government is that it provides an example in the model of a leader for others to follow. The apostle Paul was a gifted leader who recognized his opportunity to influence several generations of leaders. He told Timothy, "And the things that thou hast heard of me among many witnesses, the same commit thou to faithful men, who shall be able to teach others also" (2 Tim. 2:2). He capitalized on this modeling principle when correcting problems in the church at Corinth. "Be ye followers of me, even as I also am of Christ" (1 Cor. 11:1). Others in the Scriptures were given as being examples of excellence (1 Cor. 16:10; Phil. 2:19, 20).

Vision. Since the church takes on the characteristics of its leaders, when the congregation is led by people of great vision the church can do more because it participates in its pastors' burdens and goals. When the leadership is free to follow visions from God, then communicate that direction to the church, the church can move toward accomplishing the direction God has given it.

Results. Some advocate this form of church government because it seems to be more effective than the other two. Pragmatism by itself is never a reason to believe a doctrine or choose church government. But God has always used the "gifted man" to get the job done. When God wanted to deliver his people from an oppressive nation during the period of the judges, he raised up different judges. Later, when Israel's existence as a race was threatened, God placed Esther in a position where she could save her people from extermination. God used Noah, Abraham, David, and other well-known men to do his work. His method has not changed. Today God still is looking for the right individuals to diagnose problems and solve them.

Leadership. A study of Episcopal government reveals that its strength is also its weakness. Since everything can rise on leadership, it can also fall on leadership. A gifted man can lift a church to great outreach as he faithfully serves God. Sometimes an inferior leader may enter a place of influence in the government of the church. In this case, a great church can be destroyed or slowed down by poor leadership.

REPRESENTATIVE GOVERNMENT

Most of the governments of the free world are built upon a representative democracy. The people select leaders who are charged with representing their constituency. Some churches believe that a representative or committee is also the most biblical form of church government. Such a government often provides for a more stable ministry because it represents a large base of opinion and insight into any problem or direction that a church may take.

Many churches place the seat of authority in a group of men called the church board, the session, the deacons, or the trustees. These men are chosen for their wisdom, experience, and spirituality. But also, these men live in the business and social areas of the community. They usually know the needs and unique expressions of their town, and also they are known by the community. Their wisdom will give stability to the church and "In the multitude of counselors, there is safety" (Prov. 11:14).

Since the deacons are the only other group besides the bishops (overseers) mentioned in the New Testament that function as a group or committee (Phil. 1:1), we should examine their function. But immediately we find that more is said of their character than their duties. Since their qualifications include wisdom (Acts 6:3), we assume God wanted to use their wisdom in counseling others.

There is no specific reference or example where the deacons or any other committee other than the elders governed the church. These men served the church and advised the church, but they did not appear to be charged with church leadership, nor are they the final seat of church authority.

When a church is governed by a committee, the church sometimes tends to become more influenced by reason than revelation. Sometimes control by a committee is good in that it produces stability in a situation which otherwise might be very unstable if led by a shifting, fanatical leader. The problem comes when the committee becomes so rational that bureaucracy takes over the procedure. When this happens, a church fails to allow God to work in a supernatural way. Whereas a single leader may step out in faith, usually a committee will not take a bold step of faith as a pastor would.

CONGREGATIONAL GOVERNMENT

Congregational government, the third form of church government, is democracy at its most basic level. This style of church government recognizes the authority of the people in the church in making the decisions of the church. Historically, Congregationalists, Baptists, and other "free church" or "believer's church" groups have opted for this style of church government. The epistles that were written to churches placed the responsibility for the church on the people. Paul says little in criticism of deacons or pastors.

Church unity. Every believer has the responsibility of preserving church unity. Paul appealed to the entire church at Corinth "that ye all speak the same thing, and that there be no divisions among you, but that ye be perfectly joined together in the same mind and in the same judgment" (1 Cor. 1:10). He gave a similar responsibility to the Christians in Rome, Ephesus, and Philippi (Rom. 12:16; Eph. 4:3; Phil. 1:27). If the people were responsible for preserving unity, they must have a biblical responsibility for the church, hence they are the final seat of authority.

Church purity. The preservation of church purity, especially in matters of faith and practice, also appears to be the responsibility of each individual believer. Jude wrote his epistle not to pastors, but "to them that are sanctified by God the Father, and preserved in Jesus Christ, and called" (Jude 1), i.e., the Christians. His purpose for writing is clearly expressed in verse 3: "It was needful for me to write unto you, and exhort you that ye should earnestly contend for the faith which was once delivered unto the saints" (Jude 3). As the letter was addressed to the common Christian, anyone of us could place our name in the place of the three personal pronouns.

Church discipline. Closely related to the responsibility for purity and unity is the responsibility for correcting the erring saint. Early, Jesus makes it clear that anyone can bring a problem to the church if the problem cannot be solved with that individual (Matt. 18:15-19). When the apostle Paul discussed church discipline in Corinth (1 Cor. 5:4-13; 2 Cor. 2:6, 7; 7:11) and Thessalonica (1 Thess. 3:6-15), he wrote to the people, not to the pastors or deacons. The New Testament suggests that same authority be given to the church congregation.

Believers' priesthood. The doctrine of the priesthood of believers in another argument for congregational government. Peter identified Christians as "a royal priesthood" (1 Pet. 2:9). This means that every believer has access to authority with God. If this is so, then every believer ought to be able to discern the mind of God concerning a particular situation or decision facing the church. A congregational meeting is a meeting of priests to decide corporately what each has privately discerned to be the mind of Christ.

Indwelling Trinity. The bodies of believers are the temples of God today (1 Cor. 6:19, 20). One of the key expressions in Paul's writings recognized the indwelling presence of Christ in every believer. Advocates of congregational government argue that God is therefore able to lead a church through any and every believer. Congregational government calls on all church members to express themselves on a matter.

In a church governed under a system of congregational government, there are at least four ways church members can influence their church. On important issues raised in congregational meetings, all members can vote. On numerous occasions the people in the New Testament church made corporate decisions (Acts 1:23-26; 6:3-5; 13:2, 3; 15:2-30). They also influence the church through those with whom they fellowship and those they shun. This includes both the formal and informal acceptance of others into the church. A third way of influencing the church is through counseling and helping others with problems. Finally, the ultimate influence on a church is through leaving. Even though there are church splits or people leaving churches in our country, there is no illustration of this happening in the New Testament.

One problem with congregational government is its tendency to lack direction. Also, it is sometimes inefficient and the church often stoops to the level of the mediocre, rather than reaching for the highest standard of excellence. When a vote is taken, the issue is often modified to appeal to the majority of people. Because many church members are not themselves sure where they want their church to be five and ten years from now, they will often vote their preference without realizing how it affects the total church program.

Thus, for the most part, the congregation is passive to the greater objectives of the church while their decisions on relatively insignificant items may convince them they are moving forward. Finally, the worst fault that can be leveled against congregational government is that everyone can be wrong. In Acts 15, the church at Jerusalem wanted to impose circumcision, and might have, if Paul had not objected.

SUMMARY

The church must allow its leaders to lead. The pastorate is a leading office. This does not mean dictatorship, control, or even ownership of the property. If the people do not follow, then the failure is with the leadership. The deacons/committee must give wisdom and guidance to the pastor and to the congregation. They are a serving office while they work behind the scene: they must work together with pastors and people (1 Cor. 3:9). Christ, the head of the Church, has the final seat of authority in the church. Sheep are not leaders; they are known for following. The shepherd of the flock is Jesus Christ who originally gave the church authority for government and today guides through the pastor, deacons, and congregation to carry out his will.

THREE KINDS OF CHURCH GOVERNMENT			
Kind	*Congregational*	*Representative*	*Episcopal*
Authority	People	Board	Man/Office
Strengths	Church decides together—unity	Stability	Takes fullest advantage of gifted leader
Weaknesses	Lack of direction	Rationalistic	Poor leadership
Governmental approach	Democratic	Representative, Republican	Monarchy

CONCLUSION

In governing the local church, we must never lose sight of the nature of the church. The church is not a building or denomination, it is people assembled with Christ. The church is described as a "house of God" (1 Tim. 3:15). As such,

Christ is the designer, architect, builder, foundation, owner, and occupant. The church is also called the "Body of Christ." Christ is both the head and fullness of the body (Eph. 1:23). Church government must allow Christ to express and accomplish his will and, in the final judgment, to bring glory to himself.

DAILY READINGS

☐Monday: *Acts 5:1-16*　☐Tuesday: *Acts 6:1-15*
☐Wednesday: *Acts 11:1-18*　☐Thursday: *Acts 12:1-19*
☐Friday: *Acts 12:20—13:5*　☐Saturday: *Acts 15:1-21*
☐Sunday: *Acts 15:22-35*

FORTY-FOUR
THE ORDINANCES
OF THE CHURCH

And they continued stedfastly in the apostles' doctrine and fellowship, and in breaking of bread, and in prayers. Acts 2:42

INTRODUCTION

One of the characteristics of most religious institutions is their symbols. The basic symbols recognized by Christianity are baptism and the Lord's Supper. But within Christianity, churches of particular denominations may vary in their understanding of the number and nature of these symbols. They are primarily called memorials, ordinances, or sacraments. Some look on the sacraments and interpret them as a means of obtaining grace or favor with God. A member of a Roman Catholic church might argue he had received forgiveness of sins through the mass in which he took part, when in fact the Bible teaches there are no works a man can do to gain the forgiveness of sins or gain merit from God. Baptism and the Lord's Supper are outward symbols of an inner reality. When they are called memorials, they are simply acts whereby we remember what God has done for us.

The Bible teaches that two rites were given to the church by God, baptism and the Lord's Supper. Christians are obliged to celebrate these two outward symbols because God has accomplished the real work in their hearts. Technically, the Christian observes them in obedience to the Lord's commandment. The keeping of these memorials does not provide any special grace to the observer, yet God does honor those who obey his commands. At the very heart of these two symbols is the atoning death of Christ.

BAPTISM

Baptism should be practiced by every Christian after conversion, hence it is called the first step of faith. There are many contemporary ideas regarding the nature and the correct mode of baptism. There are many good reasons why every Christian should be baptized, but perhaps the example of Christ is a compelling one. As a new believer is baptized, he follows the example of Christ who began his public ministry with baptism.

Definition. The word *baptizo* is a Greek word transliterated into the English, "baptize." The word could be better translated "to dip or immerse." The Greek word is a form of the word *bapto,* which means "to dip," as in dyeing cloth. In the New Testament, when the Holy Spirit places a believer into the Body of Christ so that he is identified with his death, burial, and resurrection, it is called "baptism." Water baptism is the act of placing the new believer in water as a testimony that he has experienced the reality of the conversion experience. The act in itself should not be equated with salvation, as some groups teach. Baptism does not wash away sin. It is rather a symbol of the candidate's cleansing in the blood of Christ (Rev. 1:5).

The symbolic significance of baptism is threefold, as explained by the apostle Paul. First, it is a symbol of redemption, picturing the gospel. "Therefore we are buried with him by baptism into death: that like as Christ was raised up from the dead by the glory of the Father, even so we also should walk in newness of life" (Rom. 6:4). Everyone who is baptized is testifying to the fact "that Christ died for our sins according to the scriptures" (1 Cor. 15:3, 4).

Second, baptism is a symbol of the future resurrection. "For if we have been planted together in the likeness of his death, we shall be also in the likeness of his resurrection" (Rom. 6:5). This was an important concern of New Testament Christians. Some mistakenly believed that those who died prior to the return of Christ would not enjoy his presence for eternity. Paul had to teach at least two churches that the saved would be raised at the return of Christ. "For the Lord himself shall descend from heaven with a shout, with the voice of the archangel, and with the trump of God: and the dead in Christ shall rise first" (1 Thess. 4:16).

Finally, baptism is a symbol of regeneration. Everyone who is baptized testifies to the knowledge that "our old man is crucified with him, that the body of sin might be destroyed, that henceforth we should not serve sin" (Rom. 6:6). In another place, the apostle explained: "I am crucified with Christ: nevertheless I live; yet not I, but Christ liveth in me: and the life which I now live in the flesh I live by the faith of the Son of God, who loved me and gave himself for me" (Gal. 2:20).

Immersion. Most Bible-believing churches practice baptism by immersion. One of the chief reasons to immerse in water is because of the meaning of the word *baptizo,* which means "to immerse or dip." The Scriptures, however, clearly show the word sometimes to refer to ceremonial washings when no immersion was involved. "The Pharisee . . . marvelled that he [Jesus] had not washed [*baptizo*] before dinner" (Luke 11:38; Mark 7:4). Throughout the history of the church the emphasis has been placed on the significance of the rite rather than the mode of its ministration. From the same biblical passages Bible expositors draw different conclusions. Some say at Jesus' baptism that John immersed him in water. Others say that John stood with him in the river and poured or sprinkled water on him. These interpreters claim that the use of the term was to signify the religious rite practiced in the Old Testament and later by the Christian church and is not the classical meaning of the terms *baptizo* or *bapto.* They interpret Jesus coming "straightway . . . up out of the water" to be a description of his climbing the banks of the stream. When Philip baptized the Ethiopian eunuch, "they were come up out of the water" (Acts 8:39). In these two instances, Jesus and the Ethiopian, it is clear that the candidates for baptism were standing in a stream of water.

Another reason for baptism by immersion is because of its clarity in representing the symbol of death, burial, and resurrection. As we are baptized, we are placed in water to symbolize the grave, then brought up to symbolize resurrection. Hence, a threefold message of death, burial, and resurrection (Rom. 6:4-6) is symbolized in baptism.

Candidate. The Bible does not teach infant baptism nor the baptism of any other age as part of a step in the plan of salvation. The Bible teaches only believers were baptized after they were converted. On the day of Pentecost, people were saved before they were baptized and added to the church (Acts 2:41, 47). This pattern was repeated continuously in the New Testament.

Some groups argue that the candidate should be baptized in the name of Jesus only, based upon their interpretation of Acts 2:38: "Then Peter said unto them, Repent, and be baptized, every one of you in the name of Jesus Christ for the remission of sins, and ye shall receive the gift of the Holy Ghost." The phrase "in the name of Jesus Christ" modifies both the verb "repent" and "be baptized." Only as one repents can he experience the remission of sins and receive the Holy Spirit. In other places in the Book of Acts where people were "baptized in the name of Jesus," the expression is used to distinguish Christian baptism from the baptism of John the Baptist or some other group (cf. Acts 19:1-5).

The formula by which the candidate is baptized is found in the Great Commission, "baptizing them in the name of the Father, and of the Son, and of the Holy Ghost" (Matt. 28:19). Some immerse three times because of the mention of the three Persons of the Trinity, a practice dating back to Augustine. However, the word "name" is singular. The candidate is baptized once in the singular name of the triune God.

Motives. Christians are baptized to testify to what Christ has done in their lives. Baptism is a "symbolic confession" (Rom. 10:9). Everyone who has been converted should be willing to tell others what Christ has done for him (Acts 1:8).

Baptism is also a testimony of identification with Christ. Theologian A. H. Strong wrote, "Baptism symbolizes the previous entrance of the believer into the communion of Christ's death and resurrection—or, in other words, regeneration through union with Christ." This was what Paul taught the Romans when he explained the significance of this symbol (Rom. 6:3-5).

Christians are also baptized in obedience to Christ's command. Jesus commanded baptism in the Great Commission (Matt. 28:19, 20). On the day of Pentecost, baptism was the first command for the Christian to obey (Acts 2:38). A Christian who does not obey this command calls into question his love for the Lord (John 14:23). Obedience to this command is "the answer of a good conscience toward God" (1 Pet. 3:21).

THE LORD'S SUPPER

The other sacrament of the church is the Lord's Supper. It is called the final step of faith because it represents the ultimate communion of the believer and Christ. Also, it continues until we are taken home to be with Christ at the rapture.

After Jesus had eaten the Passover supper with his disciples, he instituted this ordinance of the church (1 Cor. 11:23). It is also a symbol representing the atonement for sin, specifically containing bread to represent the body of Christ and the fruit of the vine to represent his blood. It goes by the name of the Lord's supper (1 Cor. 11:20), communion (1 Cor. 10:16), the Lord's Table (1 Cor. 10:21), and ordinance (1 Cor. 11:2).

Definition. The Lord's Supper is the distinctive symbol of Christian worship instituted by the Lord on the eve of his death, being a spiritual partaking of the fruit of the vine and bread. These elements are presented in thankful memorial of Christ's sacrifice and are taken by those in good fellowship with him and one another. It is conducted as a memorial in remembrance of the atoning death of Christ and in anticipation of his return to earth.

Symbols. The two symbols in this ordinance are the bread and the cup. Jesus said concerning the bread, "This is my body, which is broken for you" (1 Cor. 11:24). Later in the meal he said, "This cup is the new testament in my blood" (1 Cor. 11:25). This does not mean, as some Christians teach, that the bread and wine become the actual body and blood of Jesus. Jesus was clearly speaking symbolically in this context. When a grandfather unfolds his wallet to show off pictures of his grandchildren, he might say, "This is my grandson." Calling the photos his grandchildren is a figure of speech, meaning that the photo is an image of his grandchildren. This is what Jesus meant when he said, "This is my body." He could have said, "This is a representation of my body," but that was unnecessary in the context. These two symbols represent several things.

Practice. The Bible gives no specific instructions regarding how often the Lord's Supper should be observed, only that it should be observed regularly (1 Cor. 11:26). It seems that in the beginning it was observed daily. Some churches observe it every week, others at the beginning or end of the month, and some quarterly. When it is observed, there are three kinds of communion practiced: open, closed, and close. Each of these groups will conduct a similar service closely following Paul's instructions in 1 Corinthians 11:23-34.

Open communion allows all believers access to the Lord's Supper. The chief argument supporting this position is that communion is the Lord's Supper, not that of some religious denomination (1 Cor. 11:20, 23). Jesus is the one that invites Christians to his supper. Those who hold this position teach that communion should not be controlled by a church. Open communion tends to reflect a believer-centered Christianity rather than an institutional-centered Christianity. It also gives everyone the opportunity to worship God and go deeper with the Lord. The believer himself judges whether or not he is to participate.

Closed communion is practiced by many denominations, whereby communion is made available only to a member of the church who is in good standing. The Lord's Supper is a time of examination and those who have sin in their lives should confess it. Those who have sin in their lives are not given access to the Lord's Supper because God will judge them. As only the church knows who is walking with God, it should not allow a person to eat or drink judgment on his head. Therefore, only members are invited to participate. To avoid the problems of Corinth, a church can be kept pure through closed communion and those who practice closed communion testify to spiritual power as a result.

Close communion is an attempt to have the best of both systems. Here the role of the church is recognized, yet the place of fellowship among Christians is also recognized. In close communion, the pastor acknowledges the responsibility of the individual in self-examination (1 Cor. 11:28). The church, possessing executive but not legislative authority, is charged with the duty, not of reinforcing rules for the administering and guarding of the ordinance but of discovering and applying the practice given in the New Testament. Most churches which practice close communion usually warn the participants that they should be baptized and in fellowship with a New Testament church before they partake of communion. But the church leaves the determination up to the individual.

CONCLUSION

God established the church for his people. He gave that church two memorials to help his people better live for him. When a person is baptized, he identifies with both Christ and his church. As he then begins observing the Lord's Supper, he is given a regular opportunity to examine his own life and relation with the Lord. Also, he is constantly reminded of the sacrifice of Christ for his sin. This reminder, together with the opportunity to regularly examine ourselves, will help us as we seek to live consistent Christian lives.

DAILY READINGS

☐Monday: *Romans 6:1-13*   ☐Tuesday: *Acts 8:26-40*
☐Wednesday: *John 1:15-34*   ☐Thursday: *1 Corinthians 10:16-33*   ☐Friday: *1 Corinthians 11:1-22*   ☐Saturday: *1 Corinthians 11:23-34*   ☐Sunday: *Matthew 26:20-46*

PART TWELVE

UNDERSTANDING THE DOCTRINE OF LAST THINGS

FORTY-FIVE
THE NATURE OF PROPHECY

Knowing this first, that no prophecy of the scripture is of any private interpretation. 2 Peter 1:20

INTRODUCTION

People seem to be more interested in the subject of Bible prophecy than ever before. Many gospel films are being produced on the subject of the second coming of Christ. The shelves of Christian bookstores are constantly being filled with titles on prophetic themes. Most ministers know that when they announce a prophecy topic for their message, many people will come out of curiosity.

People are interested in prophecy because they want to hear things they have never studied before. Also, people are concerned about their future and, since they have confidence in the Bible, they want to know what the Bible says about it. And beyond these reasons, there seems to be an "apocalyptic spirit" in the world. People feel that the time of the end is near. Perhaps this "anticipation of Armageddon" is heightened by the threat of atomic warfare or other circumstances that could end civilization, such as the prospect of polluting ourselves to death or populating ourselves out of existence or the breakdown of civilization as we know it. With any of these possibilities, the study of prophecy seems to be an answer to the natural curiosity people have about the future.

Actually, a large percentage of the Bible was prophetic when it was originally written. Of course, much has been fulfilled, but there is still much to be fulfilled. Many of the prophetic Scriptures have been ignored for many years, but Christians today are taking a deeper interest in them.

THE IMPORTANCE OF PROPHECY

Actually, prophets were men raised up of God, especially in time of backsliding and apostasy, to call Israel back to God. Prophets were primarily preachers and statesmen who spoke on behalf of God. They gave a revelation from God that included both intellectual content and emotional persuasion, with a view of convicting the heart of Israel. Often the messages included offers of hope and encouragement. The message of the prophets had a twofold thrust. Sometimes they spoke to a local circumstance. At other times their message had also long-range implications (Isa. 7:1-11; Joel 2:28-32). Eventually, the message of the prophets became books in the Bible, so we can now study their words and attempt to determine what they were saying about the future.

The message of the prophets in the Old Testament generally dealt with Israel, the covenant people of God. The messages dealt primarily with Israel's sin and failure and warned that God was going to judge them accordingly. Also, their message predicted a glorious future for Israel after God punished them.

As we see how God has fulfilled his Word in the past, it helps us place greater confidence in the promises of God for today. Many personal lessons can be applied to our lives from prophecy, for all Scripture, whether prophetic or historical, contains principles that can be applied to the lives of believers in every age.

Fulfilled prophecy. The fact that God will keep his word is an undisputed fact to the serious student of prophecy. Many contemporary prophets and prophetesses are often wrong in their predictions. They could never be compared to the Old

Testament prophets, who could never be wrong. The divinely ordained punishment of the false prophet was death by stoning (Deut. 18:20). With that in mind, to speak on behalf of God was a solemn responsibility.

God honored his word by doing what he promised. Today, we can pass through the ruins of cities God promised to destroy, or live in cities God promised to restore. Much prophecy remains to be fulfilled, but the fact that much has been fulfilled gives us great confidence. The Word of God will continue to be honored by the God of his word.

Revelation. We must study prophecy because it is included in "all Scripture" that God inspired and revealed to us (2 Tim. 3:16; Deut. 28:29; Heb. 1:1). Some have refused to study prophecy because it is difficult or because Christians disagree over various interpretations in the Book of Revelation. But if God thought it was important to give prophecy to us, then we are obligated to study it thoroughly (2 Tim. 2:15). All Scripture, including prophecy, will teach us the nature and personality of God. Those who have never studied the Book of Revelation cannot fully comprehend what it means that God is still on the throne in the midst of our personal trials. A study of Daniel reminds us that God is dealing sovereignly with the nations and great civilizations of the world. To ignore such a large percent of the Bible because it is difficult to understand, is to voluntarily reject much of what God has revealed to us about himself and his plan for our lives.

Personal applications. Bible doctrine was never taught by the apostles and prophets without personal application. Sometimes, these applications referred to the affairs of the nation, but they also applied to people. Hope, comfort, peace, soulwinning, holy living, and other areas of interest are taught in prophetic Scriptures.

Dangers. As important as the study of Bible prophecy is, the student of the Scriptures must be cautious not to fall into certain common traps. Some have gone off on a tangent by always seeking new truth. Others have become proud or exploitative with their newfound knowledge of prophetic

THE LIFE OF A CHRISTIAN IN THE LIGHT OF CHRIST'S RETURN	
1. Holy living	Titus 2:11-13
2. Purity	1 John 3:3
3. Love	1 Cor. 13:9-13
4. Peace	John 14:1
5. Comfort	1 Thess. 4:18
6. Hope	1 John 3:3
7. Witnessing	Acts 1:7, 8

truth. Others who want to grow in their understanding of prophecy have a tendency to speak on areas where the Bible is silent. Some Bible scholars have made the mistake of fixing dates and identifying the Antichrist, which have all been proven wrong. Sometimes minor differences of opinion in this area of Bible prophecy have become a major source of irritation, leading to breaks in Christian fellowship. An additional danger of prophetic studies is that some are so consumed with future events that they exclude the central focus of Scripture, Christ. The divinely inspired title of the final book of the New Testament, "The Revelation of Jesus Christ" (Rev. 1:1), is a good guideline to all prophecy; ultimately it concerns him.

Beyond these dangers, there are other reasons why people end up with wrong views of prophecy. We need to make sure our motives and presuppositions are correct in prophecy. Sometimes, people have been wrong in their study of prophecy because they do not have all the data. The apostle Paul observed, "For we know in part, and we prophecy in part" (1 Cor. 13:9). Sometimes people have been mistaken because they only study prophecy to prove a point, which leads to pulling verses out of context to prove a theory rather than studying the context to find the truth. The presence of sin in the life of the student will hinder the study of the prophetic Scriptures, as it hinders the study of every part of the Bible.

SCHOOLS OF PROPHECY

If we want to create a stir in a gathering of Christians from different groups, we should present an interpretation of a prophecy as though it were the only one that is correct. There are at least three distinct "schools of prophecy" in Christianity, each labeled according to its view of the millennium.

Amillennial. This prophetic school of interpretation does not believe in a literal kingdom of peace and prosperity here on earth that will last 1,000 years. They believe that the Old Testament predictions of the kingdom were fulfilled in a nonliteral way, either in the present church age or the experience of the church in heaven. As a result, they tend to interpret prophetic Scriptures more figuratively than literally. Most amillennial Bible students do not recognize a distinction between Israel and the church but rather argue Israel was the church of the Old Testament and the church is the Israel of the New Testament.

Postmillennial. At the turn of the century, the most popular view of Bible prophecy was the postmillennial view. Theologians believed that the world from the time of Christ's coming was getting better and better and assumed that a millennial kingdom would be established on earth as the world lived in peace. They interpreted the return of Christ as coming toward the end of this reign of peace. The existence of two major international conflicts in this century and scores of other smaller wars have shattered the hopes of most postmillennialists for a man-made peaceful world.

Premillennial. The view of prophecy, which has become increasingly popular in the last half of this century has been the premillennial position. Essentially it recognizes a distinction between Israel and the church (1 Cor. 10:32), and accepts a literal interpretation of key passages such as Revelation 20:1-10 that call for 1,000 years of peace and prosperity. The premillennial position teaches that Christ will return to the earth and set up a literal kingdom as he promised. With the establishment of Israel as a political state in 1948 and the declaration of Jerusalem as her capital in 1980, this school of interpretation has been gaining credibility in recent years. Most of the popular films and books on Bible prophecy are premillennial, as are many Bible schools and missionary societies.

INTERPRETATION OF PROPHECY

Literal interpretation. Many conservative Bible scholars will interpret the Scriptures literally until they come to a prophetic passage. Then they begin to interpret more allegorically, giving undue consideration to names, numbers, and the hidden meaning of symbols. These are important considerations as God will sometimes use these to teach us important truth, but we should not allow this emphasis to destroy the use of a consistent, literal interpretation of Bible prophecy.

The literal method is an attempt to give the same meaning to a word as the author who wrote the passage. This means we do not try to "think up" an interpretation for the Book of Daniel, but to seek the author's meaning of words and passages. By "literal interpretation" we mean the normal meaning of words or terms. Obviously, when Jesus is called a Lamb in the Bible, the writer does not mean Jesus had four legs and was covered in wool. Lamb in this case is a figure of speech and must be interpreted with the meaning that John the Baptist had in mind when he said, "Behold the Lamb of God" (John 1:29). John the Baptist meant that Jesus was the fulfillment of the typical paschal lamb in the Passover supper. This literal approach is the most secure method of determining what God intended to say. It simply asks, "In the light of the historical context of this passage and the basic rules of grammar as we understand them, what was the writer saying?" But since all Scripture has dual authorship (God and man) we must seek the mind of both authors in interpreting Scripture.

Contextual interpretation. Symbols are an important part of the prophetic Scriptures but the Christian does not have to rely upon his imagination to interpret them. The Bible often tells us the meaning of a symbol within the context of the same passage. This is illustrated in the first chapter of Revelation. The symbols of stars and candlesticks are used but they are identified as the messengers of the church (Rev. 1:26). Sometimes a parallel passage may have the divine interpretation of a symbol we would otherwise not understand.

Double fulfillment. The Old Testament prophets spoke to a contemporary problem but the message had also a long-range prediction. When Isaiah predicted that Messiah would be born of a virgin (Isa. 7:14; Matt. 1:21, 23), he spoke to an immediate setting (Isa. 7:1-14). The double fulfillment is also seen when Joel predicted, "I will pour out my spirit upon all flesh" (Joel 2:28). This applies to the outpouring of the Holy Spirit both on the day of Pentecost and in the end times.

CONCLUSION

The study of the prophetic Scriptures should be an important part of every Christian's personal Bible study. Introducing the Book of Revelation, John wrote, "Blessed is he that readeth, and they that hear the words of this prophecy, and keep those things which are written in it; for the time is at hand" (Rev. 1:3). In light of the return of Christ, each of us needs to reevaluate our own lives with a view of living closer to God's standard in our life-style. A study of the prophetic Scriptures is one of the best ways to accomplish this objective.

DAILY READINGS

☐Monday: *Revelation 1:1-8*   ☐Tuesday: *Revelation 22:1-12*
☐Wednesday: *Daniel 12:1-13*   ☐Thursday: *2 Peter 1:12-21*
☐Friday: *1 Corinthians 10:1-12*   ☐Saturday: *1 Timothy 2:1-15*
☐Sunday: *1 Thessalonians 3:1-13*

FORTY-SIX
THE SIGNS
OF THE TIMES

And as he sat upon the Mount of Olives, the disciples came unto him privately, saying, Tell us, when shall these things be? And what shall be the sign of thy coming, and of the end of the world? Matthew 24:3

INTRODUCTION

Recently a group of religious believers spent a restless night on Staten Island, New York. According to the prophetic "revelations" received by group members, that particular Saturday evening was the time when the Messiah would return. Obviously, Christ did not return, so the group members eventually returned to their homes anticipating an early explanation of their error by their leader.

This incident occurred recently, but judging from the reports of the past several years, a similar situation could repeat itself somewhere during the month you are reading this chapter. Despite the clear teaching of Jesus that no one knows the "day and hour" of his return (Matt. 24:36), many religious sects overstep this limit to biblical revelation and give dates to mark the return of Christ. Some groups, such as the Jehovah's Witnesses and Seventh-day Adventists have predicted numerous dates over the years only to have to change the date or redefine the event after the fact.

With all the fanaticism related to watching for the return of Christ, one might wonder if there are "signs of the times" that do give some warning that Christ might be soon appearing. Jesus said, "Now learn a parable of the fig tree; When his branch is yet tender, and putteth forth leaves, ye know that summer is nigh: So likewise ye, when ye shall see all these things, know that it is near, even at the doors" (Matt. 24:32, 33). Later Jesus stated two words every serious student of Bible prophecy should heed, "Watch therefore" (Matt. 24:42).

No one will ever know the date of Jesus' return until they see him coming in the clouds. Still, there are certain things happening in our world today that suggest the day of his return may be very close. We must be careful to obey the Scriptures and accurately interpret the evidences of Christ's return without abusing the Scriptures in an attempt to somehow date his coming.

THE COURSE OF THIS AGE

Two passages of Scripture present for us a prophetic history of the major trends of our age. When Jesus gave his "kingdom parables," some commentators believe he was chronologically outlining the characteristics of this present age. Later, as Jesus evaluated the seven churches of Asia, he may also have presented a second clue concerning the future history of this church age.

Kingdom parables. Much of the ministry of Jesus during his earthly life was devoted to teaching his disciples. Parables were among his favorite techniques. They enabled him to address a large group, but speak specifically to a smaller group who would understand the real message of the parable. Matthew 13 records seven such parables in which Jesus sought to teach his disciples "the mysteries of the kingdom of heaven" (Matt. 13:11). Here, Jesus outlined the progress of this current age. The following chart lists the seven parables with their central message to the disciples.

Church epistles. When Jesus appeared to John on the Isle of Patmos, the first part of his revelation was to dictate seven

THE COURSE OF THIS AGE IN MATTHEW 13		
	vv.	
Parable of the Sower	1-23	There will be a sowing of the gospel throughout the world.
Parable of the Tares	24-30; 36-43	There will be a counter-sowing by Satan.
Parable of the Mustard Seed	31, 32	There will be an outward growth of Christendom, but not necessarily the true church.
Parable of the Leaven	33-35	There will be a permeation of the gospel into all areas of life.
Parable of the Hidden Treasure *Parable of the Pearl of Great Price*	44 45, 46	God will gather to himself a peculiar people.
Parable of the Dragnet	47-51	God will end the age in judgment.

letters to the messenger to seven particular churches in Asia (Rev. 2, 3). There were far more than seven churches in that region but only seven were chosen by Christ to receive messages. The order in which they are presented is also unusual. It is not the normal order in which these churches would be visited by a traveler. Some conservative scholars believe Christ selected these seven churches in this particular order to prophetically suggest the major trends in future church history. The following chart demonstrates how the chief traits of these seven apostolic churches also characterized the major trend of seven periods of church history.

In both cases, one could argue that some parables or epistles may overlap, but the major theme illustrates the course of this present age. As one surveys the history of these last

THE CHURCH AGE IN REVELATION 2, 3			
Church	*Reference*	*Characterization*	*Period*
Ephesus	2:1-7	Apostolic church	A.D. 33-100
Smyrna	2:8-11	Persecuted church	A.D. 100-316
Pergamos	2:12-17	Worldly church	A.D. 316-500
Thyatira	2:18-29	Idol-worshiping church	Middle Ages
Sardis	3:1-6	Remnant church	Reformation
Philadelphia	3:7-13	Revived church	Awakenings
Laodicea	3:14-22	Apathetic church	Present

two millennia it is possible to see how these prophetic illusions may have been fulfilled. One of the signs of Christ's soon return is the fact that we are at the end of the age according to these two portions of Scripture. God's final judgment is all that remains to be fulfilled in this age.

ISRAEL AND PROPHECY

The energy that keeps God's prophetic clock running on schedule is the Jewish nation. God's character demands that he honor his covenant with Abraham (Gen. 12:1-6). Since God promised to give the land of Israel to the seed of Abraham, it is only natural to interpret the return of the Jews as an indication that God's timetable is coming to an end. The New Testament writers were careful not to confuse the church with Israel, recognizing they each existed as two similar yet distinct groups (1 Cor. 10:32). As we have watched the establishment and struggles of the State of Israel since 1948, we have seen Bible prophecy fulfilled before our eyes. The gathering of the Jews to a Palestinian homeland is setting the stage for Christ's return.

Restoration. God told Ezekiel he would bring his people back into the land (Ezek. 37:11-14). That promise included both the restoration of the Jews to the land that God gave Abraham, and the regeneration of that people in the land. During the past century, we have seen maps drawn outlining the boundaries of David's kingdom (following World War I) and that kingdom in part given to the Jews (1948). During the Six-

Day War of 1967, Jerusalem and other parts of the Jewish homeland were conquered and became a part of the national geography of Israel. When Israel declared Jerusalem her capital during the summer of 1980, yet another step had been taken toward the ultimate fulfillment of those prophecies concerning the restoration of the Jews in Israel.

Regeneration. The second part of Ezekiel's prophecy concerned the spiritual rebirth of the Jews. God committed himself to restore the people to their land and said, "[I] shall put my spirit in you, and ye shall live, and I shall place you in your own land; then shall ye know that I, the Lord, have spoken it, and performed it, saith the Lord" (Ezek. 37:14). Even though some Jews have returned to the land today, they are there in unbelief (Deut. 30:1-3). Many Jews could not be considered good practicing Jews and most are certainly not Christians.

The apostle Paul also recognized a future time when "all Israel shall be saved" (Rom. 11:26). While some Jews are always being saved throughout the age (Rom. 11:5), most are still in spiritual blindness (Rom. 11:25). When Jesus returns, the Bible describes a national turning to God. This national regeneration will be the second fulfillment of Ezekiel's promise.

The student of Bible prophecy must always find his authority in the Scriptures, not current events. When Bible teachers such as Drs. H. A. Ironside and C. I. Scofield taught the restoration of Israel to the land at the beginning of this century, their critics could show them maps which did not even have boundaries, let alone Jews, in the place they claimed a nation would someday be reestablished. Fifty years later the tables were turned and the teachings of Ironside and Scofield have been vindicated. Yet, the critics still reject the clear teaching of Scriptures. Present-day "anti-missionary" laws in Israel should not discourage the student of prophetic Scripture from believing in a future revival sweeping the land of Israel.

THE GROWTH OF INTERNATIONALISM

We are living in a global community where national borders do not appear as significant in the minds of people as they were even a generation or two ago. Immigration to the Western hemisphere from around the world has produced truly international cities in our land. The television, airplane, and media have greatly contributed to the cosmopolitan spirit of our day. Our society is being prepared to accept the possibility of an international government and ecumenical "state church."

World government. Daniel described the progress of world history in terms of four beasts representing kingdoms. "Thus he said, The fourth beast shall be the fourth kingdom upon earth, which shall be diverse from all kingdoms, and shall devour the whole earth, and shall tread it down, and break it in pieces" (Dan. 7:23). That beast was the Roman Empire, but it will be revived before Christ returns. This revived empire appears to be a world government that will have international control and influence.

John also described the ruler of that kingdom, observing, "It was given unto him to make war with the saints, and to overcome them: and power was given him over all kindreds, and tongues, and nations" (Rev. 13:7).

These two writers expected a world leader who would establish a world government. Today, our society appears to be moving back to that position. With many major and minor crises that have confronted world leaders in recent years, an internationalist view of world politics is becoming more popular. Some have cited organizations such as the United Nations and the European Common Market as possible patterns for an international government. It is generally agreed that such a government would demand a strong leader. As we move closer toward conditions which will exist when Jesus returns to earth, we consider them "signs" that his coming is near.

World religion. Religious leaders around the world today are eagerly hoping to establish a greater ecumenical attitude among their followers even to the end of establishing a unified church which could include all the various sects of Christianity. Some have even suggested this church should be tolerant of and include members of Hindu, Islamic, Jewish, and other non-Christian sects.

While cooperation between churches is good and a spirit of unity among Christian leaders is a biblical goal, the current religious ecumenical movement does not fit the biblical pattern for the church of Jesus Christ. It is only biblical in that it is the fulfillment of prophetic Scriptures. John calls it a "harlot church" in his vision on the Isle of Patmos (Rev. 17:1; 18:24). It was a harlot in that it prostituted its doctrine and standards of purity by compromising with the world. The harlot church is actually guilty of opposing and aggressively seeking to destroy the true followers of Christ, those who practice biblical Christianity.

This coming church will probably carry on the ancient pagan custom of interrelating the church and state into a single institution. Presumably, an international state church could be the official religion of the world and the chief religious leader would also be the chief political leader. He would be the Antichrist. Except in a few Islamic republics, the union of political and religious government is not practiced today as in the past. But as many things come full cycle, this future harlot church would be the state religion of the international state.

SUPPORTIVE CONDITIONS

Man's self-destruction. Certain conditions exist in the world today that could end civilization or destroy life as we know it. The threat of atomic annihilation is a possibility as well as the possibility of polluting ourselves out of existence, or populating ourselves into mass starvation. Of course, these will not happen because the Bible teaches Christ will end this age. He will not allow man to destroy himself. But the rapid acceleration of these dangers implies that Christ will return before they run their natural course.

Implied signs. Other conditions in the Scripture imply the return of the Lord. However, it is difficult to give an objective identification to them, so we are not sure they are "signs." Paul noted, "in the last days perilous times shall come. For men shall be lovers of their own selves, covetous, boasters, proud, blasphemers, disobedient to parents, unthankful, unholy, without natural affection, trucebreakers, false accusers, incontinent, fierce, despisers of those that are good, traitors, heady, highminded, lovers of pleasures more than lovers of God; having a form of godliness, but denying the power thereof" (2 Tim. 3:1-5). Some of these conditions have been true in every age, as they were in Timothy's day. But others seem more evident in these last times, such as the pleasure-seekers, those with a form of godliness but no power, and those disobedient to parents. These supportive conditions are only mentioned by inference and should not be considered the strong arguments for the signs of the times. But their appearance in Scripture meant they could not be left off the list.

CONCLUSION

When the robins begin to sing and flowers start to come up out of the ground, we know summer is near. When the trees begin to lose their colored leaves and the days grow shorter, we instinctively know winter is near. When we see our world conforming to the conditions which exist at the coming of Christ described in the prophetic Scriptures, we can know we are rapidly approaching the end of the church age.

The Christian who realizes the truth that Christ may return even today will seek to do all he can before Christ comes. True Christians will recognize the importance of accomplishing the will of God in daily life.

DAILY READINGS

☐Monday: *Matthew 24:1-14*   ☐Tuesday: *Matthew 24:15-28* ☐Wednesday: *Matthew 24:29-41*   ☐Thursday: *Matthew 24:42—25:13*   ☐Friday: *Matthew 25:14-30*   ☐Saturday: *Matthew 25:31-46*   ☐Sunday: *Revelation 2:1—3:22*

FORTY-SEVEN
THE RAPTURE

Then we which are alive and remain shall be caught up together with them in the clouds, to meet the Lord in the air: and so shall we ever be with the Lord. 1 Thessalonians 4:17

INTRODUCTION

One of the most unusual events to occur in this world is yet to happen. The Bible talks about the rapture of every Christian who is alive when the Lord Jesus Christ returns in the air. These Christians will be caught up in the air to meet him and, instantaneously, they will receive glorified bodies. To the Christian, this is a wonderful hope, but what will be the response of the unsaved? Instantaneously, millions of Christians will suddenly vanish from sight. What explanation will be given for their disappearance?

Only two men, as far as we know, have entered the presence of God in a similar way (without dying), Enoch and Elijah. In both cases the experience of these men typically represents the experience of all Christians living at the time of the rapture. Enoch was "translated" into the presence of God as a result of his relationship with God, a relationship that had been established by faith (Heb. 11:5). So those who are included in the coming rapture are also included because of their faith in God. In the same way, the coming of Christ to meet his saints in the air will be an indisputable act of God.

Bible scholars sometimes disagree concerning the details of the doctrine of the rapture, but that does not take away from the importance of the biblical doctrine. Apart from a belief in the rapture, it is impossible to recognize the return of Christ, apparently one of the basic presuppositions of the New Testament. A correct understanding of the rapture also gives hope and comfort at a time of disappointment or sorrow (1 Thess. 4:18). As in the study of all doctrines relating to Bible prophecy, understanding this doctrine will help us establish the right character and accomplish those things God wants us to do.

THE NATURE OF THE RAPTURE

The word "rapture" never occurs in our English Bible but the idea is described specifically in two key passages. The word comes from the Latin term *rapto*, meaning "to be caught up." The apostle Paul teaches this doctrine in 1 Corinthians 15 and 1 Thessalonians 4. In these chapters he describes a day when the dead in Christ will be raised and all who are living and know Jesus Christ as their personal Savior will be changed and will meet Christ in the air. When properly understood by the believer, the rapture will become a major motivating factor in determining the life-style of each individual.

Description. The rapture is a future event in which Christ returns for his own, for he promised, "I will come again" (John 14:1-3). The rapture is not his coming at death to take Christians to heaven. Rather, Christ will descend toward earth. "Then we who are alive and remain shall be caught up together with them in the clouds, to meet the Lord in the air" (1 Thess. 4:17). At this meeting in the air, we will be transformed and given glorified bodies. Paul describes this event: "We shall be changed, in a moment, in the twinkling of an eye" (1 Cor. 15:51, 52). All the dead in Christ will be resurrected at the time of the rapture. Paul reminds those in Thessalonica who were concerned over Christians who died that "the dead in Christ shall rise first" (1 Thess. 4:16). They too will receive glorified bodies. "The dead shall be raised incorruptible, and we shall be changed" (1 Cor. 15:52).

Every indication is that this rapture could occur at any moment and will include every believer. While our faithfulness to Christ and obedience to his Word are very definitely issues which affect the reward we will or will not receive, it is never indicated that backslidden Christians would be in danger of losing any part of their salvation (1 Cor. 3:15). Some groups teach a partial rapture theory, that only some Christians will be taken, while sinning or unbaptized Christians are left behind. The reason some accept the partial rapture theory is their belief that sin or disobedience in the Christian's life is punished in the Tribulation period. But the proper meaning of redemption is that Christ has paid the complete price for every sin. Since every sin has been punished, God cannot legally punish sinning Christians again by omitting them in the rapture. If a person is in Christ, he will be caught up with Christ in the air.

Distinction. Most evangelical Christians make a distinction between the rapture of the church and the revelation of Christ. There are a large number of similarities in these two events that make it easy to confuse them. Both the rapture and the revelation include a resurrection, both feature Christ's coming, and both include believers being gathered by Christ.

The rapture could occur at any moment (1 Thess. 4:16), where the revelation of Christ will be preceded by various events, some of which are still unfulfilled. At the rapture, Christians will meet Christ in the air (1 Thess. 4:13), but the revelation occurs on the Mount of Olives just outside Jerusalem (Zech. 14:4, 9). The changes in nature described at the revelation of Christ (Matt. 28:28-30; 2 Pet. 3:10) are unknown at the rapture of the church. Some of these distinctions are contrasted in the following chart.

Demands. Whenever we study Bible doctrine, we should ask, "What does this mean to me?" Too often, even in recent history, Christians have studied Bible prophecy to argue events or symbols, or to draw charts. When studying prophecy, Christians have failed to make practical application in their personal lives. As a result, those who believe in an imminent rapture are not those who win souls or live pure lives. But

TWO DISTINCT EVENTS	
Rapture of the Church	*Revelation of Christ*
1. Meeting in the air— 1 Thess. 4:13	1. Standing on Mt. of Olives—Zech. 14:4, 9
2. Dead in Christ raised— 1 Thess. 4:16	2. Judgment—2 Thess. 1:7
3. Imminent—Phil. 4:5	3. Preceded by signs
4. Day of Christ	4. Day of the Lord— 2 Pet. 3:10
5. Believer judged—2 Cor. 5:10	5. Unbeliever judged— 1 Thess. 5:4
6. Lower creation unchanged	6. Nature is changed— Matt. 24:29, 30
7. Message of comfort— 1 Thess. 4:18	7. Message of judgment— 1 Thess. 5:4-9
8. Blessed hope—Titus 2:13	8. Glorious appearing— Titus 2:13

since they believe that Christ could return at any time, they should be most active in serving him.

The concluding line of Paul's explanation of the rapture to the Thessalonians reads, "Wherefore comfort one another with these words" (1 Thess. 4:18). If we believe what Paul wrote concerning this doctrine, we must also apply his conclusion. The doctrine of the rapture demands we comfort one another.

A second demand of this doctrine challenges our life-style. "Let your moderation be known unto all men. The Lord is at hand" (Phil. 4:5). The word translated "moderation" here literally refers to our self-control or forbearance. If we are consistently looking for the Lord to come, then we will exercise self-discipline in soul-winning, Christian service, and obedience to Christ.

The truth about the rapture makes a third demand on our lives. The apostle John wrote, "and every man that hath this hope in him purifieth himself, even as he is pure" (1 John 3:3). God will instantaneously change us to be like Jesus at the rapture (1 Cor. 15:51). George Whitefield realized this truth and once prayed, "Lord, someday I will be like Thee.

And if someday, why not today when I can be the greatest blessing to the most people?" In the light of the imminent rapture of the church, this should represent our daily desire and prayer to God.

THE TIME OF THE RAPTURE

Good men have studied the prophetic Scriptures and arrived at different conclusions concerning when the rapture occurs in relation to the Great Tribulation. Some claim the rapture occurs after the Tribulation is over because the Church is promised tribulation on earth (John 16:1, 2; Rev. 12:12). The Tribulation is a distinct era, not just a general condition of trouble as experienced over the years of history. Others claim the rapture will occur at some point in the middle of the seven years. Usually they argue that the rapture will occur at "the last trump" (1 Cor. 15:52), when the seventh trumpet is blown in Revelation 15. The expression "the last trumpet" is a reference to the four trumpets blown in the wilderness wandering to notify Israel to move out and break camp. This more closely parallels the meaning of "the last trump" at the rapture. It is a notification to Christians that time has come to break camp and move on out. There are several arguments suggesting the rapture comes at the beginning of the Great Tribulation.

Seventieth week. Daniel provided a key to understanding Bible prophecy in his vision of seventy weeks (Dan. 9:24). More accurately, a week was "sevens of years," therefore the last week is seven years long. A gap of some unspecified duration exists between the sixty-ninth and seventieth week, but the final week (seven years) is described in terms of a single unit. Several other passages describe this week as a single unit, the entire week having the same characterization. It is a time of wrath (Rev. 14:19), judgment (Rev. 15:4), and punishment (Isa. 24:20, 21). The week will be marked with darkness (Joel 2:2) and destruction (Joel 1:15). The week is identified as an "hour of trial" (Rev. 3:10). For the church to pass through this week would conflict with the truths of John 5:24, Romans 8:1, and 1 Thessalonians 5:9. The church will not have any further condemnation, judgment, or suffering of the wrath of God. God is just and will not repunish the same sin. Since Christ has suffered our wrath, the church cannot go through the Tribulation and suffer wrath a second time.

Israel and the church. A second key argument for the pretribulation rapture of the church is the biblical distinction of Israel and the church. The church was not announced until after the rejection of the Messiah by Israel. This does not mean the church was an afterthought, but rather it is a mystery, previously kept hidden from others until this present age (Eph. 3:1, 2). God will not renew his program of salvation with Israel again until he has completed his objective with the church.

Israel and the church represent two distinct and separate programs. The rapture is part of God's program for the church, the revelation of himself to the nations is a part of God's program for Israel. These are different groups and should not be confused (1 Cor. 10:32).

If we say the church enters the Great Tribulation, we have difficulty harmonizing that idea with the unique relationship that exists between Christ and the church. Christ and his church are vitally and intricately united together. If the church goes through wrath—i.e., the Great Tribulation—then Christ must also pass through wrath a second time. This conclusion minimizes the accomplishments of Christ in his work at Calvary.

Imminence. One cannot read the New Testament and conclude the writers believed in other than an imminent return of Christ. Christ can return at any moment. Christians are exhorted to keep watching for his return (1 Thess. 5:1-8; 2 Pet. 3:8-10) and wait for it (1 Cor. 1:7; 1 Thess. 1:9, 10; Titus 2:13). These commands were as meaningful and applicable to the first century as they are today. Even if there are certain signs concerning the end time, that does not preclude the belief in the imminent return of Christ. Signs relate to general conditions on the earth when Christ returns, whereas imminency means he can come at any time.

CONCLUSION

The next significant event on God's prophetic timetable is the rapture of the church. It could occur at any moment. Just that quickly, Christ would descend to meet us in the air. We would instantaneously become like Jesus and begin our eternal existence in his presence.

DAILY READINGS

☐Monday: *1 Corinthians 15:50-58*   ☐Tuesday: *1 Thessalonians 4:13-18*   ☐Wednesday: *1 Thessalonians 5:1-11*   ☐Thursday: *2 Thessalonians 2:1-17*   ☐Friday: *Titus 2:11-15*   ☐Saturday: *2 Kings 2:1-11*   ☐Sunday: *Genesis 5:11-14; Hebrews 11:1-6*

FORTY-EIGHT
THE TRIBULATION

For then shall be great tribulation, such as was not since the beginning of the world to this time, no, nor ever shall be. Matthew 24:21

INTRODUCTION

In no other period of time in the past or future history of the world will there be so much suffering and universal destruction as in the last half of the seven years, called the Great Tribulation. This period of time will unleash more torture and misery than occurred during the Second World War that ended with an atomic holocaust. Most of the final book of the New Testament is devoted to a recounting of the events of those years. Portions of Daniel, Jeremiah, and Ezekiel also speak to the events. Among Christians, even non-Christians, great interest exists in what will happen to the world during the Great Tribulation.

The prophet Daniel prophesied concerning the seventy weeks in which God would be dealing with the nation Israel. As in the case of other Old Testament writers, the mystery of the church was kept hidden. Daniel did accurately predict the death of the Messiah and the destruction of the city of Jerusalem; after the sixty-ninth week, "shall Messiah be cut off, but not for himself: and the people of the prince that shall come shall destroy the city and the sanctuary" (Dan. 9:26).

Most historians agree Jesus was crucified about A.D. 30, and the Romans destroyed Jerusalem in A.D. 70. This ended the sixty-nine weeks that were predicted by Daniel. Then the prophet describes a gap between that time and the beginning of the Tribulation. The church age fits into that gap and has lasted almost two millennia. There is no indication of the length of the church age, also called the "age of grace." At the end of this age, "he [Antichrist] shall confirm the covenant with many for one week; and in the midst of the week he shall cause the sacrifice and oblation to cease, and for the overspreading of abominations he shall make it desolate, even until the consummation, and that determined shall be poured upon the desolate" (Dan. 9:27).

God has still a future for Israel. There is coming a period of about seven years when Israel will once again be the chief focus of God's activity. Unfortunately, much of that "week" will be devoted to judgment and the world will be in a continual state of chaos. But the period is coming. It is certain as the promises of God (Dan. 9:24-27). The Great Tribulation is as certain as the return of Christ himself (2 Thess. 2:2-4).

THE CHARACTER OF THE TRIBULATION

If the Christian did not realize he would be taken out of the world before the Tribulation begins, he could become very discouraged looking forward to those three-and-a-half years. They will be characterized by distress, judgment, darkness, suffering, and sorrow. There is no way to brighten the picture that the Bible paints concerning life in those years. Understanding what lies ahead for unbelievers who are alive at the time of the rapture has caused many people to reconsider the claims of Christ on their life.

Distress. Writing seven centuries before the birth of Christ, the prophet Zephaniah vividly described the character of the the Great Tribulation. "That day is a day of wrath, a day of trouble and distress, a day of wasteness and desolation, a day of darkness and gloominess, a day of clouds and thick darkness" (Zeph. 1:15). What was true in Judah during the invasion of Nebuchadnezzar will be multiplied in all the world during the Great Tribulation.

Judgment. Judgment characterizes much of the Great Tribulation. John saw an angel flying in heaven, "Saying with a loud voice, Fear God, and give glory to him; for the hour of his judgment is come: and worship him that made heaven, and earth, and the sea, and the fountains of water" (Rev. 14:7). The judgments of God upon the world that are manifested during the Great Tribulation will be a message to the world to repent and worship God (Rev. 15:4). Those who will not recognize the claims of Christ before the rapture will continually witness the power of God manifest in judgment throughout the Tribulation.

Darkness. Amos declared, "The day of the Lord is darkness, and not light. . . . Shall not the day of the Lord be darkness, and not light? even very dark, and no brightness in it?" (Amos 5:18, 20). Darkness is often used in the Bible to portray the state of unregenerate man, lost in the darkness of his sin until the light of the gospel shines through. As the Tribulation begins with the departure of the church (a candlestick— Rev. 1:20), the world will be placed in even greater spiritual darkness than now exists.

Suffering. One of the chief consequences of sin in the world is the problem of pain and suffering. During the Great Tribulation when sin is no longer restrained, pain and suffering will be greatly multiplied. Jesus, speaking of this period, said, "For then shall be great tribulation, such as was not since the beginning of the world to this time, no, nor ever shall be" (Matt. 24:21). Those living in the midst of this chaos will call for the rocks to fall on them and destroy them, "For the great day of his wrath is come; and who shall be able to stand?" (Rev. 6:17). Jesus accurately described this period as "the beginning of sorrows" (Matt. 24:8).

THE COURSE OF THE TRIBULATION

The Tribulation will begin with the rapture of the church and the revelation of the man of sin. At first, anti-Semitism will be minimal and a covenant will be made between the beast (Antichrist) and Israel (Dan. 9:27). The peace that is promised by Antichrist will not last. The world begins to experience three series of seven judgments of God. The chaos created by the evil forces that govern the world at that time will result in a breaking of the covenant with Israel and a threat to the very existence of the nation. As the final "week" of Daniel's vision begins, a gigantic universal state church is in control as the dominant religious movement. Israel is in the Promised Land, yet still is not regenerate, and God is about to judge the world.

Seals. The first of three series of judgments described in Revelation accompanies the breaking of the seals. As each seal on a scroll is broken, a specific judgment takes place on earth. With the breaking of the first seal, a white horseman goes forth to conquer, meaning war (Rev. 6:1, 2). The second seal brings a rider on a red horse taking peace from the earth (Rev. 6:3, 4). A black horse representing famine accompanies the third seal (Rev. 6:5, 6) and a final pale horse takes the life of a fourth of the world's population as the fourth seal is broken (Rev. 6:7, 8). The fifth seal is broken revealing martyred saints in heaven praying for vengeance (Rev. 6:9-11). With the breaking of the sixth seal, various natural phenomena occur, creating great fear in the people who remain (Rev. 6:12-17). The final seal is broken, bringing about an awesome silence in heaven for about half an hour while seven angels prepare to blow their trumpets.

SEVEN SEALS OF JUDGMENT	
1. White horse conquering	Rev. 6:1, 2
2. Red horse taking peace	Rev. 6:3, 4
3. Black horse bringing famine	Rev. 6:5, 6
4. Pale horse bringing death	Rev. 6:7, 8
5. Martyred saints praying	Rev. 6:9-11
6. Heavenly phenomena	Rev. 6:12-17
7. Silence	Rev. 8:1

The 144,000. The appearance of 144,000 Jews occurs early in the Seventieth Week. These are especially marked off by God for the special task of world evangelization (Rev. 7:1-8). As a result of their commitment and effectiveness in accomplishing this task, the Bible identifies an innumerable group of persons from every social, ethnic, and linguistic group who are saved during the Great Tribulation (Rev. 7:9-17). The prophecy concerning the success of these men should challenge us to a greater commitment to and involvement in world evangelization during this present age.

Two witnesses. During the first half of the Tribulation, two special witnesses begin to preach. Although they are not clearly identified, they do have the power of God to perform miracles similar to those of Moses and Elijah (Rev. 11:6). Some have speculated that these witnesses may be Enoch and Elijah as they have not yet died and every man has an appointment with death (Heb. 9:27). These men are killed by the beast, and their bodies are left lying in the streets of Jerusalem (Rev. 11:7). For three-and-a-half days their bodies will lie on the streets while the world celebrates their death. Then they will be resurrected and raptured into heaven (Rev. 11:8-12). Despite the evangelistic efforts of these witnesses and the 144,000 Jews, the world will continue in its sin. Many will be saved but apparently many more will choose to follow the beast.

Trumpets. As seven angels blow their trumpets in heaven to announce the transfer of ownership of the world to Christ, additional plagues occur on earth. At the blowing of the first trumpet, a third of nature is destroyed (Rev. 8:1-7). The second trumpet marks the destruction of a third of the sea (Rev. 8:8, 9). The next plague is the pollution of one third of all the earth's fresh water (Rev. 8:10, 11). This is followed by a fourth trumpet, causing the destruction of one third of the heavens (stars, etc.—Rev. 8:12, 13). The fifth trumpet is accompanied by a locust-scorpion-like creature bringing with it pain (Rev. 9:1-12). One third of the remaining population of the world is destroyed at the blowing of the sixth trumpet (Rev. 9:13-21). The great announcement is made at the blowing of the seventh trumpet but it is not yet realized. "The kingdoms of this world are become the kingdoms of our Lord and of his Christ; and he shall reign for ever and ever" (Rev. 11:15).

SEVEN TRUMPETS	
1. Nature smitten	Rev. 8:1-7
2. Sea turned to blood	Rev. 8:8, 9
3. Pollution of fresh water	Rev. 8:10, 11
4. Destruction in heavens	Rev. 8:12, 13
5. Locust-scorpions	Rev. 9:1-12
6. 1/3 population destroyed	Rev. 9:13-21
7. Great announcement	Rev. 10:15-19

Battle of Gog and Magog. During the latter half of the Tribulation, an alliance between Gog and his allies will invade Israel from the north. These nations will fail in great confusion in their attempt to destroy Israel. It will take seven months to bury the dead (Ezek. 38:1-19, 25). The geographic regions included in Ezekiel's vision of the allies is today occupied by the Russian and the Soviet-bloc countries in eastern Europe. This battle may be fought with allies attacking from the east (Rev. 16:12-16). Today, mainland China is the only nation in the world with an army or militia the size of that identified by John.

Bowl judgments. A final series of judgments precede the Battle of Armageddon. These are pictured as angels pouring out bowls or vials of judgment upon the world. As the first angel acts, people are covered with boils and sores (Rev. 16:1, 2). The destruction of all remaining sea life is contained in the second bowl (Rev. 16:5). The third bowl will turn all fresh water to blood (Rev. 16:4-7). The fourth angel will intensify the sun's heat to unbearable proportions (Rev. 16:8, 9). This will be followed with darkness and pain, perhaps as a result of sunburn and other complications of the former judgment (Rev. 16:10, 11). The sixth act here performed will effect the drying up of the Euphrates River (Rev. 16:12-16). The final bowl of judgment includes destruction caused by 125-pound hailstones (Rev. 16:17-21).

Battle of Armageddon. The world will be unable to handle the problems caused by these judgments. Many other minor

SEVEN BOWLS OF JUDGMENT	
1. Sores	Rev. 16:1, 2
2. Sea life destroyed	Rev. 16:3
3. Fresh water to blood	Rev. 16:4-7
4. Sun's heat intensified	Rev. 16:8, 9
5. Darkness and pain	Rev. 16:10, 11
6. Drying of Euphrates River	Rev. 16:12-16
7. Hail stones	Rev. 16:17-21

events will take place in these years as anti-Semitism continues to grow. Finally, demons will influence world leaders to assemble for their final battle in an attempt to destroy Israel and God (Rev. 16:14-16). While demons are identified as a source inspiring this battle, the Bible clearly identifies these leaders as responsible for their decision to organize for this battle (Rev. 19:19). Even in this great anti-God struggle, God is in control (Rev. 19:11-16). The Battle of Armageddon and the triumphant return of Christ mark the conclusion of the Great Tribulation.

CONCLUSION

Throughout the darkest days this world has yet to experience, God is still on the throne to accomplish his will. Today many Christians talk about the economic, social, and moral problems of our world as if to suggest the work of God cannot be accomplished. If God has worked in the dark days of the past, and will save people and accomplish his will in future dark days, there is no valid reason for doubting his effectiveness today. The key message to remember in any study of the Great Tribulation is clearly this: "God is still on the throne."

DAILY READINGS

☐Monday: *Revelation 6:1-17*   ☐Tuesday: *Revelation 7:1-17*
☐Wednesday: *Revelation 8:1-13*   ☐Thursday: *Revelation 9:1-21*   ☐Friday: *Revelation 11:1-19*   ☐Saturday: *Revelation 16:1-21*   ☐Sunday: *Revelation 19:1-21*

FORTY-NINE
THE MILLENNIUM

Blessed and holy is he that hath part in the first resurrection: on such the second death hath no power, but they shall be priests of God and of Christ, and shall reign with him a thousand years. Revelation 20:6

INTRODUCTION

Deep within the heart of every person is the desire to live with his fellow man in peace and harmony so that together they can enjoy the benefits of a utopian society. Plato had his *Republic*. In more contemporary times we have witnessed the world of *1984* and the dream of a thousand-year reign of the Third Reich proposed in Hitler's *Mein Kampf*. Of course, we reject the means by which these people wanted to bring peace into the world, but the desire for peace and uniformity is nevertheless there.

Perfect peace on the earth has been the ambition and goal of more than one political leader. Men representing various political and ethical persuasions have dreamed of and attempted to establish their utopias. But, true to the meaning of its name, "utopia" is to be found "no place."

In contrast, the Bible describes God's ultimate society. This theocratic kingdom will be characterized by harmony not only among men but also in nature. Its successful reign of peace lasting one thousand years is accomplished because it is the kingdom of God, and Christ himself will sit on the throne as King. The millennial reign of Christ differs from other utopian proposals in that it is the accomplishment of God, not the fulfillment of a man's goals and ambitions. As such, where men have failed in the past, God will succeed in the future.

Some claim this doctrine chiefly relates to a particular interpretation of ten verses (Rev. 20:1-10). In light of the controversy among Bible scholars, some would minimize the doctrine of the millennium. But, in a somewhat inconsistent manner, the same people would argue the importance of defending the doctrine of the virgin birth which is built upon fewer verses of Scripture. Actually, the importance of a doctrine is not determined by how many verses discuss it. If God says it once, it is enough. The importance of a doctrine is determined by its content and the meaning that God gives to it. Actually, the doctrine of the millennium has more biblical support than the ten verses in Revelation 20. The millennium is the chief theme of the prophets of Israel and Judah. Jonah stands alone in the canonical writings of the prophets as having no reference to the millennial kingdom of God. Both John the Baptist and Jesus preached on this subject. The apostles continued teaching the people concerning the kingdom of God.

THE NATURE OF THE MILLENNIUM

The word "millennium" does not appear in the Bible but again the idea is taught. This word is derived from two Latin words meaning "thousand years." That expression is used six times in Revelation 20. When we talk about the millennial reign of Christ, we are talking about the thousand-year period when Christ personally sits on the throne of David and reigns over the earth from Jerusalem.

The millennium is more than an era in history. It will be characterized by the restraining of Satan and the universal recognition of Christ as the King. The land of Palestine will in that day be the focal point of attention, particularly Jerusalem as its political capital. Nature will be released from the bondage it has experienced since the Fall of man. Righteousness will permeate all society. By anyone's definition, this kingdom will be desirable for its joys and comforts as well as the absence of sickness and death.

Restraint of Satan. Today, Satan has the liberty to work in this world, even though certain restraints are placed upon him by God. The millennium will be characterized as a time when complete restraint is placed on Satan. John saw an angel leave heaven "And he laid hold on the dragon, that old serpent, who is the Devil and Satan, and bound him a thousand years" (Rev. 20:2). While the specific details of that binding are uncertain, it is certain that Satan will be prevented from exerting any kind of evil influence until the end of the millennium. Hence, there will be no temptation to sin, no deception or counterfeit religion. No one will teach heresy and everyone will recognize the deity and rule of Jesus Christ.

Universal King. The millennium has been called the "theocratic kingdom" because it is a kingdom ruled directly by God in the person of Christ. Years before the first advent of Christ, Isaiah wrote, "For unto us a child is born, unto us a son is given: and the government shall be upon his shoulder: and his name shall be called Wonderful, Counsellor, The mighty God, The everlasting Father, The Prince of Peace" (Isa. 9:6). This Prince of Peace was prophesied to reign on the throne of David in an unending kingdom (Isa. 9:7). This will be accomplished in the millennium. Christ will be the authoritative Leader and rule in a way that all past rulers have failed to accomplish.

Palestine. God chose the land of Palestine to be the focal point of his concern in the history of the world. The Jews are God's chosen people and he gave that land to them. Throughout the years, the Jews have spent comparatively little time in the land and much of the time they lived there was filled with uncertainty. Concerning the future, God has promised, "And they shall dwell in the land that I have given unto Jacob my servant, wherein your fathers have dwelt; and they shall dwell therein, even they, and their children, and their children's children for ever: and my servant David shall be their prince forever" (Ezek. 37:25). This land will be the Jewish homeland during the millennium.

Jerusalem. A fourth characteristic of the thousand-year reign of Christ will be the place of Jerusalem in the world. "And it shall come to pass, that every one that is left of all the nations which came against Jerusalem shall even go up from year to year to worship the King, the Lord of hosts, and to keep the feast of tabernacles" (Zech. 14:16). Jerusalem will be a truly international city. The vast numbers of tourists in that city today is nothing in comparison with the crowds that will converge on the city during the reign of Christ. The city of Jerusalem will be the universal capital of the theocratic kingdom.

Nature. An additional blessing of this golden era will be the liberty once again experienced in nature. The apostle Paul talked of a future day when "the creature itself also shall be delivered from the bondage of corruption into the glorious liberty of the children of God" (Rom. 8:21). At the Fall, even the creation which God had perfectly created was made subject to the bondage of sin. At the return of Christ, deliverance from that bondage will be a part of the deliverance that Christ brings. Life in the millennium is pictured in terms of "the wolf also shall dwell with the lamb, and the leopard shall lie down with the kid; and the calf and the young lion and the fatling together; and a little child shall lead them" (Isa. 11:6). There will be no destructive vengeance in nature. There will not be "survival of the fittest," but survival of all. And children will enjoy all nature with no threat of danger to them.

Righteousness. Righteousness will be characteristic of the millennium. "In his days shall the righteous flourish" (Ps. 72:7). God has promised, "For Zion's sake will I not hold my peace, and for Jerusalem's sake I will not rest, until the righteousness thereof go forth as brightness, and the salvation thereof as a lamp that burneth" (Isa. 62:1). Much is being said today concerning morality in legislation. During Christ's reign on earth, all legislation will reflect his righteous character.

Desirable. The ultimate understatement concerning the nature of the millennium is that it will be desired of God's people (Heb. 11:10). This is true because of what exists and what does not exist in the kingdom. That which brings joy and fulfillment to life will be included in the kingdom. Those things which produce sorrow or discomfort in life will be excluded from the kingdom of God. The following chart identifies some of the specific elements of that world.

A KINGDOM TO BE DESIRED (Hebrews 11:10)	
Joy	Isa. 9:3, 4
Glory	Isa. 24:23
Comfort	Isa. 12:1, 2
Full knowledge	Isa. 11:1, 2
No sickness	Isa. 33:24

THE PURPOSE OF THE MILLENNIUM

Since God is wise and omniscient, he does not accomplish acts without reason. God has several purposes to fulfill by ushering in a thousand years of peace in the world. This period of time gives God the opportunity to reward the saints of all time. The reign will come in answer to the prayer "Thy kingdom come." God will redeem creation and rebuild the temple of David. He will finish what was previously begun. God will fulfill three important Old Testament covenants during the rule on earth (the Abrahamic, the Davidic, and the New Covenant). The millennium will also serve to complete the ministry of Christ.

Rewards. The doctrine of rewards is one of the chief motivational doctrines in Scripture. Isaiah taught concerning rewards, "Behold, the Lord God will come with strong hand, and his arm shall rule for him: behold, his reward is with him, and his work before him" (Isa. 40:10). Jesus said, "For the Son of man shall come in the glory of his Father with his angels; and then he shall reward every man according to his works" (Matt. 16:27). The apostle Paul looked forward to his "crown of righteousness, which the Lord, the righteous judge, shall give me at that day: and not to me only, but unto all them also that love his appearing" (2 Tim. 4:8). The giving of promised rewards is one of the purposes of Christ's reign on earth.

Prayer. God will keep his promise to hear and answer prayer. When his disciples wanted to know how to pray, Jesus provided a model which has become known as "The Lord's Prayer" (Matt. 6:9-13; Luke 11:1-4). When Christians pray, "Thy kingdom come," they are expressing a twofold desire. First, they seek the rule of God in their lives and in the world today. That is why we pray, "Thy will be done on earth as it is in heaven." A second desire expressed is for the actual, literal reign of Christ on the earth. God will answer both requests in the millennium. As we yield ourselves to him, he will lead and rule in our lives. When Jesus returns to establish his kingdom, he will have answered the second desire, for we will rule and reign with him.

Redeem creation. God created a harmonious and perfect world which was described as "very good" (Gen. 1:31). With the entrance of sin into the world, that creation was placed under the bondage of sin. At the return of Christ to establish his kingdom, the natural world will be delivered from that bondage. Peter described this time as "the times of restitution of all things, which God hath spoken by the mouth of all his holy prophets since the world began" (Acts 3:21). The curse will be lifted. Thorns and thistles that make work torturous will disappear. The earth will yield its strength and man will enjoy the fruit and beauty of nature.

Rebuilding of the temple. One of the things done in the millennium will be the rebuilding of the temple. The Old Testament prophets wrote, "After this I will return, and will build again the tabernacle of David, which is fallen down; and will build again the ruins thereof, and I will set it up" (Acts 15:16). Several chapters in Ezekiel deal specifically with the rebuilding of the millennial temple and the conducting of memorial sacrifices (Ezek. 40-48).

Covenants. The Lord is a covenant God and has on several occasions made covenants with Israel. Three important covenants will be fulfilled in the millennium. The Abrahamic Covenant (Gen. 12:1-3) promised that Israel would be a great nation and possess the Promised Land. The Davidic Covenant (2 Chron. 13:5; 2 Sam. 7:12-16) promised the seed of David (Christ) would rule forever on the throne of David. The New Covenant (Jer. 31:31-34) promised a spiritual rebirth for the nation Israel. These things will be accomplished in the thousand-year reign of Christ. If a person denies the existence of the millennium, he attempts to tie the hands of God behind his back so he cannot keep his promises.

Ministry of Christ. Peter described the full ministry of Christ in terms of "the sufferings of Christ, and the glory that should follow" (1 Pet. 1:11). Much of the earthly ministry of Christ would be included in the first part of that description, but his glory will be revealed in the millennium. The following chart contrasts these two aspects of Christ's ministry.

CONCLUSION

The hymn writer wrote, "Jesus shall reign where'er the sun/ Does his successive journeys run." In one sense, that truth is future and will not be realized until the millennium. In yet another sense, that truth should be realized personally as we take the gospel around the world. Someday Christ will sit on a throne in Jerusalem and rule the world, but today he simply desires to sit on the throne of our hearts and rule our lives. In the future, he will seize control of the world by winning the Battle of Armageddon. But today, he will not violate our wills. The only way that Christ will control our lives is for us to submit to his control.

DAILY READINGS

☐ Monday: *Ezekiel 40:1-49*   ☐ Tuesday: *Ezekiel 41:1—42:20*
☐ Wednesday: *Ezekiel 43:1—44:31*   ☐ Thursday: *Ezekiel*

45:1—46:24   □Friday: *Ezekiel 47:1—48:35*   □Saturday:
Isaiah 11:1—12:6   □Sunday: *Isaiah 9:1-7; Revelation
20:1-10*

"THE SUFFERINGS OF CHRIST, AND THE GLORY THAT SHOULD FOLLOW" (1 Pet. 1:11)

The Sufferings	*The Glory*
A baby, in humble clothes. Luke 2:12	A King, dressed in majestic apparel. Ps. 93:1
He was weary. John 4:6	He will be untiring. Isa. 40:28, 29
He had nowhere to lay his head. Luke 9:58	He will own all things. Heb. 1:2
He was rejected by his own. John 1:11	He will be recognized by all nations. Isa. 9:6
He was acquainted with grief. Isa. 53:3	He is the mighty God. Heb. 1:9
His royal robe was mocked. Luke 23:11	He will be clothed with a vesture dipped in the blood of his enemies. Rev. 19:13
He was smitten with a reed. Matt. 27:30	He will rule with a rod of iron. Rev. 19:15
Soldiers bowed their knee and mocked him. Mark 15:19	Every knee shall bow and acknowledge him. Phil. 2:10
He wore the crown of thorns. John 19:5	He will wear the crown of gold. Rev. 14:14
His hands were pierced with nails. John 20:25	His hands will carry a sharp sickle. Rev. 14:14
His feet were pierced with nails. Ps. 22:16	His feet will stand on the Mount of Olives. Zech. 14:4
He had no form or beauty. Isa. 53:2	He will be the fairest of ten thousand. Ps. 27:4
He was laid in the tomb. Matt. 27:59, 60	He will sit on his throne. Heb. 8:1

FIFTY
THE JUDGMENTS

The Lord recompense thy work, and a full reward be given thee of the Lord God of Israel, under whose wings thou art come to trust. Ruth 2:12

INTRODUCTION

One reason individual freedom works in a democratic society is responsibility. If a person is responsible for his actions, then personal freedom does not become license and anarchy. A person's freedom to speak his mind on a subject is limited only by a responsible attitude that prevents him from crying "Fire!" in a crowded auditorium. We must be held accountable for our actions if we would experience true liberty.

The same is true in our Christian lives. Many times we discuss the liberty or freedom we possess in Christ but seldom do we consider our accountability to God for how we exercise that liberty. "So then every one of us shall give account of himself to God" (Rom. 14:12). This principle of accountability is one of the keys to understanding the biblical doctrine of stewardship.

The Bible describes at least seven judgments by God in which people, nations, and other created beings are held accountable for their attitudes and actions. In these judgments, the plaintiffs are judged according to the standards God has established for them. These judgments are both positive and negative. Some judgments will be like criminal trials in which charges are read and proved. Then judgment is administered when some type of sentence is passed out. Other judgments will be similar to a contest in which those who have completed certain requirements will be rewarded for their work.

Understanding the judgments of God will help us in several ways. As we see how God judges, we will better understand the nature of God. Understanding those things that God judges will help us know what to avoid in our lives. Those things God rewards should be things we strive to develop as we seek to serve God.

THE CROSS

When Jesus died on Calvary, he was experiencing the judgment of God upon the sins of the world. He died in our place as our substitute. "Christ hath redeemed us from the curse of the law, being made a curse for us: for it is written, Cursed is everyone that hangeth on a tree" (Gal. 3:13). The cross was a criminal judgment by God upon the sins of the world.

Crime. The judicial charge bringing about the judgment was sin against God. Every man is a sinner because of a threefold reason. First, because of Adam's transgression everyone has been born with a sin nature (Ps. 51:2). Second, we have also committed personal sins against God. "For all have sinned and come short of the glory of God" (Rom. 3:23). In the third place, we have had sin imputed to our account in heaven (Rom. 5:19). Since man is a sinner, God is his enemy (Eph. 2:3). This is strong language, but sin is a violation of the nature of God. The crime of sin is so great that it brought about the judgment of Calvary.

Criminal. Everyone is guilty of the crime of sin. A popular gospel song reflects on this subject, "I should have been crucified." This is also the conclusion of the apostle Paul, who said "Christ. . .being made a curse for us " (Gal. 3:13). Some have commented on the significance of the circumstances surrounding the death of Christ. When given a choice by Pontius Pilate, the people decided Christ should die in the place of Barabbas, the one who was guilty of a crime that deserved death. Barabbas's name means "a father's son." The people had chosen that Christ should die for a guilty son of a father; God had long before agreed Christ would die for every guilty son and daughter of every father.

Sentence. "The wages of sin is death" (Rom. 6:23). Nothing could be more clearly taught in the Bible than the eternal consequences of sin. Its path leads to ultimate destruction both in this life and in the life to come. Sin involves the anger of God against it. Thus the Giver of life will judge sin with death—physical and eternal death. That sentence will someday be read over all those who do not accept Jesus as their Substitute (Rev. 20:11-15).

SELF-JUDGMENT

God will judge Christians for sin in their lives but he first gives them the opportunity to deal with the problem. In explaining the reasoning for the sickness and death among church members in Corinth, Paul pointed to the judgment of God upon sin (1 Cor. 11:30). He then identified self-evalation as a means of preventing this divine judgment, "For if we would judge ourselves, we should not be judged " (1 Cor. 11:31).

Place. God gave the church the ordinance of the Lord's Supper as a divinely appointed place where Christians should engage in self-evaluation. "But let a man examine himself, and so let him eat that bread, and drink of that cup" (1 Cor. 11:28). This practice keeps Christians individually in fellowship with God. It also keeps a local church in the spirit of revival. Several of history's great revivals began as church members engaged in self-evaluation, confession, and repentance.

Purpose. The chief purpose for self-evaluation (self-judgment) is to prevent oneself from becoming ineffective in the Lord's service. "When we are judged, we are chastened of the Lord, that we should not be condemned with the world" (1 Cor. 11:32). When we examine ourselves, we accomplish the same purpose without having to experience the judgment of God. The apostle Paul, always fearful of becoming ineffective in the service of Christ, constantly disciplined himself. "But I keep under my body, and bring it into subjection: lest that by any means, when I have preached to others, I myself should be a castaway" (1 Cor. 9:27).

Procedure. The apostle John outlined the procedure in self-evaluation. "If we confess our sins, he is faithful and just to forgive us our sins, and to cleanse us from all unrighteousness" (1 John 1:9). As we discover sin in our lives, our immediate response should be to confess it to God. God will forgive sin, and once again restore us to the place of fellowship from which we fell. The basis of forgiveness is the cross of Christ, hence the basis of self-judgment is the cross.

THE JUDGMENT SEAT OF CHRIST

Of all the judgments in the Bible, perhaps none has been so popular in preaching and singing throughout history as the judgment of the believer's works. The judgment is often discussed as the doctrine of rewards for Christians. This is not a judgment to determine if Christians will enter into heaven but will determine the quality and quantity of our past service on this earth. As a result of our service for Christ, we will receive a reward (Ruth 2:12).

Not everyone will obtain the same reward, and our service will be tested by God to determine the extent of the reward. Some may have nothing with which to enter heaven except their salvation (1 Cor. 3:12-15). The Bible also teaches it is possible to lose part of our reward that had been previously accrued. Therefore, it is important that we continue faithful in our service for Christ even after we have earned a prize (2 John 8). These rewards are sometimes identified as "crowns" in the Bible.

Incorruptible crown. Just as an athlete will discipline himself and his life-style to win a race and trophy, so a Christian should discipline himself in his service for Christ. In the

THE BELIEVER'S REWARDS	
1. Incorruptible crown	1 Cor. 9:25
2. Crown of righteousness	2 Tim. 4:8
3. Crown of life	Rev. 2:10
4. Crown of glory	1 Pet. 5:4
5. Crown of rejoicing	1 Thess. 2:19

early Olympic Games, the prize won by the victor was a crown of olive leaves. Naturally, with the heat of the day, the crown withered. The apostle Paul contrasts that incident with our Christian life. "Now they do it to obtain a corruptible crown; but we an incorruptible" (1 Cor. 9:25).

Crown of righteousness. A second crown the apostle identified was one which he someday expected to receive. Writing his final epistle to Timothy and expecting his death, Paul was looking forward to the coming of Christ, and if that did not happen in his lifetime, he expected to see the Lord in death. "Henceforth there is laid up for me a crown of righteousness, which the Lord, the righteous judge, shall give me at that day: and not to me only, but unto all them also that love his appearing" (2 Tim. 4:8). As we work for Christ in the light of his imminent return, we are earning a crown of righteousness. This was probably what Dwight L. Moody was thinking of when he said, "This is my coronation day" as he passed from his deathbed into eternity.

Crown of life. God has a special reward for those whose service costs them their lives. This is also called the martyr's crown. Speaking to the church that was going through severe persecution, Jesus said, "Be thou faithful unto death, and I will give thee a crown of life" (Rev. 2:10). This reward is also given to those who are victorious in enduring temptation (James 1:12). James may have been thinking of the temptation to Christians to compromise their witness rather than to endure persecution at the cost of their lives.

Crown of glory. God also has a special reward for those who serve him as pastors of local churches. Peter spoke to pastors: "And when the chief Shepherd shall appear, ye shall receive a crown of glory that fadeth not away" (1 Pet. 5:4). Being a fair and just God, he has prepared a reward for those carrying the bulk of the responsibility in the church. Often a company will recognize employees with the presentation of a plaque, watch, or some other token of appreciation. The crown of glory is Christ's token of appreciation to faithful pastors who do his will.

Crown of rejoicing. Every Christian should receive the crown of rejoicing (1 Thess. 2:19). This is the reward given for faithful witnessing and fruit bearing. Sadly, most Christians never experience the joy of leading a person to Christ. In contrast, God expects all of us to "bear fruit" (John 15:16).

GENTILE NATIONS

At Christ's second coming, all the nations of the world will pass before him to be judged (Matt. 25:32). Jesus described the scene in terms of a separation of sheep and goats. The classification is related to their treatment of those identified by Christ as "these my brethren" (Matt. 25:40, 45). These brethren may be one of the following three groups.

Israel. Some believe Jesus was referring to his fellow Jews. If that is the case, people of those nations which have sought to protect the Jews will be sheep. The others who have sought to harm the Jews or simply ignore their plight will be goats. This interpretation is in keeping with the promise of blessing in the Abrahamic Covenant to those who blessed the seed of Abraham (Gen. 12:1-3; 15:1-3).

Church. Some commentators argue that the brethren of Jesus are really the church. Jesus said, "For whosoever shall do the will of my Father which is in heaven, the same is my brother, and sister, and mother" (Matt. 12:50). In this case, the treatment of churches and Christians in those churches will be the basis of the judgment.

Oppressed. Throughout the Bible, God is portrayed as a defender of those who cannot defend themselves. Some have suggested God will judge the nations based upon their protection of the oppressed and defenseless members of their society. This would include the very young and very old, the poor and unborn.

TRIBULATION

During the Great Tribulation, God will release three major judgments upon the world (seals, trumpets, and bowls). The first of these accompanies the breaking of seven seals on a scroll which many commentators believe is the title deed of the world. The second judgment accompanies the sounding of seven trumpets, while the final series of judgments occurs as seven angels empty vials of the wrath of God upon the world. For a fuller discussion of this judgment, see Chapter 48.

THE GREAT WHITE THRONE JUDGMENT

At the end of the millennial reign of Christ, those who died unsaved will have to stand before the throne of God to be judged. "And I saw the dead, small and great, stand before God; and the books were opened; and another book was opened, which is the book of life: and the dead were judged out of those things which were written in the books, according to their works (Rev. 20:12). This judgment does not suggest these people may enter into heaven or hell on the basis of their works. All those who are judged at the Great White Throne are consigned to hell because they have rejected the gospel. The saved have already been resurrected and are enjoying fellowship with Christ. The Great White Throne judgment will determine the degree of punishment they will endure, based upon the nature of their evil work. When the book of words is opened (Rev. 20:12), a sentence of the severity of their punishment will be determined. All those sentenced will be consigned "into the lake of fire" (Rev. 20:14), where they will suffer according to their personally assigned sentence.

ANGELS

The Bible also teaches that angels are not exempt from judgment. Paul asked the Corinthians, "Know ye not that we shall judge angels?" (1 Cor. 6:3). Toward the end of the age, it will be our responsibility as Christians to represent God in the role of judge. It may be that during the Tribulation, the millennial kingdom, or eternity to follow, we will serve as judges similar to the judges who ruled before Israel's first king. As judges, we will be given a position of authority over angels.

CONCLUSION

Jesus promised, "If the Son therefore shall make you free, ye shall be free indeed" (John 8:36), but that liberty cannot be experienced and enjoyed if we do not discipline ourselves to recognize that there is a future day of judgment. Freedom can only be enjoyed by the responsible citizens of a society. In the greater Christian society, liberty is often perverted into licentiousness and lawlessness when we fail to bring ourselves under the Word of God. In the light that God will some-day settle all accounts, it is best for us to seek to accomplish faithfully the will of God as long as we are able.

DAILY READINGS

☐Monday: *Galatians 3:1-15*   ☐Tuesday: *1 Corinthians 11:23, 24*   ☐Wednesday: *1 Peter 5:1-14*   ☐ Thursday: *Revelation 20:1-15*   ☐Friday: *1 Thessalonians 2:1-20* ☐Saturday: *2 Timothy 4:1-8*   ☐Sunday: *Matthew 25:31-46*

FIFTY-ONE
THE ETERNAL ABODE
OF THE UNSAVED

But the fearful, and unbelieving, and the abominable, and murderers, and whoremongers, and sorcerers, and idolaters, and all liars, shall have their part in the lake which burneth with fire and brimstone: which is the second death. Revelation 21:8

INTRODUCTION

No one really wants to talk about hell, but it exists as a definite part of the eternal plan of God. Hell is not the devil's playground, nor is hell someone's punishment on earth. God created hell, a *real* place where *real* people will spend a *real* eternity. One of the primary dangers of false religions is their denial of this place. On the other hand, hell's existence has been a primary motivation in the lives of great Christian leaders. General William Booth, founder of the Salvation Army, vowed he would close his training schools if he could send his workers to hell for five minutes. One of America's leading pastors, Dr. Jack Hyles, often says he works hard winning souls because he believes that his father went to hell. It would be impossible to identify the missionaries who have chosen to spend their lives in a foreign culture because they believe that lost people will spend eternity in hell if they do not believe the gospel.

Liberal theologians often mock the biblical doctrine of hell. They say it is an ancient superstition, yet the existence of hell is well documented in the Word of God. When we understand the nature of hell, we begin to see why the Lord "is long-suffering toward us, not willing that any should perish, but that all should come to repentance" (2 Pet. 3:9). The realization of the nature of hell moved the rich man to concern on behalf of his family (Luke 16:27, 28). As we better understand hell, we will have a deeper burden for our lost loved ones. Though we find it hard to pray for them now, it will be impossible to cease interceding for them if we knew the fate that awaits them after death. A full awareness of hell would lead us to make every effort to present the gospel to the lost.

THE NAMES OF HELL

The Bible uses several terms to identify the various purposes and descriptions of hell. First, note that there is a difference between "hell" and the "lake of fire." When the unsaved die they go immediately to a place called hell. Later, the Bible indicates that those in hell are given up and cast into the lake of fire (Rev. 20:14). Even though they seem to be different places, the inhabitants are the same and the punishment is the same. The place of judgment for the unsaved is called the Great White Throne and the lake of fire follows it. Everyone without Christ will enter the first punishment, and no one who enters the first hell can escape entering the second (Rev. 11:15).

Sheol/grave. The common word for hell in the Old Testament is "Sheol" which means "the grave" where people go when they die. In the *King James Version*, Sheol is translated "hell" thirty-one times and "pit" three times. When both saved and unsaved died, they were said to go to Sheol, the place of the departed dead. The Hebrew word "Sheol" was translated into Greek as *hadees* (hades). Hades or Sheol is the place the Old Testament unsaved went. Jesus, in the parable of the rich man and Lazarus, said that Lazarus had gone to a place called "paradise" (Luke 23:43), and "Abraham's bosom" (Luke 16:22). Two people died, the rich man and Lazarus

(Luke 16:19-31), but in their afterlife they were treated differently.

Hades. The rich man went to hades at death and was tormented in flames (Luke 16:24). The punishment of hades is (1) burning, (2) separation/loneliness, (3) conviction by memory, (4) thirst, (5) falling, and (6) stench. The rich man could look across "a great gulf fixed" (Luke 16:26) and see where the saved were located. However, the Scripture is silent whether the saved could see the torment of the unsaved. The one thing the rich man could not do was escape his torment. He could not even send a warning to his family.

Gehenna. This word appears only twelve times in the New Testament and is translated "hell." The Lord Jesus used this term eleven times. The name is probably related to the Valley of Hinnom. During the reign of Ahaz, Israel participated in the worship of the false god Molech. In his attempt to please Molech, Ahaz actually engaged in human sacrifice, sacrificing his own son to the fiery god (2 Chron. 28:1-4). Archaeologists have learned that Molech was represented by a golden calf, being the religion of Canaan. The idol had the head of a bull, with outstretched arms. A fire burned in his hollow stomach and a child was sacrificed on the arms.

This practice was stopped during the reforms of Josiah (2 Kings 23:10), then the valley became a dumping ground for the city of Jerusalem. During the time of Jesus it was used to burn garbage. Hence, the Lord used the word *gehenna* to describe the place of eternal punishment because it was a place of filth and stench, a place of smoke and pain, a place of fire and death (Matt. 5:22; 18:8, 9; 23:33; John 5:36).

Lake of fire. John refers to hell in terms of a "lake of fire" (Rev. 20:15). Some have suggested this is nothing more than a metaphor to describe a place of suffering, but since the Bible uses flames to describe its torment, there is no reason to think the cause of suffering will be otherwise. Also, human language limits a perfect identification of the horrors of hell, as it also does when we seek to describe the glories of heaven. Only in this aspect can the "lake of fire" be considered a metaphor. It is as if John were saying, "Hell is so horrible I cannot completely describe it. Hell is like a vast sea covered in flames and that is only the beginning of the pain and suffering I saw there."

Second death. The lake of fire is also called the "second death" (Rev. 20:14; 21:8). In the Bible, death always speaks of separation, not cessation of existence. The idea behind death is not annihilation but rather the concept of eternal separation from God. Physical death is the first, where a person suffers because he is separated from his loved ones. The second death is the separation of a person from God.

Eternal retribution. Hell is also described as a place of eternal retribution or eternal punishment. Speaking of the unsaved, Jesus said, "And these shall go away into everlasting punishment: but the righteous into life eternal" (Matt. 25:46). The idea of punishment here is one of eternal duration. Eternity is incomprehensible as it confronts the human mind. We cannot comprehend limitless time, but hell will last as long as heaven, for the Scriptures describe these opposite concepts as "everlasting punishment" and "life eternal" (Matt. 25:46).

"Everlasting punishment" is used throughout the Bible to identify "duration without end." Eternal retribution would be horrible if we only thought of it as lasting a million years, but because it is eternal, a million years of time could be removed from its duration without in any way affecting the time of its duration. The worst part of hell is that its inhabitants know it will never end.

"Eternal" is described by the Hebrew word *olam* in the Old Testament and the Greek word *aion* in the New. Both words are linked to God; he is called the "eternal God." Therefore hell lasts as long as the duration of God. Eternity is beginningless and endless; it cannot be measured. It has no past, no future, no parts. Eternity is an infinite circle; we are born in the center of the circle and will die physically in the center of the circle, but remain there forever.

THE CHARACTER OF HELL

Someone described hell as a perpetual party with drinking, cursing, riotous living, and sexual freedom. Because a minister will condemn these actions does not mean they will be present in hell. As a matter of fact, a party is the farthest idea of the teaching of the Bible on hell. Others try to deny its existence, while still others attempt to redefine hell so as not to make it so bad. Regardless of the ideas of man, a real and literal hell exists.

Fire. The first torment a person encounters in reaching hell is the torment of burning. Jesus said his angels "shall cast them into a furnace of fire: there shall be wailing and gnashing of teeth" (Matt. 13:42). John the Baptist identified hell in terms of an "unquenchable fire" (Matt. 3:12). The rich man in hell acknowledged, "I am tormented in this flame" (Luke 16:24). While it is wrong to say all the torture in hell comes from the flame, it would also be wrong to explain away the literal flames of hell.

Memory. Abraham said one word to the rich man in hell that probably caused even greater torment than physical suffering: "Remember" (Luke 16:25). For eternity, the memories of lost people will function perfectly. They will remember all their injustices and sin. They will remember every instance when they rejected the convicting of the Holy Spirit. When we find ourselves inconvenienced in the midst of a problem, the problem is only complicated when we remember the opportunities that were ours to avoid the pitfall.

Thirst. The inhabitants of hell will also be tormented by one of the most painful sensations known by man, thirst. The Bible portrays the picture of a man in hell pleading for a single drop of water and being refused (Luke 16:24). Few of us have ever lived a single day without drinking something. If we were to try, many would give up. Try to imagine what it would be like to live for a week without water. The thirst of hell is in contrast to the offer of Jesus Christ, "If any man thirst, let him come unto me and drink" (John 7:37).

Separation. Hell is also referred to as "the second death." The biblical idea of death is separation. Part of the torment and misery in hell will be the "great gulf" (Luke 16:26) that separates men from their Maker. Much of what God does for us is taken for granted. Although he provides for us daily in many ways, most will never recognize God's goodness to us until it is too late. In hell, God is absent forever. Some people glibly say they anticipate meeting their friends in hell. They are seriously mistaken in their idea of hell. Many Bible scholars believe a wall of separation will surround each individual so that people are alone and isolated. It may be significant that the Bible never identifies two talking together in hell, as people will fellowship in heaven.

Darkness. Besides referring to the night, darkness has a moral description in the Bible. There is intellectual and spiritual darkness that leads to hell which is described as "outer darkness" (Matt. 8:12; 22:13). The angels that sinned were reserved in "chains of darkness" (2 Pet. 2:4). The fear that comes when walking on a strange street in thick darkness is one of the torments that will last forever. The result of darkness is "cast ye the unprofitable servant into outer darkness: there shall be weeping and gnashing of teeth" (Matt. 25:30).

Hopelessness. Hell is not a temporary place to pay for evil. Hell is the eternal abode of the unsaved. Sooner or later, the inhabitants of hell will realize they are in hell to stay. There will be no escape. Abraham told the man in hell, "They which would pass from hence to you cannot; neither can they pass to us" (Luke 16:26). Without hope, life is not worth living. In hell men will exist eternally without hope.

INHABITANTS OF HELL

"Whosoever was not found written in the book of life was cast into the lake of fire" (Rev. 20:15). Peoples from all nations, races, religions, and families will be in hell. The only thing that will keep a man out of hell is faith in Jesus Christ. The following chart identifies the known inhabitants of hell.

CONCLUSION

God established hell to punish those angels that rebelled against his authority (Matt. 25:41). Though God is not desirous of sending people to hell, men leave no choice when

THE CITIZENS OF HELL	
1. Satan	Rev. 20:10
2. The Antichrist	2 Thess. 2:8
3. The False Prophet	Rev. 19:20
4. Demons	2 Pet. 2:4
5. Judas Iscariot	Acts 1:25
6. Base Sinners	Rev. 21:8
7. All Sinners	Rev. 20:15

they continually reject the gospel. Even the man who has never heard the gospel preached has rejected various other attempts by God to point him to salvation. If the man would respond positively to these appeals, God would provide a gospel preacher to lead him to salvation.

THE MESSAGE BY GOD TO THE UNSAVED MAN	
1. Power and plan of God reflected in nature	Rom. 1:18-20
2. Conscience	Rom. 2:15
3. Providence	John 1:7; James 1:17
4. Glory of God	Ps. 19:1
5. Moral absolutes reflected in laws	Rom. 2:1, 2

None has a valid excuse for rejecting the gospel. God has offered eternal life to all who will receive it (Rom. 6:23). If we are unsure we possess eternal life, we should ask God to save us. Understanding the doctrine of hell should motivate us to do everything to get eternal life and win lost people before it is everlastingly too late.

DAILY READINGS

☐Monday: *Revelation 21:1-8*   ☐Tuesday: *Revelation 20:11-15*   ☐Wednesday: *Luke 16:19-31*   ☐Thursday: *2 Chronicles 28:1-27*   ☐Friday: *Matthew 18:1-14*   ☐Saturday: *Matthew 5:21-26*   ☐Sunday: *Matthew 25:31-36*

[1]Robert L. Sumner, *Hell Is No Joke* (Murfreesboro, TN: Sword of the Lord, 1959), p. 35.

FIFTY-TWO
THE ETERNAL HOME OF THE SAVED

For he looked for a city which hath foundations, whose builder and maker is God. Hebrews 11:10

INTRODUCTION

Most people in this world, even those who deny the existence of hell, talk about the existence of some form of paradise after death. The spiritual sung over a hundred years ago cried, "Everybody talkin' 'bout heaven ain't goin' there." One of the first references in Scripture to heaven noted Abraham "looked for a city." Just as a family moving into a new home will want to know every detail about the house, the neighborhood, area churches, schools, bus lines, and shopping centers, so we should want to know about our future home. Jesus said, "I go to prepare a place for you" (John 14:2). This chapter describes what it will be like and how we will live in it.

Someone observed that the older we become and the closer we get to moving into heaven, the more we are concerned with knowing every detail about our eternal home. For this reason, older Christians are often more concerned about the biblical doctrine of heaven than younger Christians. Actually, everyone who has received Christ as personal Savior has become a child of God (John 1:12) and now possesses eternal life (John 5:24). Everyone who is saved will go to heaven. But in the final analysis, the destination is not as important as the fact that we will live with God.

THE LOCATION OF HEAVEN

The Bible seems to teach there are "three heavens," but only one is the abode of God.

The first heaven is the atmosphere. "Heaven" refers to the air and atmosphere that surrounds every human being and all created life upon earth. "Behold the fowls of the air: for they sow not, neither do they reap" (Matt. 6:26). "And he prayed again, and the heaven gave rain" (James 5:18).

The second heaven is the stellar spaces. This is what we call outer space. "The stars shall fall from heaven" (Matt. 24:29). God described this space to Abraham, "Look now toward heaven, and tell the stars, if thou be able to number them" (Gen. 15:5).

The third heaven is the dwelling place of God. No one knows the location of God's throne and localized presence. All we can say is that heaven is where God is located. "And fire came down from God out of heaven and devoured them" (Rev. 20:9). "I will write upon him the name of my God...and the name of the city of my God, which is new Jerusalem, which cometh down out of heaven from my God" (Rev. 3:12).

References to the three heavens. The fact that "Jesus passed through the heavens" (Heb. 4:14) indicates there is more than one heaven. Also, Jesus "ascended up far above all heavens" (Eph. 4:10) means one heaven is above another. Paul taught that there were three heavens. "I knew a man in Christ above fourteen years ago, (whether in the body, I cannot tell; or whether out of the body, I cannot tell: God knoweth;) such an one caught up to the third heaven. And I knew such a man, (whether in the body, or out of the body, I cannot tell: God knoweth;) How that he was caught up into paradise, and heard unspeakable words, which it is not lawful for a man to utter" (2 Cor. 12:2-4).

The Bible teaches that all of these heavens shall pass away, "But the day of the Lord will come as a thief in the night; in the which the heavens shall pass away with a great noise, and the elements shall melt with fervent heat, the earth also and the works that are therein shall be burned up" (2 Pet. 3:10). Then the Bible describes "a new heaven" because the "first heaven" was passed away (Rev. 21:1).

THE DESCRIPTION OF HEAVEN

The splendor and beauty of heaven far outshines anything the human mind can comprehend. It will be impossible to comprehend heaven until we arrive on location, but we do know that heaven is a huge and colorful city.

The presence of God. The Bible tells us what is not in heaven to help us understand what is there. "And I saw no temple therein: for the Lord God Almighty and the Lamb are the temple of it" (Rev. 21:22). The temple was a symbol of the presence of God. Since the centralized presence of God is heaven, there is no need of a temple there. "Behold, the tabernacle of God is with men and he will dwell with them" (Rev. 21:3). In the Old Testament, the glory cloud over the tabernacle was symbolic of the presence of the glory of God. In the future is the place of the glory of God, "Having the glory of God" (Rev. 21:11) and "the city had no need of the sun, neither of the moon, to shine in it; for the glory of God did lighten it, and the Lamb is the light thereof" (Rev. 21:23).

Heaven is eternal. Heaven is the place of those who have eternal life (Titus 1:2; 3:7) and an eternal inheritance (Heb. 9:15). Therefore, heaven is described as having no day or night. This is because it is eternal and there is no time which is measured by day and night sequences in heaven. Eternity is timeless: "No need of the sun, neither of the moon" (Rev. 21:25).

Heaven has no death. Since death means separation, there is no death in heaven because we will live forever with God and those who die in Christ. "And death and hell were cast into the lake of fire. This is the second death" (Rev. 20:14). "And there shall be no more curse" (Rev. 22:3). Sin, the reason why God originally cursed the earth, is gone, therefore death, its result, is also gone.

Heaven has no tears. This means there will be no more sadness because, "God shall wipe away all tears from their eyes; and there shall be no more death, neither sorrow, nor crying, neither shall there by any pain; for the former things are passed away" (Rev. 21:4).

Heaven is a place of memory. The question is often asked, "Will we know one another in heaven?" The answer is yes! David said that he would know his son. "While the child was yet alive, I fasted and wept: for I said, Who can tell whether God will be gracious to me, that the child may live? But now he is dead, wherefore should I fast? can I bring him back again? I shall go to him, but he shall not return to me" (2 Sam. 12:22, 23). Moses and Elijah, who had been to heaven, were recognized by Peter, James, and John (Mark 9:4, 5). Also, "[We] shall sit down with Abraham, and Isaac, and Jacob, in the kingdom of heaven" (Matt. 8:11). They shall be recognized and known. The Thessalonians were concerned about Christians who had died. Paul answered, "For this we say unto you by the word of the Lord, that we which are alive and remain unto the coming of the Lord shall not prevent them which are asleep. For the Lord himself shall descend from heaven with a shout, with the voice of the archangel, and with the trump of God: and the dead in Christ shall rise first: Then we which are alive and remain shall be caught up together with them in the clouds, to meet the Lord in the air: and so shall we ever be with the Lord" (1 Thess. 4:15-17). Finally the Bible teaches, "I shall know even as also I am known" (1 Cor. 13:12).

Heaven is the largest city ever built. When people think of a city, they usually conceive a city about the size where they live. Even cities like Tokyo, New York, London, São Paulo, have not begun to approach the size of the city of God. John writes, "And the city lieth foursquare, and the length is as large as the breadth; and he measured the city with the reed, twelve thousand furlongs. The length and breadth and height of it are equal" (Rev. 21:16). This description of heaven suggests that it will be a gigantic cube, pyramid, or sphere. According to our present measurements, 12,000 furlongs would be equivalent to 1,500 miles or 2,400 kilometers. If placed in America, this city would reach from New York City to Denver, Colorado, and from the Canadian border to Florida. If the new Jerusalem takes the form of a sphere, it will be slightly larger than the moon which presently circles our globe.

Heaven will be beautiful and clean. From time to time, most every city council attempts to beautify their city. The most elaborate efforts of any city council would fail to rival the natural beauty of the city of God. Heaven will be constructed of things that are described as minerals, crystals, and metals of this present world. These colorful elements will form a cavalcade of beauty as the pure light of the Lamb shines through them.

The city itself will be built of transparent gold (Rev. 21:18). It will be surrounded by a wall of jasper; it will be as beautiful as a crystal clear diamond, as bright as a transparent icicle in the sunshine (Rev. 21:18). The wall will rest upon twelve foundations inlaid with various precious stones.

This city wall will stand some 216 feet high (Rev. 21:17) and include twelve gates, each made of simple white pearl (Rev. 21:21). The main street of the eternal city will be paved of pure transparent gold (Rev. 21:21).

The central focus of heaven will not be the walls, streets, foundations or gates, but rather the Lamb and his throne. The throne was the first thing John saw in heaven (Rev. 4:2). He saw an emerald green rainbow surrounding the throne (Rev. 4:3). John also noted, "Before the throne there was a sea of glass like crystal; and in the midst of the throne, and round about the throne" (Rev. 4:6).

The river and the tree of life. From the earliest pages of the Bible, two natural elements are described, which find their ultimate existence in heaven. Both the river (Gen. 2:10; Rev. 22:1) and the tree of life (Gen. 2:9; Rev. 22:2) were part of the original creation of God. They were placed in the original garden and now are in the paradise of God as constant symbolic reminders that God himself is the source of life. In the midst of the confusion and chaos of his circumstances, David received strength from the eternal presence of God: "There is a river, the streams whereof shall make glad the city of God, the holy place of the tabernacles of the most High" (Ps. 46:4).

The tree of life, though it is not mentioned after the Fall of man until the final chapters of Scripture, is pictured holding a place of prominence and providing for the growth of the people by its fruit. "In the midst of the street of it, and on either side of the river, was there the tree of life, which bore twelve kinds of fruits, and yielded her fruit every month; and the leaves of the tree were for the healing of the nations" (Rev. 22:2). The word "healing" means "nurture or growth."

Some would argue that it is wrong to describe heaven in specific terms. They claim that these are only heavenly symbols to represent the idea that the presence of God is beautiful. While on the surface, this sounds logical, it is also a subtle undermining of the authority of God. God could have made heaven without streets of gold or he could have used other symbols to describe his home, but the fact is that God did not choose to do that. Since he has told us there would be streets of gold in heaven, why should we not expect it to be as he described it? If language is inadequate to describe heaven, why did not God create words that approximated heaven? Also, if God chose, he could have created us with an understanding that could have comprehended heaven.

Of course, there are many things about heaven God has not told us. We may never know some things about heaven until we learn about them upon our arrival there. But what God has revealed in his Word is an adequate introduction to the city. Perhaps after we have lived several weeks, months, or years in heaven we will know our city better, much as is our experience when we move into a new city here.

THE INHABITANTS OF HEAVEN

Heaven is more than the eternal home of the saved. Many others will forever live with us there. These include God and his angels and special creations. Both Jews and Gentiles will live in heaven in perfect harmony. Citizens of every linguistic group and race will live in heaven for eternity. It will be the ultimate international community.

Angels. John "heard the voice of many angels about the throne in heaven" (Rev. 5:11). These include several kinds of angels. The seraphim, a special kind of angel who deal with God's altar, are present in heaven (Isa. 6:1-7). Another special angelic group who deal with God's throne, the cherubim, will also be there (Ps. 99:1). Both Gabriel (Rev. 22:8) and Michael (Rev. 12:7) live in heaven.

Elders. The Bible identifies twenty-four elders around the throne of God in heaven (Rev. 4:4). Much has been speculated concerning the identity of this group. One suggestion is that these men are twelve tribal leaders of Israel and the twelve apostles of Jesus. Another is that they represent the saved from both Jews and Gentiles.

Saved Israel. Hebrews 11 lists a number of individuals and groups who practiced faith in the Old Testament. "But now they desire a better country, that is, an heavenly: wherefore God is not ashamed to be called their God: for he hath prepared for them a city" (Heb. 11:16). These who have experienced saving faith have an eternal place in heaven.

Church. One of the first events after the rapture will be the marriage supper of the Lamb. This is when the church, the Bride of Christ, will be presented to her Groom, the Lord Jesus Christ. The new Jerusalem has been described as "the wedding ring of the church." The size of the church is innumerable. John writes, "After this I beheld, and, lo, a great multitude which no man could number, of all nations, and kindred, and people, and tongues, stood before the Lamb, clothed with white robes, and palms in their hands" (Rev. 7:9).

The triune God. Heaven is, of course, the eternal home of each member of the trinity of God. The Father sits upon a throne in heaven (Rev. 4:2, 3). John saw Jesus standing in heaven (Rev. 5:6). Though not as prominent, the Holy Spirit also lives in heaven and is twice quoted in John's account of his experience there (Rev. 14:13; 22:17).

THE ACTIVITIES OF HEAVEN

Heaven is often thought of in terms of angels sitting on clouds with harps and singing in choirs. At best, this is a small part of heaven. Though described as the eternal rest of the believer, heaven will be a very active place.

A life of fellowship. We will enjoy communion with the Lord Jesus Christ for all eternity. "They shall see his face" (Rev. 22:4). Christ predicts our future unity with him, "I will come again, and receive you unto myself; that where I am, there ye may be also" (John 14:3).

A life of rest. One of the results of sin was the curse of toil and sweat in a life of work. When we arrive at heaven, we will continue to work, but the agony of labor will be gone. "Blessed are the dead which die in the Lord from henceforth: Yea, saith the Spirit, that they may rest from their labours" (Rev. 14:13).

A life of service. We will work in heaven, but rather than dread the thought of labor and suffer the physical pain from grueling drudgery, we will enjoy our work. The curse will be gone, "And his servants shall serve him" (Rev. 22:3).

A life of growth. We will not "instantaneously" know everything when we arrive at heaven. We will spend a lifetime growing in knowledge and maturity. Christians will learn facts about God and his plan. They will grow in love. Also, they will learn how to serve him and grow in their ability to serve him. "The leaves of the trees were for the healing of the nations" (Rev. 22:2).

A life of worship. Jesus said at the beginning of his ministry, "The Father seeketh such to worship him" (John 4:23). Since the Father wanted people to worship him while they were on earth, it will not change when they get to heaven. "And after these things I heard a great voice of much people in heaven, saying, Alleluia; Salvation, and glory, and honour, and power, unto the Lord our God" (Rev. 19:1).

WHAT TO DO IN HEAVEN	
1. Learning	1 Cor. 13:9, 10
2. Singing	Rev. 15:3
3. Worship	Rev. 5:9
4. Serving	Rev. 22:3
5. Leading	2 Tim. 2:12; Rev. 22:5
6. Fellowship with others	Matt. 16:3
7. Eating	Rev. 2:17

CONCLUSION

God has certainly prepared a very special place for each one who desires to spend eternity with him. The Bible tells us how we can know with certainty that we have eternal life and a place in heaven with God (John 5:24). Anyone who will trust Christ as personal Savior will be admitted into heaven. The new birth is the only prerequisite to gain admission (John 3:7). What a shame it would be to know all about heaven and never see it, simply because we put off getting saved. We should receive Christ as our personal Savior right now! That way, if we never meet here, we can spend some time together in heaven.

DAILY READINGS

☐Monday: *Revelation 21:1-13*   ☐Tuesday: *Revelation 21:14-27*   ☐Wednesday: *Revelation 22:1-15*   ☐Thursday: *Matthew 13:1-23*   ☐Friday: *Matthew 13:24-32*   ☐Saturday: *Matthew 13:33-44*   ☐Sunday: *Matthew 13:45-58*